# OXFORD ENGLISH DRAMA

*General Editor:* MICHAEL CORDNER
*Associate General Editors:* PETER HOLLAND · MARTIN WIGGINS

# SHE STOOPS TO CONQUER
## AND OTHER COMEDIES

THIS edition brings together four eighteenth-century comedies that illustrate the full variety of the century's drama. Fielding's *The Modern Husband*, written before the 1737 Licensing Act that restricted political and social comment, depicts wife-pandering and widespread social corruption. In Garrick and Colman's *The Clandestine Marriage* two lovers marry in defiance of parental wishes and rue the consequences. *She Stoops to Conquer* explores the comic and not-so-comic consequences of mistaken identity, and in *Wild Oats*, the 'strolling player' Rover is a beacon of hope at a time of unrest.

NIGEL WOOD is Professor of Literature at Loughborough University. He has edited several volumes of critical essays on eighteenth-century writers, and is co-editor with David Lodge of *Modern Criticism and Theory*. He is General Editor of the 'Theory in Practice' series for the Open University Press.

MICHAEL CORDNER is Ken Dixon Professor of Drama at the University of York. He has edited George Farquhar's *The Beaux' Stratagem*, the *Complete Plays* of Sir George Etherege, and, for Oxford English Drama, *Four Restoration Marriage Plays* and Sheridan's *The School for Scandal and Other Plays*.

PETER HOLLAND is McMeel Family Professor in Shakespeare Studies at the University of Notre Dame.

MARTIN WIGGINS is a fellow of Shakespeare Institute and Lecturer in English at the University of Birmingham.

D1167058

# OXFORD ENGLISH DRAMA

OXFORD WORLD'S CLASSICS

═══

# She Stoops to Conquer
## and Other Comedies

HENRY FIELDING
*The Modern Husband*

DAVID GARRICK and GEORGE COLMAN
*The Clandestine Marriage*

OLIVER GOLDSMITH
*She Stoops to Conquer*

JOHN O'KEEFFE
*Wild Oats*

═══

*Edited with an Introduction and Notes by*
NIGEL WOOD

**OXFORD**
UNIVERSITY PRESS

# OXFORD

UNIVERSITY PRESS

Great Clarendon Street, Oxford OX2 6DP

Oxford University Press is a department of the University of Oxford.
It furthers the University's objective of excellence in research, scholarship,
and education by publishing worldwide in

Oxford New York

Auckland Cape Town Dar es Salaam Hong Kong Karachi
Kuala Lumpur Madrid Melbourne Mexico City Nairobi
New Delhi Shanghai Taipei Toronto

With offices in

Argentina Austria Brazil Chile Czech Republic France Greece
Guatemala Hungary Italy Japan Poland Portugal Singapore
South Korea Switzerland Thailand Turkey Ukraine Vietnam

Oxford is a registered trade mark of Oxford University Press
in the UK and in certain other countries

Published in the United States
by Oxford University Press Inc., New York

First published as an Oxford World's Classics paperback 2007
Reissued 2008

British Library Cataloguing in Publication Data

Data available

Library of Congress Cataloging in Publication Data

Data available

ISBN 978-0-19-955388-4

10

Typeset in Ehrhardt
by RefineCatch Limited, Bungay, Suffolk

Printed and bound in Great Britain by Clays Ltd, Elcograf S.p.A.

For Dominic Maxwell Yarrington Wood

# CONTENTS

# ACKNOWLEDGEMENTS

My labours on this volume have been invaluably assisted by several kindly helpers. Robert D. Hume, both by example and direct advice, has steered me aright, especially as concerns staging conditions; Thomas Lockwood read earlier drafts and supplied careful suggestions for improvement, all of which were adopted, and Angela Smallwood shared with me her ideas on the staging of *The Modern Husband* and how it might be adapted for contemporary performance. My greatest debt, however, is to Andrew Hagiioannu, who trawled through the complex textual history of *Wild Oats* and supplied a detailed and reliable account of its probable evolution. The staff of several libraries have given generously of their time, principally at the Beinecke, Bodleian, and Loughborough University. For their care in checking (and politely cajoling), I am particularly grateful to Martin Wiggins, Wendy di Taglia, Judith Luna, and Elizabeth Stratford. Any remaining errors are certainly my own.

# INTRODUCTION

It is unlikely that the essayist and critic Charles Lamb would have included the four comedies in this volume in his personal canon of plays. In his survey 'On the Artificial Comedy of the Last Century' (*The London Magazine*, April 1822), Congreve, Wycherley, and Farquhar represent all that is worth preserving before Sheridan and this highly selective choice is symptomatic of his desire to support comedy in its purest form, the investment in an 'idle gallantry in a fiction, a dream, the passing pageant of an evening'. Artifice is here no weakness but an attempt to allow us a freedom from 'our fire-side concerns' that were, otherwise, unshunnable, our inability to evade the 'pressure of reality' producing a compulsion only to 'confirm our experience of it'.[1] This eloquent defence of comedic wonder has been formative in our own recent theatrical preferences, with the significant exception of Goldsmith's *She Stoops to Conquer*, which remained a constant in the repertory of our own last century and *Wild Oats*, which, despite being the revelation of the Royal Shakespeare Company's 1976–7 season at the Aldwych Theatre in London, is still more studied than produced. Fielding's *The Modern Husband* has no professional stage history in an unadapted form and, whilst *The Clandestine Marriage* has been filmed (1999) and occasionally makes it to the bigger theatres, it is usually an exercise in witty sentiment on the few times it is given an airing. This is, paradoxically, the pre-eminent reason for this edition: to help re-evaluate the pressures, welcome and not so, that were placed on the writer for the stage in the eighteenth century, and also the creative solutions that resulted.

There is ample evidence that the audiences of mid-century onwards became less and less interested in vital contemporary issues. The politeness (with all that that entailed) of theatregoing was not just a free aesthetic choice; theatres sought a public's approbation as an economic necessity. Richard Tickell's 'Prologue' to Joseph Richardson's *The Fugitive* (1792) had the actor gaze out on the 'well-dress'd Pit' from whom he expects 'few perils' (l. 20):

---

[1] Charles Lamb, *Selected Prose*, ed. Adam Phillips (Harmondsworth, 1985), 142.

Not as of old, when, train'd to frown and fret,
In murky state the surly synod met.
Vain of half learning and of foreign rules,
Vamp'd from the jargon of the ancient schools.

(ll. 21–4)

The reason Tickell advances is the feminization of the pit that has produced a 'gay parterre' where 'female softness [is now] join'd to manly sense' (ll. 29, 32).[2] Certainly, at the turn of the century, the refurbishment and expansion of the two main houses established by Royal patent in 1660, Covent Garden and Drury Lane, accentuated the class (or income) divisions in a theatre audience. Whilst catered for by a staple diet of pantomimes and farces, afterpieces and entr'acte entertainments elsewhere and in the summer booths at Southwark amongst other sites, lower class theatregoers were restricted by price and probably choice to the upper gallery, significantly further from the stage.[3] Front and side boxes at Drury Lane were usually reserved for sponsors of the theatre or those with proven aristocratic credentials, leaving the pit and lower gallery to the professional classes. In 1762, the occasional provision for seating spectators on stage at Drury Lane, usually at benefits, was discontinued; Covent Garden lasted until 1781 before its audiences were safely corralled into the body of the auditorium.

This seems unpromising for artistic risk-taking yet this collection represents examples of distinct and original work. It is one of the ready clichés of eighteenth-century theatre research that Sentiment and Sensibility were the lodestones of literary as well as philosophical investigation.[4] The broadest categories may satisfy broad interpretations, yet these plays are open to a variety of emphases and shades of conclusion, as if the prevailing tendencies were a challenge to original thought and motive. The slipperiness of definition where the sentimental is concerned has been interestingly explored.[5] The culture

[2] *The Fugitive: A Comedy* (1792), pp. iii–iv.

[3] See H. W. Pedicord's analysis of this trend in his *The Theatrical Public in the Time of Garrick* (2nd edn., Carbondale, Ill., 1966), 22–36.

[4] See Frank H. Ellis's *Sentimental Comedy: Theory and Practice* (Cambridge, 1991), 3–22, and Roy Porter, *Enlightenment: Britain and the Creation of the Modern World* (London, 2000), 276–94.

[5] See especially G. J. Barker-Benfield, *The Culture of Sensibility: Sex and Society in Eighteenth-Century Britain* (Chicago, 1992), and Lawrence E. Klein, *Shaftesbury and the Culture of Politeness: Cultural Politics in Early Eighteenth-Century England* (Cambridge, 1991). Both these studies provide a sense of valuable context for the term and its vogue for describing an aesthetic and social politeness that became a self-conscious aspiration

of the heart and its powerful promptings would seem to lead to a rather narrow spectrum of possible resolutions, of unlikely happiness and improbable justice, yet what is distinctive is the trace of other logics, alternative endings, or the victims who might still have a claim on our attention if not our sympathies. If we were put to the task of typifying a Comedy of Sensibility, then John Loftis's guide in his *The Politics of Drama in Augustan England* is still the most reliable.[6] Some of the earliest examples are those supplied by Sir Richard Steele, who, in his *The Lying Lover* (1704), proclaimed its design to be 'to banish out of Conversation all Entertainment which does not proceed from Simplicity of Mind, Good-nature, Friendship, and Honour' ('Epistle Dedicatory to His Grace, The Duke of Ormond').[7] The author's own words in the 'Preface' stressed the implausibility to which he was driven in order to deliver a comic resolution—or perhaps anything comic at all: for four acts the hero is false and murders, yet 'in the fifth Act [he] awakes from his Debauch with ... Compunction and Remorse'.[8] In both his *The Tender Husband* (1705) and *The Conscious Lovers* (1722) this rather programmatic rendition of human motivation is extended and some attempt at darkening the picture evident, yet the basic problem of squaring Lamb's idea of successful comedy and the foregone conclusions of Comedies of Sensibility remain: if eleventh-hour conversions are expected, how can the plays sustain dramatic interest?

With the passing of the Licensing Act in May 1737, there were powerful reasons why dramatists might have chosen to look more into the heart for dramatic interest. Fielding and John Gay were effectively muffled by the need to submit work for perusal by the Lord Chamberlain and few managers would take a chance on his vigilance.[9]

from the mid–1730s. John Brewer has mapped its origins in medical textbooks such as George Cheyne's *The English Malady; or, a Treatise of Nervous Disorders* (1733) (*The Pleasures of the Imagination: English Culture in the Eighteenth Century* (London, 1997), 112–22). In *She Stoops to Conquer*, Marlow could be suffering from this particular malady when addressing women of his own class.

[6] *The Politics of Drama in Augustan England* (Oxford, 1963), especially pp. 190–207.
[7] *The Lying Lover: or, the Ladies Friendship. A Comedy* (1704), p. iii.
[8] ibid., p. viii.
[9] A comprehensive account of the immediate context can be found in the documents compiled by Vincent J. Liesenfeld in his *The Licensing Act of 1737* (Madison, 1984). See also Robert D. Hume, *Henry Fielding and the London Theatre, 1728–1737* (Oxford, 1988), especially pp. 242–60 and Thomas Lockwood, 'Fielding and the Licensing Act', *Huntington Library Quarterly*, 50 (1987), 379–93. Against this flow of commentary

To Samuel Johnson, there was no doubt but that this measure would adulterate stage comment: 'With warbling Eunuchs fill a licens'd Stage, And lull to Servitude a thoughtless Age' (*London: A Poem* (1738), ll. 59–60).[10] Fielding himself was to return to the whole morality of licensing in *Joseph Andrews* (1742) when he had his innocent parson, Abraham Adams, attempt to have his sermons published; the Bookseller is dubious and compares the less popular edification of the one to the safer bet of a stage play 'that had been acted twenty nights together'. His conclusion was that the Act would 'shortly bring them to the same footing', clearly implying that plays could now be truly populist entertainment, safe from polemical complexity (1.1.16). In effect, the Act lent greater power to the two main patent houses, Drury Lane and Covent Garden, the two enterprises that could both resist government interference and also gauge and/or shape popular demand. The anonymous commentator of *A Compendious History of the English Stage, from the earliest period to the present time. Containing a candid analysis of all dramatic Writings* (1800) felt that this slackening of competition had indeed harmed the art, by reducing the number of theatres:

> were there *more* theatres, and upon a smaller scale, were the salaries of actors in some cases not so enormous and in others not so illiberally low, the public would be in every respect better served than they even are at present. It would be neither a few authors, a few actors, or two or three managers, that could monopolize the favour of the town . . . (p. 44)

These might be difficult times for full-blown experimentation, but Lamb's appreciation of comic freedoms is here demonstrated in each of the comedies in the collection, as is its manipulation (as opposed to exploitation alone) of sentimental ideals.

The saving graces of complex eighteenth-century comedies lie in their linguistic and narrative detail. If we were expecting the easy glide into a routine happy ending, we might find several ingredients in their closing passages unexpected. In *The Clandestine Marriage*, Sir John is clear that it is possible to equate both sensibility and honour (5.2.411–13), and that the only aid where the risks of passion are

---

indicating the constricting effects of this legislation, Matthew Kinservik has uncovered the occasional help that the Lord Chamberlain's Office gave to comedies that allied a sense of moral reform to ridicule (see his *Disciplining Satire: The Censorship of Satiric Comedy on the Eighteenth-Century Stage* (Lewisburg, Pa., 2002)).

[10] See also his heavily ironic *A Complete Vindication of the Licensers of the Stage* (1739).

concerned would be the generosity of a Lord Ogleby and the (perhaps forced) magnanimity of a Sterling. Initially believing her to be a chambermaid, Marlow may appear to have identified his true affections for the authentic Kate Hardcastle, in Goldsmith's *She Stoops to Conquer*, yet the transition is swift. We might also hesitate to take Hastings and Miss Neville strictly at their word when they similarly come to observe no clash between duty and passion (5.3.112–21). Well may Mrs Hardcastle claim that this seems rather more like 'the whining end of a modern novel' (5.3.122–3). The fortuitous resolution of *Wild Oats* leaves out in the cold the nay-sayers, Ephraim, Gammon, and the Ruffians, yet the essential needs of friendship and kin are tested across time and space and the discovery of a location in society for Rover, the strolling player, and also the pre-eminent virtues of dramatic craft are not predictable or, indeed, universally understood to represent turn-of-the-century assumptions. The 'candid Thespian laws' that Rover invokes in the closing exordium (5.4.291) are in place only when wild oats have been spent, and the need for a strong well-motivated navy as well as a belief in social cohesion are implicit in many of Sir George's shows of exasperation. If *The Modern Husband* is taken as a special case, then that is as much to do with its date as its author. The acerbic satire on 'Modernity', carried by the Moderns in the play, is part of Fielding's project in early career, and his chosen medium was usually dramatic burlesque. This play represents one of his few excursions into full-length plot development. For those who would like to trace the novelist before the event, there is evidence here of narrative scope as well as satiric bite. This does not discount an element of unexpected compassion, however, where Mrs Modern is concerned. Her crestfallen exit and fate moves the 'compassion' of Mrs Bellamant (always an accurate barometer of approved sentiments), and Gaywit is quick to note that her 'faults are more her husband's than her own' (5.4.68, 69–70).

These plays both support and qualify Lamb's desire for comedy with little 'design' upon the reader: even if in jest, 'Laughing' comedy emerges as an art form, reflecting serious contemporary concerns.

## The Modern Husband

'Where grandeur can give licence to oppression, the people must be slaves, let them boast what liberty they please' (5.2.36–8). Bellamant's resolute defiance of Lord Richly's influence and social rank might have emerged as one of the most daring comments on place and power the young Fielding ever penned had he placed it as a resonant conclusion to his play, but *The Modern Husband* concludes rather more safely with one saved marriage and two anticipated weddings. The Bellamants have been tempted and resist (eventually), whereas their son, the Captain, disconcerts Richly by marrying his daughter. His nephew, Harry Gaywit, can now gain his inheritance and he celebrates this by gaining the hand of Emilia. The ending celebrates a degree of freedom from Richly's strategems, yet it does not quite annul that sense of pervasive opportunism evident throughout most of the play. Richly well knows that social position might sometimes only be maintained at the cost of true morality. Mr Modern prostitutes his wife to Richly so as to repair their financial losses, and, in turn, when this source of funds appears to be running dry, and Mrs Modern's charms lose their allure, she is turned into a pander in her own right by attempting to compromise the hitherto faithful Mrs Bellamant on his behalf. Bellamant's own desperate plight, to make good substantial losses in a high-profile legal case, drives him into a similar predicament. The rescue of his marriage in 4.2 is unexpected—as sudden as Captain Bellamant's successful proposal to Lady Charlotte. Modern's design to catch Richly in the act of intimacy with his wife (criminal conversation) so as to gain damages in the courts runs awry and they end the play as debauched as they began it. Although the action may be said to end fortunately, it does not quite lead to reassurance that love will always prevail and libertines be vanquished.

*The Modern Husband* signals an attempt by Henry Fielding, as his Prologue to the play makes clear, to 'restore the sinking honour of the stage' (l. 38). In this he is also distancing himself from the 'unshaped monsters of a wanton brain' (l. 6) manifest in his earliest dramatic works, the wildly successful farces, *The Author's Farce* and *Tom Thumb: A Tragedy* (both 1730), the latter known as *Tragedy of Tragedies* from 1731 onwards. Rejecting the string of local effects characteristic of broad burlesque or the popular lyricism of the ballad opera, he strove to create the taste for a more heroic comedy that took as its satiric target, 'Vice, cloth'd with Power' (p. iii), as identified in the Prologue to his first ambitious piece in this vein, *Rape upon Rape* (1730).[11] It is tempting to take Fielding at his word here, and the scope of *The Modern Husband* certainly exceeds that of his afterpieces, ballad

---

[11] *Rape upon Rape; or, The Justice Caught in his Own Trap* opened at the Little Theatre at the Haymarket on 23 June 1730. For its second run at Lincoln's Inn Fields, and thereafter at the Little Theatre, it was renamed *The Coffee-House Politician*.

operas, and farces, but the polemical strain in his work is a constant and the more regular form of this comedy not directly a matter of maturity. The play in MS draft was sent to Lady Mary Wortley Montagu, a particularly influential arbiter of taste, in September 1730, just a few months after the completion of a second edition of *Tom Thumb* (June) and a few before its expansion to the *Tragedies of Tragedies* (March 1731).[12] Throughout 1731 and early 1732 he was engaged in the staging of three farces (*The Letter-Writers* (March), *The Welsh Opera* (April; expanded as *The Grub-Street Opera* in June) and *The Lottery* (January)). At exactly the time he was establishing his reputation in the London theatre world with caricature and burlesque, he was waiting avidly for Lady Mary's opinion on quite another venture. It is rather the case that the heroic and the bathetic existed for Fielding in a complex dynamic where the contemporary instances of manic folly suggested perennial evils.[13]

The play opened at the Theatre Royal at Drury Lane on 14 February 1732, where it ran for thirteen consecutive performances plus an additional night in March. Fielding enjoyed, therefore, at least three benefit nights, and it was rapidly published by John Watts, with a reissue and 'second edition' before the year was out. This does not suggest a resistant and unheeding public. Indeed, Watts (and probably the author himself) thought so well of the piece that, in June, his next play, *The Old Debauchees*, was advertised on the title-page as 'by the author of *The Modern Husband*'. To date, however, the play has almost no further stage history.[14]

Reasons for this apparent failure are not obvious. Given that he was, in effect, barred from the stage by the provisions of the 1737 Licensing

---

[12] The date is suggested by Battestin and Probyn in their *The Correspondence of Henry and Sarah Fielding* (Oxford, 1993), 4. Fielding's care with his MS is clear from the letter to Lady Mary: 'In hope your Ladyship will honour the Scenes which I presume to lay before you with your Perusal. As they were written on a Model I never yet attempted, I am exceedingly anxious least they should find less Mercy from you than my lighter Productions' (p. 4).

[13] See his defence, in the Prologue to *The Lottery*, of caricature—at the same time as his defence of comedy's higher aims:

> . . . Farce still claims a magnifying right
> To raise the object larger to the sight,
> And show her insect fools in stronger light. (ll. 7–9)

[14] The 1995 adaptation by Paul Godfrey for the Actors Touring Company is, I believe, the only subsequent staging. Godfrey concentrates the action on the Bellamants, Moderns, and Richly. All other parts are omitted. His text can be found in *A Bucket of Eels and The Modern Husband* (London, 1995).

Act, his political animus towards the Whig administration might well have discounted any revival for a considerable time—at least until 1742 when Walpole's star was eventually dimmed. The more direct invective of the works written on his return to the Little Haymarket, such as *Pasquin* (March 1736), *The Historical Register*, and *Eurydice Hiss'd* (March–April 1737), mark a return to a Fielding at his lampooning best, but *The Modern Husband* is much more guarded and more universal cultural comment. The production of the play at Drury Lane must have seemed rather like a relaunch of his career. It is an indication both of his precocity and his ambition that his very first play, *Love in Several Masques*, ran there for four nights in February 1728—and, indeed, had attracted two of the theatre's managers to take major roles: Colley Cibber played the clueless fop, Rattle, and Robert Wilks, Merital. The intervening years had allowed Fielding the opportunity to demonstrate a flair for showmanship—but at the more popular and less grand arena of the Little Haymarket. It was only with *The Lottery* in January 1732 that he made it back to Drury Lane, and then only with a farce very much in the vein of his latter 'entertainments', such as *The Welsh Opera* (April 1731). *The Modern Husband* is a full-length play, and provided him with the opportunity—as even *Rape upon Rape* (at the Haymarket) did not—of addressing the Lord Richlys as well as the Mr Bellamants of London with a degree of seriousness and narrative power. It is tempting, especially given the benefit of hindsight, to regard the play's removal from the repertory as part of an attack of calculated prudence on Colley Cibber's behalf. As Lord Richly, he might indeed be regarded as complicit in the pillorying of the Great Man, the Prime Minister since 1721. The evidence of the dedication to Walpole would seem to suggest otherwise, but, especially in the opening paragraph, there is more than enough allusive material to suggest that he expected many to regard it as ironic over-praise in the spirit of Pope's Epistle to Augustus. To be dubbed 'great' could simply mean significant in dimension or celebrity, not morality or talent; it was, after all, the adjective most associated with Tom Thumb.[15] In the dedication itself, great is repeated adjectivally five times, and it is the disclosures about a great

---

[15] For a succinct survey of Fielding's treatment of greatness in his work, see Martin C. Battestin, *A Henry Fielding Companion* (Westport, Conn., 2000), 234–5; see also H. K. Miller, *Essays on Fielding's Miscellanies: A Commentary on Volume One* (Princeton, 1961), 42–54, and Ronald Paulson, *The Life of Henry Fielding: A Critical Biography* (Oxford, 2000), 47–55.

man that spices Captain Bravemore's advice to Captain Merit in 1.2 (see lines 21, 28, 31, and 54). In 5.4, the final riposte to Lord Richly, spoken by Captain Bellamant, is that he would dispense with a blessing on his union with Lady Charlotte Gaywit, as he 'would not kneel any longer to [him], though [he] were the great mogul' (5.4.120–2). Fielding may not have dared to face down Walpole directly, but he left enough traces for the knowing to recognize where his real allegiances lay.

The more damning reason for the play's neglect is an aesthetic one: Fielding is considered not to have written a particularly subtle or well-formed play. This perspective has been forcefully expressed by Robert D. Hume and it concerns the implausibility of the characters and the 'plot cohesion', which is 'inadequate'.[16] To be sure, the play is not a streamlined experience. Richly's levee in 1.2–3 introduces the audience to characters who do not reappear. Captain Merit's prominence in these scenes promises much, yet he reappears rather as an afterthought in 5.4 to witness Mrs Modern's final disgrace, but is given just one line. The Lady Charlotte–Captain Bellamant union discomforts Richly and, structurally, is necessary to demonstrate the limits of his social power, but for much of the play they seem rather flat characters who have stumbled in from a Restoration study in foppish stereotypes. With such a limited stage history, it would be hazardous to suggest where the play's virtues might lie, but it is certainly possible to find in Fielding's profuse plotting an attempt at a scope of mood and comment that aspires to rather more than a comedy of manners.

A particularly apt example is Richly's levee in 1.3, where Merit and Bravery (in Captains Merit and Bravemore) sue for notice from riches and arrogant privilege. The motifs of the gaming-tables, taking in specific references to Quadrille, Hazard, and Picquet, help denote a society given over to chance and lotteries, and frequently there is a packed stage, figuring a society wherein the individual rarely stands out prominently. Brean Hammond is surely accurate when he notes Fielding's determination to undermine the 'relentlessly

[16] 'Both sub-plots disappear from view for long periods . . . The Moderns and Lord Richly are simplistic monsters, really just objects of detestation. Fielding does not manage to make very clear why a husband otherwise so sensible and devoted as Mr Bellamant should be in the toils of a boring harpy [Mrs Modern].' (*Henry Fielding and the London Stage, 1728–1737* (Oxford, 1988), 123–4.)

bourgeois norms' of sentimental drama, Colley Cibber's in particular.[17] Perhaps to ask for a large measure of contemporary approval of such a risky and daring undertaking would have been presumptuous, but, on top of this, Fielding had been waging a paper war with the *Grub-Street Journal*, a self-styled censor of recent theatrical and poetic experiment. 'Dramaticus', in issue 117 (30 March 1732), found the play neither diverting nor edifying, and its gallery of characters a 'motley composition'. He refused to follow the logic implicit in finding greatness to be allied in society with roguery and monstrously immoral behaviour evident in human nature.[18] This was exactly Fielding's point: the Moderns did exist and the Richlys often prevailed.

## The Clandestine Marriage

*The Clandestine Marriage*'s popularity (and clear profitability)[19] may be judged by its impact in that first 1765–6 season: it initially ran for thirteen consecutive nights from 20 February and then for one night in each of the succeeding six weeks. It did so, also, without the safety-net of any afterpiece that might have incorporated dancing or singing. Its publication—on 4 March 1766—entailed three editions in just three weeks. To some extent, the collaboration between Garrick and Colman ensured a certain advance celebrity. David Garrick, although coming to the end of an illustrious acting career, was capable of forming theatrical taste. His managing of Drury Lane had recently steered the capital's premier house to a degree of stability, both artistic and financial. George Colman was a friend of Garrick's who had created his own following with *Polly Honeycombe* (1760) and *The Jealous Wife* (1761).

The collaboration on this venture was, however, fraught; Garrick disappointed his audience and Colman by turning down the part of Lord Ogleby at the last minute. The reason, according to Thomas

---

[17] *Professional Imaginative Writing in England, 1670–1740: 'Hackney for Bread'* (Oxford, 1997), 284.

[18] In Ronald Paulson and Thomas Lockwood (eds.), *Henry Fielding: The Critical Heritage* (London, 1969), 33, 36. See also the contributions from 'Prosaicus' and 'A.B.' in the *Journal* of 29 June (pp. 45–9). Even a champion of Fielding's, Thomas Cooke in his 'Reflections on Some Modern Plays' (*The Comedian* (June, 1732) ), observed that there were 'some Scenes independent of the main Busyness of the Play' (p. 38).

[19] Pedicord and Bergmann's figures can be found in *The Plays of David Garrick*, 7 vols. (Carbondale, Ill., 1980), i. 419.

Davies, was a fear of fatigue and his 'frequent attacks of the gout and stone'.[20] In truth, there was also a protracted rift between them about authorship. Colman had always conceived of the venture as a joint one, yet suspected that Garrick was, in private, laying claim to the lion's share.[21] The personalities involved and the enlistment of supporters for either side throughout the play's earliest stage history have provided a dense literature. The most telling documents would seem to be a manuscript of the play now to be consulted in the Folger Shakespeare Library, and a recently discovered sketch of the plot, in Garrick's hand, entitled *The Sisters*.[22] Colman would surely have brought to the project his own experience of legal business from Lincoln's Inn (where he was called to the Bar in 1757) and the Oxford circuit during 1759. There is a direct borrowing at 4.2.303 from Garrick's version of *Every Man in His Humour* (1752), itself derived from Jonson's own text (3.3.36).[23] It is, however, safer to assume that Colman took on the task of the final revision and preparation. Whilst it is always informative to identify a respective authorial responsibility, the net effect of this collaboration is a play that has at least two impulses: a frame suggested by any number of Sentimental plots of thwarted love, on the one hand, and, on the other, the satire on class and corruption of taste that gives the play its bite.

The title is quite specific in its associations. Often simply known as the Marriage Act of 1753, the Act for the better prevention of Clandestine Marriages, framed by Philip Yorke, the first Earl of Hardwicke, then Lord Chancellor, was the culmination of at least a century's concern at not only lax legislation but also loose morals. The lobbying that intensified in early century certainly derived from clear moral concern, but it affected the statute-book by also appealing to an aristocratic determination to defend legacies from unscrupulous

---

[20] *Memoirs of the Life of David Garrick* (1780), 2 vols., ii. 103.

[21] See James Boaden (ed.), *The Private Correspondence of David Garrick, with the most Celebrated Persons of his Time*, 2 vols., (1831), i. 209–12 (letter dated 4 Dec. 1765). For a fuller account of the manuscript evidence of the play's composition, see Pedicord and Bergmann, i. 413–18, and Ian McIntyre, *Garrick* (London, 1999), 373–5.

[22] These documents confirm the fact that Garrick supplied an overall scheme, including the disposition of the characters, and that Colman must have worked on the detail, especially the more satiric episodes on mercantile and legal life. The most reliable analysis of this material is still that of Frederick Bergmann, in his 'David Garrick and *The Clandestine Marriage*', *PMLA*, 67 (1952), 148–62.

[23] I here use the scene divisions and lineation of Robert Miola's Revels edition (Manchester, 2000).

gold-diggers.[24] From 1754, a marriage was only truly so if solemnized in church. A mere verbal contract would count for little. In addition, the ceremony had to be formally recorded in the parish register, signed by both parties who, if under the age of 21, also needed the consent of parents or a guardian. This secularized status of marriage also saw a victory for civil over church courts; the law made it clear that the latter's regulation had failed, and clergymen who disobeyed the law were liable for penalties of up to fourteen years' transportation. When Garrick and Colman named their play they surely intended some reference back to 1753 and the debates about the measure that were current in 1766.

The secrecy of any irregular relationship is stock comic fare, but here we have a marriage between Fanny and Lovewell, and, to top that, a pregnancy, introducing an urgency to its disclosure. A comic world is apt to condone an affair of the heart, but it would be a rare reaction to the play that ignored the at times strident contemporary concerns about sexual and moral incontinence. In February 1765, a repeal Bill, sponsored by Sir John Glynne, had been presented to the Commons and was narrowly defeated in the Lords. Its dilution of the 1753 Act effectively proposed the repeal of a residential qualification and the closer supervision of the marriages of minors by licence. Its supporters were quick to note the rights of even dependent adults (and sometimes those of anybody in love) to act upon strongly held sentiments, and the Act was almost unenforceable if the intending couple had the wit and determination to flee to Scotland (Gretna Green was a favourite border destination), where the Act was not in force. Hardwicke's arguments held their own: public and parental notice were still required, regulation meant security for the young and it was that much harder for bigamy to thrive. There is little evidence to suppose that the play was designed to enter such serious debates. Sterling may fear for the foolishness of 'silly girls' who might 'throw themselves away without the consent of their parents' (5.2.375–7), but the more Olympian generosity of Lord Ogleby exposes this as a 'Change-Alley meanness: 'I indulge my own passions too much to tyrannise over those of other people' (5.2.385–6). This indulgent conclusion delivers the implicit rebuke to the commercial spirit

[24] See Lawrence Stone, *The Family, Sex and Marriage in England, 1500–1800* (New York, 1977), 28–36; R. B. Outhwaite, *Clandestine Marriage in England, 1500–1850* (London, 1995), 112–18; and Rebecca Probert, 'The Impact of the Marriage Act of 1753: Was It Really "A Most Cruel Law for the Fair Sex"?', *Eighteenth-Century Studies*, 38 (2005), 247–62.

derived (as Garrick's 'Prologue' identifies) from Hogarth's series of paintings, *Marriage-a-la-Mode* (1745) and John Shebbeare's novel, *The Marriage Act* (1754).

Hogarth depicts a tragic narrative of blighted lives produced by an arranged marriage. Viscount Squanderfield and his bride have no pretensions to companionship, and the first plate in the series ('The Marriage Contract') shows their fathers involved in negotiations that involve merely prudential considerations. The Earl has had to abandon expensive (and fashionable) building improvements, and needs middle-class funds to maintain his lifestyle; the Alderman, scrutinizing the marriage contract, is prepared to supply this for a name and degree. The Viscount is eventually stabbed by Silvertongue, a favourite of his wife's, in a low-life tavern (Plate 5, 'The Death of the Earl'), and she commits suicide after draining a phial of laudanum (Plate 6, 'The Death of the Countess'). As a perspective on Hardwicke's legislation, even if proleptic, it is not a flattering one. The attempt to preserve an estate or climb socially is doomed once human desire is discounted. The estate will be broken up (in the final painting, her father is even prising the wedding-ring off her finger) and the name inevitably blackened by recent events.[25] Shebbeare's novel involves a clergyman who is transported after consenting to officiate in a clandestine ceremony, but the plot is otherwise very near to that of Garrick and Colman's. In place of Sterling and Mrs Heidelberg, there is Barter and his wife, who are attempting to pair their status-conscious elder daughter, Molly, with Lord Sapplin,[26] the son of the Ogleby figure, Lord Wormeaton. In a subplot reminiscent of Fanny and Lovewell, the younger daughter, Eliza, is in love with Barter's honest, yet poor, clerk, William Worthy. If the plot is similar, the tone is not. Shebbeare is principally a polemicist. *The Marriage Act* is dedicated to John, Duke of Bedford, well known as an opponent of Hardwicke's bill, but the most salient fact about the author's association with the play is that he was convicted and imprisoned in 1758 for libel against the administration, derived in part from the novel (reissued with a sharper commentary in 1755 as *Matrimony*). He also criticized the Duke of Newcastle in *Letters on the English Nation, by*

---

[25] A fuller description of the iconography can be found in Ronald Paulson, *Hogarth*, 3 vols. (New Brunswick, NJ, 1992), ii: *High Art and Low, 1732–1750*, 214–25; Mark Hallett, *Hogarth* (London, 2000), 167–96. See also Helmut Geber, 'The Clandestine Marriage and its Hogarthian Associations', *Modern Language Notes*, 72 (1957), 267–71.

[26] In the early drafts, Sapplin was originally the name given to the character that evolved into Sir John.

*Batista Angeloni, a Jesuit Resident in London* (1756). Part of his punishment was, indeed, to stand in the pillory at Charing Cross. It is highly unlikely, allowing for the public nature of the crime, that Garrick's mention in the 'Prologue' would have gone unnoticed.

It is tempting, therefore, to regard the fortunate conclusion of the action as rather more than convention. Shebbeare had concluded his narrative with a clear objection to the meddling of usually self-interested parents: 'Weigh the Disposition of Guardians against the Folly of Youth, the Circumstances of one Case against those of the other, and then see if it is not probable that more *Suckey Brightleys* will be ruined hereafter by Guardians, than have hitherto been undone by love and unequal Marriage' (ch. 69, ii. 324).[27] It is clear that the authors recognized a current preoccupation when they saw it.

*The Clandestine Marriage* provides wider social commentary, on the other hand, in Sterling's *arriviste* determination to appear to have new wealth at the same time as launder it by appealing to an old, landed, pedigree. Mrs Heidelberg's skirmishes with the English language are part of the same malaise: she wishes to bend it, as with so much else, to her will. The same might be said of Sterling's 'improvements' to the landscape. It may be fashionable to introduce fish into the 'pond' in his grounds, but plentiful 'carp and tench in the boat' simply means few, if any, in the water. That means the expensive introduction of 'turbot' or 'land-carriage mackerel' to supply what nature cannot: a profusion of life that matches Sterling's expectations and that can reproduce itself (1.2.166-9). He may well hold it as 'the chief pleasure of a country house' to make 'improvements', yet, in his hands, it is tampering. The trees that surrounded the house have been cut down so that the vista is open to unrelenting 'wind and sun'. The outhouses that promised a self-sufficiency, the laundry and brewhouse, now have become a greenhouse and pinery respectively (2.2.43-9). The move to 'improve' one's land could simply lead to the presumption that

---

[27] Opinions supporting the legislation usually claimed that all clandestine marriages were 'generally rash . . . made without any calm Thoughts or Deliberation' in Henry Gally's words, the Rector of St Giles in the Fields (*Some Considerations upon Clandestine Marriages* (1750), 12). They were also immensely difficult to substantiate and therefore were liable to provoke bigamy and, in the eyes of the law and church, illegitimacy. For Henry Stebbings, the Chancellor of the Salisbury diocese, the Act would allow marriage to flourish as a divine institution rather than merely a civil contract and work to prevent '*Traffick*' (p. 27) in personal relations. (See his *Enquiry into the Force and Operation of the Annulling Clauses in a late Act for the better preventing of Clandestine Marriages* (1754), 15-29.)

nature did not provide enough, an intervention that itself appeared ill-conceived. By 1766, there were, in any case, signs that taste was changing. Hugh Blair, the Regius Professor of Rhetoric and Belles Lettres at Edinburgh University from 1762 to 1763, made it clear that elevation of mind could not be achieved by gazing on the cultivated and contrived: 'Not the gay landscape, the flowery field, or the flourishing city; but the hoary mountain, and the solitary lake; the aged forest, and the torrent falling over the rock.'[28] Sterling has learnt the art of gardening from a variety of sources, the most identifiable being the Chinese style extolled by William Chambers in his *Designs of Chinese Buildings, Furniture, Dresses, Machines, and Utensils* (1757) and the rigorous (and untactful) application of Hogarth's 'serpentine line', regarded as a major ingredient of beauty in his *The Analysis of Beauty* (1753).[29] Whereas both Chambers and Hogarth anticipate a pleasing alertness from the onlooker, Sterling's version is formulaic and lifeless, closing vistas and tiring the eye. John Shebbeare also had an interest in gardening and, in his *Letters on the English Nation*, he has his commentator, Battista Angeloni, lament the growing trend for cluttered grounds and obvious expense: 'Alas! the bane of men of fine and elegant taste, and the cause of its sudden decline, is the belief in every rich man, who has an inclination to build, or plant, that he has a taste equal to his wealth, and to the undertaking, and a right to obtrude his opinion on the most accomplished judge, in architecture and gardening . . .' ('Letter LVII', ii. 273). Lord Ogleby could not have expressed it better.

The play is rather tougher in its net effect than could be illustrated just in the concluding sentiments. The coercive forces that confront Fanny and Lovewell are shown directly in the play in the shape of Mrs Heidelberg, but also the phalanx of uncaricatured judicial opinions on display for over a hundred lines at the start of 3.1. In Christopher Miles's admirably lucid and sunny film version of 1999, it is little surprise that this scene is trimmed (and repositioned); an abbreviation of some of the threat contained in the guardian forces congregating on the landing outside Fanny's chamber in 5.1 similarly takes the film

[28] *Lectures on Rhetoric and Belles Lettres*, 2 vols. (1783), i. 55.
[29] The most direct line of influence on Hogarth is usually taken to be Batty Langley's *New Principles of Gardening* (1728), where the serpentine path and the varied view symbolize the liberty and informality of the English character. For Hogarth, beauty derived from an intricacy that drew the spectator into its folds and contours, to lead 'the eye a wanton kind of chace' (*Analysis*, 66). It is the 'pleasure of the pursuit' that engages the attention (p. 45).

performance further from the potentially agonistic. As a comment on bourgeois taste, the play also displays a precise consciousness of the emergent cultural forces that permeated mid-century society. The rapid spread of building in what might be called suburban London affected architectural taste and, in turn, promoted consumerist ideals about personal or domestic space.[30] This became insistently so once the rage for 'improvement' took hold in the later years of the century. Wealth had to be shown to be appreciated. Garrick and Colman realized that this had a human cost.

## She Stoops to Conquer

There can rarely have been an acknowledged classic of the British stage of which so little was expected than She Stoops to Conquer. The acclaim it received on its first night at Covent Garden, 15 March 1773, was even of some surprise to its author, who, the well-attested story goes, could not bring himself to attend. Wandering in a nearby park, 'in great agitation', he was met by an incredulous friend who prevailed on him to at least show his face. His first impression on arrival in the wings was of a play that had strained the audience's patience rather too much, as he immediately heard hisses at Mrs Hardcastle's credulousness, in Act 5, scene 2, that she had travelled full fifty miles away when she was in fact in her own garden. Goldsmith need not have worried. George Colman, then in place at the theatre, is supposed to have reassured him: 'Don't be alarmed at a few squibs, when we have been sitting these two hours upon a barrel of gunpowder.'[31] Colman, as manager of the theatre, and David Garrick, similarly in charge at Drury Lane, had resisted several attempts to persuade him that the play, then known by its eventual subtitle, The Mistakes of a Night, should be included in the repertory. Goldsmith had worked steadily on the text throughout the summer of 1771. Perennially in need of some measure of financial stability, his description of the process in his letter to Bennet Langton of 7 September betrays some desperation:

[30] See Peter Thorold, The London Rich: The Creation of a Great City, from 1666 to the Present (West Hartford, Conn., 1999), especially pp. 112–45; N. McKendrick, J. Brewer, and J. H. Plumb, The Birth of a Consumer Society: The Commercialization of Eighteenth-Century England (London, 1982), 34–99, 265–85; James Raven, Judging New Wealth: Popular Publishing and Responses to Commerce in England, 1750–1800 (Oxford, 1992), 212–28.

[31] In John Watkins's Anecdotes of Men of Learning and Genius (1808), repr. in E. H. Mikhail (ed.), Goldsmith: Interviews and Recollections (Basingstoke, 1993), 163–4.

I have been almost wholly in the country at a farmer's house quite alone trying to write a Comedy. It is almost finished but when or how it will be acted, or whether it will be acted at all are questions I cannot resolve. . . . I have been trying these three months to do something to make people laugh. There have I been strolling about the hedges studying jests with a most tragical countenance.[32]

As it was, the production only just made it to the stage right at the end of the 1772–3 season, too late to allow a protracted initial run and a definite threat to an author's benefit receipts.

Goldsmith's experiences with the literary establishment of mid-century, and with the London theatre world in particular, had perhaps prepared him for some problems. He had arrived in London by 1756 from Irish village life via Dublin, Edinburgh, and (to judge by his own accounts) a lengthy European tour. His earliest literary ventures, in the main contributing to the *Monthly Review*, brought him to the notice of several powerful arbiters of taste, the most helpful being that of Samuel Johnson from 1762 onwards—and yet there is a persistent sense that he regarded himself only as a guest. His first major poem, *The Traveller, or a Prospect of Society* (1764), has its conventional passages, but it does purport to track Goldsmith's own European experiences, especially his solitariness:

> But me, not destin'd such delights to share,
> My prime of life in wandering spent and care;
> Impell'd, with steps unceasing, to pursue
> Some fleeting good, that mocks me with the view; . . .
> My fortune leads me to traverse realms alone,
> And find no spot of all the world my own.
>
> (ll. 23–6, 29–30)

The narrator-figure in *The Deserted Village* (1770) seems destined to observe that the 'rural virtues leave the land' (l. 398). This depiction of such spiritual malaise is only one of the attitudes Goldsmith struck, but he was acutely aware of how narrow the margin for literary error might be.

In one of his earliest pieces, *An Enquiry into the Present State of Polite Learning in Europe* (1759) his catalogue of reasons not to write for the stage is persuasive. Caught between the contradictory imperatives to introduce 'stage pomp' on the one hand and 'recital and simplicity' on the other, the playwright is also beset by powerful

---

[32] *The Collected Letters of Oliver Goldsmith*, ed. Katherine Balderston (Cambridge, 1928), 102.

determining forces in the culture itself: 'Our poet's performance must undergo a process truly chymical before it is presented to the public. It must be tried in the manager's fire, strained through a licenser, manager, or critic himself.'[33] Goldsmith had certainly been 'strained' by Colman and Garrick, both of whom had been offered *The Mistakes of a Night*, and had perused it very much at their leisure.[34] Other portents of doom were evident. Assembling the desired cast proved unexpectedly difficult. Mrs Abington, the first choice for the part of Kate Hardcastle and a popular leading lady at Drury Lane, dismissed the offer, perhaps on Garrick's advice. Lee Lewes, whose total stage experience consisted of Harlequin roles in pantomime, accepted Marlow on 'Gentleman' Smith's refusal. The vastly experienced Henry Woodward (some said, at the age of 56, too experienced) eventually declared himself otherwise engaged, allowing another untried talent, John Quick, to take on the onerous task of Tony Lumpkin. Garrick bought himself off from any approach by writing the Prologue. Perhaps the most awkward predicament caused by the late date was the lack of adequate funds for new costumes or props. No wonder Goldsmith feared the worst.

In the event the play prospered. It ran for twelve nights in its first season, including a performance 'By Command of their Majesties' on 5 May. There were a further six summer performances at the Haymarket presented by Samuel Foote, followed by a return to Covent Garden in the Autumn for a further seven by the end of the calendar year. What was just as reassuring was the popularity of the printed text. Within two days of its publication (25 March), a 'new edition' was announced widely in the press, and the *Morning Chronicle* for 1 April commented on how sales had been so 'rapid' that 4,000 copies had been 'disposed of' within three days.[35] To this day, it has proved to be a regular in the British and American repertoire.

It is difficult now to place oneself in the Georgian theatrical context that Goldsmith so much distrusted, but there are three major factors that account for his success. The first returns us to that scenario reported in the letter to Bennet Langton quoted above: Goldsmith

---

[33] *Collected Works of Oliver Goldsmith*, ed. Arthur Friedman, 5 vols. (Oxford, 1966), i. 323.

[34] See Goldsmith's letter to Colman (probably Jan. 1773), allowing him to decree any changes he might think fit (*Letters*, 116). The fullest account of this hiatus in Goldsmith's career can be found in John Ginger, *The Notable Man: The Life and Times of Oliver Goldsmith* (London, 1977), 302–22.

[35] For a full account, see Friedman, v. 89–97.

studied hard how to make audiences laugh. Second, he manipulated
stock comic conventions so that they appeared fresh and challenging.
Comic misrecognition has rarely been so various and so telling. Lastly,
he managed to create a rural genius, or satyr (depending very much on
your perspective) in Tony Lumpkin, who speaks in comic vein for all
who were distrustful of politeness and pretension.

In an essay that appeared just two and a half months prior to the
play's first night ('An Essay on the Theatre; or, a Comparison between
Laughing and Sentimental Comedy'), Goldsmith made great claims
for laughter as a prime effect of comedy. Appearing in the first number
of the *Westminster Magazine* (1 January 1773), it was calculated to
prepare the way for a full appreciation of his new play, but it is very
much more than just advertising. The essay's target is the cult of
Sentiment, a set of gestures taken to be threatening the comic spirit
by a misplaced attempt to excite tragic sympathies at the same time.
In this pen-picture, Sentimental Comedy is almost a contradiction
in terms, where the rationale for comedy—its ridicule of folly by an
appeal to an audience's common sense—is fatally ignored. Nobility of
sentiment is everywhere:

... a new species of Dramatic Composition has been introduced under the
name of *Sentimental* Comedy, in which the virtues of Private Life are
exhibited, rather than the Vices exposed; and the Distresses, rather than the
Faults of Mankind, make our interest in the piece. . . . In these Plays almost all
the Characters are good, and exceedingly generous . . . If they happen to have
Faults or Foibles, the Spectator is taught not only to pardon, but to applaud
them, in consideration of the goodness of their hearts.[36]

Hence it is that he felt that a rearguard action on behalf of the full-
throated guffaw needed to be fought: it ultimately allowed a colder
perspective on folly leading to its correction. Garrick's Prologue to the
play also suggests that it leads to bad art. The collage of undigested
and proverbial saws of lines 25 to 30 illustrates how formulaic the
moral of the sentimental tale had become. Horace's distinction in his
*Art of Poetry*, that comedy portrayed the risible actions of those
lower in social rank than ourselves whereas tragedy dealt with the woes
of gods and kings,[37] was little observed in sentimental pieces where

---

[36] Friedman, iii. 212.

[37] *Ars Poetica*, ll. 89–91: 'A theme for Comedy refuses to be set forth in verses of
Tragedy; likewise the feast of Thyestes scorns to be told in strains of daily life that well
nigh befit the comic sock' (trans. H. R. Fairclough, *Horace: Satires, Epistles and Ars
Poetica* (Cambridge, Mass., 1929), 458–9).

empathy was all. According to the Prologue, it therefore existed on the contemporary stage rather as 'a mawkish drab of spurious breed' (l. 13).

It is necessary, however, to look beyond Goldsmith's immediate argument here, for there are several aspects of his dramatic writing that can certainly appear sentimental. The profligate Young Honeywood in his only other play, *The Good-Natur'd Man* (1768), has a 'sentimental' fault in that, whilst he is moved to generosity by the approaches of beggars and first-time acquaintances, he finds it impossible to settle up with his tailor and grocer. The comic complications of *She Stoops to Conquer* turn on the pardonable faults of Tony's puckish mischief, Mrs Hardcastle's cupboard love and Marlow's 'Englishman's malady' (2.1.80), an extreme reticence before ladies of his own class. It is indeed hard to identify a clear corrective intent in the play. James Ogden acutely observes that, whilst he may have been 'avowedly against sentimentalism, Goldsmith [nonetheless] admits it to the sub-plot' (p. xxiii) for Hastings and Constance Neville. Several critics have also pointed out some of the flaws in Goldsmith's literary history. The stage was not awash with sentimental plays and there are even persistent doubts that sentimental (as opposed to exemplary) comedies actually existed as clearly as Goldsmith makes out.[38]

Goldsmith is not a literary historian, however, and, although the distinction between 'laughing' and 'sentimental' theatre has its frailties, it represents an aspiration borne out by the play itself. The main thrust of his thesis in 1773 was that comedy had steadily divorced itself from an engagement with the everyday. It was exemplary to a fault, and rarely held up a mirror to nature. Recent comment on the essay has given him a little more credit for providing a well-judged dramatic manifesto. Frank H. Ellis has supplied a comprehensive analysis of the sentimental in a variety of forms and concludes that, even if clearly identified sentimental stage comedies might be difficult to isolate, sentiment itself was very much *au*

---

[38] This is most cogently argued by Robert D. Hume in his 'Goldsmith and Sheridan and the Supposed Revolution of "Laughing" against "Sentimental" Comedy' in his *The Rakish Stage: Studies in English Drama, 1660–1800* (Carbondale, Ill., 1983), 312–55. See also Arthur Friedman, 'Aspects of Sentimentalism in Eighteenth-Century Literature', in Henry Knight Miller, Eric Rothstein, and G. S. Rousseau (eds.), *The Augustan Milieu: Essays Presented to Louis A. Landa* (Oxford, 1970), 247–61, and R.W. Bevis, *The Laughing Tradition* (Athens, Ga., 1980).

*courant*.[39] In the writing of the play Goldsmith had, himself, stooped
to conquer, as is evident in one of his epilogues to the play refused
by Colman: where he describes his choice of setting as containing
'No high-life scenes, no sentiment, the creature | Still stoops among
the low to copy nature' ('Second Rejected Epilogue to *She Stoops to
Conquer*', ll. 55–6).[40] This determination to risk being 'low' is part of
the shared joke of 1.2.36–8, where Tony's singing is debated by his
drinking companions at the Three Pigeons:

SECOND FELLOW I loves to hear him sing, bekeays he never gives us nothing
that's *low*.
THIRD FELLOW O damn anything that's *low*, I cannot bear it,

and it culminates in the surprisingly direct verdict on him from the
Landlord: 'Ah, bless your heart, for a sweet, pleasant—damned
mischievous son of a whore' (1.2.169–70). Horace Walpole felt that
the play was 'the lowest of all farces', wherein the 'drift tends to no
moral, no edification of any kind'.[41] Exactly, Goldsmith might have
replied.

Tony Lumpkin provides enough evidence that Goldsmith was certainly not aiming to supply studies of spiritual conversion. Throughout, he is the prime mover of the romantic plot set against the inertia
of parental authority. Most tellingly, he retains, despite his stepfather's
judgement that he is 'a mere composition of tricks and mischief'
(1.1.36), a capacity for good nature that impresses Constance (who
claims that he is 'a good-natured creature at bottom' (1.1.187)), and
even himself when he strives to recover a forlorn situation for the
lovers by being 'a more good-natured fellow than [they] thought for'
(4.1.429–31). Source-hunters have traversed long over the play and

[39] In *Sentimental Comedy: Theory and Practice* (Cambridge, 1991), 3–22. An excellent
study of Goldsmith's relations with his reviewers and how it influenced both the essay
and his plays can be found in Frank Donoghue's ' "He Never Gives Us Nothing that's
*Low*": Goldsmith's Plays and the Reviewers', *ELH*, 55 (1988), 665–84.

[40] The text consulted is that of *The Poems of Gray, Collins, and Goldsmith*, ed. Roger
Lonsdale (London, 1969).

[41] Letter to William Mason, 27 Mar. 1773, in *Goldsmith: The Critical Heritage*,
ed. G. S. Rousseau (London, 1974), 118. It is of some interest in this regard that
Covent Garden restored the 'low' bailiff scene (in Act 3) for its revival of *The Good
Natur'd Man* on 3 May 1773. So opposed had that first-night audience (29 Jan. 1768)
been to its 'low' subject-matter that the 1773 appearance was only the second ever.

there are undeniably antecedents for Tony as for the whole plot.[42] There is a clear line back to Marivaux's *Le Jeu de l'amour et du hasard* (1730), but not where Tony is concerned. Isaac Bickerstaffe's opera, *Love in a Village* (1762), has his rustic sprite, Hodge, similarly help the young lovers, Lucinda/Eustace and Rosetta/Meadows, but his own familial predicament is a matter of far greater creative emphasis in Goldsmith's version. If, indeed, one wished to develop the thesis that he borrowed unduly from Bickerstaffe, one would also have to acknowledge that the debt was a particularly open one. Bickerstaffe visited Goldsmith in that germinal summer of 1771, and had his work current throughout the 1772–3 season at Covent Garden, as there were performances on 23 January, 19 February, and 29 March. It was, therefore, possible to compare Edward Shuter's Hardcastle with his 'operatic' counterpart, Justice Woodcock, and Jane Green's Mrs Hardcastle with Margery, Hodge's buxom beauty. Just in case the analogues with others' plots might be missed, Kate Hardcastle imagines a resemblance in her plain country dress (3.1.227–8) to Cherry, a maid at a provincial inn from Farquhar's *The Beaux' Stratagem* (1707), which similarly explores the effect of the arrival of two male outsiders on a rather sleepy locality.

Goldsmith's strategy is thus a highly theatrical one. Hardcastle's 'old rambling mansion' (1.1.12–13) may as well be a roadside inn if appearances alone are consulted—and that is what happens after all in any dramatic representation. The deep, wide, and shadowy Covent Garden stage aided a certain sympathy with Mrs Hardcastle's confusion in 5.2, that she might be in Crack-skull Common and not in her own back garden. We may know that Kate Hardcastle is the daughter of the house, but, when Marlow encounters her, we actually see her behaving as a chambermaid. Alongside the earliest commentators who were quick to stress the rank implausibility of Goldsmith's plot,[43]

---

[42] The fullest account is in Susan Hamlyn's *She Stoops to Conquer: The Making of a Popular Success* (MA Thesis, Birmingham University, 1975); but see the comments of John Harrington Smith in his 'Tony Lumpkin and the Country Booby Type in Antecedent English Comedy' (*PMLA* 58 (1944), 1038–49; and *Ogden*, pp. xv–xvi, who both discover more freshness than indebtedness in Goldsmith's project. Ginger's account (pp. 296–307) emphasizes Tony's more pivotal role and his less calculating responses towards others, including Bett Bouncer.

[43] See William Woodfall's conclusion that it consisted of 'circumstances . . . the most improbable, and lugged in, the most violently, of any things we ever remember to have either read or seen' (*Monthly Review*, March 1773, in *Rousseau*, p. 117), and the anonymous notice in the *London Magazine* (March 1773) that concluded it contained 'numerous inaccuracies' and unnatural incidents 'in order *to make things meet*' (p. 122).

there were others who, nonetheless, discovered an uncanny form of natural behaviour. Thomas Davies admitted its comic excess, but traced, at the same time, 'a lively and faithful representation of nature; genius presides over every scene', whereas Sir Joshua Reynolds appreciated his accuracy in describing 'how one sentiment breeds another in the mind, preferring this to grow out of the preceding and rejecting another, though more brilliant, as breaking the chain of ideas'.[44] That, we might say, is the trick of it.

## Wild Oats

By the time John O'Keeffe (1747–1833) turned to the writing of *Wild Oats* in 1791, he had an established reputation at Covent Garden, based on some fifty afterpieces, comic operas, and a few attempts at full-scale dramas. William Hazlitt was a genuine admirer of his comedies, claiming that he was the 'English Molière':

The scale of the modern writer was smaller, but the spirit is the same. In light, careless laughter, and pleasant exaggerations of the humorous, we have no one equal to him, There is no labour or contrivance in his scenes, but the drollery of his subject seems to strike irresistibly upon his fancy, and run away with his discretion as it does with ours . . . He is himself a Modern Antique. His fancy has all the quaintness and extravagance of the old writers, with the ease and lightness, which the moderns arrogate to themselves. ('Lecture VIII: On the Comic Writers of the Last Century', in *Lectures on the English Comic Writers* [1819])[45]

Leaving aside the fact that O'Keeffe was Irish and had received an extensive training at Dublin's Smock Alley theatre before his move to London in 1781, Hazlitt's approbation accurately captures the reasons why Regency audiences so took to his plays and other pieces.

Hazlitt, however, principally bases his judgement on the afterpiece, *The Agreeable Surprise* (1784), a great popular success and even more a staple ingredient in the Covent Garden repertory through to the mid-nineteenth century than *Wild Oats*. The later play is neither a

[44] *Memoirs of the Life of David Garrick*, 2 vols. (London, 1808), in *Mikhail*, 69; *Portraits by Sir Joshua Reynolds*, ed. Frederick W. Hilles (London, 1952), in *Mikhail*, 151.
[45] *Complete Works*, vi. 166–7. This title was repeated in the review of *The Agreeable Surprise* for May 1820. O'Keeffe was to be commended 'for all the hearty laughing he has given us' (*Complete Works*, xviii. 319). Hazlitt's wider critical perspective on performance is ably discussed by James Mulvihill in his 'William Hazlitt on Dramatic Text and Performance', in *Studies in English Literature, 1500–1900*, 41 (2001), 695–709.

completely sober experience nor even a regular romantic comedy, yet the effortless and carefree enjoyment Hazlitt discovers in O'Keeffe fits the play only at certain points. There is a comic providence in Sir George and John Dory fetching up, in their 'cruizing' (1.1.1), at Lady Maria's house, and the romantically implausible reunion of Rover with his parents in the last scene has some of the poetic compensation for an intimidating world both of Shakespeare's *As You Like It* (the source of so much direct and indirect allusion in Acts 4 and 5) and, perhaps even more so, the rediscovery of kith and kin after an isolating interval of many years that renders a successful conclusion to *The Winter's Tale* so powerful, and yet recent revivals of the play have discovered more besides.

Clifford Williams's perceptive approach to the play in production, for the Royal Shakespeare Company at the Aldwych Theatre, London, from 1976, has done more than most to set the modern agenda for viewing the play in the theatre and perhaps also for study. Whilst there is a generosity in O'Keeffe's writing, in distributing dramatic interest amongst most of his characters, Williams felt that 'Rover is a man to be treated seriously' in that he is far more than the collage of quotation and allusion that makes up so much of his lines: 'Rover is "forlorn" not only because he lacks means and recognition. More importantly, he lacks parents and identity. His high spirits frequently give place to moments of melancholy and anger'.[46] It does not harm the play to note these darker psychological recesses. Jeremy Sams in 1995 was to catch these same sounds from the text, when preparing his own adaptation for the National Theatre (London). Rover is a man 'without a home, without a family, without love, sucked into a world where rootlessness (or roving) is the norm, where friends are quickly made (and lost), where love and attention can be, on a good night, magicked out of nothing'.[47] From this perspective, Rover is not just an actor but rather *homo thespius*, where humanity is regarded as role-play.

The overall effect of the work is not, however, as chilling as this might indicate. Love and faith in other people is what Rover has in abundance. John Taylor's praise of Rover, in the 'Prologue' to the 1794 edition onwards, includes a recognition of 'Nature's warm and absolute control' that 'guides ev'ry impulse of his generous soul' (ll. 27–8). This might seem rather abstract, yet it does gesture towards the overall need for generous behaviour that even Sir George Thunder

---

[46] 'Introduction', *Wild Oats or The Strolling Gentlemen* (1977), p. x.
[47] 'Introduction', *Wild Oats* (1995), p. vi.

recognizes at the play's conclusion.[48] As noted by Williams (p. xiii), though, there was an urgency in emphasizing the virtues of magnanimity in the 1790s. In setting the action where he does, out of doors and on the road, O'Keeffe can get the audience to appreciate the details of economic exploitation, homelessness, and the desperation of social exclusion. One of O'Keeffe's favourite authors, George Farquhar, achieved the same effect in the Lichfield scenes of *The Beaux' Strategem* (1707) and the Shrewsbury setting for *The Recruiting Officer* (1706). Indeed, the real advantage of tracing the sources of the plentiful allusions and quotations of the play lies not only in identifying the precise local meaning but also in noting the wash of connotations that bathe the whole. Certainly, Farquhar is in the mix, but also Rover is momentarily seen through the lens of Edgar as 'Poor Tom' in *King Lear* (the part Sim remembers Rover to have taken so well at Lymington), the unfortunate Barbarossa from John Brown's *Barbarossa: A Tragedy*, and Chamont's social disadvantage from Otway's *The Orphan*, amongst other instances of tragic potential. In part exorcism of these implied cries of rage, we have the innocent pastoralism of *As You Like It* (the play that will delight the whole community [save a handful of fundamentalists] at the close of the play's action) and Isabella's plea for magisterial mercy from *Measure for Measure* (2.1.62–5, 79–81) introduced at 4.1.27–31.

But what motivates Rover's incessant stream of quotation? For Harry Thunder, this is an 'abominable habit' (1.2.41), a sign of his impetuosity and 'volatile spirits' (1.2.45–6). As far as Jonathan Bate is concerned, the habit of storing up Shakespearian tags and reciting them at any opportune (or even inopportune) moment was very much an accomplishment of the time,[49] but Rover is not directly a common-room competitor. Far from airing knowledge, he discloses an inability to speak in his own accents—a manic counterpoint to Marlow's nervous malady in *She Stoops to Conquer*—and a defensive reflex in answer to new and partially understood social conventions. In the 1793 edition, O'Keeffe had additional material at this point: 'Tho' so devilish pleasant in his quotations, . . . on the moment he dashes in a parody whimsically opposite to every occasion as it happens.' This did not survive thereafter, and we may be grateful that it did not, as

---

[48] The play is studded with references to generous behaviour—not all in relation to Rover; see 2.1.243–5, 2.2.22–4, 3.1.53–4, 4.1.142–3, 5.4.259, 5.4.277–8, and 5.4.284.

[49] Jonathan Bate, *Shakespearean Constitutions: Politics, Theatre, Criticism 1730–1830* (Oxford, 1989), 106–7 n.

any close examination of Rover's 'habit' shows him (and, of course, O'Keeffe) as rarely parodic and often knowing in his match of words and occasion. At its simplest level the comedy comes from Rover's inability to remember his lines; that does not make the task of tracing the source-text any easier, and it produces complex evidence of O'Keeffe's working methods.

Several in-jokes for the Covent Garden faithful are included. At 3.1.100–21, there is a string of self-references to *The Agreeable Surprise*. Mary Wells had played Cowslip regularly at the theatre over the last six years and had been involved in the very scene alluded to in 1791 onwards, but now she is Jane in another play but still as mystified as Cowslip was and is, elsewhere in the repertory. At 4.1.296, the clear reference to Otway's *Venice Preserv'd* (in 5.2) implicitly includes in the same scene Joseph Holman, whose Jaffeir had been in repertory at Covent Garden since November 1790. Thomas Lewis had taken (with some success) Farquhar's Captain Plume in *The Recruiting Officer* at Covent Garden from February 1790. In April 1791, he alludes (at 1.2.63), in the character of Rover, to that same play. The effect is an expansive one, for once the source or one's own memory of recent performance is consulted, one recognizes an extra dimension to what is surely one of the thematic concerns of the play, the confusion of role and reality. This goes deep. In the 1798 text for *Dramatic Works*, O'Keeffe becomes precise in detailing the book Gammon presents to Jane as a present from Lady Amaranth (2.1.41–4): Robert Dodsley's *The Economy of Human Life* (1747). Gammon hands it on approvingly as he likes 'economy' (2.1.43), but if he had perused the book carefully he would have discovered its sense of 'economy' as defiantly opposed to monetary concerns (see note to 2.1.43). These are just a few of many such instances. The conclusion should be clear: O'Keeffe alluded tactically and thematically, and Rover's deliberately hazy recollections of past parts he had taken should not be taken to affect our appreciation of O'Keeffe's acute theatrical awareness.

Anxiety and cultural panic were especially evident at the time O'Keeffe conceived the play. Indeed, over the considerable time of rewriting and extending that 1791 text, national paranoia intensified. War was declared on post-revolutionary France in 1793 and invasion widely anticipated. Sir George's irritation at the Landlord's selfishness leads to a staunch advocacy of a strong, well-motivated, navy, a sentiment that would have struck a deep chord with the audience: 'Chatter your own private concerns, when the public good, or fear of general calamity, should be the only compass. These fellows that I'm in pursuit of, have run from their ships. If our navy's unmanned, what becomes of you and your house, you cormorant ?' (3.2.29–33). Accordingly, the clear identification throughout the 1791, 1792, and 1793 editions of the thieves in Act 5 as 'Sailors' was abandoned from 1794 in favour of 'Ruffians'.

O'Keeffe was not one who took sides in the revolutionary aftermath. The record shows that his *The Grenadier* (written in 1789) was named after Dubois, the first revolutionary to mount the broken walls of the Bastille, but that it never survived to performance: 'when the flame of liberty in Paris seemed to be converted into hell-fire, and patriotic men into demons', the Covent Garden management took the prudent view.[50] Indeed, O'Keeffe then re-called his son, Tottenham, from Paris to finish his education in England. Both *Jenny's Whim* (1794) and *She's Eloped* (destined for Drury Lane, 1798) were similarly withdrawn, but not for any Jacobin content.[51] Whenever he touched upon more controversial matters, he often simply took the quiet path. His poem, 'The Frauds of War', places the steadfast merchant ship against rascally privateers: 'skulking, prowling, thro' the flood, | Gleaners in the field of blood'.[52] On the other hand, Lady Amaranth's distrust of privilege and rank is largely unquestioned in the play. Rover is finally rewarded with position and economic security by a fortuitous twist of the plot, yet he earns this more by a display of loyal faith and humour than by obvious good breeding. It is also telling that the dramatic action should take place near Portsmouth, a port in the process of massive refurbishment in order to support not only naval defences but also to accommodate the assembly of transport ships for convicts.[53]

The title suggests that the best days have gone by and that sobriety awaits the protagonists. For both Harry and Rover, the freedoms of the strolling player must cease and social affiliation commence. O'Keeffe took a prolonged rest from the stage for fully two years immediately after *Wild Oats*, and, although he did return with modest success, he was neither as prolific nor as original again. Indeed, his health was in rapid decline. Michael Kelly, who had known him well in Dublin in the 1770s, met him in 1793, and found him 'broken down, and almost

[50] John O'Keeffe, *Recollections of the Life of John O'Keeffe*, 2 vols. (1826), ii. 144.

[51] See ibid., ii. 337–8, 352–4.

[52] In *O'Keeffe's Legacy to his Daughters, being the Poetical Works, Collected with a Memoir by Adelaide O'Keeffe* (1834), 58.

[53] See the figures given by John Winton in his *The Naval Heritage of Portsmouth* (Southampton, 1989), 68–70.

blind: but still full of pleasantry and anecdote'.[54] He did not, however, turn his back on the play; as the evidence of significant textual development or correction makes abundantly clear, he tinkered with and adapted almost every scene—and not in an incremental or teleological way. The temptation is to conclude that he may, in his *Dramatic Works* (1798), have finally got it right, yet the process of revision did not end there, even if O'Keeffe's own direct involvement did. The play was obviously cared for, not only by its author, but also by each company that chose to reenact it. The hope is that this process will continue—in performance as well as in reading.

[54] Michael Kelly, *Reminiscences*, 2 vols. (1826), ii. 37.

# NOTE ON THE TEXTS

## The Modern Husband

*The Modern Husband* exists in two forms, but not consistent with the description on the title-pages of the 'First' and 'Second' editions announced on four of the 1732 copies consulted ('First'—M.adds.108 e. 107 (3) and 'Second'—Vet. A5 e. 5413 (Bodleian), 'First'—11775 e.25 and 'Second'—613 h.19 (British Library)). In every particular they are identical. This is indicated in the notes by *1732 (1)*. Despite a common title (The | Modern Husband. | A | Comedy. | As it is acted at the THEATRE-ROYAL | in DRURY-LANE | By His MAJESTY'S Servants. | Printed for J. Watts at the Printing-Office in *Wild-Court* near *Lincoln's-Inn Fields*), there is an 'edition', another 'First', that shows minor emendations: Vet. A5. E.5413 (4) (Bodleian) and Ashley 719 (BL), indicated in the notes by *1732 (2)*. The only clear indication that one text might have been corrected is the necessary negative in the latter's 1.2.53–4: 'Or if they do speak, it will be a language not understood by the great.' There is also an occasionally more emphatic choice of phrase in this text. Consequently, I have adopted the readings of this corrected 'First' edition.

Each of these texts obeyed the prevailing convention of starting a new scene whenever new characters entered. This edition divides the action only when a new location is required. I have also included additional stage directions where it is clear that these are called for or where it may be directly inferred from the text. These are contained within square brackets. I have also reduced the number of hyphenated conjunctions within most speeches, and retained them only where the speaker is turning to address someone new or where there is a significant change of tempo.

## The Clandestine Marriage

In Harry William Pedicord and Frederick L. Bergmann's detailed investigations of the work's earliest textual history (*The Dramatic Works of David Garrick*, 7 vols. (Carbondale, Ill., 1982)), it is clear that the most intense interest in the play is evident—from both of its authors—during its first season. The editors regard the five printings of the play in 1766 as separate editions, although the actual differences are very small, and mainly confined to the correction of mistakes. A First Edition (octavo), published by T. Becket and P. A. De Hondt soon after its first performance in February 1766 (*1766 (1)*), was swiftly followed by a second octavo edition later in the year, which shows some authoritative revisions to orthography and some substantive amendments to some of the legal jargon in Act 3. As the changes are so slight elsewhere in the 'editions', it is possible to conclude that the 1766 printings followed necessary and inevitable amendments during a first run on stage rather than any significant change of heart. Noel Chevalier's Broadview Press edition (1995) is clearest in a rationale for adopting the second edition (here, *1766 (2)*) as copy-text (I have also closely consulted the third (?) edition (*1766 (3)*), yet the variants noted are slight). His observation that later editions, notably the 'New Edition' from Becket and De Hondt of 1770, and that in the 1777 *Dramatic Works of George Colman* (*1777*), work to normalize the text is due, in the main, to certain revisions and clarifications of Mrs Heidelberg's particular expressions, the original spelling of which probably represented Kitty Clive's own intonations during the first performances. This is marked in the three-volume *Dramatic Works of David Garrick* (1768—here *1768*) and its second edition of 1774 (*1774*). To clarify here is also to eradicate valuable hints as to how the character was first conceived, and it is also likely that these two later versions represent the separate opinions of the two men rather than any collaborative labour. For these reasons, I have taken *1766 (2)* as copy-text.

When modernizing the spelling of the original it would be superfluous to note the several variants between editions that in effect are concerned only with achieving a standard orthography. I have therefore only represented such variants where there would appear to be a significant choice of form.

## She Stoops to Conquer

The first texts of the play, printed for F. Newbery, all in 1773, appeared in rapid order. Thanks to the researches of William B. Todd (in his 'The First Editions of *The Good Natur'd Man* and *She Stoops to Conquer*' (*Studies in Bibliography*, 11 (1958), 133–42)), these are now to be regarded as a single edition, but with six impressions. Accidentals are regularized in this process and a few errors emended.

This would seem to suggest that the bibliographical difficulties they present are easily resolved. *1773a*, the first impression, is my copy-text, and the few necessary choices from the second impression appear as *1773b*. There are no significant choices from subsequent impressions.

There is, however, a manuscript copy of the play, not in Goldsmith's hand, that was presented to the licenser prior to performance (*L*), and that can now be found in the Larpent Collection at the Huntington Library in California. This is usually regarded as representing a preliminary, though fair, state of the text before the author introduced his final corrections. Traditionally, the printed version would take precedence as providing evidence of final intention, but there are local considerations that need to be appreciated. As Tom Davis and Susan Hamlyn make clear (in their 'What Do We Do When Two Texts Differ?', in *Evidence in Literary Scholarship*, ed. Rene Wellek and Alvaro Ribeiro (Oxford, 1979), 263–79), later editions that lay claim to authority in their derivation from prompt copies reintroduce some *L* readings. Of ninety-one variants between *1773a* and *L*, twenty-five are adopted in the Bell (1791), Inchbald (1806), and Cooke (1817) editions. It is probable that the haste with which the printed copies were provided for a voracious early market signalled more their author's need for rapid funds than a full account of the play's evolution in the playhouse, as a dramatic item. Goldsmith's care for consistent punctuation and orthography was, in any case, sporadic at best, and there is evidence to suppose that he neither revised the printed versions nor expressed a view as to whether a 'correct' text should exist (see Davis/Hamlyn and also Coleman O. Parsons, 'Textual Variations in a Manuscript of *She Stoops to Conquer*' (*Modern Philology*, 40 (1942), 57–69)). It is accepted that *1773a* and *L* may have been coexistent, the one more a literary than a dramatic record, and thus equally authoritative. I have, therefore, in line with the practice of recent editors, adopted *L* readings where I believe that they represent (*a*) a vigour that the more prudent Goldsmith did not risk in print and (*b*) a more theatrical record. In line with the format of the series, only significant and substantive variants are recorded.

Garrick's Prologue and Goldsmith's Epilogue both appeared in the press before any other printed version. Variants from the text in the *London Chronicle* (18–20 March 1773) are recorded (*LC*).

## *Wild Oats*

The base-text adopted for this edition is that found in volume ii
(pp. 3–108) of O'Keeffe's *Dramatic Works ... Published under the
Gracious Patronage of His Royal Highness, the Prince of Wales. Prepared
for the Press by the Author* (4 vols., 1798). There are three main reasons
for this choice: (*a*) it stands as the author's most considered version
after a vibrant stage history. Previous texts were obviously much
affected by playhouse use. Adelaide O'Keeffe reported an encounter
in late 1794 with Mrs Pope (Lady Amaranth in the early run) who
bemoaned the 'vile spelling, unintelligible scrawl and careless
arrangement of her pages [her script]' which had 'tried the patience of
managers and transcribers severely' ('Memoir', in *O'Keeffe's Legacy to
his Daughters, being his poetical works* [1834], p. xxiv); (*b*) it clarifies
much of the stage business and punctuation; and (*c*) extends the range
of several parts, most notably that of Rover and Harry. The following
texts have been consulted:

*1791*—*Wild Oats: or the Strolling Gentlemen. A comedy, in five acts, as performed at the Theatre Royal, Covent-Garden* (Dublin, 1791—British Library,
11777.b.64)
*1792*—*Wild Oats: ...,  as performed at the Theatre-Royal, Smock-Alley*
(Dublin, 1792—BL, 11771.a.14)
*1793*—*Wild Oats, ... as performed at the Theatre Royal, Covent Garden*
(Dublin, 1793—BL, 11785.de.14)
*1794*—*Wild Oats, ... as performed at the Theatre Royal, Covent Garden*
(London, 1794—BL, 11777.g.68)

The temptation to pursue the evolution of the play further has been
resisted. Even at the point of the play's first performance on 16 April
1791 at Covent Garden, O'Keeffe had severely curtailed sight, and, by
1798, he was totally blind and all but retired from active involvement
in the theatre world. The testimony of two further editions is of
interest when detailing its early stage history, but we must also
conclude that they represent the necessary evolution of its staging
rather more than any development of interest on the part of O'Keeffe
himself:

*Wild Oats, ... as performed at the Theatre Royal, Covent Garden. Printed ...
from the prompt book. With remarks by Mrs Inchbald* (London, 1806—BL,
1507/319 (8) )
*Wild Oats; ... A Comedy ... With Prefatory Remarks.* | *The only edition
which is faithfully* | *marked with the stage business* | *and stage directions,* | *As it is*

*performed at the Theatres Royal, by W. Oxberry, Comedian* (London, 1820—
BL, 11784.ff.21)

There are two major acts of revision and expansion: in *1794* and
*1798*. The progress from *1791* to *1793* is one mainly of correction,
although there are occasional new errors. *1793* represents both a
(partially) corrected version of preceding editions and the culmination
of attempts to clarify Rover's quotations and tidy up the punctuation
and stage business. It does, however, introduce further corrupt readings on its own account. *1794* includes for the first time quotation
marks around Rover's obvious allusions to other plays, perhaps a sign
of the growing self-consciousness on O'Keeffe's part as to the need
for an audience to acknowledge their existence during performance.
I have adopted just two pre–*1798* readings and these seem merited:
2.1.90 ('foot' for 'spot') and 5.3.102 ('suit' for 'sue').

O'Keeffe's consciousness of his patron for *1798* led him to remove
some of the racier expressions found generally in earlier texts. It could
be argued that these temper the characterization of Sir George and
John Dory, but, conversely, the earlier version could also be regarded
as an initial playing to the gallery and there are enough traces of
idiomatic flavour retained, in any case, to render their 'sea-jaw' vivid
and plausible. I have followed *1798* in excluding them, yet future
productions may consider their inclusion, according to taste.

# SELECT BIBLIOGRAPHY

## General

The most succinct account of eighteenth-century playing conditions and cultural expectations can be found in John Brewer's *The Pleasures of the Imagination: English Culture in the Eighteenth Century* (London, 1997), 325–423. Brewer is observant when noting the increased power of the theatre-manager and the actor—and the persistent commercial motive that helped foster stage spectacle and variety. Conversely, he also traces the often tacit political context that prompted a new set of theatrical conventions. For those interested in developments in design, the updated review of staging conditions in Melinda C. Finberg's edition of *Eighteenth-Century Women Dramatists* (Oxford, 2001), pp. li–lvi is essential reading. Gillian Russell has also provided a compact narrative of 'Theatrical Culture' in *The Cambridge Companion to English Literature, 1740–1830*, ed. Thomas Keymer and Jonathan Mee (Cambridge, 2004), 100–18. Two revisionist histories of gender and dramatic character provide intriguing context for the comedies in this collection. Both Misty G. Anderson's *Female Playwrights and Eighteenth-Century Comedy: Negotiating Marriage on the London Stage* (Basingstoke, 2002) and Lisa Freeman's *Character's Theater: Genre and Identity on the Eighteenth-Century Stage* (Philadelphia, 2002) question the resonance of comedy's fortunate conclusions. For Anderson (and most relevantly for the plays here in question), her use of the Marriage Act debates in unearthing deep incongruities in Elizabeth Inchbald's plays might suggest alternative reactions to those of Garrick/Colman and Goldsmith. Freeman similarly distrusts the neatness of comic resolutions in that 'seams or gaps in character motivation' will have been revealed before the fifth act (p. 149), and thus the individualized identities of the protagonists placed in a potentially ironic perspective. Frank H. Ellis wonders whether Sentimental writing accomplishes that direct sincerity usually associated with it in his *Sentimental Comedy: Theory and Practice* (Cambridge, 1991) and should be read alongside Goldsmith's apparent unsentimentality (see especially pp. 14–21).

Vincent J. Liesenfeld's *The Licensing Act of 1737* illustrates the impact of the Act by reproducing several key primary sources as well as supplying commentary on the events that led up to its codification. Leo Hughes's *The Drama's Patrons: A Study of the Eighteenth-Century London Audience* (Austin, Tex., 1971) is still a reliable authority on the commercial and cultural pressures playwrights confronted. Matthew Kinservik's work has qualified our view of such constraints, and his *Disciplining Satire: The Censorship of Satiric Comedy on the Eighteenth-Century Stage* (Lewisburg, Penn., 2002), whilst it focuses on Fielding (plus Foote and Macklin) also allows us to appreciate the legal position as 'a condition of literary production and not just repression' (p. 14) and its consequences for later drama.

## Fielding

### Editions

Texts of *The Modern Husband* have not been collated and compared until this edition; however, the Wesleyan Edition of the *Plays* will include it in the second volume.

### Biographical Studies

Martin C. and Ruthe R. Battestin's *Henry Fielding: A Life* (London, 1989) is by far the most comprehensive account, incorporating many MS materials. Part II ('Playwright and Libertine, (1727–39)', 55–254) gives a detailed account of Fielding's shifting allegiances. *The Modern Husband* is dealt with especially at pp. 127–33. Simon Varey's *Henry Fielding* (Cambridge, 1986) spares very little time on the play, yet the comments on Richly's final treatment (pp. 14–15) are a corrective to the sentimental view: 'Richly's part in the drama does not end in the ignominy that this plain speaking [Bellamant's closing libertarian notions at 5.2.36–8] might seem to predict' (p. 15). There are useful supplements to the Battestins in Pat Rogers's *Henry Fielding: A Biography* (London, 1979), 53–5, Ronald Paulson's *The Life of Henry Fielding: A Critical Biography* (Oxford, 2000), 33–97, and Harold Pagliaro's *Henry Fielding: A Literary Life* (Basingstoke, 1998), 82–5. The Life (and much more) is included in Martin C. Battestin's *A Henry Fielding Companion* (Westport, Conn., 2000).

### Critical Studies

Still reliable both in its historical and its critical judgements is Robert D. Hume's *Henry Fielding and the London Theatre, 1728–1737* (Oxford, 1988—see especially pp. 111–64). Hume also stands out against the moralism of Fielding's earliest biographers, reclaiming the play as unequivocally supporting the institution of marriage. See also his 'Marital Discord in English Comedy from Dryden to Fielding', *Modern Philology*, 74 (1977), 248–72. Earla A. Wilputte contrasts the play with Behn's *The Lucky Chance* and Haywood's *A Wife to be Lett* in her 'Wife Pandering in Three Eighteenth-Century Plays', *Studies in English Literature, 1500–1900*, 38 (1998), 447–64. Thomas Lockwood (the Wesleyan editor of the *Plays*) combines an acute sense of Fielding's dramatic qualities with an awareness of how he negotiated with the existing theatre world in two essays: (*a*) 'Fielding and the Licensing Act', *Huntington Library Quarterly*, 50 (1987), 379–93; and (*b*) 'Theatrical Fielding', in *Studies in the Literary Imagination*, 32 (1999), 105–14. Although Jill Campbell's *Natural Masques: Gender and Identity in Fielding's Plays and Novels* (Stanford, Calif., 1995) has very little room for *The Modern Husband*, the opening chapter (pp. 19–60) has some suggestive propositions about Fielding's early search for satiric form. See also her 'Fielding's Style', in *Journal of English Literary History*, 72 (2005), 407–28. Again, there is excellent cultural analysis in Angela J. Smallwood's *Fielding and the Woman Question: The Novels of Henry Fielding and Feminist Debate, 1700–1750* (Hemel Hempstead, 1989). See her sections on marriage debates at pp. 153–7, and 167–71.

## *Garrick/Colman*

### Editions

The fullest textual account hitherto can be found in Harry William Pedicord and Frederick Louis Bergmann's *The Dramatic Works of David Garrick*, 7 vols. (Carbondale, Ill., 1980–2), vol. i (*Garrick's Own Plays, 1740–1766*), text: pp. 253–336, commentary, pp. 413–25. It is rivalled by Noel Chevalier's edition of the play (alongside *The Cunning-Man* and *The Rehearsal, or Bayes in Petticoats*—Peterborough, Ont., 1993), containing also a fresh look at Sterling's ethics in the Introduction. E. R. Wood has compiled all the *Plays of David Garrick and George Colman, The Elder* (Cambridge, 1982). *The Clandestine Marriage* has just made it to DVD (dir. Christopher Miles, Ventura Distribution, 2001, VHS—1999).

### Biographical Studies

Ian McIntyre's *Garrick* (Harmondsworth, 1999) deserves the accolades it has received from many quarters; it is even-handed in the treatment of its subject's many weaknesses as well as his strengths, and the description of the relationship with Colman helps to uncover the play's rather fraught genesis (pp. 373–7). George Winchester Stone, Jr., and George M. Kahrl's *David Garrick: A Critical Biography* (Carbondale, Ill., 1979) does provide more general theatrical context. James Boaden's edition of *The Private Correspondence of David Garrick with the Most Celebrated Persons*, 2 vols. (London, 1831) is more than a Victorian curiosity; there is detailed annotation on many who came into contact with Garrick. David M. Little and George M. Kahrl's edition of *The Letters of David Garrick*, 3 vols. (London, 1963) is more comprehensive.

### Critical Studies

Cecil Price's *Theatre in the Age of Garrick* (Oxford, 1973) illustrates both graphically and textually a great deal of the contemporary theatre world; pp. 166–7 merely commences a study of Colman's involvement in the play that still needs supplementing. Jean Benedetti's *David Garrick and the Birth of Modern Theatre* (London, 2001) covers a lot of ground and uncovers new material on his managing of Drury Lane. More specifically on Garrick's writing is Frederick Bergmann's 'David Garrick and *The Clandestine Marriage*', *PMLA*, 67 (1952), 148–62, although John A. Vance's 'A Peep behind the Curtain: David Garrick, Playwright and Adaptor', *Papers on Language and Literature*, 20 (1984), 339–51, is more adventurous. Chevalier's Introduction updates many thematic areas (see above).

Perhaps the most significant contextual studies are those that help us comprehend the debates and consequences of the framing of the 1753 Marriage Act. R. B. Outhwaite's *Clandestine Marriage in England, 1500–1850* (London, 1995) looks before and after, yet its main thesis is (politely) challenged by Rebecca Probert's 'The Impact of the Marriage Act of 1753: Was it Really "A Most Cruel Law for the Fair Sex?"', *Eighteenth-Century Studies*, 38 (2005), 247–62. Katherine S. Green supplies some new material about the Act and its effect on the play in her 'David Garrick and the Marriage Habitus: *The Clandestine Marriage* Revisited', *Restoration and 18th. Century Theatre Research*, 13 (1998), 17–34.

## Goldsmith

### Editions

The first considered attempt to incorporate the Larpent material was Arthur Friedman's edition in his *Collected Works of Oliver Goldsmith*

(Oxford, 1966), 5 vols., vol. v. There is also an indispensable thematic index. Whilst not superseded in this, both Tom Davis (1979) and James Ogden (2001) in their New Mermaid editions are valuable in their comment on other textual and staging issues.

## Biographical Studies

Any serious assessment of Goldsmith's originality amidst apparently more confident figures should read *The Collected Letters of Oliver Goldsmith*, ed. Katherine C. Balderston (Cambridge, 1928). Goldsmith has been well served by several biographers who have traced common themes and preoccupations. Ricardo Quintana's *Oliver Goldsmith: A Georgian Study* (London, 1967) and John Ginger's *The Notable Man* (London, 1977) provide careful, even hesitant, narratives. Ginger (pp. 298–324) is fuller on the play itself, whilst Quintana (pp. 137–58) is extensive in his contextualizing. Samuel H. Woods, Jr.'s *Oliver Goldsmith: A Reference Guide* (London, 1982) provides a comprehensive map to his critical waxings and wanings. This, however, is easily outdistanced—with helpful commentary—by G. S. Rousseau's compilation, *Goldsmith: The Critical Heritage* (London, 1974). E. H. Mikhail has unearthed a few gems in his *Goldsmith: Interviews and Recollections* (Basingstoke, 1993—see the contributions from Thomas Davies (pp. 64–74) and that from Sir Joshua Reynolds (pp. 145–52)).

## Critical Studies

Some of the best general criticism can be found in Davis and Ogden's Introductions to their editions (see above), but recently more theoretical accounts have helped open up the play's multiple perspectives. Christopher K. Brooks is persuasive in his contention that the 'Englishman's Malady' is far more deeply embedded in the play than in Marlow's reticence alone: 'Goldsmith's Feminist Drama: *She Stoops to Conquer*, Silence and Language', *Papers on Language and Literature*, 28 (1992), 38–51. This is also part of T. G. A. Nelson's perception in his 'Stooping to Conquer in Goldsmith, Haywood and Wycherley', *Essays in Criticism*, 46 (1996), 319–39. William J. Burling notes the themes of 'entrapment' in both narrative and in the play's relationship with its audience in his 'Entrapment in Eighteenth-Century Drama from Congreve to Goldsmith', in Carl R. Kropf (ed.), *Reader Entrapment in Eighteenth-Century Literature* (New York, 1992), 177–99.

Some of the best advice on staging can be found in Katherine

Worth's *Sheridan and Goldsmith* (Basingstoke, 1992), especially ch. 5, and in Bernard Harris's contribution to *The Art of Oliver Goldsmith*, ed. Andrew Swarbrick (London, 1984), 144–67: 'Goldsmith in the Theatre'. Goldsmith's varied guises before his public have been the centrepiece of two further studies: Frank Donoghue's ' "He Never Gives Us Nothing That's Low": Goldsmith's Plays and the Reviewers', *Journal of English Literary History, 1500–1900*, 55 (1988), 665–84, and the full-length study of *Goldsmith as Journalist* (Rutherford, NJ, 1993) by Richard C. Taylor.

## O'Keeffe

### Editions

The recent renewal of theatrical interest in *Wild Oats* has helped produce two texts, both mainly based on the 1798 edition. That by Clifford Williams (New York, 1977) has a succinct 'Life' of O'Keeffe and a short essay, 'O'Keeffe and his Critics'. The Introduction by Williams is a valuable account of his rediscovery of the play's depths in the rehearsal-room. Jeremy Sams's text is more adapted (London, 1995). Claire Tomalin supplies a biographical note. Both editions have provided excellent notes. There is a facsimile reproduction of *The Plays of John O'Keeffe* edited by Frederick M. Link (New York, 1981), but the texts are not collated.

### Biographical Studies

Frederick M. Link lists a number of early biographical notices in his *John O'Keeffe: A Bibliography* (Lincoln, Neb., 1983). The *Recollections of the Life of John O'Keeffe, Written by Himself*, 2 vols. (London, 1826) is a respectful account, particularly reticent at the separation from his wife. Some extra insights might be gained by looking at his daughter, Adelaide O'Keeffe's, edition of *O'Keeffe's Legacy to his Daughter, being the Poetical Works of John O'Keeffe* (London, 1834). The revised entry in the *Dictionary of National Biography* is a careful conspectus of what has been gathered from several sources.

### Critical Studies

The introductions in the Williams and Sams editions are perceptive about the challenges in staging the play. Although not exactly authoritative, there are some indications in the 'Oxberry's' edition (1820) of how it had come to he staged by then, both in terms of costume and also set. Attempts to co-opt O'Keeffe for the Irish cause do not always convince, but Karen J. Harvey and Kevin B. Pry's 'John O'Keeffe as an Irish Playwright within the Theatrical, Social and Economic Context of his Time', *Eire-Ireland*, 22 (1987), 19–43 is a balanced account, as is Heinz Kosok's ' "George my Belov'd King, and Ireland my Honor'd Country": John O'Keeffe and Ireland', *Irish University Review*, 22 (1992), 40–54. L. W. Connolly has some careful, though necessarily sketchy, comments about possible censorship (and self-censorship) of O'Keeffe's work in his 'A Case of Political Censorship at the Little Theatre in the Haymarket in 1794: John O'Keeffe's "Jenny's Whim; or, The Roasted Emperor" ', *Restoration and 18th Century Theatre Research*, 10 (1995), 34–40, and also his 'More on John O'Keeffe and the Lord Chamberlain', *Notes and Queries*, NS 16 (1969), 190–2.

# CHRONOLOGY

1707  Fielding born at Sharpham Park, nr. Glastonbury, Somersetshire.

1717  David Garrick born in the Angel Inn, Hereford.

1728  Fielding's poem, *The Masquerade: Love in Several Masques* opens at Drury Lane.

1730  Probable birthdate of Goldsmith, at Pallas, Co. Westmeath; Fielding's *The Temple Beau* performed at Goodman's Fields, his *The Author's Farce* commences a run of 42 performances, and *Tom Thumb* a run of 41 performances, at the New Theatre in the Haymarket; *Rape upon Rape; or The Justice Caught in his Own Trap* opens at the Haymarket—as *The Coffee-House Politician*, it is revived at Lincoln's Inn Fields.

1731  Fielding's *The Tragedy of Tragedies; or The Life and Death of Tom Thumb* performed at the Haymarket; a revised version of his *The Welsh Opera; or, The Grey Mare the Better Horse*, known as *The Grub-Street Opera* commissioned by the Haymarket, but withdrawn at the last minute and never acted.

1732  Fielding's *The Lottery* and *The Modern Husband* at Drury Lane; George Colman born at Florence; John Rich opens new Covent Garden theatre.

1733  Theophilus Cibber leads a breakaway group of actors from Drury Lane to the Little Haymarket; Fielding remains loyal.

1734  The Drury Lane management accedes to Cibber's group's demands; Fielding moves to the Haymarket; he begins contributing (until 1739) to the opposition journal, *The Craftsman*.

1736  Henry Fielding's most directly satirical piece, *Pasquin*.

1737  Henry Fielding's *Eurydice; or the Devil Henpeck'd* opens in February at Drury Lane; the final performance of one of his plays at the Haymarket (23 May); the Licensing Act effectively restricts the performance of full-length plays to the two patent theatres, Drury Lane and Covent Garden (21 June)—and contributes to Fielding's move from theatre; Garrick and Samuel Johnson set out for London on 9 March.

1740  Garrick's first play, *Lethe; or, Esop in the Shades*, performed at Drury Lane.

1741  Garrick makes his debut as Richard III at Goodman's Fields; his *The Lying Valet* is performed there.

1742  Walpole resigns as Prime Minister.

1743  Garrick and Charles Macklin lead an actors' strike at Drury Lane.

1747    Garrick is joint patentee (with James Lacy) at Drury Lane; John O'Keeffe born in Dublin.

1752    Local Licensing Act requires magistrates to review and license smaller productions.

1753    Fielding dies; the Marriage Act passed.

1755    Colman graduates from Oxford and enters Lincoln's Inn to read for the Bar.

1757    Colman practises on the Oxford Circuit.

1759    Goldsmith starts to contribute to Smollett's *Critical Review*; publishes *An Enquiry into the Present State of Learning in Europe*; starts to be known as 'Dr Goldsmith'.

1760    Colman's *Polly Honeycombe*.

1761    Colman's *The Jealous Wife* performed at Drury Lane.

1762    Goldsmith's *The Citizen of the World*.

1763    David Garrick clears audience from the stage; travels on the continent to 1765; Drury Lane and Covent Garden damaged by rioters demanding reduced admission after the third act.

1764    Goldsmith's *The Traveller; or, A Prospect of Society*; O'Keeffe's first play performed at Smock Alley, Dublin: *The She Gallant*.

1765    Garrick introduces side-lights at Drury Lane.

1766    Samuel Foote granted a patent for the Haymarket; Goldsmith's *The Vicar of Wakefield*; Colman and Garrick's *The Clandestine Marriage*.

1767    Goldsmith's *The Good Natur'd Man*; Garrick's *The Dramatic Works of David Garrick*, published in three volumes. Colman buys a share in Covent Garden.

1769    Torrential rain almost ruins the Garrick festivities at Stratford-upon-Avon to celebrate the bicentennial of Shakespeare's birth.

1770    Goldsmith's *The Deserted Village*.

1771    Garrick employs Philippe Jacques de Loutherbourg to design scenery at Drury Lane.

1773    Goldsmith's *She Stoops to Conquer*.

1774    Goldsmith dies at the Temple (4 April).

1775    Garrick's *Bon Ton; or High Life above Stairs*; Drury Lane is altered and decorated by the Adam brothers.

1776    Garrick retires; Sheridan takes over Drury Lane and Colman manages the Haymarket.

1777    A sequel to *She Stoops to Conquer: Tony Lumpkin in Town* performed at the Haymarket.

1779    Garrick dies; burial in Poets' Corner.

1781   O'Keeffe moves to England from Dublin, never to return.

1782   Covent Garden altered and enlarged.

1783   George Colman revives *The Clandestine Marriage* at the Haymarket.

1786   John O'Keeffe's wife, Mary Heaphy, leaves the family; O'Keeffe's *The Agreeable Surprise* opens at Covent Garden.

1787   Attempt to defy patentees with the opening of the Royalty Theatre proves unsuccessful.

1788   Kemble manager of Drury Lane.

1789   Haymarket Theatre burns.

1791   O'Keeffe's play, *The Grenadier*, in rehearsal at Covent Garden, yet is cancelled due to the pressure of anti-French feeling; his *Wild Oats* is performed at Covent Garden and Dublin.

1792   Opening of enlarged Covent Garden.

1793   Enlarged Drury Lane opened; death of Colman.

1798   O'Keeffe's *Dramatic Works* are published in four volumes.

1833   Death of O'Keeffe.

# THE MODERN HUSBAND

## A Comedy

BY

## HENRY FIELDING

*Hæc ego non credam Venusinâ digna Lucernâ?*
*Hæc ego non agitem?—*
*Cùm Leno accipiat Moechi bona, si capiendi*
*Jus nullum Uxori, doctus spectare Lacunar,*
*Doctus & ad Calicem vigilanti stertere Naso.*

Juv. Sat. 1°

## To the Right Honourable Sir Robert Walpole,°
## Knight of the most Noble Order of the Garter

SIR,

While the peace of Europe,° and the lives and fortunes of so great a part of mankind, depend on your counsels, it may be thought an offence against the public good to divert, by trifles of this nature, any of those moments, which are so sacred to the welfare of our country.   5

But however ridiculed or exploded the muses may be, in an age when their greatest favourites are liable to the censure and correction of every boy or idiot, who shall have it in his power to satisfy the wantonness of an evil heart, at the expense of the reputation and interest of the best poet, yet has this science been esteemed, honoured,   10
protected, and often professed by the greatest persons of antiquity. Nations and the muses have generally enjoyed the same protectors.

The reason of this is obvious: as the best poets have owed their reward to the greatest heroes and statesmen of their times, so those heroes have owed to the poet that posthumous reputation, which is   15
generally the only reward that attends the greatest actions. By them the great and good blaze out to posterity, and triumph over the little malice and envy which once pursued them.

Protect therefore, sir, an art from which you may promise yourself such notable advantages: when the little artifices of your enemies,   20
which you have surmounted, shall be forgotten, when envy shall cease to misrepresent your actions, and ignorance to misapprehend them. The muses shall remember their protector, and the wise statesman the generous patron, the steadfast friend, and the true patriot; but, above all, that humanity and sweetness of temper, which shine through   25
all your actions, shall render the name of Sir Robert Walpole dear to his no longer ungrateful country. That success may attend all your counsels, that you may continue to preserve us from our enemies abroad, and to triumph over your enemies at home,° is the sincere wish of,   30

SIR, your most obliged, most obedient humble servant, Henry Fielding.

# THE CHARACTERS OF THE PLAY

## MEN

| | |
|---|---|
| Lord Richly. | Mr Cibber. |
| Mr Bellamant. | Mr Wilks. |
| Cap. Bellamant. | Mr Cibber, Jun. |
| Mr Gaywit. | Mr Mills, Jun. |
| Mr Modern. | Mr Bridgewater. |
| Lord Lazy *person who attends L. Richly's Levee.* | Mr Boman. |
| Col. Courtly *person who attends L. Richly's Levee.* | Mr Hallam, Jun. |
| Mr Woodall, *person who attends L. Richly's Levee* | Mr Harper. |
| Cap. Merit *person who attends L. Richly's Levee.* | Mr Paget. |
| Cap. Bravemore *person who attends L. Richly's Levee.* | Mr Watson. |
| John, *servant to Modern.* | Mr Berry. |
| Porter to Lord Richly. | Mr Mullart. |

## WOMEN

| | |
|---|---|
| Lady Charlotte Gaywit. | |
| Mrs Bellamant. | Mrs Cibber. |
| Mrs Modern. | Mrs Horton. |
| Emilia | Mrs Heron. |
| Lately. | Mrs Butler. |
| | Mrs Charke. |

3

# Prologue

Spoken by Mr Wilks

In early youth, our author first begun,
To combat with the follies of the town;
Her want of art, his unskilled muse bewailed,
And where his fancy pleased, his judgement failed.
Hence, your nice tastes he strove to entertain,                    5
With unshaped monsters of a wanton brain!

He taught Tom Thumb strange victories to boast,
Slew heaps of giants, and then—killed a ghost!°

To rules, or reason, scorned the dull pretence,
And fought your champion, 'gainst the cause of sense!°         10

At length, repenting frolic flights of youth,
Once more he flies to nature, and to truth:
In virtue's just defence, aspires to fame,
And courts applause without the applauder's shame!

Impartial let your praise, or censure flow,                        15
For, as he brings no friend, he hopes to find no foe.
His muse in schools too unpolite was bred,
To apprehend each critic—that can read:
For, sure, no man's capacity's less ample
Because he's been at Oxford or the Temple!°                      20
He shows but little judgement, or discerning,
Who thinks taste banished from the seats of learning.

Nor is less false, or scandalous th' aspersion,
That such will ever damn their own diversion.
But, poets damned, like thieves convicted, act,                    25
Rail at their jury, and deny the fact!
Tonight (yet strangers to the scene) you'll view,
A pair of monsters most entirely new!
Two characters scarce ever found in life.
A willing cuckold—sells his willing wife!                          30

But, from whatever clime the creatures come,
Condemn 'em not—because not found at home:
If then, true nature in his scenes you trace,
Not scenes, that comedy to farce debase;°
If modern vice detestable be shown,                              35
And vicious, as it is, he draws the town;
Though no loud laugh applaud the serious page,
Restore the sinking honour of the stage!°
The stage which was not for low farce designed,
But to divert, instruct, and mend mankind.                       40

## 1.1

*Mrs Modern's House*

*Mrs Modern at her toilet, Lately attending*

MRS MODERN Lud! this creature is longer in sticking a pin, than some people are in dressing a head. Will you never have done fumbling?

LATELY There, maam,° your ladyship is dressed.

MRS MODERN Dressed! Ay, most frightfully dressed, I am sure. If it    5 were not too late, I would begin it all again. This gown is wretchedly made, and does not become me. When was Tricksy here?

LATELY Yesterday, maam, with her bill.

MRS MODERN How! Her bill already?

LATELY She says, maam, your ladyship bid her bring it.    10

MRS MODERN Ay, to be sure, she'll not fail to remember that.

LATELY She says too, maam, that she's in great distress for her money.

MRS MODERN Oh, no doubt of that. I do not know anyone who is not.

LATELY What shall I do, maam, when she comes again?

MRS MODERN You must—you must send her away again, I think.    15

LATELY Yes, maam, but—

MRS MODERN But—but what? Don't trouble me with your impertinence, I have other things to think on. Bills! Bills! Bills! I wonder there are no laws against duns in a civilised nation. (*Knocking at the door*) Come in.    20

*Enter Footman*

FOOTMAN My Lady Ever-play, madam, gives her humble service to you, and desires your ladyship's company tomorrow se'ennight° to make a party at Quadrille with my Lady Lose-all, and Mrs Banespouse.

MRS MODERN Lately, bring the Quadrille book hither. See whether    25 I am engaged.

LATELY Here it is, maam.

MRS MODERN Run over the engagements.

LATELY Monday, February 5. at Mrs Squabble's; Tuesday, at Mrs Witless's; Wednesday, at Lady Matadore's;° Thursday, at Mrs    30 Fiddle-Faddle's; Friday, at Mrs Ruin's; Saturday, at Lady Trifle's; Sunday, at Lady Barbara Pawnjewels.

MRS MODERN What is the wench doing? See for how long I am engaged. At this rate you will not have done this hour.

LATELY Maam, your ladyship is engaged every night till Thursday    35
three weeks.

MRS MODERN My service to Lady Ever-play. I have parties every
night till Thursday three weeks, and then I shall be very glad if she
will get two more at my house. And, Tom, take the roll of visits,
and go with my chair to pay them, but remember not to call at Mrs    40
Worthy's.
    *[Exit Footman]*

MRS MODERN I intend to leave off her acquaintance, for I never see
any people of fashion at her house, which, indeed, I do not wonder
at, for the wretch is hardly ever to be found without her husband.
And truly, I think, she is not fit company for any other. Did you    45
ever see any one dress like her, Lately?

LATELY Oh, frightful! I have wondered how your laship could endure
her so long.

MRS MODERN Why, she plays at Quadrille worse than she dresses,
and one would endure a great deal in a person who loses her money.    50

LATELY Nay, now I wonder that your laship has left her off at all.

MRS MODERN Truly, because she has left off play; and now she rails
at cards for the same reason, as some women do at gallantry: from
ill success. Poor creatures! How ignorant they are, that all their
railing is only a loud proclamation that they have lost their money,    55
or a lover!

LATELY They may rail as long as they please, maam, they will never
be able to expel those two pleasures out of the world.

MRS MODERN Ah, Lately! I hope I shall be expelled out of the world
first. Those Quadrille rings° of mine are worth more money, than    60
four of the best brilliants. There is more conjuration in these dear
circles. (*Shows a ring*) These Spades, Hearts, Clubs and Diamonds.
Hark, I hear my husband coming, go you downstairs.
    *[Exit Lately]*
Husband, did I say? Sure, the wretch, who sells his wife, deserves
another name, but I must be civil to him while I despise him.    65
    *[Enter Mr Modern]*
My dear, good-morrow.

MR MODERN I hope you slept well last night, madam. That is, I hope,
you had good success at cards.

MRS MODERN Very indifferent. I had won a considerable sum if it
had not been for a cursed Sans-prendre-vole° that swept the whole    70
table. That Lady Weldon has such luck. If I were superstitious, I

should forswear playing with her, for I never played with her, but I
cheated, nor ever played with her, but I lost.

MR MODERN  Then without being very superstitious, I think, you may
suspect that she cheats too.                                                    75

MRS MODERN  Did I not know the other company.° For the very
worst of Quadrille is, one cannot cheat without a partner.° The
division of a booty gives one more pain, than the winning it can
pleasure. I am to make up accounts tomorrow with Mrs Sharpring.
But where to get the money, I know not, unless you have it, child.     80

MR MODERN  I have it? I wanted to borrow some of you. Unless you
can raise me £500 by tomorrow night, I shall be in a fair way to go
to jail the next morning.°

MRS MODERN  If the whole happiness of my life depended on it, I
could not get the tenth part.                                                  85

MR MODERN  You do not manage Lord Richly right. Men will give
anything to a woman they are fond of.

MRS MODERN  But not to a woman whom they were fond of. The
decay of Lord Richly's passion is too apparent for you not to have
observed it. He visits me seldom, and I am afraid, should I ask a     90
favour of him, it might break off our acquaintance.

MR MODERN  Then, I see no reason for your acquaintance. He dances
no longer at my house, if he will not pay the music.° But hold, I
have a thought come into my head, may oblige him to it, and make
better music for us than you imagine.                                          95

MRS MODERN  What is it?

MR MODERN  Suppose, I procured witnesses of his familiarity with
you. I should recover swingeing damages.

MRS MODERN  But then my reputation—

MR MODERN  Pooh, you will have enough to gild it. Never fear your    100
reputation, while you are rich, for gold in this world covers as many
sins, as charity in the next,° so that get a great deal, and give away a
little, and you secure your happiness in both. Besides, in this case,
all the scandal falls on the husband.°

MRS MODERN  Oh no! I shall be no more visited.—Farewell, dear      105
Quadrille; dear, dear, Sans-prendre-vole, and Matadores.

MR MODERN  You will be forced to quit these pleasures otherwise,
for your companions in 'em will quit you the very moment they
apprehend our sinking fortune. You will find that wealth has a
surer interest to introduce roguery into company, than virtue to     110
introduce poverty.

8

MRS MODERN  You will never persuade me. My reputation is dearer to
me than my life.

MR MODERN  Very strange, that a woman who made so little scruple
of sacrificing the substance of her virtue, should make so much of      115
parting with the shadow of it.

MRS MODERN  'Tis the shadow only that is valuable. Reputation is the
soul of virtue.°

MR MODERN  So far indeed that it survives long after the body is dead,
though to me, virtue has appeared nothing more than a sound, and      120
reputation is its echo. Is there not more charm in the chink of a
thousand guineas, than in ten thousand praises? But what need
more arguments, as I have been contented to wear horns for your
pleasure, it is but reasonable, you should let me show 'em for my
profit.      125

MRS MODERN  If my pleasures, Mr Modern, had been your only
inducement, you would have acted another part. How have you
maintained your figure in the world since your losses in the South
Sea,° and others? And do you upbraid me with the crimes which
you yourself have licensed, have lived by?      130

MR MODERN  Had I followed my own inclinations, I had retired, and
instead of supporting these extravagances by such methods, had
reduced my pleasures to my fortune. 'Twas you, madam, who by
your unbridled pride, and vanity ran me into debt, and then, I gave
up your person to secure my own.      135

MRS MODERN  Ha! Have I secured thy worthless person at the
expense of mine? No, wretch, 'tis at the price of thy shame, I have
purchased pleasures. Why, why do I say thy shame? The mean,
grovelling animal, whom any fear could force to render up the
honour of his wife, must be above the fear of shame. Did I not come      140
unblemished to thee? Was not my life unspotted as my fame, 'till at
thy base entreaties I gave up my innocence? Oh! that I had sooner
seen thee starve in prison, which yet I will, ere thou shalt reap the
fruits of my misfortunes. No, I will publish thy dishonour to the
world.      145

MR MODERN  Nay, but, my dear.

MRS MODERN  Despicable monster!

MR MODERN  But, child, hearken to reason.

MRS MODERN  Never, never.

MR MODERN  I own myself in the wrong. I ask ten thousand pardons. I      150
will submit to any punishment.

MRS MODERN  To upbraid me with—

MR MODERN  My dear, I am in the wrong, I say. I never will be guilty
of the like again. [*Aside*] Sure, the Grand Signior° has no slave
equal to a contented cuckold.                                    155

MRS MODERN  Leave me a while. Perhaps I may come to myself.

MR MODERN  My dear, I am obedient.

   *Exit Mr Modern*

MRS MODERN  What shall I do? Money must be raised. But how? Is
there on earth a person that would lend me twenty guineas! I have
lost Gaywit's heart too long to expect anything there, nor would my   160
love ever suffer me to ask him. Ha! Bellamant, perhaps may do it.
He is generous,° and I believe he loves me. I will try him, however.
What wretched shifts are they obliged to make use of, who would
support the appearance of a fortune which they have not!

   *Exit Mrs Modern*


## 1.2

   *The street before Lord Richly's door*

CAPTAIN MERIT  That is the door I must attack, and I have attacked a
city with less reluctance. There is more hardship in one hour's base
solicitation at a levee,° than in a whole campaign.

   [*Enter Porter*]

Does my Lord Richly see company this morning?

PORTER  Sir, I cannot tell yet, whether he does or no.            5

CAPTAIN MERIT  Nay, I have seen several gentlemen go in.

PORTER  I know not whom you may see go in. I suppose, they have
business with his lordship. I hope you will give my lord leave to be
at home to whom he pleases.

CAPTAIN MERIT  If business be a passport to his lordship, I have busi-   10
ness with him of consequence.

PORTER  Sir, I shall tell him of it.

CAPTAIN MERIT  Sir, I shall be obliged to you, to tell him now.

PORTER  I cannot carry any message now, unless I knew you.

CAPTAIN MERIT  Why, don't you know me, that my name is Merit?     15

PORTER  Sir, here are so many gentlemen come every day, that, unless
I have often new tokens to remember 'em by, it is impossible—
Stand by there, room for my Lord Lazy.

   *Lord Lazy crosses in a chair[, carried by two servants.*
   *Enter Capt. Bravemore, from the house.]*


10

CAPTAIN BRAVEMORE  Merit, good-morrow. What important affair
can have sent you hither, whom I know to shun the houses of the     20
great, as much as virtue does?

CAPTAIN MERIT  Or as much as they do poverty, for I have not been
able to advance farther than you see me. 'Sdeath, I have mounted
a breach against an armed file of the enemy,° and yet a single porter
has denied me entrance at that door. You, I see, have speeded     25
better.

CAPTAIN BRAVEMORE  Ha! Ha! Ha! Thou errant man of war. Hark'ye,
friend, there is but one key to all the great men's houses in town.

CAPTAIN MERIT  Is it not enough to cringe to power, but we must do
the same to the servants of power?     30

CAPTAIN BRAVEMORE  Sir, the servants of a great man° are all great
men. Would you get within their doors, you must bow to the porter,
and fee him too. Then to go farther, you must pay your devoirs
to his gentleman. And after you have bowed for about half an hour
to his whole family, at last you may get a bow from himself.     35

CAPTAIN MERIT  Damnation! I'd sooner be a galley-slave. Shall I, who
have spent my youth and health in my country's service, be forced
by such mean vassalage to defend my old age from cold and hunger,
while every painted butterfly wantons in the sunshine?

*Col. Courtly crosses*

'Sdeath, there's a fellow now. That fellow's father was a pimp.     40
His mother, she turned bawd, and his sister turned whore. You see
the consequence. How happy is that country, where pimping and
whoring are esteemed public services, and where grandeur, and the
gallows lie on the same road!

CAPTAIN BRAVEMORE  But leaving off railing, what is your business     45
with his lordship?

CAPTAIN MERIT  There is a company vacant in Colonel Favourite's
regiment, which by his lordship's interest I hope to gain.

CAPTAIN BRAVEMORE  But pray, by what do you hope to gain his
lordship's interest?     50

CAPTAIN MERIT  You know, Bravemore, I am little inclined to boast-
ing, but I think, my services may speak something for me.

CAPTAIN BRAVEMORE  Faith, I'm afraid you will find 'em dumb. Or
if they do speak, it will be a language not understood by the great.
Suppose you apply to his nephew, Mr Gaywit. His interest with my     55
lord may be of service to you.

CAPTAIN MERIT  I have often seen him at Mr Bellamant's, and believe
he would do anything to serve me.

CAPTAIN BRAVEMORE  But the levee is begun by this.° If you please, I'll introduce you to't.                                                                    60

CAPTAIN MERIT  What an abundance of poor wretches go to the feeding the vanity of that leviathan,° one great rogue.

## 1.3

*Lord Richly at his house, with Lord Lazy, Lord Richly, Woodall, Mr Modern and Col. Courtly*

*Enter Capt. Merit and Capt. Bravemore*

LORD RICHLY  Ha! Ha! Ha! Agreeable! Courtly, thou art the greatest droll upon earth. You'll dine with me.—Lord Lazy, will you make me happy too?

LORD LAZY  I'll make myself so, my lord.

LORD RICHLY  Mr Woodall, your servant, how long have you been in     5
town?

WOODALL  I cannot be particular. I carry no almanac about me, my lord, a week or a fortnight perhaps. Too much time to lose at this season, when a man should be driving the foxes out of his country.

COLONEL COURTLY  I hope you have brought your family to town.     10
A parliament-man should always bring his wife with him, that if he does not serve the public, she may.

LORD RICHLY  Now I think familiarity with the wife of a senator should be made a breach of privilege.°

COLONEL COURTLY  Your lordship is in the right. The person of his     15
wife should be made as sacred as his own.

WOODALL  Ay, the women would thank us damnably for such a vote, and the Colonel here is a very likely man to move it.

COLONEL COURTLY  Not I, for the women then would be as backward to be our wives, as the tradesmen are now to be our creditors.     20

WOODALL  To the fine gentlemen of us, who lay out their small fortunes in extravagance, and their slender stock of love on their wenches. I remember the time, when I was a young fellow, that men used to dress like men, but now I meet with nothing but a parcel of toupet coxcombs,° who plaster up their brains upon their periwigs.     25

LORD RICHLY  I protest thou art an errant wit, Woodall.

COLONEL COURTLY  Oh, he's one of the greatest wits of his county.

WOODALL  I have one of the greatest estates of my county, and by what I can see, that entitles a man to wit here, as well as there.

CAPTAIN MERIT (*aside to Bravemore*) Methinks, this rough spark is     30
very free with his lordship.

CAPTAIN BRAVEMORE [*aside to Merit*] You must know, this is a sort of
polite bear-baiting. There is hardly a great man in town but what is
fond of these sort of fellows; whom they take a delight in baiting
with one or more buffoons. But now for your business.     35

LORD RICHLY (*to a gentleman*) I shall see him this morning. You may
depend on my speaking about it.—Captain Bravemore, I am glad to
see you.

CAPTAIN BRAVEMORE My lord, here is a gentleman of distinguished
services. If your lordship would recommend him to Colonel     40
Favourite—

LORD RICHLY Sir, I shall certainly do it.

CAPTAIN MERIT There being a company vacant, my lord. My name is
Merit.

LORD RICHLY Mr Merit, I shall be extremely glad to serve you. Sir     45
John, your most obedient humble servant.—Lazy, what were you
saying about Mr Bellamant?

LORD LAZY We were talking, my lord, of his affair, which was heard
in our House yesterday.

LORD RICHLY I am sorry I was not there. It went against him, I     50
think.

LORD LAZY Yes, my lord, and I am afraid it affects him deeply.

COLONEL COURTLY Undone, sir, quite undone.

LORD RICHLY Upon my soul, Mrs Bellamant's a fine woman.

WOODALL Then I suppose, if her husband's undone, you'll have her     55
among you.

LORD RICHLY Woodall, thou'rt a liquorish dog. Thou would'st have
the first snap.°

WOODALL Not I, none of your town ladies for me. I always take leave
of women from the time I come out of the country till I go back     60
again.

LORD LAZY Women! Pox on him! He means foxes again.

COLONEL COURTLY He knows no difference.

WOODALL Nor you either, but, hark'ee, I fancy it is safer riding after
the one, than the other.     65

COLONEL COURTLY Thy ideas are as gross as thy person.

LORD RICHLY Hang him, sly rogue. You never knew a fox-hunter°
that did not love a wench.

WOODALL No, nor a wench of any sense that did not love a fox-
hunter.°     70

LORD RICHLY  Modern, your servant.°

MR MODERN  I would presume only to remind your lordship—

LORD RICHLY  [*to a gentleman*] Depend upon it, I will remember you.
    I hope your lady is well.

MR MODERN  Entirely at your service, my lord.                          75
        [*They talk aside*]

LORD RICHLY  I have a particular affair to communicate to her, a
    secret that I cannot send by you. You know, all secrets are not
    proper to trust a husband with.

MR MODERN  You do her too much honour, my lord. I believe you will
    find her at home any time today.                                   80

LORD RICHLY  Faith, Modern, I know not whether thou art happier in
    thy temper, or in thy wife.

MR MODERN  Um, my lord, as for my wife, I believe, she is as good as
    most wives. I believe she is a virtuous woman. That I think I may
    affirm of her.                                                     85

LORD RICHLY  That thou may'st, I dare swear, and that I as firmly
    believe as thou dost thyself. And let me tell you, a virtuous woman
    is no common jewel in this age, but prithee, hast thou heard
    anything of Mr Bellamant's affairs?

MR MODERN  No more, than that he has lost his cause,° which he        90
    seemed to expect the other night, when he was at my house.

LORD RICHLY  Then you are intimate.

MR MODERN  He visits my wife pretty often, my lord.

LORD RICHLY  Modern, you know I am your friend, and now we are
    alone let me advise you. Take care of Bellamant, take a particular  95
    care of Bellamant. He is prudent enough in his amours to pass
    upon the world for a Constant Husband;° but I know him. I know
    him. He is a dangerous man.

MR MODERN  My lord, you surprise me so that—

LORD RICHLY  I know you will excuse this freedom my friendship      100
    takes, but beware of Bellamant, as you love your honour.
        [*Enter servant*]

SERVANT  My lord, the coach is at the door.

LORD RICHLY  My dear Modern, I see the great surprise you are in,
    but you'll excuse my freedom.

MR MODERN  I am eternally obliged to your lordship.                  105

LORD RICHLY  Your humble servant.

MR MODERN  I hope your lordship will pardon my freedom, if, after
    all these obligations, I beg leave once more to remind you.

LORD RICHLY  Depend upon it, I'll take care of you.

[*Aside*]° What a world of poor chimerical devils does a levee draw
together? All gaping for favours, without the least capacity of
making a return for them.°

> But great men justly act, by wiser rules.
> A levee is the paradise of fools.°

## 2.1

*SCENE Mrs Bellamant's House*

*Enter Mrs Bellamant and Emilia*

MRS BELLAMANT (*to a servant*) Bid John put up the coach. What think you now, Emilia? Has not this morning's ramble° given you a surfeit of the town? After all the nonsense and ill-nature we have heard today, would it grieve one to part with the place one is sure to hear 'em over again in?                                                                5

EMILIA I am far from thinking any of its pleasures worth too eager a wish, and the woman who has with her, in the country, the man she loves, must be a very ridiculous creature to pine after the town.

MRS BELLAMANT And yet, my dear, I believe you know there are                    10
such ridiculous creatures.

EMILIA I rather imagine, they retire with the man they should love, than him they do, for a heart that is passionately fond of the pleasures here, has rarely room for any other fondness. The town itself is the passion of the greater part of our sex, but such I can      15
never allow a just notion of love to. A woman, that sincerely loves, can know no happiness without, nor misery with, her beloved object.

MRS BELLAMANT You talk feelingly, I protest. I wish you don't leave your heart behind you. Come, confess. I hope I have deserved     20
rather to be esteemed your confidante than your mother-in-law.°

EMILIA Would it be a crime, if it were so? But if love be a crime, I am sure you cannot upbraid me with it.

MRS BELLAMANT Though if it be a crime, I am sure you are guilty.—
Well, I approve your choice, child.                                                          25

EMILIA My choice! Excellent! I carry his picture in my eyes,° I suppose.

MRS BELLAMANT As sure as in your heart, my dear.

EMILIA Nay, but dear mamma, tell me whom you guess.

MRS BELLAMANT Hush, here's Mr Bellamant.                                            30

*Enter Bellamant*

MR BELLAMANT So soon returned, my dear? Sure, you found nobody at home.

MRS BELLAMANT Oh, my dear! I have been in such an assembly of company, and so pulled to pieces with impertinence and ill-nature.

16

Welcome, welcome the country! For sure the world is so very bad,        35
those places are best, where one has the least of it.

MR BELLAMANT What's the matter?

MRS BELLAMANT In short, I have been downright affronted.

MR BELLAMANT Who durst affront you?

MRS BELLAMANT A set of women that dare do everything, but what        40
they should do. In the first place, I was complimented with
prude, for not being at the last masquerade, with dullness, for not
entering into the taste of the town in some of its diversions. Then
had my whole dress run over,° and disliked, and to finish all, Mrs
Termagant° told me I looked frightful.        45

MR BELLAMANT Not all the paint in Italy can give her half your
beauty.

MRS BELLAMANT You are certainly the most complaisant man in the
world, and I the only wife who can retire home, to be put in a good
humour. Most husbands are like a plain-dealing° looking-glass,        50
which sullies all the compliments we have received abroad, by
assuring us we do not deserve 'em.

  [Enter servant]
  *During this speech a servant delivers a letter to Bellamant, which*
  *he reads*

EMILIA I believe though, madam, that generally happens when they
are not deserved, for a woman of true beauty can never feel any
dissatisfaction from the justice of her glass, nor she, who has your        55
worth, from the sincerity of her husband.

MRS BELLAMANT Your father seems discomposed. I wish there be no
ill news in his letter.

MR BELLAMANT My dear, I have a favour to ask of you.

MRS BELLAMANT Say to command me.        60

MR BELLAMANT I gave you a bank note° of a hundred yesterday. You
must let me have it again.

MRS BELLAMANT I am the luckiest creature in the world, that I did
not pay away some of it this morning. Emilia, child, come with me.

  *Exit Mrs Bellamant with Emilia*

MR BELLAMANT Excellent! Unhappy woman! How little doth she        65
guess, she fetches this money for a rival! That is all the little merit I
can boast towards her. To have contended by the utmost civility and
compliance, with all her desires, and the utmost caution in the
management of my amour, to disguise from her a secret, that must
have made her miserable. Let me read once more.        70

17

*SIR,*
*If you have, or ever had any value for me, send me a hundred pounds this*
*morning. Or to make 'em more welcome than the last of necessities can,*
*bring them yourself to—Yours—more than her own, Hillaria Modern.*

Why, what a farce is human life? How ridiculous is the pursuit of    75
our desires, when the enjoyment of 'em is sure to beget new ones?
      [*Enter Capt. Bellamant*]

CAPTAIN BELLAMANT  Good-morrow, sir.

MR BELLAMANT  I suppose, sir, by the gaiety of your dress, and your
countenance, I may wish you joy of something besides your father's
misfortunes.                                                          80

CAPTAIN BELLAMANT  Would you have me go into mourning for your
losses, sir?

MR BELLAMANT  You may mourn, sir. I am now unable to support
your extravagance any longer. My advice, nay, my commands have
had no effect upon you, but necessity must, and your extravagance    85
must fall of course, when it has nothing to support it.

CAPTAIN BELLAMANT  I am surprised you should call the expenses of
a gentleman, extravagance.

MR BELLAMANT  I am sorry you think the expenses of a fool, or fop,
the expenses of a gentleman, and that racehorses, cards, dice,       90
whores, and embroidery° are necessary ingredients in that amiable
composition.

CAPTAIN BELLAMANT  Faith, and they are so with most gentlemen of
my acquaintance, and give me leave to tell you, sir, these are the
qualifications which recommend a man to the best sort of people.     95
Suppose, I had stayed at the University, and followed Greek and
Latin, as you advised me: what acquaintance had I found at court?
What bows had I received at an assembly, or the opera?

MR BELLAMANT  And will you please to tell me, sir, what advantage
you have received from these? Are you the wiser, or the richer?     100
What are you? Why, in your opinion, better dressed. Where else
had been that smart toupet, that elegant sword-knot, that coat
covered with lace, and then with powder? That ever heaven should
make me father to such a dressed-up daw! A creature, who draws
all his vanity from the gifts of tailors, and periwig-makers!        105

CAPTAIN BELLAMANT  Would you not have your son dressed, sir?

MR BELLAMANT  Yes, and, if he can afford it, let him be sometimes
fine, but let him dress like a man, not affect the woman, in his habit,
or his gesture.

CAPTAIN BELLAMANT If a man will keep good company, he must      110
  comply with the fashion.
MR BELLAMANT I would no more comply with a ridiculous fashion,
  than with a vicious one, nor with that which makes a man look like a
  monkey,° than that which makes him act like any other beast.
CAPTAIN BELLAMANT Lord, sir! You are grown strangely unpolite.      115
MR BELLAMANT I shall not give myself any farther trouble with you,
  but since all my endeavours have proved ineffectual, leave you to
  the bent of your own inclinations. But I must desire you to send me
  no more bills. I assure you, I shall not answer them. You must live
  on your commission. This last misfortune has made it impossible      120
  that I should add one farthing to your income.
CAPTAIN BELLAMANT I have an affair in my view, which may add
  to it. Sir, I wish you good-morrow. When a father and son must
  not talk of money-matters, I cannot see what they have to do
  together.                                                           125
        [*Exit Capt. Bellamant*]. *Enter Mrs Bellamant and Emilia*
MRS BELLAMANT Here is the bill, my dear.
MR BELLAMANT You shall be repaid in a day or two.
MRS BELLAMANT I saw your son part hastily from you, as I came in.
  I hope you have not been angry with him.
MR BELLAMANT Why will you ever intermeddle between us?      130
MRS BELLAMANT I hope you will pardon an intercession, my dear,
  for a son-in-law,° which I should not be guilty of for a son of my
  own.
        *Enter Mr Gaywit*
MR GAYWIT Bellamant, good-morrow—Ladies, your humble servant.
MR BELLAMANT Servant, Mr Gaywit. I thought your time had been      135
  so employed, that you had forgot your friends.
MR GAYWIT I ought to excuse so long an absence, but as Bellamant
  knows that it must give myself the greatest pain, he will impute it to
  business.
MR BELLAMANT Did I not also know, that two days of thy life were      140
  never given to business yet?
MR GAYWIT Not what the grave world call so, I confess, but of what
  the gay world allow that name to, no hands were ever fuller.
MR BELLAMANT You have been making love to some new mistress, I
  suppose.                                                           145
MR GAYWIT Fie, it is only husbands make a business of love. To us
  'tis but an amusement.
MRS BELLAMANT Very fine! And to my face too!

MR GAYWIT  Mr Bellamant, madam, is so known an exception to the general mode of husbands, that what is thrown on them, cannot effect one of so celebrated a constancy.    150

MRS BELLAMANT  That's a virtue he may be celebrated for, without much envy.

MR GAYWIT  He will be envied by all men, for the cause of that constancy. Were such wives as Mrs Bellamant less scarce, such husbands as my friend would be more common.    155

EMILIA  You are always throwing the fault on us.

MRS BELLAMANT  It is commonly in us, either in our choice of our husband, or our behaviour to them. No woman, who married a man of perfect sense, was ever unhappy, but from her own folly.    160

          *Knock*

MR GAYWIT  (*looking out of the window*) Ha! A very worthy uncle of mine, my Lord Richly.

MR BELLAMANT  You'll excuse me, if I am not at home.

MR GAYWIT  Fie! To deny yourself to him, would be unprecedented.    165

MR BELLAMANT  I assure you, no, for I have often done it.

MR GAYWIT  Then, I believe, you are the only man in town that has. But it is too late, I hear him on the stairs.

MRS BELLAMANT  Come, Emilia, we'll leave the gentlemen to their entertainment. I have been surfeited with it already.    170

          *Exeunt Mrs Bellamant and Emilia. Enter Lord Richly*

LORD RICHLY  Dear Bellamant, I am your most obedient servant. I am come to ask you ten thousand pardons, that my affairs prevented my attendance the day your cause° came on. It might have been in my power to have served you beyond my single vote.

MR BELLAMANT  I am obliged to your lordship, but as I have great reason to be satisfied with the justice of your honourable house, I am contented.    175

LORD RICHLY  I hope the loss was not considerable.

MR BELLAMANT  I thought your lordship had heard.

LORD RICHLY  I think, I was told twenty thousand pound. But that's a trifle, a small retrenchment in one's expenses. Two or three dozen suits the less, and two or three dozen fewer women in a year, will soon reimburse you.    180

MR BELLAMANT  My loss is not equal to what your lordship intimates, nor can I complain of a fortune, still large enough to retire into the country with.    185

LORD RICHLY  Nay, dear Bellamant, we must not lose you so. Have

you no friend that could favour you with some comfortable snug
employment, of a thousand or fifteen hundred per annum?

MR GAYWIT  Your lordship is the properest° person in the world.      190

LORD RICHLY  Who I? I am sure no mortal would do half so much to
serve dear Jack Bellamant as myself, but I have no interest in the
least.

MR BELLAMANT  I am obliged to the good offices of my friend, but I
assure your lordship I have no intention that way. Besides, I      195
have lived long enough in the world, to see that necessity is as bad
a recommendation to favours of that kind, which as seldom fall
to those who really want them, as to those who really deserve
them.

LORD RICHLY  I can't help saying, those things are not easily obtained.   200
I heartily wish I could serve you in anything. It gives me a great
deal of uneasiness that my power is not equal to my desire. [*Aside*]
Damn it, I must turn this discourse, or he'll never have done with
it.—Oh, Bellamant! have you heard of the new opera of Mr
Crambo?°      205

MR GAYWIT  What's the name of it?

LORD RICHLY  It will be called the Humours of Bedlam.° I have read
it, and it is a most surprising fine performance. It has not one
syllable of sense in it from the first page to the last.

MR GAYWIT  It must certainly take.      210

LORD RICHLY  Sir, it shall take, if I have interest enough to support it.
I hate your dull writers of the late reigns. The design of a play is to
make you laugh, and who can laugh at sense?°

MR GAYWIT  I think, my lord, we have improved on the Italians. They
wanted only sense. We have neither sense, nor music.      215

LORD RICHLY  I hate all music but a jig.

MR GAYWIT  I don't think it would be an ill project, my lord, to turn
the best of our tragedies and comedies into operas.

LORD RICHLY  And, instead of a company of players, I would have a
company of tumblers and ballad-singers.°      220

MR BELLAMANT  Why, faith, I believe it will come to that soon, unless
some sturdy critic should oppose it.

LORD RICHLY  No critic shall oppose it. It would be very fine, truly, if
men of quality were confined to the vulgar taste. We should be
rarely diverted, if a set of pedants were to licence all our diversions.   225
The stage then would be as dull as a country pulpit.

MR GAYWIT  And the boxes in Drury Lane, as empty as the galleries
in St James's.°

MR BELLAMANT Like enough, for religion and common sense are in a
fair way to be banished out of the world together.                    230

LORD RICHLY Let 'em go, egad.

MR BELLAMANT This is, I believe, the only age that has scorned a
pretence to religion.°

LORD RICHLY Then it is the only age that hath scorned hypocrisy.

MR BELLAMANT Rather, that hypocrisy is the only religion° it wants.    235
You shall have a known rascal set up for honour—a fool for wit—
and your professed dear bosom fawning friend, who, though he
wallow in wealth, would refuse you ten guineas to preserve you
from ruin, shall lose a hundred times that sum at cards, to ruin your
wife.                                                                  240

LORD RICHLY There dear Jack Bellamant is the happiest man in the
world, by possessing a wife whom a thousand times that sum would
have no effect on.

MR BELLAMANT I look upon myself equally happy, my lord, in having
no such friend as would tempt her.                                    245

LORD RICHLY That thou hast not, I dare swear. But I thank you for
putting me in mind of it. I must engage her in my author's cause,
for I know her judgement has a great sway.

MR BELLAMANT As our stay will be so short in town, she can do you
no service. Besides, I have heard her detest partiality in those       250
affairs. You would never persuade her to give a vote contrary to her
opinion.

LORD RICHLY Detest partiality! Ha, ha, ha! I have heard a lady
declare for doing justice to a play, and condemn it the very next
minute, though I knew she had neither seen, nor read it. Those          255
things are entirely guided by favour.

MR GAYWIT Nay, I see no reason to fix the scandal on the ladies. Party
and prejudice have the same dominion over us.° Ask a man's
character of one of his party, and you shall hear he is one of the
worthiest, honestest fellows in Christendom. Ask it of one of           260
the opposite party, and you shall find him as worthless, good-for-
nothing a dog as ever was hanged.

MR BELLAMANT So that a man must labour very hard to get a general
good reputation, or a general bad one.

LORD RICHLY Well, since you allow so much, you will give me leave       265
to tempt Mrs Bellamant.

MR BELLAMANT With all my heart, my lord.

MR GAYWIT Thou art a well-bred husband, indeed, to give another
leave to tempt your wife.

MR BELLAMANT I should have been a very ill-bred one to have denied    270
it. Who's there?
  *Enter Servant*
LORD RICHLY (*aside*) If I had said more, he had granted it, rather
than have lost my favour. Poverty makes as many cuckolds as it does
thieves.
MR BELLAMANT Wait on my Lord Richly to your mistress's apart-    275
ment.—[*To Lord Richly*] I am your most obedient servant.
  [*Exit Lord Richly*]
MR GAYWIT I find, you are resolved to make your wife share your
misfortunes. It would have been civil to have given her the choice of
not being at home.
MR BELLAMANT I wanted to be alone with you. Besides, women have    280
a liberty of sending away an impertinent visitant which we have
not.
MR GAYWIT Ay, and a way of entertaining visitants too which we have
not, and he is a visitant not easily sent away, I assure you. I have
known him receive very vigorous rebuffs without retreating.    285
MR BELLAMANT You talk as if you suspected his making love to my
wife.
MR GAYWIT He does so to every woman he sees. Neither the strictest
friendship professed to her husband, nor the best reputation on her
own side, can preserve any woman he likes from his attacks, for he    290
is arrived at a happy way of regarding all the rest of mankind as his
tenants, and thinks because he possesses more than they, he is
entitled to whatever they possess.
MR BELLAMANT Insolent vanity! I wonder the spirit of mankind
has not long since crushed the tyranny of such lordly wolves, yet    295
believe me, Gaywit, there generally goes a great deal of affectation
to compose this voluptuous man. He oftener injures women in their
fame, than in their persons. This affectation of variety discovers a
sickly appetite; and many mistresses, like many dishes, are often
sent away untasted.    300
MR GAYWIT A very innocent affectation truly, to destroy a lady's
fame.
MR BELLAMANT Why aye, for we are come to an age, wherein a
woman may live very comfortably without it. As long as the
husband is content with his infamy, the wife escapes hers.    305
MR GAYWIT And I am mistaken, if many husbands in this town do
not live very comfortably by being content with their infamy, nay,
by being promoters of it. It is a modern trade, unknown to our

ancestors, a modern bubble which seems to be in a rising condition
at present.                                                                                    310

MR BELLAMANT  It is a stock-jobbing age.° Everything has its price.
Marriage is traffic° throughout; as most of us bargain to be husbands, so some of us bargain to be cuckolds, and he would be as
much laughed at, who preferred his love to his interest, at this end
of the town, as he who preferred his honesty to his interest at the      315
other.

MR GAYWIT  You, Bellamant, have had boldness enough, in contradiction to this general opinion, to choose a woman from her sense
and virtues. I wish it were in my power to follow your example—
but—                                                                                          320

MR BELLAMANT  But the opinion of the world, dear boy—

MR GAYWIT  No, my good forefathers have chosen a wife for me. I am
obliged by the settlement of Lord Richly's estate to marry Lady
Charlotte.

MR BELLAMANT  How!                                                                   325

MR GAYWIT  The estate will descend to me so encumbered, I assure
you.

MR BELLAMANT  I thought it had not been in Lord Richly's power, to
have cut off the entail.°

MR GAYWIT  Not if I marry Lady Charlotte.                                     330

MR BELLAMANT  I think you are happy in being engaged to no more
disagreeable woman.

MR GAYWIT  Lady Charlotte, is indeed pretty; but were she everything a lover could wish, or even imagine—there is a woman, my
friend—                                                                                        335

MR BELLAMANT  Nay, if you are in love with another, I pity you.

MR GAYWIT  Did'st thou know how I love, you would pity me, but
didst thou know whom, couldst thou look upon her with eyes
like mine, couldst thou behold beauty, wit, sense, good-nature, con-
tending which should adorn her most?                                        340

MR BELLAMANT  Poor Gaywit! Thou art gone indeed.

MR GAYWIT  But I suppose, the ladies have by this discharged their
visitant. Now if you please, we will attend them.

MR BELLAMANT  You will excuse me, if I leave you with 'em, which I
will not do, unless you promise I shall find you at my return.          345

MR GAYWIT  I intend to dedicate the day to your family, so dispose of
me as you please.

## 2.2

*Mrs Modern's House*

*Enter Lord Richly and Mrs Modern*

MRS MODERN  I think, I ought to blame your unkindness. I have not seen you so long.

LORD RICHLY  Do you think a week so long?

MRS MODERN  Once you would have thought so.

LORD RICHLY  Why, truly, hours in the spring of love are something 5
shorter than they are in the winter.

MRS MODERN  Barbarous man! Do you insult me, after what I have done for you?

LORD RICHLY  I fancy, those favours have been reciprocal.

MRS MODERN  Have I not given you up my virtue? 10

LORD RICHLY  And have I not paid for your virtue, madam? I am
sure, I am 1500 pounds out of pocket, which in my way of
counting, is fourteen more° than any woman's virtue is worth.
In short, our amour is at an end, for I am in pursuit of another
mistress. 15

MRS MODERN  Why do you come to torment me with her?

LORD RICHLY  Why, I would have you act like other prudent women
in a lower station: when you can please no longer with your own
person, even do it with other people's.

MRS MODERN  Monster! Insupportable! 20

LORD RICHLY  You may rave, madam, but if you will not do me a
favour, there are wiser people enow° who will. I fixed on you out of
a particular regard to you, for I think, when a man is to lay out his
money, he is always to do it with his friends.

MRS MODERN  I'll bear it no longer. (*Going*) 25

LORD RICHLY  Nor I. (*Going*)

MRS MODERN  Stay, my lord, can you be so cruel?

LORD RICHLY  Pshaw! (*Going*)

MRS MODERN  Oh! Stay! Stay! You know my necessities.

LORD RICHLY  And, I think, I propose a very good cure for 'em. 30

MRS MODERN  Lend me a hundred guineas.

LORD RICHLY  I will do more.

MRS MODERN  Generous creature!°

LORD RICHLY  I'll give you—twenty.

MRS MODERN  Do you jest with my necessity? 35

LORD RICHLY  Lookee, madam, if you will do a good-natured thing for me, I will oblige you in return as I promised you before, and I think that very good payment.

MRS MODERN  Pray, my lord, use me with decency at least.

LORD RICHLY  Why should we use more decency to an old    40
acquaintance, than you ladies do to a new lover, and have more
reason for so doing? You often belie your hearts, when you use us
ill. In using you so, we follow the dictates of our natures.

    *Enter a Servant, who delivers a letter to Mrs Modern*

MRS MODERN  [*aside*] Ha! it is Bellamant's hand, and the note° that
I desired. This is lucky, indeed.    45

    *Enter Mr Gaywit, Emilia, Lady Charlotte and Captain*
    *Bellamant*

LORD RICHLY  So! here's an end of my business for the present,
I find.

LADY CHARLOTTE  Oh, dear Modern! I am heartily glad to see you are
alive; for you must know, I thought it impossible for any one to be
alive, and not be at the rehearsal of the new opera.°    50

CAPTAIN BELLAMANT  How can you be surprised at one of no taste,
Lady Charlotte?

MRS MODERN  I suppose, it was very full.

LADY CHARLOTTE  Oh, everybody was there! All the world.

MR GAYWIT  How can that be, Lady Charlotte, when so considerable a    55
part, as Mrs Modern, was wanting?

MRS MODERN  Civil creature! When will you say such a thing?

CAPTAIN BELLAMANT  When I am as dull, madam.

LORD RICHLY  Very true! No-one makes a compliment, but those that
want wit for satire.    60

MR GAYWIT  Right, my lord. It is as great a sign of want of wit to say a
good-natured thing, as want of sense to do one.

LADY CHARLOTTE  Oh! I would not say a good-natured thing for the
world. Captain Bellamant, did you ever hear me say a good-natured
thing in your life?    65

MR GAYWIT  But I am afraid, Lady Charlotte, though wit be a sign of
ill-nature, ill-nature is not always a sign of wit.

LADY CHARLOTTE  I'll give you leave to say anything, after what I
have said this morning. Oh, dear Modern, I wish, you had seen
Emilia's dressing-box! Such japonning. He! He! He! She hath    70
varnished over a windmill ten several times,° before she discovered,
she had placed the wrong side upwards.

MRS MODERN  I have had just such another misfortune. I have laid out
thirty pounds on a chest, and now I dislike it of all things.

LADY CHARLOTTE Oh, my dear, I do not like one thing in twenty that 75
I do myself!

EMILIA You are the only person that dislikes, I dare say, Lady
Charlotte.

LADY CHARLOTTE Oh, you flattering creature! I wish you could bring
my Papa to your opinion. He says, I throw away more money in 80
work than in play.

MRS MODERN But you have not heard half my misfortune. For when
I sent my chest to be sold, what do you think I was offered for my
thirty pounds worth of work?

LADY CHARLOTTE I don't know, fifty guineas perhaps. 85

MRS MODERN Twenty shillings, as I live.

LADY CHARLOTTE Oh intolerable! Oh insufferable!

CAPTAIN BELLAMANT But are we to have no hazard° this morning?

MRS MODERN With all my heart.—Lord Richly, what say you?

LORD RICHLY My vote always goes with the majority, madam. 90

MRS MODERN Come then, the shrine is within, and you that will offer
at it, follow me.

> [*Exit Lord Richly, Mrs Modern, Lady Charlotte and Capt.
> Bellamant*]

EMILIA Mr Gaywit, are you no gamester?

MR GAYWIT No, madam, when I play, 'tis the utmost stretch of my
complaisance. 95

EMILIA I am glad I can find one who is as great an enemy to play as
myself, for I assure you, we are both of the same opinion.

MR GAYWIT I wish we were so in everything.

EMILIA Sir!

MR GAYWIT I say, madam, I wish all of my opinions were as well 100
seconded, and yet, methinks, I would not have your thoughts the
same with mine.

EMILIA Why so, pray?

MR GAYWIT Because you must have then many an unhappy hour,
which that you may ever avoid, will be still my heartiest prayer. 105

EMILIA I am obliged to you, sir.

MR GAYWIT Indeed, you are not. It is a self-interested wish, for,
believe me, to see the least affliction attend you, would give this
breast the greatest agony it is capable of feeling.

EMILIA Nay, this is so extravagant a flight, I know not what to call it. 110

MR GAYWIT Nor I. Call it a just admiration of the highest worth. Call
it the tenderest friendship if you please, though much I fear it
merits the sweetest, softest name that can be given to any of our

passions. If there be a passion pure without allay,° as tender
and soft, as violent and strong, you cannot sure miscall it by that    115
name.

EMILIA  You grow now too philosophical for me to understand you.
Besides, you would, I am sure, be best understood ironically, for
who can believe any thing of Mr Gaywit, when he hath asserted
that he is unhappy?    120

MR GAYWIT  Nay, I will leave my case to your own determination
when you know it. Suppose me obliged to marry the woman I don't
like, debarred for ever from her I love, I dote on, the delight of my
eyes, the joy of my heart. Suppose me obliged to forsake her, and
marry—another.    125

EMILIA  But I cannot suppose you obliged to that.

MR GAYWIT  Were it not an impertinent trouble, I could convince you.

EMILIA  I know not why I may not be excused a little concern for one
who hath expressed so much for me.

MR GAYWIT  Then, madam, the settlement of my whole fortune    130
obliges me to marry Lady Charlotte.

EMILIA  How! But suppose the refusal were on Lady Charlotte's side.

MR GAYWIT  That is my only hope.

EMILIA  And I can assure you, your hope is not ill-grounded.

MR GAYWIT  I know she hath expressed some dislike to me, but she is    135
a woman of that sort, that it is as difficult to be certain of her
dislike, as her affection, and whom the prospect of grandeur would
easily make obedient to her father's commands.

EMILIA  Well, if you are sincere, I pity you heartily!

MR GAYWIT  And if you are sincere, I never knew happiness till this    140
dear moment.

> *Enter Lord Richly, Mrs Modern, Lady Charlotte and*
> *Captain Bellamant*

MRS MODERN  Victoria, Victoria!°

CAPTAIN BELLAMANT  Stripped, by Jupiter!°

LADY CHARLOTTE  Eleven mains° together, Modern. You are a devil.

EMILIA  What's the matter, Lady Charlotte?    145

LADY CHARLOTTE  Oh, my dear, you never saw the like. Modern has
held in nine thousand mains in one hand, and won all the world.°

MR GAYWIT  She has always great luck at Hazard.

LORD RICHLY  Surprising today, upon my word.°

MRS MODERN  Surprising to me, for it is the first success I have    150
had this month, and I am sure, my Quadrille makes everyone a
sufficient amends for my Hazard.

LORD RICHLY You are one of those, whose winning nobody ever heard of, or whose losing no one ever saw.

CAPTAIN BELLAMANT But you forget the auction, Lady Charlotte.          155

LADY CHARLOTTE What have I to do at an auction, that am ruined and undone?

MR GAYWIT As much as many that are undone: bid out of whim, in order to raise the price, and ruin others. Or if the hammer should fall upon you, before you expect it, take a sudden dislike to the     160 goods, or dispute your own words, and leave them upon the hands of the seller.

MRS MODERN How polite is that now? Gaywit will grow shortly as well-bred, as Madcap.°

CAPTAIN BELLAMANT We shall have him there too, and he is the life     165 of an auction.

LADY CHARLOTTE Oh, the most agreeable creature in the world! He has more wit than anybody. He has made me laugh five hundred hours together. Emilia, we will just call there, and then I'll set you down at home.          170

EMILIA Let us but just call then.

LADY CHARLOTTE That caution is admirable from you, when you know I never stay above six minutes anywhere. Well, you never will reform.

LORD RICHLY I desire, Charlotte, you would be at home by        175 four.

LADY CHARLOTTE I shall very easily, my lord, for I have not above fourteen or fifteen places to call at. Come, dear creature, let us go, for I have more business than half the world upon my hands, and I must positively call at the auction.          180

MR GAYWIT Where you have no business, it seems.

LADY CHARLOTTE Impertinent! Modern, your servant.
    [*Exit Mr Gaywit, Lady Charlotte, Emilia and Captain Bellamant*]

LORD RICHLY I only waited till you were alone, madam, to renew my business.

MRS MODERN If you intend to renew your impertinence, I wish you     185 would omit both.

LORD RICHLY So, I find I have my work to do over again.

MRS MODERN But if you please, my lord, to truce with your proposals, and let Piquet be the word.°

LORD RICHLY So, you have taken money out of my daughter's hands,     190 to put it into mine.

MRS MODERN  Be not confident. I have been too hard for you before
now.

LORD RICHLY  Well, and without a compliment, I know none whom
I would sooner lose to than yourself, for to anyone who loves play    195
as well as you, and plays as ill, the money we lose, by a surprising ill
fortune, is only lent.

MRS MODERN  Methinks, my lord, you should be fearful of deterring
me by this plain-dealing.°

LORD RICHLY  I am better acquainted with your sex. It is as impos-    200
sible to persuade a woman that she plays ill, as that she looks ill.
The one may make her tear her cards, and the other break her
looking-glass.

> Her want of skill, for want of luck must pass,
> As want of beauty's owing to her glass.°                           205

# 3.1

*SCENE continues, with Lord Richly and Mrs Modern*

MRS MODERN  Can you be so cruel?

LORD RICHLY  Ridiculous! You might as well ask me for my whole estate. I am sure, I would as soon give it you.

MRS MODERN  An everlasting curse attend the cards! To be repiqued from forty, when I played but for five!° My lord, I believe you a  5
cheat.

LORD RICHLY  At your service, madam. When you have more money, if you will honour me with notice, I will be ready to receive it.

MRS MODERN  Stay, my lord. Give me the twenty guineas.

LORD RICHLY  On my conditions.  10

MRS MODERN  Any conditions.

LORD RICHLY  Then you must contrive some way or other, a meeting between me and Mrs Bellamant, at your house.

MRS MODERN  Mrs Bellamant!

LORD RICHLY  Why do you start at that name?  15

MRS MODERN  She has the reputation of the strictest virtue of any woman in town.

LORD RICHLY  Virtue! Ha, ha, ha! So have you, and so have several of my acquaintance. There are as few women who have not the reputation of virtue, as that have the thing itself.  20

MRS MODERN  And what do you propose by meeting her here?

LORD RICHLY  I am too civil to tell you plainly what I propose, though, by your question, one would imagine you expected it.

MRS MODERN  I expect anything from you, rather than civility,° my lord.  25

LORD RICHLY  Madam, it will be your own fault, if I am not civil to you. Do this for me, and I'll deny you nothing.

MRS MODERN  There is one thing, which tempts me more than your gold, which is the expectation of seeing you desert her, as you have done me.  30

LORD RICHLY  Which is a pleasure you'll certainly have; and the sooner you compass my wishes, the sooner you may triumph in your own. Nay, there is a third motive will charm thee, my dear Hillaria, more than the other two. When I have laid this passion, which hath abated that for you,° I may return to your arms with all  35
my former vigour.

MRS MODERN Excuse my incredulity, my lord, for though love can change its object, it can never return to the same again.

LORD RICHLY I may convince you of the contrary.—But to our business: fortune has declared on our side already, by sending Bellamant hither. Cultivate an acquaintance with him, and you cannot avoid being acquainted with his wife. She is the perfect shadow of her husband. They are as inseparable, as Lady Coquette and her lapdog. 40

MRS MODERN Yes, or as her ladyship and her impertinence, or her lapdog and his smell. Well, it is to me surprising, how women of fashion can carry husbands, children, and lapdogs about with 'em, three things I never could be fond of. 45

LORD RICHLY If the ladies were not fonder of their lapdogs than of their husbands, we should have no more dogs in St James's parish, than there are lions at the tower.° 50

MRS MODERN It is an uncommon bravery in you, to single out the woman who is reputed to be the fondest of her husband.

LORD RICHLY She that is fond of one man, may be fond of another. Fondness, in a woman's temper, like the love of play, may prefer one man, and one game, but will incline her to try more, especially when she expects greater profit, and there I am sure, I am superior to my rival. If flattery will allure her, or riches tempt her, she shall be mine, and those are the two great gates by which the devil enters the heart of womankind— 55

60

[Enter Mr Modern]
Pshaw! He here!—

MR MODERN I am your lordship's most obedient humble servant.

LORD RICHLY Have you seen this new opera, madam?

MRS MODERN I have heard vast commendations of it, but I cannot bear an opera, now poor La Dovi's° gone. 65

LORD RICHLY Nor I, after poor A la Fama.°

MRS MODERN Oh! *Cara* la Dovi! I protest, I have often resolved to follow her into Italy.

LORD RICHLY You will allow A la Fama's voice, I hope.

MRS MODERN But the mien of La Dovi. Then her judgement in singing the moment she entered the stage. I have wished myself all eyes. 70

LORD RICHLY And the moment A la Fama sung, I have wished myself all ears.

MR MODERN I find I am no desired part of this company. [*To Lord Richly*] I hope, your lordship will pardon me. Business of the 75 greatest consequence, requiring my attendance, prevents my waiting on your lordship according to my desires.

[*Exit Mr Modern*]

LORD RICHLY This unseasonable interruption has quite cut the thread of my design. Pox on him. A husband, like the fool in a play,° is of no use but to cause confusion.                                        80

MRS MODERN You would have an opportunity at my house, and to procure it, I must be acquainted with Mrs Bellamant. Now, there is a lucky accident which you are not apprised of: Mr Bellamant is an humble servant of mine.                                                                            85

LORD RICHLY That is lucky indeed. Could we give her a cause of suspicion that way, it were a lively prospect of my success. As persuading a thief that his companion is false, is the surest way to make him so.

MRS MODERN A very pretty comparison of your lordship's between    90
the two states.

*Enter Servant*

SERVANT Madam, Mr Bellamant desires to know, if your ladyship is at home.

MRS MODERN I am. Bring him into the dining room.

LORD RICHLY Thou dear creature, let me but succeed in this affair,    95
I'll give thee millions.

MRS MODERN More gold, and fewer promises, my lord.

LORD RICHLY An hundred guineas shall be the price of our first interview.

MRS MODERN Be punctual, and be confident. Go out the back way,    100
that he may not see you.

LORD RICHLY Adieu, my Machiavil.°

*Exeunt Lord Richly, Mrs Modern and Servant*

# 3.2

*Mrs Bellamant's House.*

*Enter Mrs Bellamant, Mr Gaywit and Emilia*

MRS BELLAMANT And so, Lady Willitt, after all her protestations against matrimony, has at last generously bestowed herself on a young fellow with no fortune, the famous Beau Smirk.

EMILIA She was proof against everything but charity.

MR GAYWIT  To which all other virtues should be sacrificed, as it is       5
the greatest.° The ladies are apt to value themselves on their virtue,
as a rich citizen does on his purse, and I do not know which is of the
greatest use to the public.

MRS BELLAMANT  Nor I, which are the oftenest bankrupts.

MR GAYWIT  And as, in the city, they suspect a man who is ostenta-      10
tious of his riches; so should I the woman, who makes the most
noise of her virtue.

MRS BELLAMANT  We are all the least solicitous about perfections,
which we are well assured of our possessing. Flattery is never so
agreeable as to our blind side. Commend a fool for his wit,       15
or a knave for his honesty, and they will receive you into their
bosoms.

EMILIA  Nay, I have known a pretty lady who was vain of nothing but
her false locks, and have seen a pair of squinting eyes, that never
smiled at a compliment made to any other feature.       20

MR GAYWIT  Yes, madam, and I know a pretty gentleman, who obliges
me very often with his ill-spelt songs, and a very ugly poet, who
hath made me a present of his picture.

EMILIA  Well, since you see it is so agreeable to flatter one's blind side,
I think you have no excuse to compliment on the other.       25

MR GAYWIT  Then I shall have a very good excuse to make you no
compliment at all. But this I assure you, Emilia: the first imper-
fection I discover, I will tell you of it with the utmost sincerity.

EMILIA  And I assure you with the utmost sincerity, I shall not thank
you for it.       30

MRS BELLAMANT  Then, without any flattery, you are two of the most
open plain-dealers I have met with.

*Enter Lady Charlotte*

LADY CHARLOTTE  Dear Mrs Bellamant, make some excuse for me.
I see, Emilia is going to chide me for staying so long. When did
she know the fatigue I had this afternoon. I was just going into       35
my coach, when Lady Twitter came in, and forced me away to a
fan-shop. Well, I have seen a set of the prettiest fans today. My dear
creature, where did you get that lace?° I never saw anything so
ravishing.

EMILIA  I cannot see anything so extraordinary in it.       40

LADY CHARLOTTE  It could not cost less than ten pound a yard.—Oh!
Mr Gaywit, are you here?

EMILIA  He goes with us to the play.

LADY CHARLOTTE  Oh hateful! How can you bear him? I would as

soon to the chapel with Lady Prude. I saw the ridiculous creature 45
cry at a tragedy.

MRS BELLAMANT Do you think he need be ashamed of that, Lady
Charlotte?

LADY CHARLOTTE I would as soon laugh at a comedy, or fall asleep at
an opera. 50

MRS BELLAMANT What is the play tonight?

LADY CHARLOTTE I never know that. Miss Rattle and I saw four acts
the other night, and came away without knowing the name. I think,
one only goes to see the company,° and there will be a great deal
tonight, for the Duchess of Simpleton sent to me° this morning. 55
Emilia, you must go with me after the play. I must make just fourteen visits between nine and ten. Yesterday was the first payment°
I have made since I came to town, and I was able to compass no
more than three and forty; though I only found my Lady Sober at
home, and she was at Quadrille.—Lud, Mrs Bellamant, I think you 60
have left off play, which is to me surprising, when you played so
very well.

MRS BELLAMANT And yet I believe, you hardly ever saw me
win.

LADY CHARLOTTE I never mind whether I win or no, if I make no 65
mistakes.

MR GAYWIT Which you never fail of doing as often as you play.

LADY CHARLOTTE Do you hear him?

EMILIA Oh, he sets up for a plain-dealer. That is, one who shows his
wit at the expense of his breeding. 70

LADY CHARLOTTE Yes, and at the expense of his truth.°

EMILIA Never mind him, Lady Charlotte. You will have the town on
your side.

MR GAYWIT Yes, they will all speak for you that play against you.

LADY CHARLOTTE This is downright insupportable. 75

[Enter Capt. Bellamant]

LADY CHARLOTTE Oh, here's Captain Bellamant shall be my
voucher!°

CAPTAIN BELLAMANT That you may be assured of, Lady Charlotte,
for I have so implicit a faith in your ladyship, that I know you are in
the right before you speak. 80

LADY CHARLOTTE Mr Gaywit does not allow me to play at Quadrille.

CAPTAIN BELLAMANT He may as well deny that your ladyship sees.
Besides, I do not lay a great deal of weight on his judgement, whom
I never saw play at all.

LADY CHARLOTTE Oh, abominable! Then he does not live at all. I  85
wish my whole life was one party at Quadrille.

CAPTAIN BELLAMANT As a Spaniard's is a game at chess,°
egad.

MRS BELLAMANT I never intend to sacrifice my time entirely to play,
till I can get no one to keep me company for nothing.  90

MR GAYWIT Right, madam, I think the votaries° to gaming, should be
such as want helps for conversation, and none should have always
cards in their hands, but those who have nothing but the weather in
their mouths.°

MRS BELLAMANT Thus gaming would be of service to the [re]public  95
of wit,° by taking away the encouragers of nonsense, as a war is of
service to a nation, by taking the idle people out of it.

LADY CHARLOTTE Intolerable! Mrs Bellamant an advocate against
play?
     [Enter Lord Richly]

LORD RICHLY Who is an advocate against play?  100

LADY CHARLOTTE Mrs Bellamant, my lord.

LORD RICHLY She is grown a perfect deserter from the Beau Monde.
She has declared herself against Mr Crambo too.

LADY CHARLOTTE Against dear Mr Crambo?

MRS BELLAMANT I am only for indulging reason in our entertain-  105
ments, my lord. I must own, when I see a polite audience pleased at
seeing Bedlam on the stage,° I cannot forbear thinking them fit for
no other place.

LORD RICHLY Now, I am never entertained better.

LADY CHARLOTTE Nor I. Oh dear Bedlam! I have gone there once a  110
week for a long time. I am charmed with those delightful creatures,
the Kings, and the Queens.°

CAPTAIN BELLAMANT And your ladyship has contributed abundance
of lovers, all Kings, no doubt, for he that could have the boldness to
attempt you, might with much less madness dream of a throne.  115

LADY CHARLOTTE Well, I should like to be a Queen. I fancy, 'tis very
pretty to be a Queen.

CAPTAIN BELLAMANT Were I a King, Lady Charlotte, you should
have your wish.

LADY CHARLOTTE Ay, but then, I must have you too. I would not  120
have an odious filthy he-creature° for the world.

MR GAYWIT (aside) Faith, you cannot easily find any, who is less of the
he-creature.

EMILIA But, Lady Charlotte, we shall be too late for the play.

LADY CHARLOTTE I believe the first act is over, so we'll go. I don't    125
    believe, I ever saw the first act of a play in my life, but do you think,
    I'll suffer you in my coach?
MR GAYWIT At least, you'll suffer me to put this lady into it.
CAPTAIN BELLAMANT And me to put your ladyship in.
LADY CHARLOTTE Dear Mrs Bellamant, your most obedient    130
    servant.
            [*Exeunt Capt. Bellamant and Lady Charlotte*]
LORD RICHLY Shall I have the honour, in the meantime, of entertain-
    ing you at Piquet?°
MRS BELLAMANT Your lordship has such a vast advantage over me.
LORD RICHLY None in the least. But if you think so, madam, I'll give    135
    you what points you please.°
MRS BELLAMANT For one party° then, my lord. Get cards there.
    Your lordship will excuse me a moment.
            [*Exit Mrs Bellamant*]
LORD RICHLY Charming woman! And thou art mine, as surely as
    I wish thee. Let me see, she goes into the country in a fortnight.    140
    Now, if I compass my affair in a day or two, I shall be weary of her
    by that time, and her journey will be the most agreeable thing that
    can happen.

# 3.3

*Mr Modern's House*

*Enter Mrs Modern and Mr Bellamant*

MRS MODERN Is it not barbarous, nay, mean, to upbraid me with what
    nothing but the last necessity could have made me ask of you?
MR BELLAMANT You wrong me. I lament my own necessities, not
    upbraid yours. My misfortune is too public for you not to be
    acquainted with it, and what restrains me from supporting the    5
    pleasures of the best wife in the world, may, I think, justly excuse
    me from supporting those of a mistress.
MRS MODERN Do you insult me with your wife's virtue? You, who
    have robbed me of mine? Yet Heaven will, I hope, forgive me this
    first slip,° and, if henceforth I ever listen to the siren persuasions of    10
    your false ungrateful sex, may I—
MR BELLAMANT But hear me, madam.
MRS MODERN Would I had never heard, nor seen, nor known you.

37

MR BELLAMANT  If I alone have robbed you of your honour, it is you
alone have robbed me of mine.                                    15

MRS MODERN  Your honour! Ridiculous! The virtue of a man!

MR BELLAMANT  Madam, I say, my honour. If to rob a woman who
brought me beauty, fortune, love and virtue, if to hazard the making
her miserable be no breach of honour, robbers and murderers may
be honourable men. Yet, this I have done, and this I do still for you.  20

MRS MODERN  We will not enter into a detail, Mr Bellamant, of what
we have done for one another. Perhaps the balance may be on your
side. If so, it must be still greater, for I have one request which must
not be denied.

MR BELLAMANT  You know, if it be in my power to grant, it is not in  25
my power to deny you.

MRS MODERN  Then for the sake of my reputation, and to prevent any
jealousy in my husband: bring me acquainted with Mrs Bellamant.

MR BELLAMANT  Ha!

MRS MODERN  By which means we shall have more frequent  30
opportunities together.

MR BELLAMANT  Of what use your acquaintance can be, I know not.

MRS MODERN  Do you scruple it? This is too plain an evidence of your
contempt of me. You will not introduce a woman of stained virtue
to your wife. Can you, who caused my crime, be the first to con-  35
demn me for it?

MR BELLAMANT  Since you impute my caution to so wrong a cause, I
am willing to prove your error.

MRS MODERN  Let our acquaintance begin this night then. Try if you
cannot bring her hither now.                                     40

MR BELLAMANT  I will try, nay, and I will succeed, for oh, I have
sacrificed the best of wives to your love!

MRS MODERN  I envy, not admire her, for an affection which any
woman might preserve to you.

MR BELLAMANT  I fly to execute your commands.°                   45

MRS MODERN  Stay—I—

MR BELLAMANT  Speak.

MRS MODERN  I must ask one last favour of you—and yet I know not
how. Though it be a trifle, and I will repay it—only to lend me
another hundred guineas.                                         50

MR BELLAMANT  Your request, madam, is always a command. I shall
think time flies with wings of lead° till I return.

MRS MODERN  And I shall think you fly on golden wings,° my dear
gallant.

[*Exit Mr Bellamant*]

Thou ass, to think that the heart of a woman is to be won by gold, as 55
well as her person, but thou wilt find, though a woman often sells
her person she always gives her heart.

## 3.4

*Mrs Bellamant's House*

*Lord Richly and Mrs Bellamant at Piquet*

LORD RICHLY Six parties successively!° Sure, fortune will change
soon, or I shall believe she is not blind.°

MRS BELLAMANT No, my lord, you either play with too great neg-
ligence, or with such ill-luck that I shall press my victory no farther
at present. Besides I can't help thinking five points place the odds 5
on my side.°

LORD RICHLY Can you change this note,° madam?

MRS BELLAMANT Let it alone, my lord.

LORD RICHLY Excuse me, madam, if I am superstitiously observant
to pay my losings, before I rise from the table. Besides, madam, it 10
will give me an infinite pleasure to have the finest woman in the
world in my debt. Do but keep it till I have the honour of seeing
you again. Nay, madam, I must insist on it, though I am forced to
leave it in your hands thus. [*Gives Mrs Bellamant a bank-bill*]

[*Exit Lord Richly*]

MRS BELLAMANT What can this mean? I am confident too that he lost 15
the last party designedly. I observed him fix his eyes steadfastly
on mine, and sigh, and seem careless of his game. It must be so.
He certainly hath a design on me. I will return him this note
immediately, and am resolved never to see him more.

*Enter Mr Bellamant*

My dear, where have you been all day? I have not had one moment 20
of your company since dinner.

MR BELLAMANT I have been upon business of very great consequence, my dear.

MRS BELLAMANT Is it fit for me to hear?

MR BELLAMANT No, my dear, it would only make you uneasy. 25

MRS BELLAMANT Nay, then I must hear it, that I may share your
concern.

MR BELLAMANT Indeed, it would rather aggravate it. It is not in your power to assist me, for since you will know it, an affair hath happened, which makes it necessary for me to pay an hundred guineas this very evening. 30

MRS BELLAMANT Is that all?

MR BELLAMANT That indeed was once a trifle, but now it makes me uneasy.

MRS BELLAMANT So it doth not me, because it is in my power to supply you. Here is a note for that sum, but I must be positively 35 repaid within a day or two. It is only a friend's money trusted in my hands.

MR BELLAMANT My dear, sure when heaven gave me thee, it gave me a cure for every malady of the mind, and it hath made thee still the 40 instrument of all its good to me.

MRS BELLAMANT Be assured, I desire no greater blessing than the continual reflection of having pleased you.

MR BELLAMANT Are you engaged, my love, this evening?

MRS BELLAMANT Whatever engagement I have, it is in your power to 45 break.

MR BELLAMANT If you have none, I will introduce you to a new acquaintance: One whom I believe you never visited, but must know by sight: Mrs Modern.

MRS BELLAMANT It is equal to me° in what company I am, when 50 with you. My eyes are so delighted with that principal figure, that I have no leisure to contemplate the rest of the piece. I'll wait on you immediately.

[*Exit Mrs Bellamant*]

MR BELLAMANT What a wretch am I! Have I either honour or gratitude, and can I injure such a woman? How do I injure her! 55 While she perceives no abatement in my passion, she is not injured by its inward decay. Nor can I give her a secret pain, while she hath no suspicion of my secret pleasures. Have I not found too an equal return of passion in my mistress? Does she not sacrifice more for me than a wife can? The gallant is, indeed, indebted for the favours 60 he receives, but the husband pays dearly for what he enjoys. I hope, however, this will be the last hundred pounds I shall be asked to lend. My wife's having this dear note was as lucky as it was unexpected. Ha, the same I gave this morning to Mrs Modern! Amazement, what can this mean? 65

*Enter Mrs Bellamant*

My dear, be not angry at my curiosity, but pray tell me, how came
you by this?

MRS BELLAMANT  Pardon me, my dear, I have a particular reason for
not telling you.

MR BELLAMANT  And I have as particular a reason for asking it.        70

MRS BELLAMANT  I beg you not to press me. Perhaps you will oblige
me to sacrifice a friend's reputation.

MR BELLAMANT  The secret shall rest in my bosom, I assure you.

MRS BELLAMANT  But suppose, I should have promised not to suffer
it from my own.        75

MR BELLAMANT  A husband's command breaks any promise.

MRS BELLAMANT  I am surprised to see you so solicitous about a
trifle.

MR BELLAMANT  I am rather surprised to find you so tenacious of
one. Besides, be assured, you cannot have half the reason to        80
suppress the discovery, as I to insist upon it.

MRS BELLAMANT  What is your reason?

MR BELLAMANT  The very difficulty you make in telling it.

MRS BELLAMANT  Your curiosity shall be satisfied then, but I beg you
would defer it now. I may get absolved from my promise of secrecy.        85
I beg you would not urge me to break my trust.

MR BELLAMANT  (*aside*) She certainly hath not discovered my
falsehood. That were impossible. Besides, I may satisfy myself
immediately by Mrs Modern.

MRS BELLAMANT  What makes you uneasy? I assure you, there is        90
nothing in this worth your knowing.

MR BELLAMANT  I believe it. At least, I shall give up my curiosity to
your desire.

MRS BELLAMANT  I am ready to wait on you.

MR BELLAMANT  I must make a short visit first on what I told you,        95
and will call on you immediately.

[*Exit Mr Bellamant*]

MRS BELLAMANT  What can have given him this curiosity I know not,
but should I have discovered the truth,° who can tell into what
suspicions it might have betrayed him? His jealous honour might
have resolved on some fatal return to Lord Richly, had he taken it        100
in the same way as I do, whereas by keeping the secret, I preserve
him every way from danger. For I myself will secure his honour
without exposing his person. I will myself give Lord Richly his
discharge. How nearly have I been unawares to the brink of ruin!

For, surely, the lightest suspicion of a husband is ruin, indeed!   105
     When innocence can scarce our lives defend,
     What dangers must the guilty wife attend?

# 4.1

*SCENE, Mrs Modern's House.*

*Enter Mr Modern and Mrs Modern.*

MR MODERN  In short, madam, you shall not drive a separate trade
at my expense.° Your person is mine, I bought it lawfully in the
church,° and unless I am to profit by the disposal, I shall keep it all
for my own use.

MRS MODERN  This insolence is not to be borne.                              5

MR MODERN  Have I not winked at all your intrigues? Have I not
pretended business, to leave you and your gallants together? Have
I not been the most obsequious, observant—

MRS MODERN  Out with it! You know what you are.

MR MODERN  Do you upbraid me with your vices, madam?                       10

MRS MODERN  My vices! Call it obedience to a husband's will. Can
you deny that you have yourself persuaded me to the undertaking?
Can you forget the arguments you used to convince me that virtue
was the lightest of bubbles?

MR MODERN  I own it all, and had I felt the sweets of your pleasures,       15
as at first, I had never once upbraided you with them. But as I must
more than share the dishonour, it is surely reasonable I should
share the profit.

MRS MODERN  And have you not?

MR MODERN  What if I have?                                                  20

MRS MODERN  Why do you complain then?

MR MODERN  Because I find those effects no more. Your cards run
away with the lucre of your other pleasures, and you lose to the
knaves of your own sex, what you get from the fools of ours.

MRS MODERN  'Tis false, you know I seldom lose, nor indeed can I           25
considerably, for I have not lately had it in my power to stake high.
Lord Richly, who was the fountain of our wealth, hath long been
dry to me.

MR MODERN  I hope, madam, this new gallant will turn to a better
account.                                                                    30

MRS MODERN  Our amour is yet too young to expect any thing from
thence.

MR MODERN  As young as it is, I have reason to believe it is grown
to perfection. Whatever fruits I may expect from him, it is not

impossible, from what hath already happened, but I may expect 35
some from you, and that is not golden fruit.° I am sure if women
sprung from the earth, as some philosophers think,° it was from the
clay of Egypt, not the sands of Peru.° Serpents and crocodiles are
the only fruit they produce.

MRS MODERN (*laughing*) Very true, and a wife contains the whole ten 40
plagues° of her country.

MR MODERN Why had I not been born a Turk, that I might have
enslaved my wife, or a Chinese, that I might have sold her!°

MRS MODERN That would have been only the custom of the country.
You have done more. You have sold her in England, in a country, 45
where women are as backward to be sold to a lover, as to refuse him,
and where cuckold is almost the only title of honour that can't be
bought.

MR MODERN This ludicrous behaviour, madam, as ill becomes the
present subject, as the entertaining new gallants doth the tender- 50
ness you this morning expressed for your reputation. In short, it is
impossible that your amours should be secret long, and however
careless you have been of me whilst I have had my horns in my
pocket, I hope you'll take care to gild them when I am to wear them
in public.° 55

MRS MODERN What would you have me do?

MR MODERN Suffer me to discover you together. By which means
we may make our fortunes easy all at once. One good discovery
in Westminster Hall° will be of greater service than his utmost
generosity. The law will give you more in one moment, than his 60
love for many years.

MRS MODERN Don't think of it.

MR MODERN Yes, and resolve it. Unless you agree to this, madam,
you must agree immediately to break up our house, and retire into
the country. 65

MRS MODERN Racks and tortures are in that name.°

MR MODERN But many more are in that of a prison, so you must
resolve either to quit the town, or submit to my reasons.

MRS MODERN When reputation is gone, all places are alike. When I
am despised in it, I shall hate the town as much as now I like it. 70

MR MODERN There are other places and other towns. The whole
world is the house of the rich, and they may live in what apartment
of it they please.

MRS MODERN I cannot resolve.°

MR MODERN But I can. If you will keep your reputation, you shall 75 carry it into the country, where it will be of service. In town it is of none. Or if it be, 'tis, like clogs, only to those that walk on foot; and the one will no more recommend you in an assembly than the other.

MRS MODERN You never had any love for me.

MR MODERN Do you tax me with want of love for you? Have I not for 80 your sake stood the public mark of infamy? Would you have had me poorly kept you, and starved you? No. I could not bear to see you want, therefore have acted the part I've done, and yet while I have winked at the giving up your virtue, have I not been the most industrious to cry it up everywhere? 85

MRS MODERN So has Lord Richly, and so have all his creatures, a common trick among you: to blazon out the reputation of women, whose virtue you have destroyed, and as industriously blacken them who have withstood you. A deceit so stale, that your commendation would sully a woman of honour. 90

MR MODERN I have no longer time to reason with you, so I shall leave you to consider on what I have said.

*Exit Mr Modern*

MRS MODERN What shall I do! Can I bear to be the public scorn of all the malicious and ugly of my own sex, or to retire with a man whom I hate and despise? Hold! There is a small glimpse of 95 hope that I may avoid them both. I have reason to think Bellamant's love as violent as he avers it. Now could I persuade him to fly away with me—impossible! He hath still too much tenderness for his wife.

*[Enter Lord Richly]*

LORD RICHLY What success, my angel? 100

MRS MODERN Hope all, my lord, that lovers wish or husbands fear. She will be here.

LORD RICHLY When?

MRS MODERN Now, tonight, instantly.

LORD RICHLY Thou glory of intrigue, what words shall thank thee? 105

MRS MODERN No words at all, my lord. A hundred pounds must witness the first interview.

LORD RICHLY They shall, and if she yields, a thousand.

MRS MODERN That you must not expect yet.

LORD RICHLY By heaven I do. I have more reason to expect it than 110 you imagine. I have not been wanting to my desires, since I left you. Fortune too seems to have watched for me. I got her to Piquet, threw away six parties,° and left her a bank note of a hundred for the payment of six pound.

MRS MODERN  And did she receive it?                                          115

LORD RICHLY  With the same reluctancy that a lawyer or physician
would a double fee, or a court-priest a plurality.°

MRS MODERN  Then there is hope of success, indeed.

LORD RICHLY  Hope? There is certainty. The next attack must carry
her.                                                                         120

MRS MODERN  You have a hundred friends in the garrison, my
lord.

LORD RICHLY  And if some of them do not open the gates for me, the
devil's in it. I have succeeded often by leaving money in a lady's
hands. She spends it, is unable to pay, and then I, by virtue of my          125
mortgage,° immediately enter upon the premises.

MRS MODERN  You are very generous,° my lord.

LORD RICHLY  My money shall always be the humble servant of my
pleasures, and it is the interest of men of fortune to keep up the
price of beauty, that they may have it more among themselves.                130

MRS MODERN  I am as much pleased, as surprised, at this your prospect of success, and from this day forward I will think with you, all
virtue to be only pride, caprice, and the fear of shame.

LORD RICHLY  Virtue, like the ghost in Hamlet, is here, there, everywhere, and nowhere at all.° Its appearance is as imaginary as that of        135
a ghost, and they are much the same sort of people, who are in love
with one, and afraid of the other. It is a ghost which hath seldom
haunted me, but I have had the power of laying it.

MRS MODERN  Yes, my lord. I am a fatal instance of that power.

LORD RICHLY  And the dearest, I assure you, which is some sacrifice       140
to your vanity; and shortly I will make an offering to your revenge,
the two darling passions of your sex.

MRS MODERN  But how is it possible for me to leave you together,
without the most abrupt rudeness?

LORD RICHLY  Never regard that. As my success is sure, she will          145
hereafter thank you for a rudeness so seasonable.

MRS MODERN  Mr Bellamant too will be with her.

LORD RICHLY  He will be as agreeably entertained with you in the
next room, and as he does not suspect the least design in me, he will
be satisfied with my being in her company.                                   150

MRS MODERN  Sure, you will not attempt his wife while he is in the
house.

LORD RICHLY  Pish! He is in that dependence on my interest, that,
rather than forfeit my favour, he would be himself her pander. I
have made twenty such men subscribe themselves cuckolds by the            155
prospect of one place, which not one of them ever had.

MRS MODERN So that your fools are not caught like the fish in the water by a bait, but like the dog in the water by a shadow.°

LORD RICHLY Besides I may possibly find a pretence of sending him away.  160

MRS MODERN Go then to the chocolate house, and leave a servant to bring you word of their arrival. It will be better you should come in to them than they find you here.

LORD RICHLY I will be guided by you in all things, and be assured the consummation of my wishes shall be the success of your 165 own.

    *Exit Lord Richly*

MRS MODERN That they shall, indeed, though in a way you little imagine. This forwardness of Mrs Bellamant's meets my swiftest wishes. Could I once give Bellamant reason to suspect his wife, I despair not of the happiest effect of his passion for me.  170

    [*Enter Mr Bellamant*]

Ha! He's here and alone. [*To Mr Bellamant*] Where's Mrs Bellamant?

MR BELLAMANT She will be here immediately, but I chose a few moments' privacy with you, first to deliver you this, and next to ask you one question, which do not be startled at. Pray, how did you employ that note you received this morning?  175

MRS MODERN Nay, if you expect an account of me, perhaps you will still do so. So, let me return you this.

MR BELLAMANT Do not so injuriously mistake me. Nothing but the most extraordinary reason could force me to ask you. Know then, that the very note you had of me this morning, I received within 180 this hour from my wife.

MRS MODERN Ha! Ha! Ha!

MR BELLAMANT Why do you laugh, madam?

MRS MODERN Out of triumph, to see what empty politicians men are found, when they oppose their weak heads to ours! On my 185 conscience, a parliament of women would be of very great service to the nation.

MR BELLAMANT Were all ladies [as] capable as Mrs Modern, I should be very ready to vote on their side.

MRS MODERN Nay, nay, sir, you must not leave out your wife, 190 especially you that have the best wife in the world, ha, ha, ha.

MR BELLAMANT Forgive me, madam, if I have been too partial to a woman, whose whole business hath been to please me.

MRS MODERN Oh! You have no reason to be ashamed of your good opinion. You are not singular in it, I assure you. Mrs Bellamant will 195 have more votes than one.

MR BELLAMANT I am indifferent how many she has, since I am sure she will make interest° but for one.

MRS MODERN 'It is the curse of fools to be secure, and that be thine and Altamont's',° ha, ha, ha.                                                                                                 200

MR BELLAMANT I cannot guess your meaning.

MRS MODERN Then to introduce my explanation, the note you lent me, I lost at Piquet to Lord Richly.

MR BELLAMANT To Lord Richly!

MRS MODERN Who perhaps might dispose of it to some who might                    205
lend it to others, who might give it to those who might lose it to your wife.

MR BELLAMANT I know not what to suppose.

MRS MODERN Nor I. For sure, one cannot suppose, especially since you have the best wife in the world. One cannot suppose, that it          210
could be a present from Lord Richly to herself, that she received it, that in return she hath sent him an assignation to meet her here.

MR BELLAMANT Suppose! Hell and damnation. No!

MRS MODERN But certainly, one could not affirm that this is truth.            215

MR BELLAMANT Affirm!°

MRS MODERN And yet all this is true, as true as she is false. Nay, you shall have an instance! An immediate undeniable instance. You shall see it with your own eyes, and hear it with your own ears.

MR BELLAMANT Am I alive?                                                                              220

MRS MODERN If all the husbands of these best wives in the world are dead, we are a strange nation of ghosts. If you will be prudent, and be like the rest of your brethren, keep the affair secret. I assure you I'll never discover it.°

MR BELLAMANT Secret! Yes, as inward fire, till sure destruction shall        225
attend its blaze. But why do I rage? It is impossible. She must be innocent.

MRS MODERN Then Lord Richly is still a greater villain to belie that innocence to me. But give yourself no pain of anxiety since you are so shortly to be certain. Go fetch her hither. Lord Richly will be        230
here almost as soon as you. Then feign some excuse to leave the room, I will soon follow you, and convey you where you shall have an opportunity of being a witness either to her innocence or her guilt.

MR BELLAMANT This goodness, my sweetest creature, shall bind me        235
yours for ever.

MRS MODERN To convince you that is all I desire, I am willing to

leave the town and reputation at once, and retire with you wherever
you please.

MR BELLAMANT That must be the subject of our future thoughts.    240
I can think of nothing now but satisfaction in this affair.

*Exit Mr Bellamant*

MRS MODERN Do you demur° to my offer, sir! Oh, the villain! I find, I
am to be only a momentary object of his looser pleasures, and his
wife yet sits nearest his heart. But I shall change the angel form she
wears into a devil's. Nor shall my revenge stop there. But at present    245
I must resolve my temper into a calm. Lately!

[*Enter Lately*]

MRS MODERN Come hither, Lately, get me some citron-water.° I am
horribly out of order.

LATELY Yes, madam.

MRS MODERN To be slighted in this manner, insupportable! What is    250
the fool doing?

LATELY There is no citron-water left. Your ladyship drank the last
half-pint this morning.

MRS MODERN Then bring the cinnamon-water, or the surfeit-water,
or the aniseed-water, or the plague-water,° or any water.    255

LATELY Here, madam. (*Brings the bottle and glass and fills*)

MRS MODERN (*drinks. Looks in the glass*) Lord, how—Lord, how I
look—Oh, frightful! I am quite shocking.

LATELY In my opinion your ladyship never looked better.

MRS MODERN Go, you flatterer. I look like my Lady Grim.    260

LATELY Where are your ladyship's little eyes, your short nose, your
wan complexion, and your low forehead?

MRS MODERN Which nature, in order to hide, hath carefully placed
between her shoulders, so that if you view her behind, she seems to
walk without her head, and lessen the miracle of St Dennis.°    265

LATELY Then her left hip is tucked up under her arm, like the hilt
of a beau's sword, and her disdainful right is never seen, like its
blade.

MRS MODERN Then she has two legs, one of which seems to be the
dwarf of the other, and are alike in nothing but their crookedness.    270

LATELY And yet she thinks herself a beauty.

MRS MODERN She is, indeed, the perfection of ugliness.

LATELY And a wit I warrant you.

MRS MODERN No doubt she must be very quick-sighted, for her eyes
are almost crept into her brain.    275

BOTH He, he, he.

MRS MODERN And yet the detestable creature hath not had sense enough, with all her deformity to preserve her reputation.

LATELY I never heard, I own, anything against that.

MRS MODERN You hear, you fool, you dunce, what should you hear? 280
Have not all the town heard of a certain colonel?

LATELY Oh! Lud! What a memory I have! Oh! yes, madam, she has been quite notorious. It is surprising, a little discretion should not preserve her from such public—

MRS MODERN If she had my discretion, or yours, Lately. 285

LATELY Your ladyship will make me proud, indeed, madam.

MRS MODERN I never could see any want of sense in you, Lately. I could not bear to have an insensible creature about me. I know several women of fashion I could not support for a tiring woman.° What think you of Mrs Charmer? 290

LATELY Think of her! That were I a man, she should be the last woman I attacked. I think her an ugly, ungenteel, squinting, flirting, impudent, odious, dirty puss.°

MRS MODERN Upon my word, Lately, you have a vast deal of wit too.

LATELY I am beholden for all my wit, as well as my clothes, to your 295
ladyship. I wish your ladyship wore out as much clothes as you do wit. I should soon grow rich.

MRS MODERN You shall not complain of either. [*Knocking*] Oh! They are come, and I will receive them in another room.

*Exit Mrs Modern*

LATELY I know not whether my talent of praise, or of slander, is of 300
more service to me. Whether I get more by flattering my lady, or abusing all her acquaintance.

[*Enter John*]

JOHN So, Mrs Lately, you forget your old acquaintance, but times are coming when I may be as good as another, and you may repent your inconstancy. 305

LATELY Odious fellow!

JOHN I would have you to know, I look on myself to be as good as your new sweetheart, though he has more lace on his livery, and may be a year or two younger, and as good a man I am too. And so you may tell him. Why does not he stay at home? What does he come into 310
our family for?

LATELY Who gave you authority to enquire, sirrah?

JOHN Marry, that did you, when you gave me a promise to marry me. Well, I shall say no more, but times are a-coming, when you may wish you had not forsaken me. I have a secret. 315

LATELY  A secret! Oh, let me hear it.

JOHN  No, no, mistress, I shall keep my secrets as well as you can yours.

LATELY  Nay, now you are unkind. You know, though I suffer Tom Brisk to visit me, you have my heart still.    320

JOHN  Ah! You do but say so! You know too well how much I love you. Then I'll tell you, my dear, I am going to the devil for you.

LATELY  The devil, you are. Going to the devil for me! What does the fool mean?

JOHN  Ay, I am to get a hundred pounds that you may marry me.    325

LATELY  A hundred pounds! And how are you to get a hundred pounds, my dear John?

JOHN  Only by a little swearing.

LATELY  What are you to swear?

JOHN  Nay, if I tell you, it would be double perjury,° for I have sworn    330
already, I would not trust it with anybody.

LATELY  Oh, but you may trust me!

JOHN  And if you should trust somebody else.

LATELY  The devil fetch me, if I do.

JOHN  Then my master is to give me an hundred pound to swear that    335
he is a cuckold.

LATELY  What's this?

JOHN  Why, my master has offered me an hundred pound, if I discover my lady and Mr Bellamant in a proper manner. And let me
but see them together, I'll swear to the manner, I warrant you.    340

LATELY  But can you do this with a safe conscience?

JOHN  Conscience, pshaw. Which would you choose, a husband with a
hundred pound, or a safe conscience? Come, give me a dram° out
of your mistress's closet, and there I'll tell you more.

LATELY  Come along with me.    345

## 4.2

*SCENE changes to another apartment*

*Enter Lord Richly, Mr Bellamant, Mrs Bellamant and Mrs Modern*

LORD RICHLY  Well, madam, you have drawn a most delightful sketch of life.

MRS MODERN  Then it is still life, for I dare swear there never were such people breathing.

MRS BELLAMANT  Don't you believe then, madam, it is possible for a       5
married couple to be happy in one another, without desiring any other company?

MRS MODERN  Indeed, I do not know what it may have been in the plains of Arcadia° but truly, in those of Great Britain, I believe not.       10

LORD RICHLY  I must subscribe to that too.

MRS BELLAMANT  Mr Bellamant, what say you?

MR BELLAMANT  Oh! My dear, I am entirely of your mind.

LORD RICHLY  This is a miracle almost equal to the other, to see a husband and wife of the same opinion. I must be a convert too, for       15
it would be the greatest miracle of all to find Mrs Bellamant in the wrong.

MRS BELLAMANT  It would be a much greater to find want of complaisance in Lord Richly.

MR BELLAMANT (*aside*) Hell and damnation!       20

MRS MODERN  Nay, madam, this is hardly so, for I have heard his lordship say the same in your absence.

LORD RICHLY  Dear Bellamant, I believe, I have had an opportunity to serve you this afternoon. I have spoke to Lord Powerful. He says, he is very willing to do for you.° Sir Peter, they tell me, is given       25
over,° and I fancy, you may find my lord at home now.

MR BELLAMANT  I shall take another opportunity, my lord, a particular affair now preventing me.

LORD RICHLY  The loss of an hour hath been often the loss of a place, and, unless you have something of greater consequence, I must       30
advise you as a friend.

MR BELLAMANT (*aside*) I shall find a method of thanking you.

MRS MODERN (*aside to Mr Bellamant*) Make this a handle to slip out. I'll come into the next room to you.

MR BELLAMANT  My lord, I am very much obliged to your friendship.       35

My dear, I'll call on you in my return. Mrs Modern, I am your humble servant.

[*Exit Mr Bellamant*]

LORD RICHLY I wish you success. You may command anything in my power to forward it.

MRS BELLAMANT Mr Bellamant is more indebted to your lordship, than he will be ever able to pay. 40

LORD RICHLY Mr Bellamant, madam, has a friend, who is able to pay more obligations than I can lay on him.

MRS MODERN I am forced to be guilty of a great piece of rudeness, by leaving you one moment. 45

LORD RICHLY (*aside*) And I shall not be guilty of losing it.

MRS BELLAMANT (*aside*) What can this mean?

[*Exit Mrs Modern*]

LORD RICHLY And can you, madam, think of retiring from the general admiration of mankind?

MRS BELLAMANT With pleasure, my lord, to the particular 50 admiration of him who is to me all mankind.

LORD RICHLY Is it possible any man can be so happy?

MRS BELLAMANT I hope, my lord, you think Mr Bellamant so.

LORD RICHLY If he be, I pity him much less for his losses, than I envy him the love of her in whose power it may be to redress them. 55

MRS BELLAMANT You surprise me, my lord. In my power!

LORD RICHLY Yes, madam, for whatever is in the power of man, is in yours. I am sure, what little assistance mine can give, is readily at your devotion. My interest and fortune are all in these dear hands. In short, madam, I have languished a long time for an opportunity 60 to tell you, that I have the most violent passion for you.

MRS BELLAMANT My Lord, I have been unwilling to understand you, but now your expression leaves me no other doubt but whether I hate or despise you most.

LORD RICHLY Are these the ungrateful returns you give my love? 65

MRS BELLAMANT Is this the friendship you have professed to Mr Bellamant?

LORD RICHLY I'll make his fortune. Let this be an instance of my future favours.

(*Puts a bank note in her hand; she throws it away*)

MRS BELLAMANT And this of my reception of them. Be assured, my 70 lord, if you ever renew this unmannerly attack on my honour, I will be revenged. My husband shall know his obligations to you.

LORD RICHLY I have gone too far to retreat, madam. If I cannot be

the object of your love, let me be obliged to your prudence. How
many families are supported by this method which you start          75
at? Does not many a woman in this town drive her husband's
coach?°

MRS BELLAMANT  My lord, this insolence is intolerable, and from this
hour I never will see your face again.

    (*A noise without*)

LORD RICHLY  Hey! What is the meaning of this?                       80

    *Enter Mr Modern with [John and] servants, Mr Bellamant and*
    *Mrs Modern*

MR MODERN  Come out, strumpet, show thy face and thy adulterer's
before the world. Thou shalt be a severe example of the vengeance
of an injured husband.

LORD RICHLY  I have no farther business here at present, for I fear,
more husbands have discovered injuries, than one.                    85

    *Exit Lord Richly*

MRS BELLAMANT  Protect me, heavens! What do I see!°

MR BELLAMANT  This was a masterpiece° of my evil genius.

MRS MODERN  Sir, this insult upon my reputation shall not go unre-
venged. I have relations, brothers, who will defend their sister's
fame from the base attacks of a perfidious husband, from any shame   90
he would bring on her innocence.

MR MODERN  Thou hast a forehead that would defend itself from
any shame whatsoever, that you have grafted on my forehead,° I
thank you, and this worthy gentleman.

MRS MODERN  Sir, you shall smart for the falsehood of this           95
accusation.

    *Exit Mrs Modern*

MR MODERN  [*Calling after*] Madam, you shall smart for the truth of
it. This honest man, (*pointing to John*) is evidence of the fact, of
your dishonour and mine. And for you, sir, (*to Bellamant*) you may
depend upon it, I shall take the strictest satisfaction which the law 100
will give me. So, I shall leave you at present, to give satisfaction to
your wife.

    [*Exeunt Mr Modern, John and servants*]

MR BELLAMANT  (*after some pause*) When the criminal turns his own
accuser, the merciful judge becomes his advocate. Guilt is too
plainly written in my face to admit of a denial, and I stand prepared 105
to receive what sentence you please.

MRS BELLAMANT  As you are your own accuser, be your own judge.
You can inflict no punishment on yourself equal to what I feel.

MR BELLAMANT Death has no terrors equal to that thought. Ha! I
   have involved thee too in my ruin, and thou must be the wretched   110
   partaker of my misfortunes.

MRS BELLAMANT While I was assured of your truth,° I could have
   thought that happiness enough, yet, I have still this to comfort me,
   the same moment that has betrayed your guilt, has discovered my
   innocence.   115

MR BELLAMANT (to himself) Oh, thou ungrateful fool! What stores
   of bliss hast thou in one vicious moment destroyed!—Oh, my
   angel! How have I requited all your love and goodness? For what
   have I forsaken thy tender virtuous passion?

MRS BELLAMANT For a new one. How could I be so easily deceived?   120
   How could I imagine there was such truth in man, in that
   inconstant fickle sex, who are so prone to change, that to indulge
   their fondness for variety, they would grow weary of a paradise to
   wander in a desert?

MR BELLAMANT How weak is that comparison to show the difference   125
   between thee, and every other woman!

MRS BELLAMANT I once had that esteem of you, but, hereafter, I shall
   think all men the same. And when I have weaned myself off my love
   for you, will hate them all alike.

MR BELLAMANT Thy sentence is too just. I own, I have deserved it. I   130
   never merited so good a wife. Heaven saw it had given too much,
   and thus has taken the blessing from me.

MRS BELLAMANT You will soon think otherwise. If absence from me
   can bring you to those thoughts, I am resolved to favour them.

MR BELLAMANT Thou shalt enjoy thy wish. We will part, part this   135
   night, this hour. Yet, let me ask one favour, the ring which was a
   witness of our meeting, let it be so of our separation. Let me bear
   this as a memorial of our love. This shall remind me of all the
   tender moments we have had together, and serve to aggravate my
   sorrows. Henceforth, I'll study only to be miserable. Let Heaven   140
   make you happy, and curse me as it pleases.

MRS BELLAMANT It cannot make me more wretched than you have
   made me.

MR BELLAMANT Yet, do believe me when I swear, I never injured
   you with any other woman. Nay, believe me when I swear how   145
   much soever I may have deserved the shame I suffer, I did not now
   deserve it.

MRS BELLAMANT And must we part?

MR BELLAMANT Since it obliges you.°

MRS BELLAMANT  That I may have nothing to remember you by, take    150
back this, and this, and this, and all the thousand embraces
thou hast given me,° till I die in thy loved arms and thus we part for
ever.

MR BELLAMANT  Ha!°

MRS BELLAMANT  Oh! I forgive thee all. Forget it as a frightful dream.    155
It was no more, and I awake to real joy.

MR BELLAMANT  Oh! let me press thee to my heart; for every moment
that I hold thee thus, gives bliss beyond expression, a bliss no vice
can give. Now life appears desirable again. Yet shall I not see thee
miserable? Shall I not see my children suffer for their father's    160
crime?°

MRS BELLAMANT  Indulge no more uneasy thoughts. Fortune may
have blessings yet in store for us and them.

MR BELLAMANT  Excellent goodness! My future days shall have no
wish, no labour, but for thy happiness, and from this hour, I'll never    165
give thee cause of a complaint.

    And whatsoever rocks our fates may lay
    In life's hard passage to obstruct our way;
    Patient, the toilsome journey I'll abide;
    And bless my fortune with so dear a guide.    170

# 5.1

*SCENE Mr Bellamant's House*

*Enter Emilia, speaking to a servant*

EMILIA  It is very strange you will not give me the liberty of denying myself, that you will force me to be at home, whether I will or no.

SERVANT  I had no such order from your ladyship.

EMILIA  Well, well, go wait upon her up.°

[*Exit servant*]

I am but in an ill humour to receive such a visit. I must try to make                    5
it as short as I can.

[*Enter Lady Charlotte*]

LADY CHARLOTTE  Emilia, good-morrow. Am not I an early creature? I have been so frightened with some news I have heard. I am heartily concerned for you, my dear. I hope the fright has not done you any mischief.                    10

EMILIA  I am infinitely obliged to you, Lady Charlotte.

LADY CHARLOTTE  Oh! I could not stay one moment. You see, I hurried into my chair to you half-undressed. Never was creature in such a pickle, so frightful. Lud! I was obliged to draw all the curtains round me.                    15

EMILIA  I don't perceive you had any reason for that, Lady Charlotte.

LADY CHARLOTTE  Why, did you ever see anything so hideous, so odious as this gown? Well, Emilia, you certainly have the prettiest fancy in the world. I like what you have on now, better than Lady Pinup's,° though hers cost so much more. Some people have the                    20
strangest way of laying out their money. You remember our engagement tonight.

EMILIA  You must excuse me. It will look very odd to see me abroad on this occasion.

LADY CHARLOTTE  Not odd in the least. Nobody minds these things.°                    25
There's no rule upon such occasions. Sure, you don't intend to stay at home, and receive formal visits.

EMILIA  No, but I intend to stay at home, and receive no visits.

LADY CHARLOTTE  Why, child, you will be laughed at by all the town. There never was such a thing done in the world. Staying at home is                    30
quite left off upon all occasions. A woman scarce stays at home a week for the death of a husband. Dear Emilia, don't be so awkward. I can make no excuse for you. Lady Polite will never forgive you.

EMILIA  That I shall be sorry for, but I had rather not be forgiven by
her, than by myself.                                                      35

*Enter Captain Bellamant*

CAPTAIN BELLAMANT  Sister, goodmorrow. Lady Charlotte abroad so
early!

LADY CHARLOTTE  You may well be surprised. I have not been out at
this hour, these fifty years.°

CAPTAIN BELLAMANT  You will never be able to hold it out till          40
night.

EMILIA (*aside*) I am sure if she should take it in her head to stay with
me, I shall not, and unless some dear creature, like herself, should
come and take her away, I seem to be in danger.

LADY CHARLOTTE (*to Bellamant, after a whisper*) Don't tell me of      45
what I said last night. Last night was last year, an age ago, and I
have the worst memory in the world.

CAPTAIN BELLAMANT  You seem to want one, egad!

LADY CHARLOTTE  Indeed, I do not. A memory would be of no use to
me, for I was never of the same mind twice in my life. And though     50
I should remember what I said at one time, I should as certainly
remember not to do it at another.

CAPTAIN BELLAMANT  You dear agreeable creature! Sure, never two
people were so like one another as you and I are. We think alike, we
act alike, and some people think, we are very much alike in the face.  55

LADY CHARLOTTE  Do you hear him, Emilia? He has made one of the
most shocking compliments to me. I believe, I shall never be able to
bear a looking-glass again.

CAPTAIN BELLAMANT  Faith, and if it was not for the help of a
looking-glass, you would be the most unhappy creature in the          60
world.

LADY CHARLOTTE  Impertinent!

CAPTAIN BELLAMANT  For then you would be the only person
debarred from seeing the finest face in the world.

EMILIA  Very fine, indeed.°                                            65

LADY CHARLOTTE  Civil enough. I think, I begin to endure the
wretch again now.

CAPTAIN BELLAMANT  Keep but in that mind half an hour.

LADY CHARLOTTE  Emilia, good-morrow, you will excuse the short-
ness of my visit.                                                      70

EMILIA  No apologies on that account, Lady Charlotte.

LADY CHARLOTTE  You are a good creature, and know the continual

hurry of business I am in. (*to Capt. Bellamant*) Don't you follow
me, you thing, you!

CAPTAIN BELLAMANT (*aside*) Indeed, Lady Charlotte, but I shall,    75
and I hope to some purpose.

   [*Exeunt Lady Charlotte and Capt. Bellamant*]

EMILIA So, I am once more left to my own thoughts. Heaven knows,
they are like to afford me little entertainment. Oh! Gaywit! Too
much I sympathise with thy uneasiness. Didst thou know the pangs
I feel on thy account, thy generous heart would suffer more on    80
mine.°

   [*Enter Gaywit*]

Ha, my words have raised a spirit!

MR GAYWIT I hope, madam, you will excuse a visit at so unseasonable
an hour.

EMILIA Had you come a little earlier, you had met a mistress here.    85

MR GAYWIT I met the lady you mean, madam, at the door, and
Captain Bellamant with her.

EMILIA You are the most cavalier lover I know. You are no more
jealous of a rival with your mistress, than the most polite husband is
of one with his wife.    90

MR GAYWIT A man should not be jealous of his friend, madam, and
I believe, Captain Bellamant will be such to me in the highest
manner. I wish I were so blessed in another heart, as he appears to
be in Lady Charlotte's. I wish I were as certain of gaining the
woman I do love, as of losing her I do not.    95

EMILIA I suppose, if your amour be of any date,° you can easily guess
at the impressions you have made.

MR GAYWIT No, nor can she guess at the impression she has made on
me, for, unless my eyes have done it, I never acquainted her with
my passion.    100

EMILIA And that your eyes have done it, you may be assured, if you
have seen her often. The love that can be concealed, must be very
cold indeed, but, methinks, it is something particular in you to
desire to conceal it.

MR GAYWIT I have been always fearful to disclose a passion, which I    105
know not whether it be in my power to pursue. I would not even
have given her the uneasiness to pity me, much less have tried to
raise her love.

EMILIA If you are so tender of her, take care you never let her suspect
so much generosity. That may give her a secret pang.    110

MR GAYWIT  Heaven forbid it should, one equal to those I feel, lest, while I am endeavouring to make my addresses practicable, she should unadvisedly receive those of another.

EMILIA  If she can discover your love as plain as I can, I think you may be easy on that account.                                                                                              115

MR GAYWIT  He must dote like me who can conceive the ecstasy these words have given.
            *Knocking*

EMILIA  Come in.
            *Enter servant*

SERVANT  Your honour's servant, sir, is below.

MR GAYWIT  I come to him. Madam, your most obedient servant. I go   120
on business which will by noon give me the satisfaction of thinking I have preserved the best of fathers to the best of women.
            *Exit Mr Gaywit*

EMILIA  I know he means mine, but why do I mention that, when every action of his life leaves me no other doubt than whether it convinces me more of his love, or of his deserving mine?                         125

## 5.2

*Lord Richly's House*

*Enter Lord Richly and servant*

LORD RICHLY  Desire Mr Bellamant to walk in.
            *[Exit servant]*

What can the meaning of this visit be? Perhaps, he comes to make me proposals concerning his wife, but my love shall not get so far the better of my reason, as to lead me to an extravagant price. I'll not go above two thousand, that's positive.                                          5
            *[Enter Mr Bellamant]*

LORD RICHLY  My dear Bellamant!

MR BELLAMANT  My lord, I have received an obligation from you, which I thus return.
            *(Gives him a bank-bill)°*

LORD RICHLY  Pshaw! Trifles of this nature can hardly be called obligations. I would do twenty times as much for dear Jack   10
Bellamant.

MR BELLAMANT  The obligation indeed was to my wife, nor hath she

made you a small return, since it is to her entreaty you owe your
present safety, your life.

LORD RICHLY I am not apprised of the danger, but would owe my     15
safety to no-one, sooner than to Mrs Bellamant.

MR BELLAMANT Come, come, my lord; this prevarication is low and
mean. You know, you have used me basely, villainously, and under
the cover of acquaintance and friendship have attempted to corrupt
my wife. For which, but that I would not suffer the least breath of     20
scandal to sully her reputation, I would exact such vengeance on
thee—

LORD RICHLY Sir, I must acquaint you, that this is a language I have
not been used to.

MR BELLAMANT No, the language of flatterers and hireling syco-     25
phants has been what you have dealt in. Wretches, whose honour
and love are as venal° as their praise. Such your title might awe, or
your riches bribe to silence. Such you should have dealt with, and
not have dared to injure a man of honour.

LORD RICHLY This is such presumption!     30

MR BELLAMANT No, my lord, yours was the presumption. Mine is
only justice, nay, and mild too, unequal to your crime which
requires a punishment from my hand, not from my tongue.

LORD RICHLY Do you consider who I am?

MR BELLAMANT Were you as high as heraldry could lift you, you     35
should not injure me unpunished. Where grandeur can give
licence to oppression, the people must be slaves, let them boast
what liberty they please.°

LORD RICHLY Sir, you shall hear of this.

MR BELLAMANT I shall be ready to justify my words by any action     40
you dare provoke me to. And be assured of this, if ever I discover
any future attempts of yours to my dishonour, your life shall be its
sacrifice. Henceforward, my lord, let us behave, as if we had never
known one another.

    *Exit Mr Bellamant*

LORD RICHLY Here's your man of sense now. He was half ruined     45
in the House of Lords a few days ago, and is in a fair way of going
the other step in Westminster Hall° in a few days more, yet, has
the impudence to threaten a man of my fortune and quality,
for attempting to debauch his wife, which many a fool, who rides
in his coach and six, would have had sense enough to have     50
winked at.

*Enter Mr Gaywit*

MR GAYWIT  Your lordship is contemplative.

LORD RICHLY  So, nephew, by this early visit, I suppose you had ill
luck last night, for where fortune frowns on you, she always smiles
on me, by blessing me with your company.                                55

MR GAYWIT  I have long since put it out of the power of fortune to do
me either favour or injury. My happiness is now in the power of
another mistress.

LORD RICHLY  And thou art too pretty a fellow not to have that mistress in your power.                                                    60

MR GAYWIT  The possession of her, and in her of all my desires,
depends on your consent.

LORD RICHLY  You know, Harry, you have my consent to possess all
the women in town, except those few that I am particular with.
Provided you fall not foul on mine, you may board and plunder          65
what vessels you please.

MR GAYWIT  This is a vessel, my lord, neither to be taken by force, nor
hired by gold. I must buy her for life, or not board at all.

LORD RICHLY  Then the principal thing to be considered, is her
cargo. To marry a woman merely for her person, is buying an            70
empty vessel, and a woman is a vessel, which a man will grow
cursed weary of in a long voyage.

MR GAYWIT  My lord, I have had some experience in women, and I
believe, that I never could be weary of the woman I now love.

LORD RICHLY  Let me tell you, I have had some experience too, and    75
I have been weary of forty women that I have loved.

MR GAYWIT  And, perhaps, in all that variety, you may not have found
one of equal excellence with her I mean.

LORD RICHLY  And pray, who is this paragon you mean?

MR GAYWIT  Must I, my lord, when I have painted the finest woman in   80
the world, be obliged to write Miss Bellamant's name to the picture?

LORD RICHLY  Miss Bellamant!

MR GAYWIT  Yes, Miss Bellamant.

LORD RICHLY  You know Mr Bellamant's losses. You know what happened yesterday, which may entirely finish his ruin, and the con-      85
sequence of his ruin must be the ruin of his daughter, which will
certainly throw her virtue into your power, for poverty as surely
brings a woman to capitulation, as scarcity of provisions does a
garrison.

MR GAYWIT  I cannot take this advice, my lord. I would not take       90 advantage from the misfortunes of any, but surely, not of the woman I love.

LORD RICHLY  Well, sir, you shall ask me no more, for, if my consent to your ruin will oblige you, you have it.

MR GAYWIT  My lord, I shall ever remember this goodness, and will    95
be ready to sign any instrument° to secure a very large fortune to Lady Charlotte when you please.

    [*Exit Gaywit*]

LORD RICHLY  Now if he takes my consent from my own word, I may deny it afterwards, so I gain the whole estate for my daughter, and bring an entire destruction upon Bellamant and his whole family.    100
Charming thought! That would be a revenge, indeed. Nay, it may accomplish all my wishes too. Mrs Bellamant may be mine at last.

    *Enter Mr Modern*

MR MODERN  My lord, I was honoured with your commands.

LORD RICHLY  I believe I shall procure the place for you, sir.

MR MODERN  My obligations to your lordship are so infinite, that I    105
must always be your slave.°

LORD RICHLY  I am concerned for your misfortune, Mr Modern.

MR MODERN  It is a common misfortune, my lord, to have a bad wife. I am something happier than my brethren in the discovery.

LORD RICHLY  That, indeed, may make you amends more ways than    110
one. I cannot dissuade you from the most rigorous prosecution, for, though dear Jack Bellamant be my particular friend, yet in cases of this nature, even friendship itself must be thrown up. Injuries of this kind are not to be forgiven.

MR MODERN  Very true, my lord. He has robbed me of the affections    115
of a wife, whom I have loved as tenderly as myself. Forgive my tears, my lord. I have lost all I hold dear in this world.

LORD RICHLY  I pity you, indeed, but comfort yourself with the hopes of revenge.

MR MODERN  Alas, my lord! What revenge can equal the dishonour    120
he has brought upon my family? Think on that, my lord. On the dishonour I must endure. I cannot name the title they will give me.

LORD RICHLY  It is shocking, indeed!

MR MODERN  My ease for ever lost, my quiet gone, my honour stained, my honour, my lord. Oh, 'tis a tender wound!    125

LORD RICHLY  Laws cannot be too rigorous against offences of this nature. Juries cannot give too great damages.° To attempt the wife of a friend. To what wickedness will men arrive? Mr Modern, I

own, I cannot blame you in pushing your revenge to the utmost
extremity.                                                                    130

MR MODERN  That I am resolved on. I have just received an appointment from your lordship's nephew, Mr Gaywit, I suppose to give
me some advice in the affair.

LORD RICHLY (*aside*) Ha! That must be to dissuade him from the
prosecution.—Mr Modern, if you please, I'll set you down.° I have    135
some particular business with him. Besides, if he knows anything
that can be of service to you, my commands shall enforce the discovery. Bid the coachman pull up.

MR MODERN  I am the most obliged of all your lordship's slaves.


# 5.3

*Another Apartment.*

*Enter Lady Charlotte, Captain Bellamant and servant*

LADY CHARLOTTE  My lord gone out! Then d'ye hear, I am at home
to nobody!

CAPTAIN BELLAMANT  That's kind, indeed, Lady Charlotte, to let me
have you all to myself.

LADY CHARLOTTE  You! You confident thing! How came you here?      5
Don't you remember, I bade you not to follow me?

CAPTAIN BELLAMANT  Yes, but it's so long ago, that I'm surprised
you should remember it.

LADY CHARLOTTE  Indeed, sir, I always remember to avoid what I
don't like. I suppose you don't know that I hate you of all things.    10

CAPTAIN BELLAMANT  Not I, upon my soul! The Duce take me, if
I did not think, you had liked me, as well as I liked you, ha, ha.

LADY CHARLOTTE  I like you, impossible! Why don't you know, that
you are very ugly?

CAPTAIN BELLAMANT  Pshaw! That's nothing. That will all go off. A   15
month's marriage takes off the homeliness of a husband's face, as
much as it does the beauty of a wife's.

LADY CHARLOTTE  And so you would insinuate that I might be your
wife? O horrible! Shocking thought!

CAPTAIN BELLAMANT  Nay, madam, I am as much frightened at the     20
thoughts of marriage, as you can be.

LADY CHARLOTTE  Indeed, sir, you need not be under any apprehensions of that kind, upon my account.

CAPTAIN BELLAMANT Indeed, but I am, madam, for what an unconsolable creature would you be, if I should take it in my head to marry any other woman.   25

LADY CHARLOTTE [*to the audience*] Well, he has such an excessive assurance that I am not really sure, whether he is not agreeable. Let me die, if I am not under some sort of suspense about it, and yet I am not neither. For to be sure, I don't like the thing°—and yet   30 methinks, I do too—and yet I do not know what I should do with him neither. Hi! Hi! Hi! This is the foolishest circumstance that ever I knew in my life.°

CAPTAIN BELLAMANT Very well! Sure, marriage begins to run in your head at last, madam.   35

LADY CHARLOTTE A propos,° do you know that t'other day, Lady Betty Shuttlecock and I laid down the prettiest scheme of matrimony,° that ever entered into the taste of people of condition.

CAPTAIN BELLAMANT O, pray let's hear it!

LADY CHARLOTTE In the first place then, whenever she or I marry, I   40 am resolved positively to be mistress of myself. I must have my house to myself, my coach to myself, my servants to myself, my table, time, and company to myself. Nay, and sometimes when I have a mind to be out of humour, my bed to myself.

CAPTAIN BELLAMANT Right, madam, for a wife and a husband   45 always together, are, to be sure, the flattest company in the world.

LADY CHARLOTTE O detestable! Then I will be sure to have my own humour in everything, to go, come, dine, dance, play, sup, at all hours, and in whatever company I have a mind to. And if ever he   50 pretends to put on a grave face, upon my enjoying any one of those articles,° I am to burst out in his face a-laughing. Won't that be prodigious pleasant? Ha! Ha! Ha!

CAPTAIN BELLAMANT O charmingly charming! Ha, ha, what a contemptible creature is a woman that never does anything without   55 consulting her husband?

LADY CHARLOTTE Nay, there you're mistaken again, sir, for I would never do anything without consulting my husband.

CAPTAIN BELLAMANT How so, dear madam?

LADY CHARLOTTE Because sometimes one may happen to be so low   60 in spirits, as not to know one's own mind, and then, you know, if a foolish husband should happen to say a word on either side, why one determines on the contrary without any farther trouble.

CAPTAIN BELLAMANT Right, madam, and a thousand to one, but the

happy rogue, your husband, might warm his indolent inclinations      65
too from the same spirit of contradiction, ha, ha.

LADY CHARLOTTE Well, I am so passionately fond of my own
humour that let me die, if a husband were to insist upon my never
missing any one diversion this town affords, I believe in my conscience, I should go twice a day to church, to avoid 'em.      70

CAPTAIN BELLAMANT O fie! You could not be so unfashionable a
creature!

LADY CHARLOTTE Ay, but I would though. I do not care what I do,
when I'm vexed.

CAPTAIN BELLAMANT Well! Let me perish, this is a most delectable      75
scheme. Don't you think, madam, we shall be vastly happy?

LADY CHARLOTTE We, what we? Pray, who do you mean, sir?

CAPTAIN BELLAMANT Why, Lady Betty Shuttlecock and I. Why, you
must know this is the very scheme she laid down to me last night,
which so vastly charmed me, that we resolved to be married upon it      80
tomorrow morning.

LADY CHARLOTTE What do you mean?

CAPTAIN BELLAMANT Only to take your advice, madam, by allowing
my wife all the modish privileges, that you seem so passionately
fond of.      85

LADY CHARLOTTE Your wife? Why, who's to be your wife, pray? You
don't think of me, I hope.

CAPTAIN BELLAMANT One would think, you thought I did, for you
refuse me as oddly, as if I had asked you the question. Not, but I
suppose, you would have me think now, you have refused me in      90
earnest.

LADY CHARLOTTE Ha! Ha! Ha! That's well enough. Why, sweet sir,
do you really think I am not in earnest?

CAPTAIN BELLAMANT No faith, I can't think you're so silly, as to
refuse me in earnest, when I only asked you in jest.      95

BOTH Ha! Ha! Ha!

LADY CHARLOTTE Ridiculous!

CAPTAIN BELLAMANT Delightful! Well, after all, I am a strange
creature to be so merry, when I am just going to be married.

LADY CHARLOTTE And had you ever the assurance to think I would      100
have you?

CAPTAIN BELLAMANT Why, faith! I don't know, but I might, if I had
ever made love to you. Well, Lady Charlotte, your servant. I suppose you'll come and visit my wife, as soon as ever she sees
company.      105

LADY CHARLOTTE  What do you mean?

CAPTAIN BELLAMANT  Seriously what I say, madam. I am just now going to my lawyer to sign my marriage articles with Lady Betty Shuttlecock.

LADY CHARLOTTE  And are you going in earnest?  110

CAPTAIN BELLAMANT  Positively. Seriously.

LADY CHARLOTTE  Then I must take the liberty to tell you, sir, you are the greatest villain, that ever lived upon the face of the earth.

CAPTAIN BELLAMANT  Ha! What do I see?
    *She bursts into tears*
Is it possible! O my dear, dear Lady Charlotte! Can I believe myself  115
the cause of these transporting tears! O, till this instant never did I taste of happiness!

LADY CHARLOTTE  Ha! Ha! Nor I upon my faith, sir! Ha! Ha!

CAPTAIN BELLAMANT  Hey-day! What do you mean?

LADY CHARLOTTE  That you are one of the silliest animals, that ever  120
opened his lips to a woman. Ha! Ha! O I shall die! Ha! Ha!
    *Enter a Servant*

SERVANT  Sir, here's a letter for you.

CAPTAIN BELLAMANT  (*aside*) So, it's come in good time. If this does not give her a turn, egad, I shall have all my plague to go over again.—Lady Charlotte, you'll give me leave.  125

LADY CHARLOTTE  O, sir! Billet doux° are exempt from ceremony. Ha! ha!

CAPTAIN BELLAMANT  (*after reading to himself*) Ha! Ha! Well, my dear Lady Charlotte, I am vastly glad to see you are so easy. Upon my soul, I was afraid you was really in love with me. But since I need  130
have no farther apprehensions of it, I know you won't take it ill, if I obey the summons of my wife, that is to be. Lady Betty has sent for me. You'll excuse me if I am confined a week or two, with my wife for the present. When that's over, you and I will laugh and sing, and coquette as much as ever we did, and so dear Lady Charlotte, your  135
humble servant.
    *Exit Capt. Bellamant*

LADY CHARLOTTE  What can the creature mean? I know not what to think of him! Sure it can't be true! But if it should be true—I can't believe it true—and yet it may be true too. I am resolved to be satisfied. Here, who's there! Will nobody hear? Who's there, I say.  140
    *Enter Servant*
Desire Captain Bellamant to step back again.

SERVANT  He's just gone out, madam.

LADY CHARLOTTE Then it's certainly true. Get me a chair this
moment. This instant. Go, run, fly! [*Exit Servant*] I am in such a
hurry, I don't know what I do. O hideous! I look horridly frightful.  145
But I'll follow him just as I am. I'll go to Lady Betty's. If I find him
there, I shall certainly faint. I must take a little hartshorn° with me.
> *Exit Lady Charlotte*


# 5.4

*Enter Mr Gaywit and Mrs Modern, meeting in his lodgings*

MR GAYWIT This is exactly the time I appointed her to meet me here.
Ha, she comes! You are punctual as a young lover to his first
appointment.

MRS MODERN Women commonly begin to be most punctual, when
men leave it off. Our passions seldom reach their meridian, before  5
yours set.°

MR GAYWIT We can no more help the decrease of our passions, than
you the increase of yours, and, though, like the sun I was obliged to
quit your hemisphere, I have left you a moon to shine in it.°

MRS MODERN What do you mean?  10

MR GAYWIT I suppose you are by this no stranger to the fondness of
the gentleman I introduced to you, nor will you shortly be to his
generosity. He is one who has more money than brains, and more
generosity than money.

MRS MODERN Oh! Gaywit! I am undone. You will too soon know  15
how, will hear it perhaps with pleasure, since it is too plain by
betraying me to your friend, I have no longer any share in your love.

MR GAYWIT Blame not my inconstancy, but your own.

MRS MODERN By all our joys I never loved another.

MR GAYWIT Nay, will you deny what conviction has long since con-  20
strained you to own? Will you deny your favours to Lord Richly?

MRS MODERN He had indeed my person, but you alone my heart.

MR GAYWIT I always take a woman's person to be the strongest assurance of her heart. I think, the love of a mistress who gives up her
person, is no more to be doubted than the love of a friend who gives  25
you his purse.°

MRS MODERN By heavens, I hate and despise him equal with my
husband. And as I was forced to marry the latter by the commands

of my parents, so I was given up to the former by the entreaties of
my husband.                                                                30

MR GAYWIT  By the entreaties of your husband!

MRS MODERN  Hell and his blacker soul both know the truth of what I
say: that he betrayed me first, and has ever since been the pander of
our amour. To you my own inclinations led me. Lord Richly has
paid for his pleasures. To you, they have still been free. He was my    35
husband's choice, but you alone were mine.

MR GAYWIT  And have you not complied with Bellamant too?

MRS MODERN  Oh, blame not my necessities! He is indeed that
generous creature you have spoke him.

MR GAYWIT  And have you not betrayed this generous creature to a       40
wretch?

MRS MODERN  I see you know it all. By heavens, I have not. It was his
own jealousy, not my design. Nay, he importuned me to have discovered Lord Richly in the same manner. Oh, think not any hopes
could have prevailed on me to blast my fame.° No reward could        45
make me amends for that loss. Thou shalt see by my retirement I
have a soul too great to encounter shame.

MR GAYWIT  I will try to make that retirement easy to you, and call me
not ungrateful for attempting to discomfit your husband's purpose,
and preserve my friend.                                                   50

MRS MODERN  I myself will preserve him. If my husband pursues his
intentions, my woman will swear that the servant owned he was
hired to be a false evidence against us.

MR GAYWIT  Then since the story is already public, forgive this last
blush I am obliged to put you to.                                         55

MRS MODERN  What do you mean?

MR GAYWIT  These witnesses must inform you.

        *Enter Mr Bellamant, Mrs Bellamant, Emilia and Capt. Merit*°

MRS MODERN  Distraction! Tortures!

MR GAYWIT  I have with difficulty brought myself to give you this
shock, which nothing but the preservation of the best of friends     60
could have extorted, and which you shall be made amends for.

MR BELLAMANT  Be not shocked, madam. It shall be your husband's
fault, if you are farther uneasy on this account.

MR GAYWIT  Come, madam, you may yourself reap a benefit from
what I have done, since it may prevent your being exposed in         65
another place.°

MRS MODERN  All places to me are equal, except this.

        *Exit Mrs Modern*

MRS BELLAMANT  Her misfortunes move my compassion.

MR GAYWIT  It is generous in you, madam, to pity the misfortunes of a
woman whose faults are more her husband's than her own.                    70

    *Enter Lord Richly and Mr Modern*

LORD RICHLY  Mr Gaywit, upon my word, you have the most splen-
did levee I have seen.

MR GAYWIT  I am sorry, my lord, you have increased it by one who
should grace the keeper of Newgate's levee,° a fellow whose company is scandalous to your lordship, as it is odious to us all.            75

MR BELLAMANT  His lordship is not the only man who goes abroad
with his cuckold.

LORD RICHLY  Methinks you have invited a gentleman to a very
scurvy entertainment.

MR GAYWIT  You'll know, my lord, very shortly, wherefore he was       80
invited, and how much you yourself are obliged to his kind
endeavours, for would his wife have consented to his entreaties, this
pretended discovery had fallen on you, and you had supplied that
gentleman's place.

LORD RICHLY  A discovery fallen on me!                                 85

CAPTAIN MERIT  Yes, my lord, the whole company are witnesses
to Mrs Modern's confession of it, that he betrayed her to your
embraces with a design to discover you in them.

MR MODERN  My lord, this is a base design to ruin the humblest of
your creatures in your lordship's favour.                               90

LORD RICHLY  How it should have that effect I know not, for I do not
understand a word of what this gentleman means.

MR GAYWIT  We shall convince your lordship. In the meantime I
must beg you to leave this apartment. You may prosecute what
revenge you please, but at law we shall dare to defy you.° The        95
damages will not be very great, which are given to a voluntary
cuckold.°

EMILIA  Though I see not why, for it is surely as much a robbery to
take away a picture unpaid for, from the painter who would sell it,
as from the gentleman who would keep it.                              100

MR MODERN  You may have your jest, madam, but I will be paid
severely for it. I shall have a time of laughing in my turn.

    [*Exit Mr Modern. Enter Captain Bellamant and Lady
    Charlotte*]

MR GAYWIT  He will find his mistake, and our conquest soon enough.
And now, my lord, I hope you will ratify that consent you gave me
this morning, and complete my happiness with this lady.              105

LORD RICHLY Truly, nephew, you misunderstood me, if you imagined I promised any such thing. However, though you know I might insist on my brother's will, yet let Mr Bellamant give his daughter a fortune equal to yours, and I shall not oppose it. And till then I shall not consent. 110

MR GAYWIT Hah!

CAPTAIN BELLAMANT I hope your lordship has not determined to deny every request, and therefore I may hope your blessing. (*Kneels*)

LORD RICHLY What does this mean?

CAPTAIN BELLAMANT Charlotte, my lord, has given me this right. 115 Your daughter—

LORD RICHLY What of her?

CAPTAIN BELLAMANT Is my wife.

LORD RICHLY Your wife!

CAPTAIN BELLAMANT Nay, if you will not give me your blessing, you 120 may let it alone. I would not kneel any longer to you, though you were the great mogul.°

LORD RICHLY Very well! This is your doing, Mr Bellamant, or rather my own. Confusion! My estate, my title, and my daughter, all contribute to aggrandise the man I must hate,° because he knows I 125 would have wronged him! Well, sirs, whatever pleasures you may seem to take at my several disappointments, I shall take very little trouble to be revenged on any of you, being heartily convinced, that in a few months you will be so many mutual plagues to one another.
[*Exit Lord Richly*]

MR BELLAMANT Methinks, I might have been consulted on this 130 affair.

LADY CHARLOTTE We had no time for consultation. Our amour has been of a very short date.°

CAPTAIN BELLAMANT All our love is to come, Lady Charlotte.

LADY CHARLOTTE I expect a deal of love after marriage, for what I 135 have bated° you before it.

CAPTAIN BELLAMANT I never asked you the question till I was sure of you.

LADY CHARLOTTE Then you knew my mind better than myself, for I never resolved to have you, till I had you. 140

MR GAYWIT Now, my dear Emilia, there is no bar in our way to happiness. Lady Charlotte has made my lord's consent unnecessary too. Your father has already blessed me with his, and it is now in your power to make me the happiest of mankind.

EMILIA I suppose, you follow my brother's method, and never ask till    145
you are sure of obtaining.

MR BELLAMANT Gaywit, my obligations to you are beyond my power
of repaying, and while I give you what you ask, I am still heaping
greater favours on myself.

MR GAYWIT Think not so, when you bestow on me more than any    150
man can merit.

MR BELLAMANT Then take the little all I have, and may you be as
happy with her, as I am in these arms, (*embracing Mrs Bellamant*)
whence the whole world should never estrange me more.

MRS BELLAMANT I am too happy in that resolution.    155

MR GAYWIT Lady Charlotte! I made a promise this day to your
father in your favour, which I am resolved to keep, though he hath
broken his. I know, your good nature and good sense will forgive
a fault which love has made me commit, love, which directs our
inclinations in spite of equal and superior charms.    160

LADY CHARLOTTE No excuses, dear sir, my inclinations were as
whimsical° as yours.

CAPTAIN BELLAMANT You have fairly got the start, Lady Charlotte.

MR GAYWIT My Bellamant! My friend! My father! What a transport
do I feel from the prospect of adding to your future happiness! Let    165
us henceforth be one family, and have no other contest but to outvie
in love.

MR BELLAMANT My son! Oh! What happiness do I owe to thy friendship, and may the example of my late misfortune warn thee to fly all
such encounters, and since we are setting out together in the road    170
to happiness, take this truth from an experienced traveller.

> However slight the consequence may prove,
> Which waits unmarried libertines° in love,
> Be from all vice divorced before you wed,
> And bury falsehood in the bridal bed.    175

# Epilogue

Spoken by Mrs Heron

As malefactors, on their dying day,
Have always something, at the tree,° to say;
So I, before to exile I go down,
With my hard hapless fate would warn the town.

Fatal Quadrille! Fly! Fly the tempting evil!                    5
For when our last stake's lost, 'tis sure the devil!
With cursed Quadrille avoid my fatal shame,
Or if you can't—at least—play all the game
Of spotless fame, be chary as your lives!
Keep wide of proof, and you're the best of wives!              10
Husbands most faults, not public made, connive at;
The trip's a trifle—when the frailty's private.
What can a poet hope, then, that reveals 'em?
The fair might like the play, whose plot conceals 'em;
For who would favour plays to be thus used,                    15
None ever were by operas abused!
Or could they warble scandal out at random,
Where were the harm, while none could understand 'em?
But I no more must hear those melting strains
Condemned, alas! to woods and lonely plains!                   20
Gay Masquerades, now, turned to Country-Fairs,°
And croaking rooks supply soft eunuch airs.
No Ring, no Mall—no rat, tat, tat, at doors;°
And, O hard fate! for dear Quadrille—All-Fours.°
No more new plays! But that's a small offence,                 25
Your taste will shortly banish them from hence.
Yet ere I part, methinks, it were to wrong you,
Not to bequeath some legacies among you.
My reputation, I for prudes intend,
In hopes their strictness what's amiss will mend.              30
My young gallants, let ancient maidens kill,
And take my husband—any soul that will!
Our author to the spotless fair I give,
For his chaste wife to grant him a reprieve:

73

Whatever faults to me may be imputed,                     35
In her you view your virtues unpolluted.
In her sweet mind, even age and wandering youth
Must own the transports of connubial truth:
Thus each extreme is for instruction meant,
And ever was the stage's true intent,                      40
To give reward to virtue, vice its punishment.

# Epilogue

## Spoken by Mrs Heron

In dull retirement e're I go to grieve,
Ladies, I am returned, to take my leave:
Prudes, I suppose, will, with their old good nature,
Show their great virtue, and condemn the creature:
They fail not at th' unfortunate to flout,                          5
Not because naughty—but because—found out.
Why, faith—if these discoveries succeed,
Marriage will soon become a trade, indeed!
This trade, I'm sure, will flourish in the nation,
'Twill be esteemed below no man of fashion,                         10
To be a member of the—cuckold's corporation!°
What int'rest will be made! What mighty doing!
To be directors for the year ensuing!°
And 'tis exceeding difficult to say,
Which end of this chaste town would win the day:                    15
Oh! Should no chance this corporation stop,
Where should we find one house, without a shop?
How would a wife hung out, draw beaux in throngs!
To hire your dears, like dominoes, at Long's!°
There would be dainty days! When every ninny,                       20
Might put them on and off—for half a guinea!
Oh, to behold th' embroidered trader grin,°
My wife's at home—Pray, gentlemen, walk in!
Money alone men will no more importune,
When ev'ry beauty makes her husband's fortune!                      25
While juries value virtue at this rate,
Each wife is (when discovered) an estate!°
A wife with gold, is mixing gall with honey,
But here you lose your wife by what you get your money.°

And now, t'obey a dull poetic sentence,                             30
In lonely woods, I must pursue repentance!
Ye virgins pure, ye modest matrons, lend
Attentive ears to your departing friend;
If fame, unspotted, be the thing you drive at,

75

Be virtuous, if you can, if not, be private—   35
But hold!—Why should I leave my sister-sinners,
To dwell 'mongst innocents, or young beginners?
Frailty will better with the frail go down;
So hang the stupid bard!—I'll stay in town.

## FINIS

# THE CLANDESTINE MARRIAGE

## A Comedy

BY

### DAVID GARRICK and GEORGE COLMAN

Huc adhibe vultus, et in una parce duobus:
Vivat, et ejusdem simus uterque parens!

*Ovid*°

# Advertisement

Hogarth's *Marriage-a-la-mode*° has before furnished materials to the author of a novel, published some years ago, under the title of *The Marriage-Act*°, but, as that writer pursued a very different story, and as his work was chiefly designed for a political satire, very little use could be made of it for the service of this comedy.                                    5

In justice to the person, who has been considered as the sole author, the party, who has hitherto lain concealed, thinks it incumbent on him to declare, that the disclosure of his name was, by his own desire, reserved till the publication of the piece.°

Both the authors, however, who have before been separately          10
honoured with the indulgence of the public, now beg leave to make their joint acknowledgements for the very favourable reception of the *Clandestine Marriage*.°

# THE CHARACTERS OF THE PLAY

| | |
|---|---|
| Lord Ogleby | Mr King. |
| Sir John Melvil | Mr Holland. |
| Sterling | Mr Yates. |
| Lovewell | Mr Powell. |
| Canton | Mr Baddeley. |
| Brush | Mr Palmer. |
| Serjeant Flower | Mr Love. |
| Traverse | Mr Lee. |
| Trueman | Mr Aickin. |
| Mrs Heidelberg | Mrs Clive. |
| Miss Sterling | Miss Pope. |
| Fanny | Mrs Palmer. |
| Betty | Mrs [Abington]° |
| Chambermaid | Miss Plym. |
| Trusty | Miss Mills. |

## Characters of the Epilogue

| | |
|---|---|
| Lord Minum | Mr Dodd. |
| Colonel Trill | Mr Vernon. |
| Sir Patrick Mahony | Mr Moody. |
| Miss Crotchet | Mrs— |
| Mrs Quaver | Mrs Lee. |
| First Lady | Mrs Bradshaw. |
| Second Lady | Miss Mills. |
| Third Lady | Mrs Dorman. |

# Prologue

Written by Mr GARRICK

Spoken by Mr HOLLAND

Poets and painters, who from nature draw
Their best and richest stores, have made this law:
That each should neighbourly assist his brother,
And steal with decency from one another.
Tonight, your matchless Hogarth gives the thought,                    5
Which from his canvas to the stage is brought.
And who so fit to warm the poet's mind,
As he who pictured morals and mankind?°
But not the same their characters and scenes;
Both labour for one end, by different means:                          10
Each, as it suits him, takes a separate road,
Their one great object, marriage-a-la-mode!
Where titles deign with cits to have and hold,°
And change rich blood for more substantial gold!
And honoured trade from interest turns aside,°                        15
To hazard happiness for titled pride.
The painter dead, yet still he charms the eye;
While England lives, his fame can never die:
But he, who struts his hour upon the stage,°
Can scarce extend his fame for half an age;                          20
Nor pen nor pencil can the actor save,
The art, and artist, share one common grave.

O let me drop one tributary tear,
On poor Jack Falstaff's grave, and Juliet's bier!°
You to their worth must testimony give;                              25
'Tis in your hearts alone their fame can live.
Still as the scenes of life will shift away,
The strong impressions of their art decay.
Your children cannot feel what you have known;
They'll boast of Quins and Cibbers of their own:°                    30
The greatest glory of our happy few,
Is to be felt, and be approved by YOU.

# 1.1

*SCENE A room in Sterling's house.*

*Miss Fanny and Betty meeting*

BETTY (*running in*)  Ma'am! Miss Fanny! Ma'am!

FANNY  What's the matter? Betty!

BETTY  Oh la! Ma'am! as sure as I'm alive, here is your husband—

FANNY  Hush! my dear Betty! if anybody in the house should hear
you, I am ruined.                                                    5

BETTY  Mercy on me! it has frighted me to such a degree, that my
heart is come up to my mouth. But as I was a-saying, Ma'am, here's
that dear, sweet—

FANNY  Have a care, Betty.

BETTY  Lord! I'm bewitched, I think. But as I was a-saying, Ma'am,   10
here's Mr Lovewell just come from London.

FANNY  Indeed!

BETTY  Yes, indeed, and indeed, Ma'am, he is. I saw him crossing the
courtyard in his boots.

FANNY  I am glad to hear it. But pray now, my dear Betty, be cautious.  15
Don't mention that word again, on any account. You know, we have
agreed never to drop any expressions of that sort for fear of an
accident.

BETTY  Dear Ma'am, you may depend upon me. There is not a more
trustier creature on the face of the earth, than I am. Though I say   20
it, I am as secret as the grave, and if it's never told, till I tell it, it
may remain untold till doomsday for Betty.

FANNY  I know you are faithful, but in our circumstances we cannot be
too careful.

BETTY  Very true, Ma'am!—and yet I vow and protest, there's more    25
plague than pleasure with a secret; especially if a body mayn't
mention it to four or five of one's particular acquaintance.

FANNY  Do but keep this secret a little while longer, and then, I hope
you may mention it to anybody. Mr Lovewell will acquaint the
family with the nature of our situation as soon as possible.          30

BETTY  The sooner, the better, I believe, for if he does not tell it,
there's a little tell-tale, I know of, will come and tell it for him.

FANNY (*blushing*)  Fie, Betty!

BETTY  Ah! you may well blush. But you're not so sick, and so pale,
and so wan, and so many qualms°—                                       35

FANNY  Have done! I shall be quite angry with you.

BETTY  Angry! Bless the dear puppet! I am sure I shall love it, as much as if it was my own. I meant no harm, heaven knows.

FANNY  Well, say no more of this. It makes me uneasy All I have to ask of you, is to be faithful and secret, and not to reveal this matter, till     40
we disclose it to the family ourselves.

BETTY  Me reveal it! If I say a word, I wish I may be burned. I would not do you any harm for the world, and as for Mr Lovewell, I am sure I have loved the dear gentleman ever since he got a tide-waiter's place° for my brother. But let me tell you both, you must     45
leave off your soft looks to each other, and your whispers, and your glances, and your always sitting next to one another at dinner, and your long walks together in the evening. For my part, if I had not been in the secret, I should have known you were a pair of loviers at least, if not man and wife, as—     50

FANNY  See there now! again. Pray be careful.

BETTY  Well—well—nobody hears me. Man and wife—I'll say so no more. What I tell you is very true for all that—

LOVEWELL  (calling within)  William!

BETTY  Hark! I hear your husband—     55

FANNY  What!

BETTY  I say, here comes Mr Lovewell. Mind the caution I give you. I'll be whipped now, if you are not the first person he sees or speaks to in the family. However, if you chose it, it's nothing at all to me. As you sow, you must reap; as you brew, so you must bake. I'll even     60
slip down the back-stairs, and leave you together.
            *Exit*

FANNY  (alone)  I see, I see I shall never have a moment's ease till our marriage is made public. New distresses crowd in upon me every day. The solicitude of my mind sinks my spirits, preys upon my health, and destroys every comfort of my life. It shall be revealed,     65
let what will be the consequence.
            *Enter Lovewell*

LOVEWELL  My love! How's this? In tears? Indeed this is too much. You promised me to support your spirits, and to wait the determin-ation of our fortune with patience. For my sake, for your own, be comforted! Why will you study to add to our uneasiness and     70
perplexity?

FANNY  Oh, Mr Lovewell! the indelicacy of a secret marriage grows every day more and more shocking to me. I walk about the house like a guilty wretch: I imagine myself the object of the suspicion of

the whole family; and am under the perpetual terrors of a shameful   75
detection.

LOVEWELL Indeed, indeed, you are to blame. The amiable delicacy
of your temper, and your quick sensibility, only serve to make
you unhappy. To clear up this affair properly to Mr Sterling, is the
continual employment of my thoughts. Everything now is in a fair   80
train. It begins to grow ripe for a discovery; and I have no doubt of
its concluding to the satisfaction of ourselves, of your father, and
the whole family.

FANNY End how it will, I am resolved it shall end soon, very soon. I
would not live another week in this agony of mind to be mistress of   85
the universe.

LOVEWELL Do not be too violent neither. Do not let us disturb
the joy of your sister's marriage with the tumult this matter may
occasion! I have brought letters from Lord Ogleby and Sir John
Melvil to Mr Sterling. They will be here this evening, and, I dare   90
say, within this hour.

FANNY I am sorry for it.

LOVEWELL Why so?

FANNY No matter. Only let us disclose our marriage immediately!

LOVEWELL As soon as possible.   95

FANNY But directly.

LOVEWELL In a few days, you may depend on it.

FANNY Tonight—or tomorrow morning.

LOVEWELL That, I fear, will be impracticable.

FANNY Nay, but you must.   100

LOVEWELL Must! why?

FANNY Indeed, you must. I have the most alarming reasons for it.

LOVEWELL Alarming indeed! for they alarm me, even before I am
acquainted with them. What are they?

FANNY I cannot tell you.   105

LOVEWELL Not tell me?

FANNY Not at present. When all is settled, you shall be acquainted
with everything.

LOVEWELL Sorry they are coming! Must be discovered! What can
this mean? Is it possible you can have any reasons that need be   110
concealed from me?

FANNY Do not disturb yourself with conjectures, but rest assured,
that though you are unable to divine the cause, the consequence of
a discovery, be it what it will, cannot be attended with half the
miseries of the present interval.   115

LOVEWELL  You put me upon the rack. I would do anything to make you easy. But you know your father's temper. Money (you will excuse my frankness) is the spring of all his actions, which nothing but the idea of acquiring nobility or magnificence can ever make him forgo, and these he thinks his money will purchase. You know too your aunt's, Mrs Heidelberg's, notions of the splendour of high life, her contempt for everything that does not relish of what she calls Quality,° and that, from the vast fortune in her hands, by her late husband, she absolutely governs Mr Sterling and the whole family. Now, if they should come to the knowledge of this affair too abruptly, they might, perhaps, be incensed beyond all hopes of reconciliation.

FANNY  But if they are made acquainted with it otherwise than by ourselves, it will be ten times worse: and a discovery grows every day more probable. The whole family have long suspected our affection. We are also in the power of a foolish maid-servant; and if we may even depend on her fidelity, we cannot answer for her discretion. Discover it therefore immediately, lest some accident should bring it to light, and involve us in additional disgrace.

LOVEWELL  Well, well. I meant to discover it soon, but would not do it too precipitately. I have more than once sounded Mr Sterling about it, and will attempt him more seriously the next opportunity. But my principal hopes are these: my relationship to Lord Ogleby, and his having placed me with your father, have been, you know, the first links in the chain of this connection between the two families; in consequence of which, I am at present in high favour with all parties. While they all remain thus well-affected to me, I propose to lay our case before the old Lord; And, if I can prevail on him to mediate in this affair, I make no doubt but he will be able to appease your father; and, being a lord and a man of quality, I am sure he may bring Mrs Heidelberg into good humour at any time. Let me beg you, therefore, to have but a little patience, as, you see, we are upon the very eve of a discovery, that must probably be to our advantage.

FANNY  Manage it your own way. I am persuaded.

LOVEWELL  But, in the meantime, make yourself easy.

FANNY  As easy as I can, I will. We had better not remain together any longer at present. Think of this business, and let me know how you proceed.

LOVEWELL  Depend on my care! But, pray, be cheerful.

FANNY  I will.
       *(As she is going out, enter Sterling)*
STERLING  Hey-day! who have we got here?
FANNY (*confused*)  Mr Lovewell, sir!
STERLING  And where are you going, hussy!                           160
FANNY  To my sister's chamber, sir!
       *Exit*
STERLING  Ah, Lovewell! What! always getting my foolish girl yonder
    into a corner! Well, well. let us but once see her elder sister fast°
    married to Sir John Melvil, we'll soon provide a good husband for
    Fanny, I warrant you.                                           165
LOVEWELL  Would to heaven, sir, you would provide her one of my
    recommendation!
STERLING  Yourself? eh, Lovewell!
LOVEWELL  With your pleasure, sir!
STERLING  Mighty well!                                              170
LOVEWELL  And I flatter myself, that such a proposal would not be
    very disagreeable to Miss Fanny.
STERLING  Better and better!
LOVEWELL  And if I could but obtain your consent, sir—
STERLING  What! you marry Fanny? No, no, that will never do,       175
    Lovewell! You're a good boy, to be sure I have a great value for you,
    but can't think of you for a son-in-law. There's no Stuff° in the
    case, no money, Lovewell!
LOVEWELL  My pretensions to fortune, indeed, are but moderate, but
    though not equal to splendour, sufficient to keep us above distress.  180
    Add to which, that I hope by diligence to increase it, and have love,
    honour—
STERLING  But not the Stuff, Lovewell! Add one little round o to the
    sum total of your fortune, and that will be the finest thing you
    can say to me. You know I've a regard for you, would do anything to  185
    serve you, anything on the footing of friendship, but—
LOVEWELL  If you think me worthy of your friendship, sir, be assured,
    that there is no instance in which I should rate your friendship so
    highly.
STERLING  Psha! psha! that's another thing, you know. Where money   190
    or interest is concerned, friendship is quite out of the question.
LOVEWELL  But where the happiness of a daughter is at stake, you
    would not scruple, sure, to sacrifice a little to her inclinations.
STERLING  Inclinations! why, you would not persuade me that the girl
    is in love with you, eh, Lovewell?                              195

LOVEWELL I cannot absolutely answer for Miss Fanny, sir, but am sure that the chief happiness or misery of my life depends entirely upon her.

STERLING Why, indeed now if your kinsman, Lord Ogleby, would come down handsomely for you,—but that's impossible. No, no, 'twill never do. I must hear no more of this. Come, Lovewell, promise me that I shall hear no more of this.

LOVEWELL (*hesitating*) I am afraid, sir, I should not be able to keep my word with you, if I did promise you.

STERLING Why, you would not offer to marry her without my consent, would you, Lovewell?

LOVEWELL (*confused*) Marry her, sir?

STERLING Ay, marry her, sir!—I know very well that a warm speech or two from such a dangerous young spark, as you are, will go much farther towards persuading a silly girl to do what she has more than a month's mind to do, than twenty grave lectures from fathers or mothers, or uncles or aunts, to prevent her. But you would not, sure, be such a base fellow, such a treacherous young rogue, as to seduce my daughter's affections, and destroy the peace of my family in that manner. I must insist on it, that you give me your word not to marry her without my consent.

LOVEWELL Sir, I, I, as to that—I, I, I beg, sir—Pray, sir, excuse me on this subject at present.

STERLING Promise then, that you will carry this matter no further without my approbation.

LOVEWELL You may depend on it, sir, that it shall go no further.

STERLING Well, well, that's enough. I'll take care of the rest, I warrant you. Come, come, let's have done with this nonsense! What's doing in town? Any news upon 'Change?°

LOVEWELL Nothing material.°

STERLING Have you seen the currants, the soap, and Madeira, safe in the warehouses? Have you compared the goods with the invoice and bills of lading, and are they all right?

LOVEWELL They are, sir!

STERLING And how are stocks?

LOVEWELL Fell one and an half this morning.

STERLING Well, well, some good news from America,° and they'll be up again. But how are Lord Ogleby and Sir John Melvil? When are we to expect them?

LOVEWELL Very soon, sir! I came on purpose to bring you their commands. Here are letters from both of them. (*Giving Sterling letters*)

STERLING  Let me see, let me see—'Slife, how his Lordship's letter is
perfumed! It takes my breath away. (*Opening it*) And French paper
too! with a fine border of flowers and flourishes, and a slippery
gloss on it that dazzles one's eyes. (*Reading*) 'My dear Mr Sterling'    240
Mercy on me! His Lordship writes a worse hand than a boy at his
exercise But how's this? Eh! (*Reading*) 'with you tonight' 'Lawyers
tomorrow morning' Tonight! that's sudden indeed. Where's my
sister Heidelberg? she should know of this immediately. Here John!
Harry! Thomas! (*Calling the servants*) Hark ye, Lovewell!    245

LOVEWELL  Sir!

STERLING  Mind now, how I'll entertain his Lordship and Sir John:
we'll show your fellows at the other end of the town how we live
in the city.—They shall eat gold, and drink gold, and lie in gold.°
(*Calling*) Here cook! butler! What signifies your birth and educa-    250
tion, and titles? Money, money, that's the stuff that makes the great
man° in this country.

LOVEWELL  Very true, sir!

STERLING  True, sir? Why then, have done with your nonsense of
love and matrimony. You're not rich enough to think of a wife yet.    255
A man of business should mind nothing but his business. Where
are these fellows? (*Calling*) John! Thomas! Get an estate, and a wife
will follow of course. Ah! Lovewell! an English merchant is the
most respectable character in the universe.° 'Slife, man, a rich
English merchant may make himself a match for the daughter of a    260
Nabob.° Where are all my rascals? Here, William!

    *Exit calling*

LOVEWELL  (*alone*)  So! As I suspected. Quite averse to the match, and
likely to receive the news of it with great displeasure. What's best
to be done? Let me see! Suppose I get Sir John Melvil to interest
himself in this affair. He may mention it to Lord Ogleby with a    265
better grace than I can, and more probably prevail on him to inter-
fere in it. I can open my mind also more freely to Sir John. He told
me, when I left him in town, that he had something of consequence
to communicate, and that I could be of use to him. I am glad of it,
for the confidence he reposes in me, and the service I may do him,    270
will ensure me his good offices. Poor Fanny! It hurts me to see her
so uneasy, and her making a mystery of the cause adds to my
anxiety. Something must be done upon her account; for at all
events, her solicitude shall be removed.

    *Exit*

# 1.2

*Another chamber*

*Enter Miss Sterling, and Miss Fanny*

MISS STERLING  Oh, my dear sister, say no more! This is downright
hypocrisy. You shall never convince me that you don't envy
me beyond measure. Well, after all it is extremely natural. It is
impossible to be angry with you.

FANNY  Indeed, sister, you have no cause.                                    5

MISS STERLING  And you really pretend not to envy me?

FANNY  Not in the least.

MISS STERLING  And you don't in the least wish that you was just in
my situation?

FANNY  No, indeed, I don't. Why should I?                                   10

MISS STERLING  Why should you? What! on the brink of marriage,
fortune, title—But I had forgot—There's that dear sweet creature
Mr Lovewell in the case. You would not break your faith with your
true love now for the world, I warrant you.

FANNY  Mr Lovewell! always Mr Lovewell! Lord, what signifies Mr           15
Lovewell, sister?

MISS STERLING  Pretty peevish soul! Oh, my dear, grave, romantick°
sister! A perfect philosopher in petticoats! Love and a cottage!°
Eh, Fanny! Ah, give me indifference and a coach and six!

FANNY  And why not the coach and six without the indifference? But,       20
pray, when is this happy marriage of yours to be celebrated? I long
to give you joy.

MISS STERLING  In a day or two—I can't tell exactly. (*Aside*) Oh, my
dear sister! I must mortify her a little.—I know you have a pretty
taste. Pray, give me your opinion of my jewels. How d'ye like the         25
style of this esclavage? (*Showing jewels*)

FANNY  Extremely handsome indeed, and well fancied.

MISS STERLING  What d'ye think of these bracelets? I shall have a
miniature of my father, set round with diamonds, to one, and Sir
John's to the other. And this pair of earrings! set transparent!          30
Here, the tops, you see, will take off to wear in a morning, or in an
undress. How d'ye like them? (*Shows jewels*)

FANNY  Very much, I assure you.—Bless me; sister, you have a prodigious quantity of jewels. You'll be the very Queen of Diamonds.

MISS STERLING  Ha! ha! ha! very well, my dear! I shall be as fine as a     35
little queen indeed. I have a bouquet to come home tomorrow,

made up of diamonds, and rubies, and emeralds, and topazes, and
amethysts—jewels of all colours, green, red, blue, yellow, inter-
mixed, the prettiest thing you ever saw in your life! The jeweller
says, I shall set out with as many diamonds as anybody in town,          40
except Lady Brilliant, and Polly *What d'ye-call-it*, Lord Squander's
kept mistress.°

FANNY  But what are your wedding-clothes, sister?

MISS STERLING  Oh, white and silver to be sure, you know. I bought
them at Sir Joseph Lutestring's,° and sat above an hour in the          45
parlour behind the shop, consulting Lady Lutestring about gold
and silver stuffs, on purpose to mortify her.

FANNY  Fie, sister! how could you be so abominably provoking?

MISS STERLING  Oh, I have no patience with the pride of your city-
knights'° ladies. Did you never observe the airs of Lady Lutestring    50
dressed in the richest brocade out of her husband's shop, playing
crown-whist at Haberdasher's-Hall,° while the civil smirking Sir
Joseph, with a snug wig trimmed round his broad face as close
as a new-cut yew-hedge, and his shoes so black that they shine
again,° stands all day in his shop, fastened to his counter like a bad   55
shilling?°

FANNY  Indeed, indeed, sister, this is too much. If you talk at this rate,
you will be absolutely a bye-word in the city. You must never venture on the inside of Temple Bar° again.

MISS STERLING  Never do I desire it. Never, my dear Fanny, I promise   60
you. Oh, how I long to be transported to the dear regions of
Grosvenor-Square!° Far far from the dull districts of Aldersgate,
Cheap, Candlewick, and Farringdon Without and Within!° My
heart goes pit-a-pat at the very idea of being introduced at court!
Gilt chariot! Piebald horses! Laced liveries! And then the whispers    65
buzzing round the circle: 'Who is that young Lady! Who is she?'—
'Lady Melvil, Ma'am!' Lady Melvil! my ears tingle at the sound,
and then at dinner, instead of my father perpetually asking, 'Any
news upon 'Change?', to cry, 'Well, Sir John! anything new from
Arthur's'?'° or, to say to some other woman of quality, 'Was your    70
Ladyship at the Duchess of Rubber's last night? Did you call in at
Lady Thunder's? In the immensity of crowd I swear I did not see
you. Scarce a soul at the opera last Saturday. Shall I see you at
Carlisle House° next Thursday?'—Oh, the dear Beau-Monde! I
was born to move in the sphere of the great world.                      75

FANNY  And so, in the midst of all this happiness, you have no compassion for me, no pity for us poor mortals in common life.

MISS STERLING (*affectedly*) You? You're above pity. You would not change conditions with me. You're over head and ears in love, you know. Nay, for that matter, if Mr Lovewell and you come together, 80 as I doubt not you will, you will live very comfortably, I dare say. He will mind his business, you'll employ yourself in the delightful care of your family, and, once in a season, perhaps you'll sit together in a front-box at a benefit play,° as we used to do at our dancing-master's, you know, and perhaps I may meet you in the summer 85 with some other citizens at Tunbridge.° For my part, I shall always entertain a proper regard for my relations. You shan't want my countenance, I assure you.

FANNY  Oh, you're too kind, sister!

    (*Enter Mrs Heidelberg*)

MRS HEIDELBERG (*at entering*) Here this evening! I vow and pertest 90 we shall scarce have time to provide for them. (*To Miss Sterling*) Oh, my dear! I am glad to see you're not quite in dish-abille. Lord Ogleby and Sir John Melvil will be here tonight.

MISS STERLING  Tonight, Ma'am?

MRS HEIDELBERG  Yes, my dear, tonight. Do, put on a smarter cap, 95 and change those ordinary ruffles! Lord, I have such a deal to do, I shall scarce have time to slip on my Italian lutestring. Where is this dawdle of a housekeeper? (*enter Mrs Trusty.*) Oh, here, Trusty! do you know that people of qualaty are expected here this evening?

TRUSTY  Yes, Ma'am. 100

MRS HEIDELBERG  Well, do you be sure now that everything is done in the most genteelest manner, and to the honour of the fammaly.

TRUSTY  Yes, Ma'am.

MRS HEIDELBERG  Well, but mind what I say to you.

TRUSTY  Yes, Ma'am. 105

MRS HEIDELBERG  His Lordship is to lie in the chintz bedchamber, d'ye hear? And Sir John in the blue damask room. His Lordship's valet-de-shamb in the opposite—

TRUSTY  But Mr Lovewell is come down, and you know that's his room, Ma'am. 110

MRS HEIDELBERG  Well, well, Mr Lovewell may make shift, or get a bed at the George. But hark ye, Trusty!

TRUSTY  Ma'am!

MRS HEIDELBERG  Get the great dining-room in order as soon as possible. Unpaper the curtains,° take the civers off the couch 115 and the chairs, and put the china figures on the mantlepiece immediately.

TRUSTY  Yes, Ma'am.

MRS HEIDELBERG  Be gone then! fly, this instant! Where's my brother
Sterling?                                                              120

TRUSTY  Talking to the butler, Ma'am.

MRS HEIDELBERG  Very well.

    *Exit Trusty*

    Miss Fanny! I pertest I did not see you before. Lord, child, what's
the matter with you?

FANNY  With me? Nothing, Ma'am.                                        125

MRS HEIDELBERG  Bless me! Why your face is as pale, and black, and
yellow—of fifty colours, I pertest. And then you have dressed yourself as loose and as big—I declare there is not such a thing to be
seen now, as a young woman with a fine waist You all make yourselves as round as Mrs Deputy Barter. Go, child! You know the      130
qualaty will be here by and by. Go, and make yourself a little more
fit to be seen.

    *Exit Fanny*

    She is gone away in tears, absolutely crying, I vow and pertest. This
ridiculous Love! We must put a stop to it. It makes a perfect nataral°
of the girl.                                                          135

MISS STERLING (*affectedly*)  Poor soul! she can't help it.

MRS HEIDELBERG  Well, my dear! Now I shall have an opportunity
of convincing you of the absurdity of what you was telling me
concerning Sir John Melvil's behaviour to you.

MISS STERLING  Oh, it gives me no manner of uneasiness. But,      140
indeed, Ma'am, I cannot be persuaded but that Sir John is an
extremely cold lover. Such distant civility, grave looks, and lukewarm professions of esteem for me and the whole family! I have
heard of flames and darts, but Sir John's is a passion of mere ice
and snow.                                                             145

MRS HEIDELBERG  Oh, fie, my dear! I am perfectly ashamed of you.
That's so like the notions of your poor sister! What you complain
of as coldness and indifference, is nothing but the extreme gentility
of his address, an exact pictur of the manners of qualaty.

MISS STERLING  Oh, he is the very mirror of complaisance, full of   150
formal bows and set speeches! I declare, if there was any violent
passion on my side, I should be quite jealous of him.

MRS HEIDELBERG  I say jealus indeed. Jealus of who, pray?

MISS STERLING  My sister Fanny. She seems a much greater favourite
than I am, and he pays her infinitely more attention, I assure you.   155

MRS HEIDELBERG  Lord! d'ye think a man of fashion, as he is, can't distinguish between the genteel and the wulgar part of the famaly? Between you and your sister, for instance, or me and my brother? Be advised by me, child! It is all politeness and good-breeding. Nobody knows the qualaty better than I do.                                    160

MISS STERLING In my mind the old lord, his uncle, has ten times more gallantry about him than Sir John. He is full of attentions to the ladies, and smiles, and grins, and leers, and ogles, and fills every wrinkle in his old wizen face with comical expressions of tenderness. I think he would make an admirable sweetheart.                    165

    *Enter Sterling*

STERLING (*at entering*) No fish? Why the pond was dragged but yesterday morning There's carp and tench in the boat. Pox on't, if that dog Lovewell had any thought, he would have brought down a turbot, or some of the land-carriage mackerel.°

MRS HEIDELBERG Lord, brother, I am afraid his lordship and Sir        170
John will not arrive while it's light.

STERLING I warrant you. But, pray, sister Heidelberg, let the turtle be dressed tomorrow, and some venison, and let the gardener cut some pineapples, and get out some ice. I'll answer for wine, I warrant you. I'll give them such a glass of Champagne as they never drank  175
in their lives, no, not at a Duke's table.

MRS HEIDELBERG Pray now, brother, mind how you behave. I am always in a fright about you with people of qualaty. Take care that you don't fall asleep directly after supper, as you commonly do. Take a good deal of snuff; and that will keep you awake, and don't  180
burst out with your horrible loud horse-laughs. It is monstrous wulgar.

STERLING Never fear, sister! [*looking off*] Who have we here?

MRS HEIDELBERG It is Mons. Cantoon, the Swish gentleman, that lives with his Lordship, I vow and pertest.                              185

    *Enter Canton*

STERLING Ah, Mounseer! your servant. I am very glad to see you, Mounseer.

CANTON Mosh oblige to Mons. Sterling. Ma'am, I am yours Matemoiselle, I am yours. (*bowing round*)

MRS HEIDELBERG Your humble servant, Mr Cantoon!                       190

CANTON I kiss your hands, Matam!

STERLING Well, Mounseer! and what news of your good family! when are we to see his Lordship and Sir John?

CANTON Mons. Sterling! Milor Ogelby and Sir Jean Melvile will be here in one quarter-hour.                                               195

STERLING  I am glad to hear it.

MRS HEIDELBERG  O, I am perdigious glad to hear it. Being so late I was afeard of some accident. Will you please to have anything, Mr Cantoon, after your journey?

CANTON  No, I tank you, Ma'am.                    200

MRS HEIDELBERG  Shall I go and show you the apartments, sir?

CANTON  You do me great honour, Ma'am.

MRS HEIDELBERG  Come then! (*to Miss Sterling*) Come, my dear!
      *Exeunt*

STERLING  Pox on't, it's almost dark. It will be too late to go round the garden this evening. However, I will carry them to take a peep at my    205 fine canal at least. I am determined.
      *Exit*

## 2.1

*An antechamber to Lord Ogleby's bed-chamber. A table with cups of chocolate,° and a small case for medicines.*

*Enter Brush, Lord Ogleby's valet-de-chambre, and Sterling's chambermaid*

BRUSH  You shall stay, my dear, I insist upon it.

CHAMBERMAID  Nay, pray, sir, don't be so positive.° I can't stay indeed.

BRUSH  You shall take one cup to our better acquaintance.

CHAMBERMAID  I seldom drinks chocolate; and if I did, one has  5
no satisfaction, with such apprehensions about one. If my lord
should wake, or the Swish gentleman should see one, or Madam
Heidelberg should know of it, I should be frighted to death.
Besides, I have had my tea already this morning. (*In a fright*) I'm
sure I hear my lord.  10

BRUSH  No, no, madam, don't flutter yourself. The moment my lord
wakes, he rings his bell, which I answer sooner or later, as it suits
my convenience.

CHAMBERMAID  But should he come upon us without ringing—

BRUSH  I'll forgive him if he does. This key (*takes a phial out of the*  15
*case*) locks him up till I please to let him out.

CHAMBERMAID  Law, sir! that's potecary's-stuff.

BRUSH  It is so, but without this he can no more get out of bed than
he can read without spectacles. (*Sips*) What with qualms,° age,
rheumatism, and a few surfeits in his youth, he must have a great  20
deal of brushing, oiling, screwing, and winding up to set him
a-going for the day.

CHAMBERMAID  (*sips*)  That's prodigious indeed. (*Sips*) My lord seems
quite in a decay.

BRUSH  Yes, he's quite a spectacle, (*sips*) a mere corpse, till he is  25
revived and refreshed from our little magazine here. When the
restorative pills, and cordial waters warm his stomach, and get into
his head, vanity frisks in his heart, and then he sets up for the lover,
the rake, and the fine gentleman.

CHAMBERMAID  (*sips*)  Poor gentleman!—[*Frightened*] But should the  30
Swish gentleman come upon us.

BRUSH  Why then, the English gentleman would be very angry. No
foreigner must break in upon my privacy. (*Sips*) But I can assure

you Monsieur Canton is otherwise employed. He is obliged to skim
the cream of half a score newspapers for my lord's breakfast. Ha, 35
ha, ha. Pray, madam, drink your cup peaceably. My lord's chocolate
is remarkably good; he won't touch a drop but what comes from
Italy.°

CHAMBERMAID (*sipping*) 'Tis very fine indeed! [*Sips*] And charmingly perfumed. It smells for all the world like our young ladies' 40
dressing-boxes.

BRUSH You have an excellent taste, madam, and I must beg of you to
accept of a few cakes for your own drinking, (*takes them out of a
drawer in the table*) and, in return, I desire nothing but to taste the
perfume of your lips. (*Kisses her*) A small return of favours, madam, 45
will make, I hope, this country and retirement agreeable to both.
(*He bows, she curtsies*) Your young ladies are fine girls, faith, (*sips*)
though, upon my soul, I am quite of my old lord's mind about
them; and were I inclined to matrimony, I should take the youngest.
(*Sips*)

CHAMBERMAID Miss Fanny's the most affablest and the most best- 50
natered creter!

BRUSH And the eldest a little haughty or so.

CHAMBERMAID More haughtier and prouder than Saturn° himself.
But this I say quite confidential to you, for one would not hurt a
young lady's marriage, you know. (*Sips*) 55

BRUSH By no means, but you can't hurt it with us. We don't consider
tempers. We want money, Mrs Nancy. Give us enough of that, we'll
abate you a great deal in other particulars. Ha, ha, ha.
    *Bell rings*

CHAMBERMAID Bless me, here's somebody. O! 'tis my lord Well, your
servant, Mr Brush. I'll clean the cups in the next room. 60

BRUSH Do so. But never mind the bell. I shan't go this half hour. Will
you drink tea with me in the afternoon?

CHAMBERMAID Not for the world, Mr Brush. I'll be here to set all
things to rights, but I must not drink tea indeed,—and so, your
servant. 65
    *Exit Chambermaid with teaboard. Bell rings again.*

BRUSH It is impossible to stupefy one's self in the country for a week
without some little flirting with the Abigails.° This is much the
handsomest wench in the house, except the old citizen's youngest
daughter, and I have not time enough to lay a plan for her. (*Bell
rings*) And now I'll go to my lord, for I have nothing else to do. 70
(*Going*)

*Enter Canton with newspapers in his hand*

CANTON  Monsieur Brush, Maistre Brush. My lor stirra yet?

BRUSH  He has just rung his bell. I am going to him.

CANTON  *Depechez vous donc.*

*Exit Brush*

(*Puts on spectacles*) I wish de deviel had all dese papiers. I forget, as
fast as I read. De *Advertise* put out of my head de *Gazette*, de      75
*Gazette* de *Chronique*,° and so dey all go *l'un apres l'autre*. I must get
some *nouvelle* for my lor, or he'll be *enragée contre moi—Voyons*.
(*Reads in the papers*) Here is noting but Anti-Sejanus° & *Advertise*.

*Enter Maid with chocolate things*

Vat you vant, child?—

CHAMBERMAID  Only the chocolate things, sir.                             80

CANTON  O ver well. Dat is good girl, and ver prit too!

*Exit Maid*

LORD OGLEBY  (*within*) Canton, he, he (*coughs*) Canton!

CANTON  I come, my lor. Vat shall I do? I have no news He vil make
great tintamarre!

LORD OGLEBY  (*within*) Canton, I say, Canton! Where are you?          85

*Enter Lord Ogleby, leaning on Brush*

CANTON  Here, my lor. I ask pardon, my lor, I have not finish de
papers—

LORD OGLEBY  Dem your pardon, and your papers. I want you here,
Canton.

CANTON  Den I run. Dat is all.                                          90

*Canton shuffles along. Lord Ogleby leans upon Canton too, and
comes forward*

LORD OGLEBY  You Swiss are the most unaccountable mixture. You
have the language and the impertinence of the French, with the
laziness of Dutchmen.

CANTON  'Tis very true, my lor. I can't help.

LORD OGLEBY  (*cries out*) O diavolo!                                   95

CANTON  You are not in pain, I hope, my lor.

LORD OGLEBY  Indeed but I am, my lor. That vulgar fellow Sterling,
with his city politeness, would force me down his slope last night
to see a clay-coloured ditch, which he calls a canal; and what with
the dew, and the east wind, my hips and shoulders are absolutely   100
screwed to my body.

CANTON  A littel veritable eau d'arquibusade vil set all to right again.

*Lord Ogleby sits down, Brush gives him chocolate*

LORD OGLEBY  Where are the palsy-drops,° Brush?

BRUSH (*pouring out*)  Here, my lord!

LORD OGLEBY  *Quelle nouvelle avez vous*, Canton?                              105

CANTON  A great deal of papier, but no news at all.

LORD OGLEBY  What! Nothing at all, you stupid fellow?

CANTON  Yes, my lor, I have littel advertise here vil give you more plaisir den all de lyes about noting at all. *La voila!* (*Puts on his spectacles*)

LORD OGLEBY  Come read it, Canton, with good emphasis, and good    110
discretion.

CANTON  I vil, my lor. (*Canton reads*) 'Dere is no question, but dat de Cosmetique Royale vil utterlie take away all heats, pimps, frecks & oder eruptions of de skin, and likewise de wrinque of old age, &c. &c.' A great deal more, my lor 'Be sure to ask for de Cosmetique    115
Royale, signed by de Docteur own hand—Dere is more raison for dis caution dan good men vil tink' *Eh bien*, my lor!

LORD OGLEBY  *Eh bien*, Canton! Will you purchase any?

CANTON  For you, my lor?

LORD OGLEBY  For me, you old puppy! for what?                                  120

CANT  My lor?

LORD OGLEBY  Do I want cosmetics?

CANTON  My lor!

LORD OGLEBY  Look in my face. Come, be sincere. Does it want the assistance of art?                                                          125

CANTON (*with his spectacles*)  *En verité, non.*—'Tis very smoose and brillian. But I tote dat you might take a little by way of prevention.

LORD OGLEBY  You thought like an old fool, monsieur, as you generally do. The surfeit-water,° Brush! (*Brush pours out*) What do you think, Brush, of this family, we are going to be connected    130
with?—Eh!

BRUSH  Very well to marry in, my lord; but it would not do to live with.

LORD OGLEBY  You are right, Brush. There is no washing the Blackamoor white. Mr Sterling will never get rid of Blackfriars,°    135
always taste of the Borachio,° and the poor woman his sister is so busy and so notable, to make one welcome, that I have not yet got over her first reception. It almost amounted to suffocation! I think the daughters are tolerable. Where's my cephalic snuff? (*Brush gives him a box*)

CANTON  Dey tink so of you, my lor, for dey look at noting else, *ma foi!*    140

LORD OGLEBY  Did they? Why, I think they did a little Where's my glass? (*Brush puts one on the table*) The youngest is delectable.

(*Takes snuff*)

CANTON  O, *ouy*, my lor —very delect, inteed. She made *doux yeux* at
you, my lor.

LORD OGLEBY  She was particular. The eldest, my nephew's lady, will    145
be a most valuable wife. She has all the vulgar spirits of her father,
and aunt, happily blended with the termagant qualities of her
deceased mother. Some peppermint water, Brush! How happy
is it,° Cant, for young ladies in general, that people of quality
overlook everything in a marriage contract but their fortune.    150

CANTON  *C'est bien heureux, et commode aussi.*

LORD OGLEBY  Brush, give me that pamphlet by my bedside (*Brush
goes for it*) Canton, do you wait in the antechamber, and let nobody
interrupt me till I call you.

CANTON  Mush goot may do your lordship!    155

LORD OGLEBY  (*to Brush, who brings the pamphlet*) And now, Brush,
leave me a little to my studies.

    *Exit Brush*

What can I possibly do among these women here, with this confounded rheumatism? It is a most grievous enemy to gallantry and
address. (*Gets off his chair*)—He! Courage, my lor! By heavens, I'm    160
another creature (*Hums and dances a little*) It will do, faith. Bravo,
my lor! These girls have absolutely inspired me. If they are for a
game of romps,° *me voila pret*! (*Sings and dances*) O, that's an ugly
twinge, but it's gone. I have rather too much of the lily this morning
cin my complexion; a faint tincture of the rose will give a delicate    165
spirit to my eyes for the day.

    *Unlocks a drawer at the bottom of the* [*looking-*] *glass, and
    takes out rouge. While he's painting himself, a knocking at the
    door*

Who's there? I won't be disturbed.

CANTON  (*offstage*) My lor, my lor, here is Monsieur Sterling to pay
his *devoir* to you this morn in your *chambre*.

LORD OGLEBY  (*softly*) What a fellow! (*Aloud*) I am extremely    170
honoured by Mr Sterling. Why don't you see him in, monsieur?
(*Softly*) I wish he was at the bottom of his stinking canal. (*Door
opens*) Oh, my dear Mr Sterling, you do me a great deal of
honour.

    *Enter Sterling and Lovewell*

STERLING  I hope, my lord, that your lordship slept well in the night. I    175
believe there are no better beds in Europe than I have. I spare no
pains to get 'em, nor money to buy 'em. His Majesty, God bless

him, don't sleep upon a better out of his palace, and if I had said
*in*, too, I hope no treason, my lord.

LORD OGLEBY Your beds are like everything else about you,  180
incomparable! They not only make one rest well, but give one
spirits, Mr Sterling.

STERLING What say you then, my lord, to another walk in the
garden? You must see my water by daylight, and my walks, and my
slopes, and my clumps,° and my bridge, and my flowering trees,  185
and my bed of Dutch tulips. Matters looked but dim last night,
my lord. I feel the dew in my great toe, but I would put on a
cut shoe that I might be able to walk you about. I may be laid up
tomorrow.

LORD OGLEBY (*aside*) I pray heaven you may!  190

STERLING What say you, my lord!

LORD OGLEBY I was saying, sir, that I was in hopes of seeing the
young ladies at breakfast. Mr Sterling, they are, in my mind,
the finest tulips in this part of the world. He, he.

CANTON Bravissimo, my lor! Ha, ha, he.  195

STERLING They shall meet your lordship in the garden. We won't
lose our walk for them. I'll take you a little round before breakfast,
and a larger before dinner, and in the evening you shall go to the
Grand Tower,° as I call it. Ha, ha, ha.

LORD OGLEBY Not a foot, I hope, Mr Sterling. Consider your gout,  200
my good friend. You'll certainly be laid by the heels for your
politeness. He, he, he.

CANTON (*laughing very heartily*) Ha, ha, ha. 'Tis admirable! *En
verité*!—

STERLING If my young man (*indicating Lovewell*) here, would but  205
laugh at my jokes, which he ought to do, as mounseer does at yours,
my lord, we should be all life and mirth.

LORD OGLEBY What say you, Cant? Will you take my kinsman under
your tuition? You have certainly the most companionable laugh
I ever met with, and never out of tune.  210

CANTON But when your lorship is out of spirits.

LORD OGLEBY Well said, Cant! But here comes my nephew, to play
his part.

    *Enter Sir John Melvil*

Well, Sir John, what news from the island of Love?° Have you been
sighing and serenading this morning?  215

SIR JOHN I am glad to see your lordship in such spirits this morning.

LORD OGLEBY I'm sorry to see you so dull, sir.—What poor things,

Mr Sterling, these very young fellows are! They make love with faces, as if they were burying the dead, though, indeed, a marriage sometimes may be properly called a burying of the living eh, Mr Sterling?          220

STERLING  Not if they have enough to live upon, my lord. Ha, ha, ha.

CANTON  Dat is all Monsieur Sterling tink of.

SIR JOHN (*aside to Lovewell*) Prithee, Lovewell, come with me into the garden. I have something of consequence for you, and I must communicate it directly.          225

LOVEWELL (*aside*) We'll go together. If your Lordship and Mr Sterling please, we'll prepare the ladies to attend you in the garden.

*Exeunt Sir John Melvil and Lovewell*

STERLING  My girls are always ready. I make 'em rise soon, and to bed early. Their husbands shall have 'em with good constitutions, and good fortunes, if they have nothing else, my lord.          230

LORD OGLEBY  Fine things, Mr Sterling!

STERLING  Fine things, indeed, my lord! Ah, my lord, had not you run off your speed in your youth, you had not been so crippled in your age, my lord.          235

LORD OGLEBY (*half-laughing*) Very pleasant, I protest! He, he, he.

STERLING  Here's mounseer now, I suppose, is pretty near your Lordship's standing; but having little to eat, and little to spend, in his own country, he'll wear three of your lordship out. Eating and drinking kills us all.          240

LORD OGLEBY  Very pleasant, I protest. (*aside*) What a vulgar dog!

CANTON  My lor so old as me! He is shicken to me, and look like a boy to *pauvre* me.

STERLING  Ha, ha, ha. Well said, mounseer! Keep to that, and you'll live in any country of the world. Ha, ha, ha. But, my lord, I will wait upon you into the garden. We have but a little time to breakfast. I'll go for my hat and cane, fetch a little walk with you, my lord, and then for the hot rolls and butter!          245

LORD OGLEBY  I shall attend you with pleasure.

*Exit Sterling*

Hot rolls and butter, in July! I sweat with the thoughts of it. What a strange beast it is!          250

CANTON  *C'est un barbare.*

LORD OGLEBY  He is a vulgar dog, and, if there was not so much money in the family, which I can't do without, I would leave him and his hot rolls and butter directly. Come along, monsieur!          255

*Exeunt*

## 2.2

*The Garden*

*Enter Sir John Melvil and Lovewell*

LOVEWELL  In my room this morning? Impossible.

SIR JOHN  Before five this morning, I promise you.

LOVEWELL  On what occasion?

SIR JOHN  I was so anxious to disclose my mind to you, that I could
not sleep in my bed. But I found that you could not sleep neither.    5
The bird was flown, and the nest long since cold. Where was you,
Lovewell?

LOVEWELL  Pooh! prithee! ridiculous!

SIR JOHN  Come now! Which was it? Miss Sterling's maid? A pretty
little rogue! Or Miss Fanny's Abigail? A sweet soul too! Or—    10

LOVEWELL  Nay, nay, leave trifling, and tell me your business.

SIR JOHN  Well, but where was you, Lovewell?

LOVEWELL  Walking, writing—What signifies where I was?

SIR JOHN  Walking! Yes, I dare say. It rained as hard as it could pour.
Sweet refreshing showers to walk in! No, no, Lovewell Now would    15
I give twenty pounds to know which of the maids—

LOVEWELL  But your business! Your business, Sir John!

SIR JOHN  Let me a little into the secrets of the family.

LOVEWELL  Psha!

SIR JOHN  Poor Lovewell! He can't bear it, I see. She charged you not    20
to kiss and tell. Eh, Lovewell! However, though you will not honour
me with your confidence, I'll venture to trust you with mine. What
d'ye think of Miss Sterling?

LOVEWELL  What do I think of Miss Sterling?

SIR JOHN  Ay; what d'ye think of her?    25

LOVEWELL  An odd question! But I think her a smart, lively girl, full
of mirth and sprightliness.

SIR JOHN  All mischief and malice, I doubt.

LOVEWELL  How?

SIR JOHN  But her person: what d'ye think of that?    30

LOVEWELL  Pretty and agreeable.

SIR JOHN  A little grisette thing.

LOVEWELL  What is the meaning of all this?

SIR JOHN  I'll tell you. You must know, Lovewell, that, notwithstanding all appearances—(*Seeing Lord Ogleby, Sterling, Mrs Heidelberg,*    35

*Miss Sterling and Fanny*) We are interrupted. When they are gone,
I'll explain.

> *Enter Lord Ogleby, Sterling, Mrs Heidelberg, Miss Sterling,*
> *and Fanny*

LORD OGLEBY  Great improvements° indeed, Mr Sterling! Wonder-
ful improvements! The four seasons in lead, the flying Mercury,
and the basin with Neptune in the middle, are all in the very          40
extreme of fine taste. You have as many rich figures as the man at
Hyde Park Corner.°

STERLING  The chief pleasure of a country house is to make
improvements, you know, my lord. I spare no expense, not I. This is
quite another-guess sort of a place than it was when I first took it,   45
my lord. We were surrounded with trees. I cut down above fifty to
make the lawn before the house, and let in the wind and the sun,
smack-smooth,° as you see. Then I made a greenhouse out of the
old laundry, and turned the brewhouse into a pinery. The high
octagon summer-house, you see yonder, is raised on the mast of a       50
ship, given me by an East India captain, who has turned many
a thousand of my money.° It commands the whole road. All the
coaches and chariots, and chaises, pass and repass under your
eye. I'll mount you up there in the afternoon, my lord. 'Tis the
pleasantest place in the world to take a pipe and a bottle, and so you  55
shall say, my lord.

LORD OGLEBY  Ay, or a bowl of punch, or a can of flip,° Mr Sterling!
For it looks like a cabin in the air. If flying chairs were in use, the
captain might make a voyage to the Indies in it still, if he had but a
fair wind.                                                             60

CANTON  Ha! ha! ha! ha!

MRS HEIDELBERG  My brother's a little comacal in his ideas, my lord!
But you'll excuse him. I have a little gothic dairy,° fitted up entirely
in my own taste. In the evening I shall hope for the honour of your
lordship's company to take a dish of tea there, or a sullabub warm      65
from the cow.

LORD OGLEBY  I have every moment a fresh opportunity of admiring
the elegance of Mrs Heidelberg, the very flower of delicacy, and
cream of politeness.

MRS HEIDELBERG  O my lord!                                             70

> *Leering at each other*

LORD OGLEBY  O madam!

STERLING  How d'ye like these close walks,° my lord?

LORD OGLEBY  A most excellent serpentine!° It forms a perfect maze,
and winds like a true-lover's knot.

STERLING  Ay, here's none of your straight lines here, but all taste:    75
zig-zag crinkum-crankum,° in and out, right and left, to and again,
twisting and turning like a worm, my lord!

LORD OGLEBY  Admirably laid out indeed, Mr Sterling! one can
hardly see an inch beyond one's nose anywhere in these walks. You
are a most excellent economist of your land, and make a little go a    80
great way. It lies together in as small parcels as if it was placed in
pots out at your window in Gracechurch Street.°

CANTON  Ha! ha! ha! ha!

LORD OGLEBY  What d'ye laugh at, Canton?

CANTON  Ah! *que cette similitude est drôle*! So clever what you say,    85
mi lor.

LORD OGLEBY  (*to Fanny*)  You seem mightily engaged, madam. What
are those pretty hands so busily employed about?

FANNY  Only making up a nosegay, my lord! Will your lordship do me
the honour of accepting it? (*Presenting it*)    90

LORD OGLEBY  I'll wear it next my heart, madam! (*Aside*) I see the
young creature dotes on me.

MISS STERLING  Lord, sister! you've loaded his lordship with a bunch
of flowers as big as the cook or the nurse carry to town on Monday
morning for a beaupot.° Will your lordship give me leave to present    95
you with this rose and a sprig of sweet-briar?

LORD OGLEBY  The truest emblems of yourself, madam! All sweetness and poignancy. (*Aside*) A little jealous, poor soul!

STERLING  Now, my lord, if you please, I'll carry you to see my
ruins.°    100

MRS HEIDELBERG  You'll absolutely fatigue his lordship with over-
walking, brother!

LORD OGLEBY  Not at all, madam! We're in the garden of Eden, you
know; in the region of perpetual spring, youth, and beauty. (*Leering
at the women*)

MRS HEIDELBERG  (*aside*)  Quite the man of qualaty, I pertest.    105

CANTON  Take my arm, mi lor! (*Lord Ogleby leans on him*)

STERLING  I'll only show his lordship my ruins, and the cascade, and
the Chinese bridge,° and then we'll go in to breakfast.

LORD OGLEBY  Ruins, did you say, Mr Sterling?

STERLING  Ay, ruins, my lord! And they are reckoned very fine ones    110
too. You would think them ready to tumble on your head. It has just

cost me a hundred and fifty pounds to put my ruins in thorough repair. This way, if your lordship pleases.

LORD OGLEBY (*going, stops*) What steeple's that we see yonder? The parish-church, I suppose.

STERLING Ha! ha! ha! that's admirable. It is no church at all, my lord! It is a spire that I have built against a tree, a field or two off, to terminate the prospect.° One must always have a church, or an obelisk, or a something, to terminate the prospect, you know. That's a rule in taste, my lord!

LORD OGLEBY Very ingenious, indeed! For my part, I desire no finer prospect than this I see before me. (*Leering at the women*) Simple, yet varied; bounded, yet extensive.—Get away, Canton! (*Pushing away Canton*) I want no assistance. I'll walk with the ladies.

STERLING This way, my lord!

LORD OGLEBY Lead on, sir! We young folks here will follow you. Madam! Miss Sterling! Miss Fanny! I attend you.

> *Exit, after Sterling, gallanting Fanny, Miss Sterling and Mrs Heidelberg*

CANTON (*following*) He is cock o'de game, *ma foy*!

> *Exit Canton*

SIR JOHN At length, thank heaven, I have an opportunity to unbosom. I know you are faithful, Lovewell, and flatter myself you would rejoice to serve me.

LOVEWELL Be assured, you may depend on me.

SIR JOHN You must know then, notwithstanding all appearances, that this treaty of marriage between Miss Sterling and me will come to nothing.

LOVEWELL How!

SIR JOHN It will be no match, Lovewell.

LOVEWELL No match?

SIR JOHN No.

LOVEWELL You amaze me. What should prevent it?

SIR JOHN I.

LOVEWELL You! Wherefore?

SIR JOHN I don't like her.

LOVEWELL Very plain indeed! I never supposed that you was extremely devoted to her from inclination, but thought you always considered it as a matter of convenience, rather than affection.

SIR JOHN Very true. I came into the family without any impressions on my mind, with an unimpassioned indifference ready to receive

one woman as soon as another. I looked upon love, serious, sober
love, as a chimæra, and marriage as a thing of course, as you know    150
most people do. But I, who was lately so great an infidel in love, am
now one of its sincerest votaries. In short, my defection from Miss
Sterling proceeds from the violence of my attachment to another.

LOVEWELL  Another! So! So! Here will be fine work. And pray who is
she?    155

SIR JOHN  Who is she! Who can she be, but Fanny, the tender, amiable,
engaging Fanny?

LOVEWELL  Fanny! What Fanny?

SIR JOHN  Fanny Sterling. Her sister. Is not she an angel, Lovewell?

LOVEWELL  [aside] Her sister? Confusion!—You must not think of it,    160
Sir John.

SIR JOHN  Not think of it? I can think of nothing else. Nay, tell me,
Lovewell, was it possible for me to be indulged in a perpetual
intercourse with two such objects as Fanny and her sister, and not
find my heart led by insensible attraction towards Her? You seem    165
confounded Why don't you answer me?

LOVEWELL  Indeed, Sir John, this event gives me infinite concern.

SIR JOHN  Why so? Is not she an angel, Lovewell?

LOVEWELL  I foresee that it must produce the worst consequences.
Consider the confusion it must unavoidably create. Let me per-    170
suade you to drop these thoughts in time.

SIR JOHN  Never, never, Lovewell!

LOVEWELL  You have gone too far to recede. A negotiation, so nearly
concluded, cannot be broken off with any grace. The lawyers, you
know, are hourly expected; the preliminaries almost finally settled    175
between Lord Ogleby and Mr Sterling; and Miss Sterling herself
ready to receive you as a husband.

SIR JOHN  Why the banns have been published, and nobody has
forbidden them, 'tis true. But you know either of the parties may
change their minds even after they enter the church.    180

LOVEWELL  You think too lightly of this matter. To carry your
addresses so far, and then to desert her—and for her sister too!
It will be such an affront to the family, that they can never put up
with it.

SIR JOHN  I don't think so, for as to my transferring my passion from    185
her to her sister, so much the better! For then, you know, I don't
carry my affections out of the family.

LOVEWELL  Nay, but prithee be serious, and think better of it.

SIR JOHN I have thought better of it already, you see. Tell me honestly, Lovewell, can you blame me? Is there any comparison between them? 190

LOVEWELL As to that now—why that—that is just—just as it may strike different people. There are many admirers of Miss Sterling's vivacity.

SIR JOHN Vivacity! a medley of Cheapside pertness, and White-chapel° pride.—No, no, if I do go so far into the city for a wedding-dinner, it shall be upon turtle at least. 195

LOVEWELL But I see no probability of success; for granting that Mr Sterling would have consented to it at first, he cannot listen to it now. Why did not you break this affair to the family before? 200

SIR JOHN Under such embarrassed circumstances as I have been, can you wonder at my irresolution or perplexity? Nothing but despair, the fear of losing my dear Fanny, could bring me to a declaration even now, and yet, I think I know Mr Sterling so well, that, strange as my proposal may appear, if I can make it advantageous to him as a money transaction, as I am sure I can, he will certainly come into it. 205

LOVEWELL But even suppose he should, which I very much doubt, I don't think Fanny herself would listen to your addresses. 210

SIR JOHN You are deceived a little in that particular.

LOVEWELL You'll find I am in the right.

SIR JOHN I have some little reason to think otherwise.

LOVEWELL You have not declared your passion to her already?

SIR JOHN Yes, I have. 215

LOVEWELL Indeed! And—and—and how did she receive it?

SIR JOHN I think it is not very easy for me to make my addresses to any woman, without receiving some little encouragement.

LOVEWELL Encouragement! Did she give you any encouragement?

SIR JOHN I don't know what you call encouragement, but she blushed, and cried and desired me not to think of it any more. Upon which I pressed her hand, kissed it, swore she was an angel, and I could see it tickled her to the soul. 220

LOVEWELL And did she express no surprise at your declaration?

SIR JOHN Why, faith, to say the truth, she was a little surprised, and she got away from me too, before I could thoroughly explain myself. If I should not meet with an opportunity of speaking to her, I must get you to deliver a letter from me. 225

LOVEWELL I! A letter! I had rather have nothing—

SIR JOHN Nay, you promised me your assistance, and I am sure you    230
cannot scruple to make yourself useful on such an occasion. You
may, without suspicion, acquaint her verbally of my determined
affection for her, and that I am resolved to ask her father's consent.

LOVEWELL As to that, I—your commands, you know—that is, if
she—Indeed, Sir John, I think you are in the wrong.    235

SIR JOHN Well, well, that's my concern. Ha! There she goes, by
heaven! Along that walk yonder, d'ye see? I'll go to her immediately.

LOVEWELL You are too precipitate. Consider what you are doing.

SIR JOHN I would not lose this opportunity for the universe.

LOVEWELL Nay, pray don't go! Your violence and eagerness may    240
overcome her spirits. The shock will be too much for her.
(*Detaining him*)

SIR JOHN Nothing shall prevent me. Ha! now she turns into another
walk! Let me go! (*Breaks from him*) I shall lose her. (*Going, turns
back*) Be sure now to keep out of the way! If you interrupt us, I shall
never forgive you.    245

*Exit Sir John Melvil hastily*

LOVEWELL 'Sdeath! I can't bear this. In love with my wife! Acquaint
me with his passion for her! Make his addresses before my face! I
shall break out before my time. This was the meaning of Fanny's
uneasiness. She could not encourage him—I am sure she could
not. Ha! they are turning into the walk, and coming this way. Shall    250
I leave the place? Leave him to solicit my wife! I can't submit to it.
They come nearer and nearer. If I stay it will look suspicious. It
may betray us, and incense him. They are here. I must go. I am the
most unfortunate fellow in the world.

*Exit Lovewell. Enter Fanny and Sir John Melvil*

FANNY Leave me, Sir John, I beseech you leave me! Nay, why will you    255
persist to follow me with idle solicitations, which are an affront to
my character, and an injury to your own honour?

SIR JOHN I know your delicacy, and tremble to offend it, but let
the urgency of the occasion be my excuse! Consider, madam, that
the future happiness of my life depends on my present application    260
to you! Consider that this day must determine my fate; and these
are perhaps the only moments left me to incline you to warrant
my passion, and to entreat you not to oppose the proposals I mean
to open to your father.

FANNY For shame, for shame, Sir John! Think of your previous    265
engagements! Think of your own situation, and think of mine!
What have you discovered in my conduct that might encourage

you to so bold a declaration? I am shocked that you should venture
to say so much, and blush that I should even dare to give it a
hearing. Let me be gone!                                              270

SIR JOHN  Nay, stay, madam! but one moment! Your sensibility is too
great. Engagements! What engagements have even been pretended
on either side than those of family convenience? I went on in the
trammels of matrimonial negotiation with a blind submission to
your father and Lord Ogleby; but my heart soon claimed a right      275
to be consulted. It has devoted itself to you, and obliges me to plead
earnestly for the same tender interest in yours.

FANNY  Have a care, Sir John! Do not mistake a depraved will for a
virtuous inclination. By these common pretences of the heart, half
of our sex are made fools, and a greater part of yours despise them   280
for it.

SIR JOHN  Affection, you will allow, is involuntary. We cannot always
direct it to the object on which it should fix, but when it is once
inviolably attached, inviolably as mine is to you, it often creates
reciprocal affection. When I last urged you on this subject, you     285
heard me with more temper, and I hoped with some compassion.

FANNY  You deceived yourself. If I forbore to exert a proper spirit,
nay, if I did not even express the quickest resentment of your
behaviour, it was only in consideration of that respect I wish to pay
you, in honour to my sister: and be assured, sir, woman as I am, that  290
my vanity could reap no pleasure from a triumph, that must result
from the blackest treachery to her. (*Going*)

SIR JOHN  One word, and I have done. (*Stopping her*) Your impatience
and anxiety, and the urgency of the occasion, oblige me to be brief
and explicit with you. I appeal therefore from your delicacy to      295
your justice. Your sister, I verily believe, neither entertains any real
affection for me, or tenderness for you. Your father, I am inclined to
think, is not much concerned by means of which of his daughters
the families are united. Now as they cannot, shall not be connected,
otherwise than by my union with you, why will you, from a false      300
delicacy, oppose a measure so conducive to my happiness, and, I
hope, your own?—I love you, most passionately and sincerely love
you, and hope to propose terms agreeable to Mr Sterling. If then
you don't absolutely loathe, abhor, and scorn me, if there is no
other happier man—                                                    305

FANNY  Hear me, sir! Hear my final determination. Were my father
and sister as insensible as you are pleased to represent them; were
my heart forever to remain disengaged to any other, I could not

listen to your proposals. What! You on the very eve of a marriage
with my sister, I living under the same roof with her, bound not          310
only by the laws of friendship and hospitality, but even the ties of
blood, to contribute to her happiness, and not to conspire against
her peace—the peace of a whole family—and that my own too!
Away! Away, Sir John! At such a time, and in such circumstances,
your addresses only inspire me with horror. Nay, you must detain          315
me no longer. I will go.

SIR JOHN  Do not leave me in absolute despair! (*Falling on his knees*)
Give me a glimpse of hope!

FANNY  I cannot. (*Struggling to go*) Pray, Sir John!

SIR JOHN  Shall this hand be given to another? (*Kissing her hand*) No, I      320
cannot endure it. My whole soul is yours, and the whole happiness
of my life is in your power.

    *Enter Miss Sterling*

FANNY  Ha! My sister is here. Rise for shame, Sir John!

SIR JOHN  (*rising*)  Miss Sterling!

MISS STERLING  I beg pardon, sir! You'll excuse me, madam! I have         325
broke in upon you a little unopportunely, I believe. But I did
not mean to interrupt you. I only came, sir, to let you know that
breakfast waits, if you have finished your morning's devotions.

SIR JOHN  I am very sensible, Miss Sterling, that this may appear
particular,° but—                                                        330

MISS STERLING  Oh dear, Sir John, don't put yourself to the trouble
of an apology. The thing explains itself.

SIR JOHN  It will soon, madam! In the meantime I can only assure
you of my profound respect and esteem for you, and make no doubt
of convincing Mr Sterling of the honour and integrity of my             335
intentions. And—and—your humble servant, madam!

    *Exit Sir John Melvil in confusion*

MISS STERLING  Respect? Insolence! Esteem? Very fine truly! And
you, madam! My sweet, delicate, innocent, sentimental° sister! Will
you convince my papa too of the integrity of your intentions?

FANNY  Do not upbraid me, my dear sister! Indeed, I don't deserve it.    340
Believe me, you can't be more offended at his behaviour than I am,
and I am sure it cannot make you half so miserable.

MISS STERLING  Make me miserable! You are mightily deceived,
madam! It gives me no sort of uneasiness, I assure you. A base
fellow! As for you, Miss, the pretended softness of your disposition,    345
your artful good nature, never imposed upon me. I always knew you
to be fly, and envious, and deceitful.

FANNY Indeed you wrong me.

MISS STERLING Oh, you are all goodness, to be sure! Did not I find him on his knees before you? Did not I see him kiss your sweet hand? Did not I hear his protestations? Was not I witness of your dissembled modesty? No, no, my dear, don't imagine that you can make a fool of your elder sister so easily. 350

FANNY Sir John, I own, is to blame; but I am above the thoughts of doing you the least injury. 355

MISS STERLING We shall try that, madam! I hope, Miss, you'll be able to give a better account to my papa and my aunt, for they shall both know of this matter, I promise you.

*Exit Miss Sterling*

FANNY How unhappy I am! My distresses multiply upon me. Mr Lovewell must now become acquainted with Sir John's behaviour to me, and in a manner that may add to his uneasiness. My father, instead of being disposed by fortunate circumstances to forgive any transgression, will be previously incensed against me. My sister and my aunt will become irreconcilably my enemies, and rejoice in my disgrace. Yet, at all events, I am determined on a discovery, I dread it, and am resolved to hasten it. It is surrounded with more horrors every instant, as it appears every instant more necessary. 360 365

*Exit Fanny*

## 3.1

*A hall*

*Enter a servant, leading in Sergeant° Flower and Counsellors*
*Traverse and Trueman, all booted*

SERVANT This way, if you please, gentlemen! My master is at breakfast with the family at present, but I'll let him know, and he will
wait on you immediately.

FLOWER Mighty well, young man, mighty well.

SERVANT Please to favour me with your names, gentlemen.          5

FLOWER Let Mr Sterling know, that Mr Sergeant Flower, and two°
other gentlemen of the bar, are come to wait on him according to
his appointment.

SERVANT I will, sir. (*Going*)

FLOWER And harkee, young man! (*Servant returns*) Desire my ser-   10
vant, Mr Sergeant Flower's servant, to bring in my green and gold
saddle-cloth and pistols, and lay them down here in the hall with
my portmanteau.

SERVANT I will, sir.

        *Exit servant*

FLOWER Well, gentlemen, the settling these marriage articles° falls   15
conveniently enough, almost just on the eve of the circuits.° Let
me see: the Home, the Midland, and Western. Ay, we can all cross
the country well enough to our several destinations.—Traverse,
when do you begin at Hertford?

TRAVERSE The day after tomorrow.                                 20

FLOWER That is commission-day° with us at Warwick too. But my
clerk has retainers for every cause in the paper,° so it will be time
enough if I am there the next morning. Besides, I have about half a
dozen cases that have lain by me ever since the spring assizes, and I
must tack opinions to them° before I see my country-clients again,   25
so I will take the evening before me and then *currente calamo*,° as
I say, eh, Traverse!

TRAVERSE True, Mr Sergeant, and the easiest thing in the world too,
for those country attorneys are such ignorant dogs, that, in the case
of the devise of an estate° to A. and his heirs for ever, they'll make a   30
query, whether he takes in fee or in tail.°

FLOWER Do you expect to have much to do on the Home circuit these
assizes?

TRAVERSE Not much *nisi prius*° business, but a good deal on the crown side,° I believe.—The gaols are brimful, and some of the felons in good circumstances, and likely to be tolerable clients. Let me see: I am engaged for three highway robberies, two murders, one forgery, and half a dozen larcenies, at Kingston.

FLOWER A pretty decent gaol-delivery!° Do you expect to bring off Darkin, for the robbery on Putney Common? Can you make out your *alibi*?°

TRAVERSE Oh, no! The crown witnesses are sure to prove our identity.° We shall certainly be hanged, but that don't signify.— But, Mr Sergeant, have you much to do? Any remarkable cause on the Midland this circuit?

FLOWER Nothing very remarkable, except two rapes, and Rider and Western at Nottingham, for *crim. con.*,° but, on the whole, I believe a good deal of business. Our associate tells me, there are above thirty *venires* for Warwick.

TRAVERSE Pray, Mr Sergeant, are you concerned in Jones and Thomas at Lincoln?

FLOWER I am—for the plaintiff.

TRAVERSE And what do you think on't?

FLOWER A nonsuit.

TRAVERSE I thought so.

FLOWER Oh, no manner of doubt on't, *luce clarius*.° We have no right in us. We have but one chance.

TRAVERSE What's that?

FLOWER Why, my Lord Chief does not go the circuit this time, and my brother Puzzle being in the commission, the cause will come on before him.°

TRUEMAN Ay, that may do. Indeed, if you can but throw dust in the eyes of the defendant's council . . .

FLOWER True.—Mr Trueman, I think you are concerned for Lord Ogleby in this affair?

TRUEMAN I am, sir I have the honour to be related to his Lordship, and hold some courts for him in Somersetshire, go the Western circuit and attend the sessions at Exeter, merely because his Lordship's interest and property lie in that part of the kingdom.

FLOWER Ha!—And pray, Mr Trueman, how long have you been called to the bar?

TRUEMAN About nine years and three quarters.

FLOWER Ha! I don't know that I ever had the pleasure of seeing you before. I wish you success, young gentleman!

*Enter Sterling*

STERLING  Oh, Mr Sergeant Flower, I am glad to see you Your     75
servant, Mr Sergeant! Gentlemen, your servant! Well, are all
matters concluded? Has that snail-paced conveyancer, old Ferret
of Gray's Inn, settled the articles at last? Do you approve of what
he has done? Will his tackle hold?° Tight and strong? Eh, master
Sergeant?     80

FLOWER  My friend Ferret's slow and sure, sir. But then, *serius aut*
*citius*, as we say. Sooner or later, Mr Sterling, he is sure to put his
business out of hand° as he should do. My clerk has brought the
writings, and all other instruments along with him, and the settlement is, I believe, as good a settlement as any settlement on the face     85
of the earth!

STERLING  But that damned mortgage of £60,000: there don't appear
to be any other encumbrances,° I hope?

TRAVERSE  I can answer for that, sir, and that will be cleared off
immediately on the payment of the first part of Miss Sterling's     90
portion. You agree, on your part, to come down with £80,000—

STERLING  Down on the nail.° Ay, ay, my money is ready tomorrow if
he pleases. He shall have it in India-bonds,° or notes, or how he
chooses. Your lords, and your dukes, and your people at the court-
end of the town stick at payments sometimes—debts unpaid, no     95
credit lost with them—but no fear of us substantial fellows, eh, Mr
Sergeant!—

FLOWER  Sir John having, last term, according to agreement, levied a
fine, and suffered a recovery,° has thereby cut off the entail of the
Ogleby estate° for the better effecting the purposes of the present     100
intended marriage; on which above-mentioned Ogleby estate, a
jointure of £2000 per ann. is secured to your eldest daughter, now
Elizabeth Sterling, spinster, and the whole estate, after the death of
the aforesaid Earl, descends to the heirs male of Sir John Melvil
on the body of the aforesaid Elizabeth Sterling, lawfully to be     105
begotten.

TRAVERSE  Very true, and Sir John is to be put in immediate possession of as much of his Lordship's Somersetshire estate, as lies in
the manors of Hogmore and Cranford, amounting to between two
and three thousands per ann., and at the death of Mr Sterling, a     110
further sum of seventy thousand.

*Enter Sir John Melvil*

STERLING  Ah, Sir John! Here we are, hard at it, paving the road to
matrimony. We'll have no jolts; all upon the nail, as easy as the new

pavement—First the lawyers, then comes the doctor. Let us but dispatch the long-robe,° we shall soon set pudding-sleeves° to work, I warrant you.                                                    115

SIR JOHN I am sorry to interrupt you, sir, but I hope that both you and these gentlemen will excuse me. Having something very particular for your private ear, I took the liberty of following you, and beg you will oblige me with an audience immediately.            120

STERLING Ay, with all my heart—Gentlemen, Mr Sergeant, you'll excuse it. Business must be done, you know. The writings will keep cold till tomorrow morning.

FLOWER I must be at Warwick, Mr Sterling, the day after.

STERLING Nay, nay, I shan't part with you tonight, gentlemen, I   125
promise you My house is very full, but I have beds for you all, beds for your servants, and stabling for all your horses. Will you take a turn in the garden, and view some of my improvements before dinner? Or will you amuse yourselves in the green, with a game of bowls and a cool tankard? My servants shall attend you. Do you   130
choose any other refreshment? Call for what you please. Do as you please. Make yourselves quite at home, I beg of you.—Here, Thomas, Harry, William, wait on these gentlemen!

> *Sterling follows Flower, Traverse and Trueman out, bawling and talking, and then returns to Sir John*

And now, sir, I am entirely at your service. What are your commands with me, Sir John?                                                135

SIR JOHN After having carried the negotiation between our families to so great a length, after having assented so readily to all your proposals, as well as received so many instances of your cheerful compliance with the demands made on our part, I am extremely concerned, Mr Sterling, to be the involuntary cause of any   140
uneasiness.

STERLING Uneasiness! What uneasiness? Where business is transacted as it ought to be, and the parties understand one another, there can be no uneasiness. You agree, on such and such conditions, to receive my daughter for a wife. On the same conditions I agree   145
to receive you as a son-in-law, and as to all the rest, it follows of course, you know, as regularly as the payment of a bill after acceptance.°

SIR JOHN Pardon me, sir; more uneasiness has arisen than you are aware of. I am myself, at this instant, in a state of inexpressible   150
embarrassment. Miss Sterling, I know, is extremely disconcerted

too, and, unless you will oblige me with the assistance of your
friendship, I foresee the speedy progress of discontent and animos-
ity through the whole family.

STERLING What the deuce is all this? I don't understand a single    155
syllable.

SIR JOHN In one word then: it will be absolutely impossible for me to
fulfil my engagements in regard to Miss Sterling.

STERLING How, Sir John? Do you mean to put an affront upon my
family? What! refuse to—    160

SIR JOHN Be assured, sir, that I neither mean to affront, nor forsake
your family. My only fear is, that you should desert me; for the
whole happiness of my life depends on my being connected with
your family by the nearest and tenderest ties in the world.

STERLING Why, did not you tell me, but a moment ago, that it was    165
absolutely impossible for you to marry my daughter?

SIR JOHN True. But you have another daughter, sir.

STERLING Well?

SIR JOHN Who has obtained the most absolute dominion over my
heart. I have already declared my passion to her. Nay, Miss Sterling    170
herself is also apprised of it, and, if you will but give a sanction
to my present addresses, the uncommon merit of Miss Sterling
will no doubt recommend her to a person of equal, if not superior
rank to myself, and our families may still be allied by my union with
Miss Fanny.    175

STERLING Mighty fine, truly! Why, what the plague do you make
of us, Sir John? Do you come to market for my daughters, like
servants at a statute-fair?° Do you think that I will suffer you, or
any man in the world, to come into my house, like the Grand
Signior,° and throw the handkerchief first to one, and then to    180
t'other, just as he pleases? Do you think I drive a kind of African
slave-trade° with them? And—

SIR JOHN A moment's patience, sir! Nothing but the excess of my
passion for Miss Fanny should have induced me to take any step
that had the least appearance of disrespect to any part of your    185
family; and even now I am desirous to atone for my transgression,
by making the most adequate compensation that lies in my power.

STERLING Compensation! What compensation can you possibly make
in such a case as this, Sir John?

SIR JOHN Come, come, Mr Sterling. I know you to be a man of sense,    190
a man of business, a man of the world. I'll deal frankly with you;

and you shall see that I do not desire a change of measures for my own gratification, without endeavouring to make it advantageous to you.

STERLING  What advantage can your inconstancy be to me, Sir John?    195

SIR JOHN  I'll tell you, sir. You know that by the articles at present subsisting between us, on the day of my marriage with Miss Sterling, you agree to pay down the gross sum of eighty thousand pounds?

STERLING  Well?    200

SIR JOHN  Now if you will but consent to my waiving that marriage—

STERLING  I agree to your waiving that marriage? Impossible, Sir John!

SIR JOHN  I hope not, sir; as on my part, I will agree to waive my right to thirty thousand pounds of the fortune I was to receive with her.    205

STERLING  Thirty thousand, d'ye say?

SIR JOHN  Yes, sir; and accept of Miss Fanny with fifty thousand, instead of fourscore.

STERLING  Fifty thousand. (*Pausing*)

SIR JOHN  Instead of fourscore.    210

STERLING  Why, why, there may be something in that. Let me see; Fanny with fifty thousand instead of Betsey with fourscore. But how can this be, Sir John? For you know I am to pay this money into the hands of my Lord Ogleby, who, I believe, between you and me, Sir John, is not overstocked with ready money at present, and    215
threescore thousand of it, you know, is to go to pay off the present encumbrances on the estate, Sir John.

SIR JOHN  That objection is easily obviated. Ten of the twenty thousand, which would remain as a surplus of the fourscore, after paying off the mortgage, was intended by his Lordship for my use,    220
that we might set off with some little *éclat*° on our marriage; and the other ten for his own. Ten thousand pounds, therefore, I shall be able to pay you immediately; and, for the remaining twenty thousand, you shall have a mortgage on that part of the estate which is to be made over to me, with whatever security you shall    225
require for the regular payment of the interest, 'till the principal is duly discharged.

STERLING  Why, to do you justice, Sir John, there is something fair and open in your proposal, and since I find you do not mean to put an affront upon the family—    230

SIR JOHN  Nothing was ever farther from my thoughts, Mr Sterling. And after all, the whole affair is nothing extraordinary. Such things happen every day, and, as the world has only heard generally of a treaty between the families, when this marriage takes place, nobody will be the wiser, if we have but discretion enough to keep our own counsel. 235

STERLING True, true; and since you only transfer from one girl to the other, it is no more than transferring so much stock, you know.

SIR JOHN The very thing. 240

STERLING Odso! I had quite forgot. We are reckoning without our host here. There is another difficulty.

SIR JOHN You alarm me. What can that be?

STERLING I can't stir a step in this business without consulting my sister Heidelberg. The family has very great expectations from her, 245 and we must not give her any offence.

SIR JOHN But if you come into this measure, surely she will be so kind as to consent.

STERLING I don't know that. Betsey is her darling, and I can't tell how far she may resent any slight that seems to be offered to her 250 favourite niece. However, I'll do the best I can for you. You shall go and break the matter to her first, and, by that time that I may suppose that your rhetoric has prevailed on her to listen to reason, I will step in to reinforce your arguments.

SIR JOHN I'll fly to her immediately. You promise me your 255 assistance?

STERLING I do.

SIR JOHN (going) Ten thousand thanks for it! And now success attend me!

STERLING Harkee, Sir John! 260

*Sir John returns*

STERLING Not a word of the thirty thousand to my sister, Sir John.

SIR JOHN (going) Oh, I am dumb, I am dumb, sir.

STERLING You remember it is thirty thousand.

SIR JOHN To be sure I do. 265

STERLING But Sir John! One thing more.

*Sir John returns*

My lord must know nothing of this stroke of friendship between us.

SIR JOHN Not for the world. (*Offering to go*) Let me alone! Let me alone!

STERLING (*holding him*) And when everything is agreed, we must give 270 each other a bond to be held fast to the bargain.

SIR JOHN  To be sure. A bond by all means! A bond, or whatever you please.

*Exit Sir John Melvil, hastily*

STERLING  I should have thought of more conditions. He's in a humour to give me everything. Why, what mere children are your fellows of quality; that cry for a plaything one minute, and throw it by the next! As changeable as the weather, and as uncertain as the stocks.° Special fellows to drive a bargain! And yet they are to take care of the interest of the nation truly! Here does this whirligig man° of fashion offer to give up thirty thousand pounds in hard money, with as much indifference as if it was a china orange.° By this mortgage, I shall have a hold on his *terrafirma*, and if he wants more money, as he certainly will, let him have children by my daughter or no, I shall have his whole estate in a net for the benefit of my family. Well; thus it is, that the children of citizens, who have acquired fortunes, prove persons of fashion; and thus it is, that persons of fashion, who have ruined their fortunes, reduce the next generation to cits. 275

*Exit Sterling*

## 3.2

*Another apartment*

*Enter Mrs Heidelberg and Miss Sterling*

MISS STERLING  This is your gentle-looking, soft-speaking, sweet-smiling, affable Miss Fanny for you!

MRS HEIDELBERG  My Miss Fanny! I disclaim her. With all her arts she never could insinuate herself into my good graces, and yet she has a way with her, that deceives man, woman, and child, except you and me, niece. 5

MISS STERLING  O ay, she wants nothing but a crook in her hand, and a lamb under her arm, to be a perfect picture of innocence and simplicity.

MRS HEIDELBERG  Just as I was drawn at Amsterdam, when I went over to visit my husband's relations. 10

MISS STERLING  And then she's so mighty good to servants: 'pray, John, do this, pray, Tom, do that, thank you, Jenny', and then so humble to her relations: 'to be sure, Papa! as my Aunt pleases, my

Sister knows best'. But with all her demureness and humility she    15
has no objection to be Lady Melvil, it seems, nor to any wickedness
that can make her so.

MRS HEIDELBERG She Lady Melvil? Compose yourself, niece! I'll
ladyship her indeed. A little creepin', cantin'—She shan't be the
better for a farden of my money. But tell me, child, how does    20
this intriguing with Sir John correspond with her partiality to
Lovewell? I don't see a concatunation, here.

MISS STERLING There I was deceived, madam. I took all their
whisperings and stealing into corners to be the mere attraction of
vulgar minds; but, behold, their private meetings were not to con-    25
trive their own insipid happiness, but to conspire against mine! But
I know whence proceeds Mr Lovewell's resentment to me. I could
not stoop to be familiar with my father's clerk, and so I have lost his
interest.

MRS HEIDELBERG My spurrit to a T. My dear child! (Kissing her) Mr    30
Heidelberg lost his election for member of parliament, because I
would not demean myself to be slobbered about by drunken shoe-
makers, beastly cheesemongers, and greasy butchers and tallow-
chandlers. However, niece, I can't help diffuring a little in opinion
from you in this matter. My experunce and sagucity makes me    35
still suspect, that there is something more between her and that
Lovewell, notwithstanding this affair of Sir John. I had my eye
upon them the whole time of breakfast. Sir John, I observed,
looked a little confounded, indeed, though I knew nothing of what
had passed in the garden. You seemed to sit upon thorns too: but    40
Fanny and Mr Lovewell made quite another-guess sort of a figur;
and were as perfet a pictur of two distressed lovers, as if it had been
drawn by Raphael Angelo. As to Sir John and Fanny, I want a
matter of fact.

MISS STERLING Matter of fact, madam! Did not I come unexpectedly    45
upon them? Was not Sir John kneeling at her feet, and kissing her
hand? Did not he look all love, and she all confusion? Is not that
matter of fact? And did not Sir John, the moment that Papa was
called out of the room to the lawyermen, get up from breakfast, and
follow him immediately? And I warrant you that by this time he has    50
made proposals to him to marry my sister. Oh, that some other
person, an earl, or a duke, would make his addresses to me, that I
might be revenged on this monster!

MRS HEIDELBERG Be cool, child! You *shall* be Lady Melvil, in spite of

all their caballins,° if it costs me ten thousand pounds to turn the    55
scale. Sir John may apply to my brother, indeed; but I'll make them
all know who governs in this fammaly.

MISS STERLING (*disordered*)  As I live, madam, yonder comes Sir John.
A base man! I can't endure the sight of him. I'll leave the room this
instant.    60

MRS HEIDELBERG  Poor thing! Well, retire to your own chamber,
child. I'll give it him, I warrant you; and, by and by, I'll come and
let you know all that has passed between us.

MISS STERLING  Pray do, madam! (*Looking back*) A vile
wretch!    65

*Exit Miss Sterling in a rage. Enter Sir John Melvil*

SIR JOHN (*bowing very respectfully*)  Your most obedient humble
servant, madam!

MRS HEIDELBERG (*dropping a half-curtsy, and pouting*)  Your servant,
Sir John!

SIR JOHN  Miss Sterling's manner of quitting the room on my    70
approach, and the visible coolness of your behaviour to me, madam,
convince me that she has acquainted you with what passed this
morning.

MRS HEIDELBERG (*pouting*)  I am very sorry, Sir John, to be made
acquainted with anything that should induce me to change the    75
opinion, which I could always wish to entertain of a person of
quallaty.

SIR JOHN  It has always been my ambition to merit the best opinion
from Mrs Heidelberg; and when she comes to weigh all circumstances, I flatter myself—    80

MRS HEIDELBERG  You *do* flatter yourself, if you imagine that I can
approve of your behaviour to my niece, Sir John. (*Warmly*) And
give me leave to tell you, Sir John, that you have been drawn into an
action much beneath you, Sir John; and that I look upon every
injury offered to Miss Betty Sterling, as an affront to myself, Sir    85
John.

SIR JOHN  I would not offend you for the world, madam, but when I
am influenced by a partiality for another, however ill-founded,
I hope your discernment and good sense will think it rather a
point of honour to renounce engagements, which I could not    90
fulfil so strictly as I ought; and that you will excuse the change in
my inclinations, since the new object, as well as the first, has the
honour of being your niece, madam.

MRS HEIDELBERG  I disclaim her as a niece, Sir John. Miss Sterling

disclaims her as a sister, and the whole fammaly must disclaim her,    95
for her monstrus baseness and treachery.

SIR JOHN  Indeed she has been guilty of none, madam. Her hand and
heart are, I am sure, entirely at the disposal of yourself, and Mr
Sterling.

*Enter Sterling behind*

And if you should not oppose my inclinations, I am sure of Mr    100
Sterling's consent, madam.

MRS HEIDELBERG  Indeed!

SIR JOHN  Quite certain, madam.

STERLING (*behind*)  So, they seem to be coming to terms already! I
may venture to make my appearance.    105

MRS HEIDELBERG  To marry Fanny?

*Sterling advances by degrees*

SIR JOHN  Yes, madam.

MRS HEIDELBERG  My brother has given his consent, you say?

SIR JOHN  In the most ample manner, with no other restriction than
the failure of your concurrence, madam. (*Sees Sterling*) Oh, here's    110
Mr Sterling, who will confirm what I have told you.

MRS HEIDELBERG  What! Have you consented to give up your own
daughter in this manner, brother?

STERLING  Give her up? No, not give her up, sister; only in case that
you—(*aside to Sir John*) Zounds, I am afraid you have said too    115
much, Sir John.

MRS HEIDELBERG  Yes, yes. I see now that it is true enough what my
niece told me. You are all plottin and caballin against her. Pray, does
Lord Ogleby know of this affair?

SIR JOHN  I have not yet made him acquainted with it, madam.    120

MRS HEIDELBERG  No, I warrant you. I thought so. And so, his
Lordship and myself truly are not to be consulted 'till the last.

STERLING  What! Did not you consult my Lord? Oh, fie for shame,
Sir John!

SIR JOHN  Nay, but Mr Sterling—    125

MRS HEIDELBERG  We, who are the persons of most consequence and
experunce in the two fammalies, are to know nothing of the matter,
'till the whole is as good as concluded upon. But his Lordship, I
am sure, will have more generosaty than to countenance such a
perceeding. And I could not have expected such behaviour from    130
a person of your quallaty, Sir John. And, as for you, brother—

STERLING  Nay, nay, but hear me, sister!

MRS HEIDELBERG  I am perfetly ashamed of you. Have you no

spurrit? no more concern for the honour of our fammaly than to
consent— 135

STERLING Consent? I consent? As I hope for mercy, I never gave my
consent. Did I consent, Sir John?

SIR JOHN Not absolutely, without Mrs Heidelberg's concurrence. But
in case of her approbation—

STERLING Ay, I grant you, if my sister approved. (*To Mrs Heidelberg*) 140
But that's quite another thing, you know.

MRS HEIDELBERG Your sister approve, indeed!—I thought you knew
her better, brother Sterling! What! Approve of having your eldest
daughter returned upon your hands, and exchanged for the
younger? I am surprised how you could listen to such a scandalus 145
proposal.

STERLING I tell you, I never did listen to it. Did not I say that I would
be governed entirely by my sister, Sir John? And unless she agreed
to your marrying Fanny—

MRS HEIDELBERG I agree to his marrying Fanny? Abominable! The 150
man is absolutely out of his senses. Can't that wise head of yours
foresee the consequence of all this, brother Sterling? Will Sir John
take Fanny without a fortune? No. After you have settled the largest
part of your property on your youngest daughter, can there be an
equal portion left for the eldest? No. Does not this overturn the 155
whole systum of the fammaly? Yes, yes, yes. You know I was always
for my niece Betsey's marrying a person of the very first quallaty.
That was my maxum. And, therefore, much the largest settlement
was of course to be made upon her. As for Fanny, if she could, with
a fortune of twenty or thirty thousand pounds, get a knight, or 160
a member of parliament, or a rich common–council–man° for a
husband, I thought it might do very well.

SIR JOHN But if a better match should offer itself, why should not it
be accepted, madam?

MRS HEIDELBERG What! At the expense of her elder sister! Oh fie, 165
Sir John! How could you bear to hear of such an indignaty, brother
Sterling?

STERLING I! Nay, I shan't hear of it, I promise you. I can't hear of it
indeed, Sir John.

MRS HEIDELBERG But you *have* heard of it, brother Sterling. You 170
know you have; and sent Sir John to propose it to me. But if you can
give up your daughter, I shan't forsake my niece, I assure you. Ah!
If my poor dear Mr Heidelberg, and our sweet babes had been alive,
he would not have behaved so.

STERLING Did I, Sir John? Nay speak! (*Aside to Sir John*) Bring me    175
off, or we are ruined.

SIR JOHN Why, to be sure, to speak the truth—

MRS HEIDELBERG To speak the truth, I'm ashamed of you both. But
have a care what you are about, brother! Have a care, I say. The
lawyers are in the house, I hear; and if everything is not settled to    180
my liking, I'll have nothing more to say to you, if I live these
hundred years. I'll go over to Holland, and settle with Mr Vander-
spracken, my poor husband's first cousin; and my own fammaly
shall never be the better for a farden of my money, I promise you.

    *Exit Mrs Heidelberg*

STERLING I thought so. I knew she never would agree to it.    185

SIR JOHN 'Sdeath, how unfortunate! What can we do, Mr Sterling?

STERLING Nothing.

SIR JOHN What! Must our agreement break off, the moment it is
made then?

STERLING It can't be helped, Sir John. The family, as I told you    190
before, have great expectations from my sister; and if this matter
proceeds, you hear yourself that she threatens to leave us. My
brother Heidelberg was a warm man; a very warm man; and died
worth a Plum° at least, a Plum! Ay, I warrant you, he died worth a
Plum and a half.    195

SIR JOHN Well; but if I—

STERLING And then, my sister has three or four very good mortgages,
a deal of money in the three per cents.° and old South Sea
annuities,° besides large concerns in the Dutch and French funds.
The greatest part of all this she means to leave to our family.    200

SIR JOHN I can only say, sir—

STERLING Why, your offer of the difference of thirty thousand was
very fair and handsome to be sure, Sir John.

SIR JOHN Nay, but I am even willing to—

STERLING Ay, but if I was to accept it against her will, I might lose    205
above a hundred thousand; so, you see, the balance is against you,
Sir John.

SIR JOHN But is there no way, do you think, of prevailing on Mrs
Heidelberg to grant her consent?

STERLING I am afraid not. However, when her passion is a little    210
abated, for she's very passionate, you may try what can be done, but
you must not use my name any more, Sir John.

SIR JOHN Suppose I was to prevail on Lord Ogleby to apply to her, do
you think that would have any influence over her?

STERLING  I think he would be more likely to persuade her to it, than    215
   any other person in the family. She has a great respect for Lord
   Ogleby. She loves a lord.
SIR JOHN  I'll apply to him this very day. And if he should prevail on
   Mrs Heidelberg, I may depend on your friendship, Mr Sterling?
STERLING  Ay, ay, I shall be glad to oblige you, when it is in my power;    220
   but as the account stands now, you see it is not upon the figures.°
   And so your servant, Sir John.
   *Exit Sterling*
SIR JOHN  What a situation am I in! Breaking off with her whom I was
   bound by treaty to marry. Rejected by the object of my affections;
   and embroiled with this turbulent woman, who governs the whole    225
   family. And yet opposition, instead of smothering, increases my
   inclination. I must have her. I'll apply immediately to Lord Ogleby;
   and, if he can but bring over the aunt to our party, her influence will
   overcome the scruples and delicacy of my dear Fanny, and I shall be
   the happiest of mankind.    230
   *Exit Sir John Melvil*

# 4.1

*A room*

*Enter Sterling, Mrs Heidelberg and Miss Sterling*

STERLING  What! Will you send Fanny to town, sister?

MRS HEIDELBERG  Tomorrow morning. I've given orders about it already.

STERLING  Indeed?

MRS HEIDELBERG  Positively.°                                                    5

STERLING  But consider, sister, at such a time as this, what an odd appearance it will have.

MRS HEIDELBERG  Not half so odd, as her behaviour, brother. This time was intended for happiness, and I'll keep no incendaries° here to destroy it. I insist on her going off tomorrow morning.      10

STERLING  I'm afraid this is all your doing, Betsey.

MISS STERLING  No indeed, Papa. My aunt knows that it is not. For all Fanny's baseness to me, I am sure I would not do, or say anything, to hurt her with you or my aunt for the world.

MRS HEIDELBERG  Hold your tongue, Betsey! I will have my way.   15
When she is packed off, every thing will go on as it should do. Since they are at their intrigues, I'll let them see that we can act with vigur on our part; and the sending her out of the way shall be the purlimunary step to all the rest of my perceedings.

STERLING  Well, but sister—                                                     20

MRS HEIDELBERG  It does not signify talking, brother Sterling, for I'm resolved to be rid of her, and I will. (*To Miss Sterling*) Come along, child! The post-shay° shall be at the door by six o'clock in the morning, and if Miss Fanny does not get into it, why I will, and so there's an end of the matter. (*Bounces out with Miss Sterling*)   25

*Mrs Heidelberg returns*

MRS HEIDELBERG  One word more, brother Sterling! I expect that you will take your eldest daughter in your hand,° and make a formal complaint to Lord Ogleby of Sir John Melvil's behaviour. Do this, brother. Show a proper regard for the honour of your fammaly yourself, and I shall throw in my mite to the raising of it.   30
If not—but now you know my mind. So act as you please, and take the consequences.

*Exit Mrs Heidelberg*

STERLING  The devil's in the woman for tyranny. Mothers, wives,

mistresses, or sisters, they always will govern us. As to my sister
Heidelberg, she knows the strength of her purse, and domineers    35
upon the credit of it. (*Mimicking*) 'I will do this' and, 'you shall do
that' and, 'you must do t'other, or else the fammaly shan't have a
farden of.' So absolute with her money! But to say the truth, nothing but money *can* make us absolute,° and so we must even make
the best of her.    40

    *Exit Sterling*


# 4.2

    *Scene changes to the garden*

    *Enter Lord Ogleby and Canton*

LORD OGLEBY What! Mademoiselle Fanny to be sent away! Why?
    Wherefore? What's the meaning of all this?

CANTON *Je ne sais pas.*° I know noting of it.

LORD OGLEBY It can't be; it shan't be. I protest against the measure.
    She's a fine girl, and I had much rather that the rest of the family    5
    were annihilated than that she should leave us. Her vulgar father,
    that's the very abstract of 'Change-Alley,° the aunt, that's always
    endeavouring to be a fine lady and the pert sister, forever showing
    that she is one, are horrid company indeed, and without her would
    be intolerable. Ah, *la petite Fanchon*!° She's the thing. Isn't she,    10
    Cant?

CANTON Dere is very good sympatie entre vous,° and dat young lady,
    mi lor.

LORD OGLEBY I'll not be left among these Goths and Vandals,° your
    Sterlings, your Heidelbergs, and Devilbergs. If she goes, I'll posi-    15
    tively go too.

CANTON In de same post-chay, mi lor? You have no object° to dat I
    believe, nor Mademoiselle neider too. Ha, ha, ha.

LORD OGLEBY Prithee hold thy foolish tongue, Cant. Does thy Swiss
    stupidity imagine that I can see and talk with a fine girl without    20
    desires? My eyes are involuntarily attracted by beautiful objects.°
    I fly as naturally to a fine girl—

CANTON As de fine girl to you, my lor, ha, ha, ha. You alway fly
    togedre like un pair de pigeons.

LORD OGLEBY (*mocks him*) Like un pair de pigeons. *Vous êtes un sot*,°    25
    Monsieur Canton. Thou art always dreaming of my intrigues,

and never seest me *badiner*,° but you suspect mischief, you old fool, you.

CANTON  I am fool, I confess, but not always fool in dat, my lor, he, he, he.                                                                                                                                     30

LORD OGLEBY  He, he, he. Thou art incorrigible, but thy absurdities amuse one. Thou art like my rappee here, (*takes out his box*) a most ridiculous superfluity, but a pinch of thee now and then is a most delicious treat.

CANTON  You do me great honeur, my lor.                                                                                                  35

LORD OGLEBY  'Tis fact, upon my soul. Thou art properly my cephalic snuff, and art no bad medicine against megrims, vertigoes, and profound thinking ha, ha, ha.

CANTON  Your flatterie, my lor, vil make me too prode.°

LORD OGLEBY  The girl has some little partiality for me, to be sure.          40
But prithee, Cant, is not that Miss Fanny yonder?

CANTON (*looking with a glass°*) *En verité*, 'tis she, my lor. 'Tis one of de pigeons, de pigeons d'amour.

LORD OGLEBY (*smiling*) Don't be ridiculous, you old monkey.

CANTON  I am monkeé, I am ole,° but I have eye, I have ear, and a little          45
understand, now and den.

LORD OGLEBY  *Taisez-vous bête!*°

CANTON  *Elle vous attend*,° my lor. She vil make a love to you.

LORD OGLEBY  Will she? Have at her then! A fine girl can't oblige me more. Egad, I find myself a little *enjouée*. Come along, Cant! She          50
is but in the next walk, but there is such a deal of this damned crinkum-crankum,° as Sterling calls it, that one sees people for half an hour before one can get to them. *Allons*, Monsieur Canton, *allons donc!*

> *Exeunt Lord Ogleby and Canton, singing in French*

> *Another part of the garden°*
> *Lovewell and Fanny*

LOVEWELL  My dear Fanny, I cannot bear your distress. It overcomes          55
all my resolutions, and I am prepared for the discovery.

FANNY  But how can it be effected before my departure?

LOVEWELL  I'll tell you. Lord Ogleby seems to entertain a visible partiality for you; and notwithstanding the peculiarities of his behaviour, I am sure that he is humane at the bottom. He is vain to          60
an excess; but, withal, extremely good-natured, and would do anything to recommend himself to a lady. Do you open the whole affair° of our marriage to him immediately. It will come with more irresistible persuasion from you than from myself; and I doubt not

but you'll gain his friendship and protection at once. His influence   65
and authority will put an end to Sir John's solicitations, remove
your aunt's and sister's unkindness and suspicions, and, I hope,
reconcile your father and the whole family to our marriage.

FANNY  Heaven grant it! Where is my lord?

LOVEWELL  I have heard him and Canton since dinner singing   70
French songs under the great walnut-tree by the parlour door.
If you meet with him in the garden, you may disclose the whole
immediately.

FANNY  Dreadful as the task is, I'll do it. Anything is better than this
continual anxiety.   75

LOVEWELL  By that time the discovery is made, I will appear to
second you. Ha! here comes my lord. Now, my dear Fanny, sum-
mon up all your spirits, plead our cause powerfully, and be sure of
success. (*Going*)

FANNY  Ah, don't leave me!   80

LOVEWELL  Nay, you must let me.

FANNY  Well; since it must be so, I'll obey you, if I have the power. Oh
Lovewell!

LOVEWELL  Consider; our situation is very critical. Tomorrow
morning is fixed for your departure, and if we lose this opportunity,   85
we may wish in vain for another. He approaches. I must retire.
Speak, my dear Fanny, speak, and make us happy!
      *Exit Lovewell*

FANNY  Good heaven, what a situation am I in! What shall I do? What
shall I say to him? I am all confusion.
      *Enter Lord Ogleby, and Canton*

LORD OGLEBY  To see so much beauty so solitary, madam, is a satire   90
upon mankind,° and 'tis fortunate that one man has broke in upon
your reverie for the credit of our sex. I say *one*, madam, for poor
Canton here, from age and infirmities, stands for nothing.

CANTON  Noting at all, inteed.

FANNY  Your lordship does me great honour. I had a favour to request,   95
my lord!

LORD OGLEBY  A favour, madam! To be honoured with your commands, is an inexpressible favour done to me, madam.

FANNY  If your lordship could indulge me with the honour of a
moment's—(*Aside*) What is the matter with me?   100

LORD OGLEBY  The girl's confused. He! Here's something in the
wind faith. I'll have a *tete-a-tete* with her. (*To Canton*) *Allez-vous
en!*°

CANTON I go. Ah, *pauvre* Mademoiselle! My lor, have *pitié* upon de poor *pigeonne*!

LORD OGLEBY (*smiling*) I'll knock you down Cant, if you're impertinent.

CANTON Den I mus avay. (*Shuffles along*) (*Aside*) You are mosh please, for all dat.

*Exit Canton*

FANNY (*aside*) I shall sink with apprehension.

LORD OGLEBY What a sweet girl! She's a civilized being, and atones for the barbarism of the rest of the family.

FANNY (*curtsies, and blushes*) My lord! I—

LORD OGLEBY (*addressing her*) I look upon it, madam, to be one of the luckiest circumstances of my life, that I have this moment the honour of receiving your commands, and the satisfaction of confirming with my tongue, what my eyes perhaps have but too weakly expressed: that I am, literally, the humblest of your servants.

FANNY I think myself greatly honoured, by your lordship's partiality to me; but it distresses me, that I am obliged in my present situation to apply to it for protection.

LORD OGLEBY I am happy in your distress, madam, because it gives me an opportunity to show my zeal. Beauty to me, is a religion, in which I was born and bred a bigot, and would die a martyr. (*Aside*) I'm in tolerable spirits, faith!

FANNY There is not perhaps at this moment a more distressed creature than myself. Affection, duty, hope, despair, and a thousand different sentiments,° are struggling in my bosom; and even the presence of your lordship, to whom I have flown for protection, adds to my perplexity.

LORD OGLEBY Does it, madam? Venus forbid!° (*Aside and smiling*) My old fault; the devil's in me, I think, for perplexing young women. Take courage, madam! Dear Miss Fanny, explain. You have a powerful advocate in my breast, I assure you: my heart, madam. I am attached to you by all the laws of sympathy, and delicacy. By my honour, I am.

FANNY Then I will venture to unburden my mind. Sir John Melvil, my lord, by the most misplaced, and mistimed declaration of affection for me, has made me the unhappiest of women.

LORD OGLEBY How, madam! Has Sir John made his addresses to you?

FANNY He has, my lord, in the strongest terms. But I hope it is needless to say, that my duty to my father,° love to my sister, and

regard to the whole family, as well as the great respect I entertain
for your lordship, (*curtsying*) made me shudder at his addresses.          145

LORD OGLEBY Charming girl! Proceed, my dear Miss Fanny,
proceed!

FANNY In a moment. Give me leave, my lord! But if what I have to
disclose should be received with anger or displeasure—

LORD OGLEBY Impossible, by all the tender powers! Speak, I beseech          150
you, or I shall divine the cause before you utter it.

FANNY Then, my lord, Sir John's addresses are not only shocking
to me in themselves, but are more particularly disagreeable to me at
this time, as—as—(*hesitating*)

LORD OGLEBY As what, madam?          155

FANNY As—Pardon my confusion. I am entirely devoted to another.

LORD OGLEBY (*aside*) If this is not plain, the devil's in it. But tell me,
my dear Miss Fanny, for I must know; tell me the how, the when,
and the where. Tell me.

> *Enter Canton hastily*

CANTON My lor, my lor, my lor!          160

LORD OGLEBY Damn your Swiss impertinence! How durst you interrupt me in the most critical melting moment that ever love and
beauty honoured me with?

CANTON I demande pardonne, my lor! Sir John Melvil, my lor,
sent me to beg you to do him the honour to speak a little to your          165
lorship.

LORD OGLEBY I'm not at leisure. I'm busy. Get away, you stupid old
dog, you Swiss rascal, or I'll—

CANTON *Fort bien,*° my lor.

> *Canton goes out [on] tiptoe*

LORD OGLEBY By the laws of gallantry, madam, this interruption          170
should be death; but as no punishment ought to disturb the
triumph of the softer passions, the criminal is pardoned and
dismissed. Let us return, madam, to the highest luxury of exalted
minds: a declaration of love from the lips of beauty.

FANNY [*aside*] The entrance of a third person has a little relieved me,          175
but I cannot go through with it. And yet I must open my heart with
a discovery, or it will break with its burden.

LORD OGLEBY (*aside*) What passion in her eyes! I am alarmed to
agitation. I presume, madam (and as you have flattered me, by
making me a party concerned, I hope you'll excuse the presump-          180
tion) that—

FANNY Do you excuse my making you a party concerned, my lord,

and let me interest your heart in my behalf, as my future happiness
or misery in a great measure depend—
LORD OGLEBY  Upon me, madam?                                                    185
FANNY (*sighs*)  Upon you, my lord.
LORD OGLEBY  There's no standing this. I have caught the infection.
Her tenderness dissolves me. (*Sighs*)
FANNY  And should you too severely judge of a rash action which
passion prompted, and modesty has long concealed.                              190
LORD OGLEBY (*taking her hand*)  Thou amiable creature. Command
my heart, for it is vanquished. Speak but thy virtuous wishes, and
enjoy them.
FANNY  I cannot, my lord. Indeed, I cannot. Mr Lovewell must tell
you my distresses, and when you know them, pity and protect me!               195
      *Exit Fanny, in tears*
LORD OGLEBY  How the devil could I bring her to this? It is too much,
too much. I can't bear it. I must give way to this amiable weakness.
(*Wipes his eyes*) My heart overflows with sympathy, and I feel every
tenderness I have inspired. (*Stifles the tear*) How blind have I been
to the desolation I have made! How could I possibly imagine that a             200
little partial attention and tender civilities to this young creature
should have gathered to this burst of passion! Can I be a man and
withstand it? No, I'll sacrifice the whole sex to her.° But here comes
the father, quite apropos. I'll open the matter° immediately, settle
the business with him, and take the sweet girl down to Ogleby                  205
House tomorrow morning. But what the devil! Miss Sterling too!
What mischief's in the wind now?
      *Enter Sterling and Miss Sterling*
STERLING  My lord, your servant! I am attending my daughter here
upon rather a disagreeable affair. Speak to his lordship, Betsey!
LORD OGLEBY  Your eyes, Miss Sterling,—for I always read the eyes            210
of a young lady—betray some little emotion. What are your com-
mands, madam?
MISS STERLING  I have but too much cause for my emotion, my lord!
LORD OGLEBY  I cannot commend my kinsman's behaviour, madam.
He has behaved like a false knight, I must confess. I have heard of           215
his apostasy.° Miss Fanny has informed me of it.
MISS STERLING  Miss Fanny's baseness has been the cause of Sir
John's inconstancy.
LORD OGLEBY  Nay, now, my dear Miss Sterling, your passion trans-
ports you too far. Sir John may have entertained a passion for                 220
Miss Fanny, but believe me, my dear Miss Sterling, believe me,

Miss Fanny has no passion for Sir John. She has a passion, indeed,
a most tender passion. (*Conceitedly*) She has opened her whole soul
to me, and I know where her affections are placed.

MISS STERLING Not upon Mr Lovewell, my lord; for I have great    225
reason to think that her seeming attachment to him, is, by his
consent, made use of as a blind to cover her designs upon Sir
John.

LORD OGLEBY (*smiling*) Lovewell! No, poor lad! She does not think of
him.    230

MISS STERLING Have a care, my lord, that both the families are not
made the dupes of Sir John's artifice and my sister's dissimulation!
You don't know her. Indeed, my Lord, you don't know her. A base,
insinuating, perfidious! It is too much. She has been beforehand
with me, I perceive. Such unnatural behaviour to me! But since    235
I see I can have no redress, I am resolved that some way or other I
will have revenge.

   *Exit Miss Sterling*

STERLING This is foolish work, my lord!

LORD OGLEBY I have too much sensibility° to bear the tears of
beauty.    240

STERLING It is touching indeed, my lord, and very moving for a
father.

LORD OGLEBY To be sure, sir! You must be distressed beyond measure! Wherefore, to divert your too exquisite feelings, suppose we
change the subject, and proceed to business.    245

STERLING With all my heart, my lord!

LORD OGLEBY You see, Mr Sterling, we can make no union in our
families by the proposed marriage.

STERLING And very sorry I am to see it, my lord.

LORD OGLEBY Have you set your heart upon being allied to our    250
house, Mr Sterling?

STERLING 'Tis my only wish, at present, my omnium,° as I may call
it.

LORD OGLEBY Your wishes shall be fulfilled.

STERLING Shall they, my lord! But how, how?    255

LORD OGLEBY I'll marry in your family.

STERLING What! My sister Heidelberg?

LORD OGLEBY You throw me into a cold sweat, Mr Sterling. No, not
your sister, but your daughter.

STERLING My daughter!    260

LORD OGLEBY Fanny!—Now the murder's out!

STERLING  What you, my lord?

LORD OGLEBY  Yes. I, I, Mr Sterling!

STERLING (*smiling*)  No, no, my lord. That's too much.

LORD OGLEBY  Too much? I don't comprehend you.                    265

STERLING  What, you, my lord, marry my Fanny! Bless me, what will
the folks say?

LORD OGLEBY  Why, what will they say?

STERLING  That you're a bold man, my lord. That's all.

LORD OGLEBY  Mr Sterling, this may be city wit for ought I know. Do    270
you court my alliance?

STERLING  To be sure, my lord.

LORD OGLEBY  Then I'll explain. My nephew won't marry your
eldest daughter, nor I neither. Your youngest daughter won't marry
him. I will marry your youngest daughter.                          275

STERLING  What! With a younger daughter's fortune, my lord?

LORD OGLEBY  With any fortune, or no fortune at all, sir. Love is the
idol of my heart, and the demon Interest° sinks before him. So, sir,
as I said before, I will marry your youngest daughter; your youngest
daughter will marry me.                                            280

STERLING  Who told you so, my lord?

LORD OGLEBY  Her own sweet self, sir.

STERLING  Indeed?

LORD OGLEBY  Yes, sir. Our affection is mutual, your advantage
double and treble. Your daughter will be a Countess directly. I shall   285
be the happiest of beings, and you'll be father to an Earl instead of
a Baronet.°

STERLING  But what will my sister say? And my daughter?

LORD OGLEBY  I'll manage that matter. Nay, if they won't consent, I'll
run away with your daughter in spite of you.                       290

STERLING  Well said, my lord! Your spirit's good. I wish you had my
constitution! But if you'll venture, I have no objection, if my sister
has none.

LORD OGLEBY  I'll answer for your sister, sir. Apropos! The lawyers
are in the house. I'll have articles drawn, and the whole affair    295
concluded tomorrow morning.

STERLING  Very well, and I'll dispatch Lovewell to London immediately for some fresh papers I shall want, and I shall leave you
to manage matters with my sister. You must excuse me, my lord,
but I can't help laughing at the match. He! he! he! what will the   300
folks say?

*Exit Sterling*

LORD OGLEBY  What a fellow am I going to make a father of? He has no more feeling than the post in his warehouse.° But Fanny's virtues tune me to rapture again, and I won't think of the rest of the family.                                                                     305
    *Enter Lovewell hastily*

LOVEWELL  I beg your lordship's pardon, my lord. Are you alone, my lord?

LORD OGLEBY  No, my lord, I am not alone! I am in company, the best company.

LOVEWELL  My lord!                                                    310

LORD OGLEBY  I never was in such exquisite enchanting company since my heart first conceived,° or my senses tasted pleasure.

LOVEWELL  (*looking about*)  Where are they, my lord?

LORD OGLEBY  In my mind, sir.

LOVEWELL  (*smiling*)  What company have you there, my lord?        315

LORD OGLEBY  My own ideas, sir, which so crowd upon my imagination, and kindle it to such a delirium of ecstasy, that wit, wine, music, poetry, all combined, and each perfection, are but mere mortal shadows of my felicity.

LOVEWELL  I see that your lordship is happy, and I rejoice at it.   320

LORD OGLEBY  You shall rejoice at it, sir. My felicity shall not selfishly be confined, but shall spread its influence to the whole circle of my friends. I need not say, Lovewell, that you shall have your share of it.

LOVEWELL  Shall I, my lord? Then I understand you. You have heard.  325
Miss Fanny has informed you.

LORD OGLEBY  She has. I have heard, and she shall be happy. 'Tis determined.

LOVEWELL  Then I have reached the summit of my wishes. And will your lordship pardon the folly?                                    330

LORD OGLEBY  O yes, poor creature, how could she help it? 'Twas unavoidable. Fate and necessity.

LOVEWELL  It was indeed, my lord. Your kindness distracts me.

LORD OGLEBY  And so it did the poor girl, faith.

LOVEWELL  She trembled to disclose the secret, and declare her      335
affections?

LORD OGLEBY  The world, I believe, will not think her affections ill-placed.

LOVEWELL  (*bowing*)  You are too good, my lord. And do you really excuse the rashness of the action?                                 340

LORD OGLEBY  From my very soul, Lovewell.

LOVEWELL (*bowing*) Your generosity overpowers me. I was afraid of her meeting with a cold reception.

LORD OGLEBY More fool you then.

    'Who pleads her cause with never-failing beauty,    345
    Here finds a full redress.'°

(*strikes his breast*)

She's a fine girl, Lovewell.

LOVEWELL Her beauty, my lord, is her least merit. She has an understanding.

LORD OGLEBY Her choice convinces me of that.    350

LOVEWELL (*bowing*) That's your lordship's goodness. Her choice was a disinterested one.

LORD OGLEBY No, no, not altogether. It began with interest, and ended in passion.

LOVEWELL Indeed, my lord, if you were acquainted with her good-    355
ness of heart, and generosity of mind, as well as you are with the inferior beauties of her face and person—

LORD OGLEBY I am so perfectly convinced of their existence, and so totally of your mind touching every amiable particular of that sweet girl, that were it not for the cold unfeeling impediments of the law,    360
I would marry her tomorrow morning.

LOVEWELL My lord!

LORD OGLEBY I would, by all that's honourable in man, and amiable in woman.

LOVEWELL Marry her! Who do you mean, my lord?    365

LORD OGLEBY Miss Fanny Sterling, that is. The Countess of Ogleby that shall be.

LOVEWELL I am astonished.

LORD OGLEBY Why, could you expect less from me?

LOVEWELL I did not expect this, my lord.    370

LORD OGLEBY Trade and accounts have destroyed your feeling.

LOVEWELL (*sighs*) No, indeed, my lord.

LORD OGLEBY The moment that love and pity entered my breast, I was resolved to plunge into matrimony, and shorten the girl's tortures. I never do anything by halves; do I, Lovewell?    375

LOVEWELL No, indeed, my lord. (*Sighs*) What an accident!

LORD OGLEBY What's the matter, Lovewell? Thou seem'st to have lost thy faculties. Why don't you wish me joy, man?

LOVEWELL (*sighs*) O, I do, my lord.

LORD OGLEBY She said, that you would explain what she had not    380
power to utter, but I wanted no interpreter for the language of love.

LOVEWELL  But has your lordship considered the consequences of
your resolution?

LORD OGLEBY  No, sir; I am above consideration, when my desires
are kindled.                                                               385

LOVEWELL  But consider the consequences, my lord, to your nephew,
Sir John.

LORD OGLEBY  Sir John has considered no consequences himself, Mr
Lovewell.

LOVEWELL  Mr Sterling, my lord, will certainly refuse his daughter to   390
Sir John.

LORD OGLEBY  Sir John has already refused Mr Sterling's daughter.

LOVEWELL  But what will become of Miss Sterling, my lord?

LORD OGLEBY  What's that to you? You may have her, if you will. I
depend upon Mr Sterling's city-philosophy,° to be reconciled to        395
Lord Ogleby's being his son-in-law, instead of Sir John Melvil,
Baronet. Don't you think that your master may be brought to that,
without having recourse to his calculations? Eh, Lovewell!

LOVEWELL  But, my lord, that is not the question.

LORD OGLEBY  Whatever is the question, I'll tell you my answer. I am   400
in love with a fine girl, whom I resolve to marry.

> *Enter Sir John Melvil*

What news with you, Sir John? You look all hurry and impatience,
like a messenger after a battle.

SIR JOHN  After a battle, indeed, my lord. I have this day had a severe
engagement, and wanting your lordship as an auxiliary,° I have at      405
last mustered up resolution to declare, what my duty to you and to
myself have demanded from me some time.

LORD OGLEBY  To the business then, and be as concise as possible;
for I am upon the wing, eh, Lovewell? (*He smiles and Lovewell
bows*)

SIR JOHN  I find 'tis in vain, my lord, to struggle against the force of   410
inclination.

LORD OGLEBY  Very true, nephew. I am your witness, and will second
the motion, shan't I, Lovewell? (*Smiles and Lovewell bows*)

SIR JOHN  Your lordship's generosity encourages me to tell you that
I cannot marry Miss Sterling.                                           415

LORD OGLEBY  I am not at all surprised at it. She's a bitter potion,
that's the truth of it; but as you were to swallow it, and not I, it was
your business, and not mine. Anything more?

SIR JOHN  But this, my lord: that I may be permitted to make my
addresses to the other sister.                                          420

LORD OGLEBY O yes. By all means. Have you any hopes there, nephew?—[*Aside*] Do you think he'll succeed, Lovewell? (*Smiles and winks at Lovewell*)

LOVEWELL ([*Aside*] *gravely*) I think not, my lord.

LORD OGLEBY [*Aside*] I think so too, but let the fool try.

SIR JOHN Will your lordship favour me with your good offices to 425 remove the chief obstacle to the match, the repugnance of Mrs Heidelberg?

LORD OGLEBY Mrs Heidelberg! Had not you better begin with the young lady first? It will save you a great deal of trouble, (*smiles*) won't it, Lovewell? But do what you please, it will be the same 430 thing to me, (*conceitedly*) won't it, Lovewell? Why don't you laugh at him?

LOVEWELL (*forces a smile*) I do, my lord.

SIR JOHN And your lordship will endeavour to prevail on Mrs Heidelberg to consent to my marriage with Miss Fanny? 435

LORD OGLEBY I'll go and speak to Mrs Heidelberg, about the adorable Fanny, as soon as possible.

SIR JOHN Your generosity transports me.

LORD OGLEBY (*aside*) Poor fellow, what a dupe! He little thinks who's in possession of the town. 440

SIR JOHN And your lordship is not offended at this seeming inconstancy.

LORD OGLEBY Not in the least. Miss Fanny's charms will even excuse infidelity. I look upon women as the *ferae naturae*,°—lawful game—and every man who is qualified, has a natural right to 445 pursue them. Lovewell as well as you, and I as well as either of you. Every man shall do his best, without offence to any. What say you kinsmen?

SIR JOHN You have made me happy, my lord.

LOVEWELL And me, I assure you, my lord. 450

LORD OGLEBY And I am superlatively so. *Allons donc.*° To horse and away, boys! You to your affairs, and I to mine. (*Sings*) Suivons l'amour!°

*Exeunt Lord Ogleby, Lovewell and Sir John Melvil severally*

# 5.1

*Fanny's apartment*

*Enter Lovewell and Fanny, followed by Betty*

FANNY Why did you come so soon, Mr Lovewell? The family is not yet in bed, and Betty certainly heard somebody listening near the chamber-door.

BETTY My mistress is right, sir! Evil spirits are abroad; and I am sure you are both too good, not to expect mischief from them. 5

LOVEWELL But who can be so curious, or so wicked?

BETTY I think we have wickedness, and curiosity enough in this family, sir, to expect the worst.

FANNY I do expect the worst. Prithee, Betty, return to the outward door, and listen if you hear anybody in the gallery; and let us know 10 directly.

BETTY I warrant you, madam. The Lord bless you both!

*Exit Betty*

FANNY What did my father want with you this evening?

LOVEWELL He gave me the key of his closet, with orders to bring from London some papers relating to Lord Ogleby. 15

FANNY And why did not you obey him?

LOVEWELL Because I am certain that his lordship has opened his heart to him about you, and those papers are wanted merely on that account. But as we shall discover all tomorrow, there will be no occasion for them, and it would be idle in me to go. 20

FANNY Hark! Hark! Bless me, how I tremble! I feel the terrors of guilt. Indeed, Mr Lovewell, this is too much for me.

LOVEWELL And for me too, my sweet Fanny. Your apprehensions make a coward of me. But what can alarm you? Your aunt and sister are in their chambers, and you have nothing to fear from the rest of 25 the family.

FANNY I fear everybody, and everything, and every moment. My mind is in continual agitation and dread. Indeed, Mr Lovewell, this situation may have very unhappy consequences. (*Weeps*)

LOVEWELL But it shan't. I would rather tell our story this moment to 30 all the house, and run the risk of maintaining° you by the hardest labour, than suffer you to remain in this dangerous perplexity. What! Shall I sacrifice all my best hopes and affections, in your dear health and safety, for the mean, and in such a case, the meanest consideration of our fortune! Were we to be abandoned by all our 35 relations, we have that in our hearts and minds, will weigh against the most affluent circumstances. I should not have proposed the secrecy of our marriage, but for your sake, and with hopes that the most generous sacrifice you have made to love and me, might be less injurious to you, by waiting° a lucky moment of reconciliation.    40

FANNY  Hush! Hush! For heaven's sake, my dear Lovewell, don't be so warm! Your generosity gets the better of your prudence. You will be heard, and we shall be discovered. I am satisfied, indeed I am. Excuse this weakness, this delicacy, this what you will. My mind's at peace. Indeed it is. Think no more of it, if you love me!    45

LOVEWELL  That one word has charmed me, as it always does, to the most implicit obedience. It would be the worst of ingratitude in me to distress you a moment. (*Kisses her*)
    *Re-enter Betty*

BETTY (*in a low voice*)  I'm sorry to disturb you.

FANNY  Ha! What's the matter?    50

LOVEWELL  Have you heard anybody?

BETTY  Yes, yes, I have, and they have heard you too, or I am mistaken. If they had seen you too, we should have been in a fine quandary.

FANNY  Prithee don't prate now, Betty!

LOVEWELL  What did you hear?    55

BETTY  I was preparing myself, as usual, to take me a little nap.

LOVEWELL  A nap!

BETTY  Yes, sir, a nap, for I watch much better so than wide awake; and when I had wrapped this handkerchief round my head, for fear of the earache, from the key-hole, I thought I heard a kind of a sort    60 of a buzzing, which I first took for a gnat, and shook my head two or three times, and went so with my hand—

FANNY  Well, well, and so?

BETTY  And so, madam, when I heard Mr Lovewell a little loud, I heard the buzzing louder too, and pulling off my handkerchief    65 softly, I could hear this sort of noise. (*Makes an indistinct noise like speaking*)

FANNY  Well, and what did they say?

BETTY  Oh! I could not understand a word of what was said.

LOVEWELL  The outward door is locked?

BETTY  Yes; and I bolted it too, for fear of the worst.    70

FANNY  Why did you? They must have heard you, if they were near.

BETTY  And I did it on purpose, madam, and coughed a little too, that they might not hear Mr Lovewell's voice. When I was silent, they were silent, and so I came to tell you.

FANNY  What shall we do?                                                        75

LOVEWELL  Fear nothing. We know the worst. It will only bring on
  our catastrophe a little too soon, but Betty might fancy this noise.
  She's in the conspiracy, and can make a man of a mouse at any time.

BETTY  I can distinguish a man from a mouse, as well as my betters. I
  am sorry you think so ill of me, sir.                                          80

FANNY  He compliments you. Don't be a fool! (*To Lovewell*) Now you
  have set her tongue a-running, she'll mutter for an hour. I'll go and
  hearken myself.
        *Exit Fanny*

BETTY  (*half aside, and muttering*) I'll turn my back upon no girl, for
  sincerity and service.                                                        85

LOVEWELL  Thou art the first in the world for both; and I will reward
  you soon, Betty, for one 70 and the other.

BETTY  I'm not marcenary neither. I can live on a little, with a good
  carreter.°
        *Re-enter Fanny*

FANNY  All seems quiet. Suppose, my dear, you go to your own room.             90
  I shall be much easier then, and tomorrow we will be prepared for
  the discovery.

BETTY  (*half aside, and muttering*) You may discover, if you please, but,
  for my part, I shall still be secret.

LOVEWELL  Should I leave you now, if they still are upon the watch,            95
  we shall lose the advantage of our delay. Besides, we should consult
  upon tomorrow's business. Let Betty go to her own room, and lock
  the outward door after her. We can fasten this; and when she thinks
  all safe, she may return and let me out as usual.

BETTY  Shall I, madam?                                                         100

FANNY  Do! Let me have my way tonight, and you shall command me
  ever after. I would not have you surprised here for the world. Pray
  leave me! I shall be quite myself again, if you will oblige me.

LOVEWELL  I live only to oblige you, my sweet Fanny! I'll be gone this
  moment. (*Going*)                                                            105

FANNY  Let us listen first at the door, that you may not be intercepted.
  Betty shall go first, and if they lay hold of her—

BETTY  They'll have the wrong sow by the ear,° I can tell them that.
  (*Going hastily*)

FANNY  Softly, softly. Betty, don't venture out, if you hear a noise!
  Softly, I beg of you! See, Mr Lovewell, the effects of indiscretion!         110

LOVEWELL  But love, Fanny, makes amends for all.
        *Exeunt Fanny and Lovewell, all softly*

## 5.2

*SCENE changes to a gallery, which leads to several bed-chambers*

*Enter Miss Sterling, leading Mrs Heidelberg in a night-cap*°

MISS STERLING This way, dear madam, and then I'll tell you all.

MRS HEIDELBERG Nay, but niece, consider a little. Don't drag me out in this figur. Let me put on my fly-cap!° If any of my lord's fammaly, or the counsellors-at-law, should be stirring, I should be perdigus disconcarted.°  5

MISS STERLING But, my dear madam, a moment is an age, in my situation. I am sure my sister has been plotting my disgrace and ruin in that chamber. O she's all craft and wickedness!

MRS HEIDELBERG Well, but softly, Betsey! You are all in emotion. Your mind is too much flustrated.° You can neither eat nor drink, 10 nor take your natural rest. Compose yourself, child, for if we are not as wary-some as they are wicked, we shall disgrace ourselves and the whole fammaly.

MISS STERLING (*she pretends to be bursting into tears all this speech*) We are disgraced already, madam. Sir John Melvil has forsaken me. 15 My lord cares for nobody but himself; or, if for anybody, it is my sister. My father, for the sake of a better bargain, would marry me to a Change-broker;° so that if you, madam, don't continue my friend—if you forsake me—if I am to lose my best hopes and con-solation—in your tenderness—and affect—ions—I had better—at 20 once—give up the matter—and let my sister enjoy—the fruits of her treachery—trample with scorn upon the rights of her elder sister, the will of the best of aunts, and the weakness of a too interested° father.

MRS HEIDELBERG Don't Betsey. Keep up your spurrit. I hate whim- 25 pering. I am your friend. Depend upon me in every partickler. But be composed, and tell me what new mischief you have discovered.

MISS STERLING I had no desire to sleep, and would not undress myself, knowing that my Machiavel sister would not rest till she had broke my heart: I was so uneasy that I could not stay in my 30 room, but when I thought that all the house was quiet, I sent my maid to discover what was going forward. She immediately came back and told me that they were in high consultation; that she had heard only, for it was in the dark, my sister's maid conduct Sir John Melvil to her mistress, and then lock the door. 35

MRS HEIDELBERG And how did you conduct yourself in this
dalimma?°

MISS STERLING I returned with her, and could hear a man's voice,
though nothing that they said distinctly, and you may depend
upon it, that Sir John is now in that room, that they have settled      40
the matter, and will run away together before morning, if we don't
prevent them.

MRS HEIDELBERG Why the brazen slut! Has she got her sister's
husband (that is to be) locked up in her chamber! At night too?
I tremble at the thoughts!      45

MISS STERLING Hush, madam! I hear something.

MRS HEIDELBERG You frighten me. Let me put on my fly-cap.
I would not be seen in this figur for the world.

MISS STERLING 'Tis dark, madam. You can't be seen.

MRS HEIDELBERG I protest there's a candle coming, and a man      50
too.

MISS STERLING Nothing but servants. Let us retire a moment!

    *Miss Sterling and Mrs Heidelberg retire*

    *Enter Brush half-drunk, laying hold of the Chambermaid, who
    has a candle in her hand*

CHAMBERMAID Be quiet Mr Brush; I shall drop down with terror!

BRUSH But my sweet, and most amiable chambermaid, if you have no
love, you may hearken to a little reason; that cannot possibly do      55
your virtue any harm.

CHAMBERMAID But you will do me harm, Mr Brush, and a great deal
of harm too. Pray, let me go. I am ruined if they hear you. I tremble
like an asp.°

BRUSH But they shan't hear us, and if you have a mind to be ruined, it      60
shall be the making of your fortune, you little slut, you! Therefore,
I say it again, if you have no love, hear a little reason!

CHAMBERMAID I wonder at your impurence,° Mr Brush, to use me
in this manner. This is not the way to keep me company, I assure
you. You are a town rake I see, and now you are a little in liquor, you      65
fear nothing.

BRUSH Nothing, by heavens, but your frowns, most amiable chambermaid. I am a little electrified, that's the truth on't. I am not used
to drink Port, and your master's is so heady, that a pint of it oversets
a claret-drinker.      70

CHAMBERMAID Don't be rude! Bless me! I shall be ruined. What will
become of me?

BRUSH I'll take care of you, by all that's honourable.

CHAMBERMAID  You are a base man to use me so. I'll cry out, if you
don't let me go. (*Pointing*) That is Miss Sterling's chamber, that      75
Miss Fanny's, and that Madam Heidelberg's.

BRUSH  And that my Lord Ogleby's, and that my Lady what d'ye
call'em. I don't mind such folks when I'm sober, much less when I
am whimsical.° Rather above that too.

CHAMBERMAID  More shame for you, Mr Brush! You terrify me. You       80
have no modesty.

BRUSH  O but I have, my sweet spider-brusher!° For instance, I reverence Miss Fanny. She's a most delicious morsel and fit for a prince.
With all my horrors of matrimony, I could marry her myself. But
for her sister—                                                          85

MISS STERLING  There, there, madam, all in a story!

CHAMBERMAID  Bless me, Mr Brush! I heard something!

BRUSH  Rats, I suppose, that are gnawing the old timbers of this
execrable old dungeon. If it was mine, I would pull it down, and fill
your fine canal up with the rubbish; and then I should get rid of two    90
damned things at once.

CHAMBERMAID  Law! Law! How you blaspheme! We shall have the
house upon our heads for it.

BRUSH  No, no, it will last our time. But, as I was saying, the eldest
sister, Miss Jezabel°—                                                   95

CHAMBERMAID  Is a fine young lady for all your evil tongue.

BRUSH  No, we have smoked her already; and unless she marries our
old Swiss, she can have none of us. No, no, she won't do. We are a
little too nice.

CHAMBERMAID  You're a monstrous rake, Mr Brush, and don't care      100
what you say.

BRUSH  Why, for that matter, my dear, I am a little inclined to
mischief; and if you won't have pity upon me, I will break open that
door and ravish Mrs Heidelberg.

MRS HEIDELBERG  (*coming forward*) There's no bearing this. You      105
profligate monster!

CHAMBERMAID  Ha! I am undone!

BRUSH  Zounds! Here she is, by all that's monstrous. (*Runs off*)

MISS STERLING  A fine discourse you have had with that fellow!

MRS HEIDELBERG  And a fine time of night it is to be here with that    110
drunken monster.

MISS STERLING  What have you to say for yourself?

CHAMBERMAID  I can say nothing. I am so frightened, and so
ashamed, but indeed I am vartuous. I am vartuous indeed.

MRS HEIDELBERG Well, well, don't tremble so, but tell us what you 115
know of this horrable plot here.

MISS STERLING We'll forgive you, if you'll discover all.

CHAMBERMAID Why, madam, don't let me betray my fellow-
servants. I shan't sleep in my bed, if I do.

MRS HEIDELBERG Then you shall sleep somewhere else tomorrow 120
night.

CHAMBERMAID O dear! What shall I do?

MRS HEIDELBERG Tell us this moment, or I'll turn you out of doors
directly.

CHAMBERMAID Why, our butler has been treating us below in his 125
pantry. Mr Brush forced us to make a kind of a holiday night
of it.

MISS STERLING Holiday! For what?

CHAMBERMAID Nay I only made one.

MISS STERLING Well, well; but upon what account? 130

CHAMBERMAID Because, as how, madam, there was a change in the
family they said, that his honour, Sir John was to marry Miss Fanny
instead of your ladyship.

MISS STERLING And so you made a holiday for that. Very fine!

CHAMBERMAID I did not make it, ma'am. 135

MRS HEIDELBERG But do you know nothing of Sir John's being to
run away with Miss Fanny tonight?

CHAMBERMAID No, indeed, ma'am!

MISS STERLING Nor of his being now locked up in my sister's
chamber? 140

CHAMBERMAID No, as I hope for marcy, ma'am.

MRS HEIDELBERG Well, I'll put an end to all this directly. Do you run
to my brother Sterling—

CHAMBERMAID Now, ma'am! 'Tis so very late, ma'am.

MRS HEIDELBERG I don't care how late it is. Tell him there are 145
thieves in the house. That the house is o'fire. Tell him to come here
immediately. Go, I say!

CHAMBERMAID I will, I will, though I'm frightened out of my wits.
    *Exit Chambermaid*

MRS HEIDELBERG Do you watch here, my dear; and I'll put myself in
order, to face them. We'll plot 'em, and counter-plot 'em too. 150
    *Exit Mrs Heidelberg into her chamber*

MISS STERLING I have as much pleasure in this revenge, as in being
made a countess! Ha! They are unlocking the door. (*Retires*) Now
for it!

*Fanny's door is unlocked, and Betty comes out with a candle.*
*Miss Sterling approaches her.*

BETTY (*calling within*) Sir, sir! Now's your time. All's clear. (*Seeing Miss Sterling*) Stay, stay, not yet, we are watched. 155

MISS STERLING And so you are, Madam Betty!

*Miss Sterling lays hold of her, while Betty locks the door, and puts the key in her pocket*

BETTY (*turning round*) What's the matter, madam?

MISS STERLING Nay, that you shall tell my father and aunt, madam.

BETTY I am no tell-tale, madam, and no thief. They'll get nothing from me. 160

MISS STERLING You have a great deal of courage, Betty; and considering the secrets you have to keep, you have occasion for it.

BETTY My mistress shall never repent her good opinion of me, ma'am.

*Enter Sterling*

STERLING What is all this? What's the matter? Why am I disturbed in this manner? 165

MISS STERLING This creature, and my distresses, sir, will explain the matter.

*Re-enter Mrs Heidelberg, with another head-dress*

MRS HEIDELBERG Now I'm prepared for the rancounter.° Well, brother, have you heard of this scene of wickedness? 170

STERLING Not I. But what is it? Speak! I was got into my little closet. All the lawyers were in bed, and I had almost lost my senses in the confusion of Lord Ogleby's mortgages, when I was alarmed with a foolish girl, who could hardly speak. And whether it's fire, or thieves, or murder, or a rape, I am quite in the dark. 175

MRS HEIDELBERG No, no, there's no rape, brother! All parties are willing, I believe.

MISS STERLING Who's in that chamber? (*Detaining Betty, who seemed to be stealing away*)

BETTY My mistress.

MISS STERLING And Who is with your mistress? 180

BETTY Why, who should there be?

MISS STERLING Open the door then, and let us see!

BETTY The door is open, madam. (*Miss Sterling goes to the door*) I'll sooner die than peach!°

*Exit Betty, hastily*

MISS STERLING The door's locked; and she has got the key in her pocket. 185

MRS HEIDELBERG  There's impudence, brother! Piping hot from your
daughter Fanny's school!

STERLING  But, zounds! what is all this about? You tell me of a sum
total, and you don't produce the particulars.                          190

MRS HEIDELBERG  Sir John Melvil is locked up in your daughter's
bed-chamber. There is the particular!

STERLING  The devil he is? That's bad!

MISS STERLING  And he has been there some time too.

STERLING  Ditto!                                                       195

MRS HEIDELBERG  Ditto! Worse and worse, I say. I'll raise the house,
and expose him to my lord, and the whole family.

STERLING  By no means! We shall expose ourselves, sister! The best
way is to insure privately.° Let me alone! I'll make him marry her
tomorrow morning.                                                      200

MISS STERLING  Make him marry her! This is beyond all patience!
You have thrown away all your affection; and I shall do as much by
my obedience. Unnatural fathers make unnatural children.° My
revenge is in my own power, and I'll indulge it. Had they made
their escape, I should have been exposed to the derision of the        205
world, but the deriders shall be derided; and so,—Help! Help,
there! Thieves! Thieves!

MRS HEIDELBERG  Tit-for-tat, Betsey! You are right, my girl.

STERLING  Zounds! you'll spoil all. You'll raise the whole family. The
devil's in the girl.                                                   210

MRS HEIDELBERG  No, no; the devil's in you, brother. I am ashamed
of your principles. What! Would you connive at your daughter's
being locked up with her sister's husband? (*Cries out*) Help!
Thieves! Thieves, I say!

STERLING  Sister, I beg you! Daughter, I command you. If you have     215
no regard for me, consider yourselves! We shall lose this opportunity of ennobling our blood, and getting above twenty per cent. for
our money.°

MISS STERLING  What, by my disgrace and my sister's triumph! I
have a spirit above such mean considerations; and to show you       220
that it is not a low-bred, vulgar Change-Alley° spirit—Help! Help!
Thieves! Thieves! Thieves, I say!

STERLING  Ay, ay, you may save your lungs. The house is in an
uproar. Women at best have no discretion; but in a passion
they'll fire a house, or burn themselves in it, rather than not be     225
revenged.

*Enter Canton, in a nightgown and slippers.*

CANTON  Eh, diable! vat is de raison of dis great noise, this tintamarre?

STERLING  Ask those ladies, sir; tis of their making.

LORD OGLEBY (*calls within*) Brush! Brush! Canton! Where are you?   230
What's the matter? (*Rings a bell*) Where are you?

STERLING  'Tis my lord calls, Mr Canton.

CANTON  I com, mi lor!

    *Exit Canton*

    *Lord Ogleby still rings*

FLOWER (*calls within*) A light! A light here! Where are the servants?
Bring a light for me, and my brothers.   235

STERLING  Lights here! Lights for the gentlemen!

    *Exit Sterling*

MRS HEIDELBERG  My brother feels, I see. Your sister's turn will
come next.

MISS STERLING  Ay, ay, let it go round, madam! It is the only comfort
I have left.   240

    *Re-enter Sterling, with lights, before Sergeant Flower (with one*
    *boot and a slipper) and Traverse.*

STERLING  This way, sir! This way, gentlemen!

FLOWER  Well, but, Mr Sterling, no danger I hope. Have they made a
burglarious entry? Are you prepared to repulse them? I am very
much alarmed about thieves at circuit-time.° They would be
particularly severe with us gentlemen of the bar.   245

TRAVERSE  No danger, Mr Sterling? No trespass, I hope?

STERLING  None, gentlemen, but of those ladies' making.

MRS HEIDELBERG  You'll be ashamed to know, gentlemen, that all
your labours and studies about this young lady are thrown away. Sir
John Melvil is at this moment locked up with this lady's younger   250
sister.

FLOWER  The thing is a little extraordinary, to be sure. But, why were
we to be frightened out of our beds for this? Could not we have
tried this cause tomorrow morning?

MISS STERLING  But, sir, by tomorrow morning, perhaps, even your   255
assistance would not have been of any service. The birds now in
that cage would have flown away.

    *Enter Lord Ogleby (in his robe de chambre and night cap),*
    *leaning on Canton*

LORD OGLEBY  I had rather lose a limb than my night's rest. What's
the matter with you all?

STERLING  Ay, ay, 'tis all over! Here's my lord too.   260

LORD OGLEBY  What is all this shrieking and screaming? Where's my
angelic Fanny. She's safe, I hope!

MRS HEIDELBERG  Your angelic Fanny, my lord, is locked up with
your angelic nephew in that chamber.

LORD OGLEBY  My nephew! Then will I be excommunicated.                     265

MRS HEIDELBERG  Your nephew, my lord, has been plotting to run
away with the younger sister; and the younger sister has been
plotting to run away with your nephew, and if we had not watched
them and called up the fammaly, they had been upon the scamper
to Scotland° by this time.                                                 270

LORD OGLEBY  Look'ee, ladies! I know that Sir John has conceived a
violent passion for Miss Fanny; and I know, too, that Miss Fanny
has conceived a violent passion for another person; and I am so well
convinced of the rectitude of her affections, that I will support
them with my fortune, my honour, and my life. Eh, shan't I, Mr          275
Sterling? (*Smiling*) What say you?

STERLING  (*sulkily*) To be sure, my lord. (*Aside*) These bawling
women have been the ruin of everything.

LORD OGLEBY  But come, I'll end this business in a trice. If you,
ladies, will compose yourselves, and Mr Sterling will insure Miss       280
Fanny from violence, I will engage to draw her from her pillow with
a whisper through the keyhole.

MRS HEIDELBERG  The horrid creatures! I say, my lord, break the
door open.

LORD OGLEBY  Let me beg of your delicacy not to be too precipitate!     285
(*Advancing towards the door*) Now to our experiment!

MISS STERLING  Now, what will they do? My heart will beat through
my bosom.

        *Enter Betty, with the key*

BETTY  There's no occasion for breaking open doors, my Lord; we
have done nothing that we ought to be ashamed of, and my mistress       290
shall face her enemies. (*Going to unlock the door*)

MRS HEIDELBERG  There's impudence.

LORD OGLEBY  The mystery thickens. (*To Betty*) Lady of the bed-
chamber! Open the door, and entreat Sir John Melvil (for
these ladies will have it that he is there,) to appear and answer to    295
high crimes and misdemeanours. Call Sir John Melvil into the
court!

        *Enter Sir John Melvil, on the other side*

SIR JOHN  I am here, my lord.

MRS HEIDELBERG  Heyday!

MISS STERLING Astonishment!                                                    300

SIR JOHN What is all this alarm and confusion? There is nothing but
hurry in the house. What is the reason of it?

LORD OGLEBY Because you have been in that chamber. *Have* been?
Nay you *are* there at this moment, as these ladies have protested, so
don't deny it.                                                                 305

TRAVERSE This is the clearest *alibi* I ever knew, Mr Sergeant.

FLOWER *Luce clarius.*°

LORD OGLEBY Upon my word, ladies, if you have often these
frolics, it would be really entertaining to pass a whole summer
with you. But come, (*to Betty*) open the door, and entreat your    310
amiable mistress to come forth, and dispel all our doubts with her
smiles.

BETTY (*opening the door*) Madam, (*pertly*) you are wanted in this
room.

*Enter Fanny, in great confusion*

MISS STERLING You see she's ready dressed, and what confusion    315
she's in!

MRS HEIDELBERG Ready to pack off, bag and baggage! Her guilt
confounds her!

FLOWER Silence in the court, ladies!

FANNY I *am* confounded, indeed, madam!                                        320

LORD OGLEBY Don't droop, my beauteous lily, but with your own
peculiar modesty declare your state of mind! (*Smiling*) Pour
conviction into their ears, and raptures into mine.

FANNY I am at this moment the most unhappy, most distressed—the
tumult is too much for my heart, and I want the power to reveal    325
a secret, which to conceal has been the misfortune and misery of
my—my—(*faints away*)

LORD OGLEBY She faints. Help, help! For the fairest, and best of
women!

(*Speaking all at once*)

BETTY (*running to her*) O my dear mistress! Help, help, there!    330

(*Speaking all at once*)

SIR JOHN Ha! Let me fly to her assistance.

(*Speaking all at once*)

*Lovewell rushes out from the chamber*

LOVEWELL My Fanny in danger! I can contain no longer. Prudence
were now a crime. All other cares are lost in this! Speak, speak, to
me, my dearest Fanny! Let me but hear thy voice, open your eyes,
and bless me with the smallest sign of life!                                   335

*During this speech they are all in amazement*

MISS STERLING Lovewell! I am easy.

MRS HEIDELBERG I am thunderstuck!

LORD OGLEBY I am petrified!

SIR JOHN And I undone!

FANNY (*recovering*) O Lovewell! Even supported by thee, I dare not    340
look my father nor his lordship in the face.

STERLING What now! Did not I send you to London, sir?

LORD OGLEBY Eh!—What!—How's this?—By what right and title,
have you been half the night in that lady's bed-chamber?

LOVEWELL By that right that makes me the happiest of men, and by a    345
title which I would not forgo, for any the best of kings could give
me.

BETTY I could cry my eyes out to hear his magnimity.°

LORD OGLEBY I am annihilated!

STERLING I have been choked with rage and wonder, but now I can    350
speak. Zounds, what have you to say to me? Lovewell, you are a
villain. You have broke your word with me.

FANNY Indeed, sir, he has not. You forbade him to think of me, when
it was out of his power to obey you. We have been married these
four months.    355

STERLING And he shan't stay in my house four hours. What baseness
and treachery! As for you, you shall repent this step as long as you
live, madam.

FANNY Indeed, sir, it is impossible to conceive the tortures I have
already endured in consequence of my disobedience. My heart    360
has continually upbraided me for it; and though I was too weak to
struggle with affection, I feel that I must be miserable forever
without your forgiveness.

STERLING Lovewell, you shall leave my house directly; (*to Fanny*) and
you shall follow him, madam.    365

LORD OGLEBY And if they do, I will receive them into mine. Look
ye, Mr Sterling, there have been some mistakes, which we had all
better forget for our own sakes; and the best way to forget them is
to forgive the cause of them; which I do from my soul. Poor girl! I
swore to support her affection with my life and fortune. 'Tis a debt    370
of honour, and must be paid. You swore as much too, Mr Sterling;
but your laws in the city will excuse *you*, I suppose, for you never
strike a balance without errors excepted.°

STERLING I am a father, my lord; but for the sake of all other fathers,
I think I ought not to forgive her, for fear of encouraging other silly    375

girls like herself to throw themselves away without the consent of
their parents.

LOVEWELL I hope there will be no danger of that, sir. Young ladies
with minds, like my Fanny's, would startle at the very shadow of
vice; and, when they know to what uneasiness only an indiscretion     380
has exposed her, her example, instead of encouraging, will rather
serve to deter them.°

MRS HEIDELBERG Indiscretion, quoth-a! A mighty pretty delicat
word to express disobedience!

LORD OGLEBY For my part, I indulge my own passions too much to    385
tyrannise over those of other people. Poor souls, I pity them. And
you must forgive them too. Come, come, melt a little of your flint,
Mr Sterling!

STERLING Why, why, as to that, my lord—to be sure, he is a relation
of yours my lord. What say *you*, sister Heidelberg?                    390

MRS HEIDELBERG The girl's ruined, and I forgive her.

STERLING Well, so do I then. (*To Lovewell and Fanny, who seem
preparing to speak*) Nay, no thanks; there's an end of the matter.

LORD OGLEBY But, Lovewell, what makes you dumb all this
while?                                                                  395

LOVEWELL Your kindness, my lord. I can scarce believe my own
senses. They are all in a tumult of fear, joy, love, expectation, and
gratitude. I ever was, and am now more, bound in duty to your
lordship. For you, Mr Sterling, if every moment of my life, spent
gratefully in your service, will in some measure compensate the     400
want of fortune, you perhaps will not repent your goodness to
me. And you, ladies, I flatter myself, will not for the future suspect
me of artifice and intrigue. I shall be happy to oblige, and serve you.
As for you, Sir John—

SIR JOHN No apologies to me, Lovewell, I do not deserve any. All I    405
have to offer in excuse for what has happened, is my total ignorance
of your situation. Had you dealt a little more openly with me, you
would have saved me, and yourself, and that lady, (who I hope will
pardon my behaviour) a great deal of uneasiness. Give me leave,
however, to assure you, that light and capricious as I may have       410
appeared, now my infatuation is over, I have sensibility° enough to
be ashamed of the part I have acted, and honour enough to rejoice
at your happiness.

LOVEWELL And now, my dearest Fanny, though we are seemingly the
happiest of beings, (*to the audience*) yet all our joys will be damped,    415
if his lordship's generosity and Mr Sterling's forgiveness should

not be succeeded by the indulgence, approbation, and consent of
these our best benefactors.

# FINIS.

# Epilogue
## Written by Mr GARRICK.

*An Assembly.*

*Several persons at cards, at different tables;*
*among the rest Col. Trill, Lord Minum, Mrs Quaver, Sir Patrick*
*Mahony at the Quadrille table.*

COLONEL TRILL  Ladies, with Leave—

SECOND LADY  Pass!

THIRD LADY  Pass!

MRS QUAVER  You must do more.

COLONEL TRILL  Indeed I can't.                                        5

MRS QUAVER  I play in Hearts.

COLONEL TRILL  Encore?

SECOND LADY  What luck!

COLONEL TRILL  Tonight at Drury Lane is played
   A Comedy, and *toute nouvelle*—a Spade!                     10
   Is not Miss Crotchet at the play?

MRS QUAVER  My niece
   Has made a party, sir, to damn the piece.
     *At the Whist table*

LORD MINUM  I hate a playhouse—Trump!—It makes me sick.

FIRST LADY  We're two by Honours, ma'am.°                           15

LORD MINUM  And we the odd trick.
   Pray do you know the author, Colonel Trill?

COLONEL TRILL  I know no poets, heaven be praised!—Spadille!°

FIRST LADY  I'll tell you who, my lord! (*Whispers my lord*)

LORD MINUM  What, he again?                                         20
   'And dwell such daring Souls in little Men?'°
   Be whose it will, they down our throats will cram it!

COLONEL TRILL  O, no.—I have a Club—the best.—We'll damn it.

MRS QUAVER  O bravo, Colonel! Music is my flame.

LORD MINUM  And mine, by Jupiter!—We've won the game.              25

COLONEL TRILL  What, do you love all music?

MRS QUAVER  No, not Handel's.°
   And nasty plays—

LORD MINUM  Are fit for Goths and Vandals.
     *All rise from the table and pay*

*From the Piquet table*

SIR PATRICK  Well, faith and troth! That Shakespeare was no fool!  30
COLONEL TRILL  I'm glad you like him, sir!—So ends the Pool!°
    *All pay and rise from table*

### SONG *by the Colonel*

> I hate all their nonsense,
> Their Shakespeares and Jonsons,
> Their plays, and their playhouse, and bards:
> 'Tis singing, not saying;  35
> A fig for all playing,
> But playing, as we do, at cards!
>
> I love to see Jonas,°
> Am pleased too with Comus;°
> Each well the spectator rewards.  40
> So clever, so neat in
> Their tricks, and their cheating!
> Like them we would fain deal our cards.

SIR PATRICK  King Lare is touching!—And how fine to see°
  Ould Hamlet's Ghost!—'To be, or not to be.'—°  45
  What are your op'ras to Othello's roar?°
  Oh, he's an angel of a Blackamoor!
LORD MINUM  What, when he chokes his wife?—
COLONEL TRILL  And calls her whore?°
SIR PATRICK  King Richard calls his horse—and then Macbeth,°  50
  When e'er he murders—takes away the breath.
  My blood runs cold at ev'ry syllable,
  To see the dagger—that's invisible.°
    *All laugh*
SIR PATRICK  Laugh if you please, a pretty play—
LORD MINUM  Is pretty.  55
SIR PATRICK  And when there's wit in't—
COLONEL TRILL  To be sure 'Tis witty.
SIR PATRICK  I love the playhouse now—so light and gay,
  With all those candles, they have ta'en away!°
    *All laugh*
  For all your game, what makes it so much brighter?  60
COLONEL TRILL  Put out the light, and then—°
LORD MINUM  'Tis so much lighter.

SIR PATRICK  Pray do you mane, sirs, more than you express?
COLONEL TRILL  Just as it happens—
LORD MINUM  Either more, or less.                                                65
MRS QUAVER (*to Sir Patrick*) An't you asham'd, sir?
SIR PATRICK  Me!—I seldom blush.—
    For little Shakespeare, faith! I'd take a push!°
LORD MINUM  News, news!—here comes Miss Crotchet from the
play.                                                                            70
       *Enter Miss Crotchet*
MRS QUAVER  Well, Crotchet, what's the news?
MISS CROTCHET  We've lost the day.
COLONEL TRILL  Tell us, dear miss, all you have heard and seen.
MISS CROTCHET  I'm tired—a chair—here, take my Capuchin!°
LORD MINUM  And isn't it damn'd, miss?                                           75
MISS CROTCHET  No, my lord, not quite:
    But we shall damn it.
COLONEL TRILL  When?
MISS CROTCHET  Tomorrow night.
    There is a party of us, all of fashion,                     80
    Resolved to exterminate this vulgar passion:
    A playhouse, what a place!—I must forswear it.
    A little mischief only makes one bear it.
    Such crowds of city folks!—so rude and pressing!
    And their horse-Laughs, so hideously distressing!           85
    When e'er we hiss'd, they frowned and fell a-swearing,
    Like their own Guildhall Giants—fierce and staring!°
COLONEL TRILL  What said the folks of fashion? Were they cross?
LORD MINUM  The rest have no more judgement than my horse.
MISS CROTCHET  Lord Grimly swore 'twas execrable stuff.                          90
    Says one, 'Why so, my lord?'—My Lord took snuff.
    In the first act Lord George began to doze,
    And criticised the author—through his nose;
    So loud indeed, that as his lordship snored,
    The pit turned round, and all the brutes encored.           95
    Some lords, indeed, approved the author's jokes.
LORD MINUM  We have among us, miss, some foolish folks.
MISS CROTCHET  Says poor Lord Simper—Well, now to my mind
    The piece is good;—but he's both deaf and blind.
SIR PATRICK  Upon my soul a very pretty story!                                   100
    And quality appears in all its glory!—
    There was some merit in the piece, no doubt;

MISS CROTCHET  O, to be sure!—if one could find it out.

COLONEL TRILL  But tell us, miss, the subject of the play.

MISS CROTCHET  Why, 'twas a marriage—yes, a marriage—Stay!  105
    A lord, an aunt, two sisters, and a merchant—
    A baronet—ten lawyers—a fat sergeant—°
    Are all produced—to talk with one another;
    And about something make a mighty pother;
    They all go in, and out; and to, and fro;  110
    And talk, and quarrel—as they come and go—
    Then go to bed, and then get up—and then—
    Scream, faint, scold, kiss,—and go to bed again.
       *All laugh*
    Such is the play—Your judgement! never sham it.

COLONEL TRILL  Oh damn it!

MRS QUAVER           Damn it!

FIRST LADY              Damn it!

MISS CROTCHET                Damn it!

LORD MINUM                    Damn it!  115

SIR PATRICK  Well, faith, you speak your minds, and I'll be free—
    Good night! This company's too good for me. (*Going*)

COLONEL TRILL  Your judgement, dear Sir Patrick, makes us proud.
       *All laugh*

SIR PATRICK  Laugh if you please, but pray don't laugh too loud.
       *Exit Sir Patrick*

RECITATIVE

COLONEL TRILL
    Now the barbarian's gone, miss, tune your tongue,  120
    And let us raise our spirits high with song!

RECITATIVE

MISS CROTCHET
    Colonel, *de tout mon coeur*—I've one in petto,°
    Which you shall join, and make it a duetto.

RECITATIVE

LORD MINUM      *Bella Signora, et Amico mio!*
    I too will join, and then we'll make a trio.—  125

COLONEL TRILL
    Come all and join the full-mouthed chorus,
    And drive all tragedy and comedy before us!
    *All the company rise, and advance to the front of the stage*

AIR

COLONEL TRILL
                    Would you ever go to see a tragedy?
MISS CROTCHET              Never, never.
COLONEL TRILL              A comedy?                                    130
LORD MINUM            Never, never,
                              Live for ever!
                    Tweedle-dum and Tweedle-dee!
COLONEL TRILL,
LORD MINUM,                Live for ever!
AND MISS            Tweedle-dum and Tweedle-dee!                        135
CROTCHET
                          CHORUS
                    Would you ever go to see, &c.

# SHE STOOPS TO CONQUER

### or,

## The Mistakes of a Night°

## A Comedy

BY

## OLIVER GOLDSMITH

## To SAMUEL JOHNSON,° L.L.D.

Dear Sir,

By inscribing this slight performance to you, I do not mean so much to compliment you as myself. It may do me some honour to inform the public, that I have lived many years in intimacy with you.° It may serve the interests of mankind also to inform them, that the greatest wit may be found in a character, without impairing the most unaffected piety.° 5

I have, particularly, reason to thank you for your partiality to this performance. The undertaking a comedy, not merely sentimental,° was very dangerous, and Mr Colman,° who saw this piece in its various stages, always thought it so. However I ventured to trust it to the public; and though it was necessarily delayed till late in the season,° I have every reason to be grateful. 10

I am, dear sir, your most sincere friend, and admirer, OLIVER GOLDSMITH. 15

# Prologue

By David Garrick, Esq.

*Enter Mr.* WOODWARD,° *dressed in black, and holding a handkerchief to his eyes.*

Excuse me, sirs, I pray—I can't yet speak—
I'm crying now—and have been all the week!
'Tis not alone this mourning suit, good masters;
I've that within—for which there are no plasters!°
Pray would you know the reason why I'm crying?                        5
The Comic muse, long sick, is now a-dying!
And, if she goes, my tears will never stop;
For as a player, I can't squeeze out one drop:
I am undone, that's all—shall lose my bread—
I'd rather, but that's nothing—lose my head.                         10
When the sweet maid is laid upon the bier,°
Shuter and I shall be chief mourners here.°
To her a mawkish drab of spurious breed,°
Who deals in sentimentals will succeed!
Poor Ned and I are dead to all intents,                              15
We can as soon speak Greek as sentiments!
Both nervous grown, to keep our spirits up,
We now and then take down a hearty cup.°
What shall we do, if Comedy forsake us?
They'll turn us out, and no one else will take us.°                  20
But why can't I be moral?—Let me try—
My heart thus pressing—fixed my face and eye—
With a sententious look, that nothing means,
(Faces are blocks, in sentimental scenes)°
Thus I begin—All is not gold that glitters,                          25
Pleasure seems sweet, but proves a glass of bitters.
When ign'rance enters, folly is at hand;
Learning is better far than house and land.
Let not your virtue trip, who trips may stumble,
And virtue is not virtue, if she tumble.°                            30
I give it up—morals won't do for me;
To make you laugh I must play tragedy.
One hope remains—hearing the maid was ill,

A doctor comes this night to show his skill.°
To cheer her heart, and give your muscles motion,                    35
He in five draughts prepared, presents a potion:°
A kind of magic charm—for be assured,
If you will swallow it, the maid is cured:
But desp'rate the Doctor, and her case is,
If you reject the dose, and make wry faces!                          40
This truth he boasts, will boast it while he lives,
No pois'nous drugs are mixed in what he gives;
Should he succeed, you'll give him his degree;
If not, within he will receive no fee!
The college you, must his pretensions back,                          45
Pronounce him regular, or dub him quack.

# THE CHARACTERS OF THE PLAY

### MEN

Sir Charles Marlow          Mr Gardner
Young Marlow (his Son)      Mr Lewes
Hardcastle                 Mr Shuter
Hastings                   Mr Dubellamy
Tony Lumpkin               Mr Quick
Diggory                    Mr Saunders

### WOMEN

Mrs Hardcastle             Mrs Green
Miss Hardcastle            Mrs Bulkely
Miss Neville               Mrs Kniveton
Maid                       Miss Willems
*Landlord, Servants, &c. &c.*

# 1.1

*A chamber in an old-fashioned house.*

*Enter Mrs Hardcastle and Mr Hardcastle*

MRS HARDCASTLE I vow, Mr Hardcastle, you're very particular. Is there a creature in the whole country, but ourselves, that does not take a trip to town now and then, to rub off the rust a little? There's the two Miss Hoggs, and our neighbour, Mrs Grigsby, go to take a month's polishing every winter. 5

HARDCASTLE Ay, and bring back vanity and affectation to last them the whole year. I wonder why London cannot keep its own fools at home. In my time, the follies of the town crept slowly among us, but now they travel faster than a stage-coach. Its fopperies come down, not only as inside passengers, but in the very basket.° 10

MRS HARDCASTLE Ay, *your* times were fine times, indeed. You have been telling us of *them* for many a long year. Here we live in an old rambling° mansion, that looks for all the world like an inn, but that we never see company. Our best visitors are old Mrs Oddfish, the curate's wife, and little Cripplegate, the lame dancing-master, and 15 all our entertainment your old stories of Prince Eugene and the Duke of Marlborough.° I hate such old-fashioned trumpery.

HARDCASTLE And I love it. I love everything that's old: old friends, old times, old manners, old books, old wine, and, I believe, Dorothy, (*taking her hand*) you'll own I have been pretty fond of an old 20 wife.

MRS HARDCASTLE Lord, Mr Hardcastle, you're forever at your Dorothy's and your old wife's. You may be a Darby, but I'll be no Joan,° I promise you. I'm not so old as you'd make me, by more than one good year. Add twenty to twenty, and make money of that.° 25

HARDCASTLE Let me see; twenty added to twenty, makes just fifty and seven.

MRS HARDCASTLE It's false, Mr Hardcastle. I was but twenty when I was brought to bed of Tony, that I had by Mr Lumpkin, my first husband—and he's not come to years of discretion yet.° 30

HARDCASTLE Nor ever will, I dare answer for him. Ay, you have taught *him* finely.

MRS HARDCASTLE No matter. Tony Lumpkin has a good fortune. My son is not to live by his learning. I don't think a boy wants much learning to spend fifteen hundred a year. 35

HARDCASTLE Learning, quotha! A mere composition of tricks and mischief.

MRS HARDCASTLE Humour, my dear, nothing but humour.° Come, Mr Hardcastle, you must allow the boy a little humour.

HARDCASTLE I'd sooner allow him an horse-pond.° If burning the    40
footmen's shoes, frighting the maids, and worrying the kittens, be humour, he has it. It was but yesterday he fastened my wig to the back of my chair, and when I went to make a bow, I popped my bald° head in Mrs Frizzle's face.

MRS HARDCASTLE And am I to blame? The poor boy was always too    45
sickly to do any good.° A school would be his death. When he comes to be a little stronger, who knows what a year or two's Latin may do for him?

HARDCASTLE Latin for him! A cat and fiddle.° No, no, the ale-house
and the stable are the only schools he'll ever go to.    50

MRS HARDCASTLE Well, we must not snub the poor boy now, for I believe we shan't have him long among us. Anybody that looks in his face may see he's consumptive.

HARDCASTLE Ay, if growing too fat be one of the symptoms.

MRS HARDCASTLE He coughs sometimes.    55

HARDCASTLE Yes, when his liquor goes the wrong way.

MRS HARDCASTLE I'm actually afraid of his lungs.

HARDCASTLE And truly so am I, for he sometimes whoops like a speaking trumpet.°

*Tony hallooing behind the scenes°*

O there he goes! A very consumptive figure, truly.    60

*Enter Tony, crossing the stage.°*

MRS HARDCASTLE Tony, where are you going, my charmer? Won't you give papa and I a little of your company, lovee?

TONY I'm in haste, mother. I cannot stay.

MRS HARDCASTLE You shan't venture out this raw evening, my dear.
You look most shockingly.    65

TONY I can't stay, I tell you. The Three Pigeons expects me down every moment. There's some fun going forward.

HARDCASTLE Ay; the ale-house, the old place. I thought so.

MRS HARDCASTLE A low, paltry set of fellows.°

TONY Not so low neither. There's Dick Muggins the exciseman,°    70
Jack Slang the horse doctor,° Little Aminadab° that grinds the music box,° and Tom Twist that spins the pewter platter.°

MRS HARDCASTLE Pray, my dear, disappoint them for one night at least.

TONY As for disappointing *them*, I should not so much mind, but I   75
can't abide to disappoint *myself*.

MRS HARDCASTLE (*detaining him*) You shan't go.

TONY I will, I tell you.

MRS HARDCASTLE I say you shan't.

TONY We'll see which is strongest, you or I.   80
    *Exit Tony, hauling Mrs Hardcastle out*

HARDCASTLE Ay, there goes a pair that only spoil each other. But
is not the whole age in a combination to drive sense and discretion
out of doors? There's my pretty darling Kate; the fashions of the
times have almost infected her too. By living a year or two in town,
she is as fond of gauze,° and French frippery, as the best of them.   85
    *Enter Miss Hardcastle*
Blessings on my pretty innocence! Dressed out as usual my Kate.
Goodness! What a quantity of superfluous silk has thou got about
thee, girl! I could never teach the fools of this age, that the indigent°
world could be clothed out of the trimmings of the vain.

MISS HARDCASTLE You know our agreement, sir. You allow me the   90
morning to receive and pay visits, and to dress in my own manner;
and in the evening, I put on my housewife's dress° to please you.

HARDCASTLE Well, remember I insist on the terms of our agreement,
and, by the bye, I believe I shall have occasion to try your obedience
this very evening.   95

MISS HARDCASTLE I protest, sir, I don't comprehend your meaning.

HARDCASTLE Then, to be plain with you, Kate, I expect the young
gentleman I have chosen to be your husband from town this very
day. I have his father's letter, in which he informs me his son is set
out, and that he intends to follow himself shortly after.   100

MISS HARDCASTLE Indeed! I wish I had known something of this
before. Bless me, how shall I behave? It's a thousand to one I shan't
like him. Our meeting will be so formal, and so like a thing of
business, that I shall find no room for friendship or esteem.

HARDCASTLE Depend upon it, child, I'll never control your choice,   105
but Mr Marlow, whom I have pitched upon, is the son of my old
friend, Sir Charles Marlow, of whom you have heard me talk so
often. The young gentleman has been bred a scholar, and is
designed for an employment in the service of his country. I am told
he's a man of an excellent understanding.   110

MISS HARDCASTLE Is he?

HARDCASTLE Very generous.°

MISS HARDCASTLE  I believe I shall like him.

HARDCASTLE  Young and brave.

MISS HARDCASTLE  I'm sure I shall like him.    115

HARDCASTLE  And very handsome.

MISS HARDCASTLE  My dear Papa, say no more (*kissing his hand*) he's mine. I'll have him.

HARDCASTLE  And to crown all, Kate, he's one of the most bashful and reserved young fellows in all the world.    120

MISS HARDCASTLE  Eh! You have frozen me to death again. That word reserved, has undone all the rest of his accomplishments. A reserved lover, it is said, always makes a suspicious husband.

HARDCASTLE  On the contrary, modesty seldom resides in a breast that is not enriched with nobler virtues. It was the very feature in    125
his character that first struck me.

MISS HARDCASTLE  He must have more striking features to catch me, I promise you. However, if he be so young, so handsome, and so everything you mention, I believe he'll do still. I think I'll have him.    130

HARDCASTLE  Ay, Kate, but there is still an obstacle. It's more than an even wager, he may not have *you*.

MISS HARDCASTLE  My dear Papa, why will you mortify one so? Well, if he refuses, instead of breaking my heart at his indifference, I'll only break my glass for its flattery, set my cap to some newer    135
fashion,° and look out for some less difficult admirer.

HARDCASTLE  Bravely resolved! In the meantime I'll go prepare the servants for his reception. As we seldom see company, they want as much training as a company of recruits, the first day's muster.°

*Exit Hardcastle*

MISS HARDCASTLE  Lud, this news of Papa's, puts me all in a flutter.    140
Young, handsome; these he put last, but I put them foremost. Sensible, good-natured—I like all that. But then reserved, and sheepish—that's much against him. Yet can't he be cured of his timidity, by being taught to be proud of his wife? Yes, and can't I— But I vow I'm disposing of the husband, before I have secured the    145
lover.

*Enter Miss Neville*

I'm glad you're come, Neville, my dear. Tell me, Constance, how do I look this evening? Is there anything whimsical about me? Is it one of my well-looking days, child? Am I in face today?

MISS NEVILLE  Perfectly, my dear. Yet now I look again—bless me!    150

Sure no accident has happened among the canary birds or the goldfishes? Has your brother or the cat been meddling? Or has the last novel been too moving?°

MISS HARDCASTLE  No, nothing of all this. I have been threatened—I can scarce get it out—I have been threatened with a lover.    155

MISS NEVILLE  And his name—

MISS HARDCASTLE  Is Marlow.

MISS NEVILLE  Indeed!

MISS HARDCASTLE  The son of Sir Charles Marlow.

MISS NEVILLE  As I live, the most intimate friend of Mr Hastings, *my*    160
admirer. They are never asunder. I believe you must have seen him when we lived in town.

MISS HARDCASTLE  Never.

MISS NEVILLE  He's a very singular character, I assure you. Among women of reputation and virtue, he is the modestest man alive,    165
but his acquaintance give him a very different character among creatures of another stamp, you understand me.

MISS HARDCASTLE  An odd character, indeed. I shall never be able to manage him. What shall I do? Pshaw, think no more of him, but trust to occurrences° for success. But how goes on your own affair    170
my dear? Has my mother been courting you for my brother Tony, as usual?

MISS NEVILLE  I have just come from one of our agreeable tête-à-têtes. She has been saying a hundred tender things, and setting off°
her pretty monster as the very pink° of perfection.    175

MISS HARDCASTLE  And her partiality is such, that she actually thinks him so. A fortune like yours is no small temptation. Besides, as she has the sole management of it, I'm not surprised to see her unwilling to let it go out of the family.

MISS NEVILLE  A fortune like mine, which chiefly consists in jewels, is    180
no such mighty temptation. But at any rate if my dear Hastings be but constant, I make no doubt to be too hard for her at last. However, I let her suppose that I am in love with her son, and she never once dreams that my affections are fixed upon another.

MISS HARDCASTLE  My good brother holds out stoutly. I could almost    185
love him for hating you so.

MISS NEVILLE  It is a good-natured creature at bottom, and I'm sure would wish to see me married to anybody but himself. [*Bell rings*]
But my aunt's bell rings for our afternoon's walk round the improvements.° *Allons.*° Courage is necessary as our affairs are critical.°    190

168

MISS HARDCASTLE  Would it were bedtime° and all were well.°
    *Exeunt Miss Hardcastle and Miss Neville*

## 1.2

*An alehouse room. Several shabby fellows, with punch and*
*tobacco. Tony at the head of the table, a little higher than*
*the rest, a mallet in his hand*

ALL  Hurrah, hurrah, hurrah, bravo.

FIRST FELLOW  Now, gentlemen, silence for a song. The 'Squire is
  going to knock himself down for a song.°

ALL  Ay, a song, a song.

TONY  Then I'll sing you, gentlemen, a song I made upon this    5
  ale-house, the Three Pigeons.

SONG

    Let schoolmasters puzzle their brain,
      With grammar, and nonsense, and learning;
    Good liquor, I stoutly maintain,
      Gives genus a better discerning.°    10
    Let them brag of their Heathenish Gods,
      Their Lethes, their Styxes, and Stygians;°
    Their Quis, and their Quæs, and their Quods,°
      They're all but a parcel of Pigeons.
    Toroddle, toroddle, toroll.    15

    When Methodist preachers come down,°
      A preaching that drinking is sinful,
    I'll wager the rascals a crown,
      They always preach best with a skinful.
    But when you come down with your pence,    20
      For a slice of their scurvy religion,
    I'll leave it to all men of sense,
      But you my good friend are the pigeon.
    Toroddle, toroddle, toroll.

    Then come, put the jorum about,    25
      And let us be merry and clever,

> Our hearts and our liquors are stout,
>     Here's the Three Jolly Pigeons for ever.
> Let some cry up woodcock or hare,
>     Your bustards, your ducks, and your widgeons;    30
> But of all the birds in the air,
>     Here's a health to the Three Jolly Pigeons.
> Toroddle, toroddle, toroll.

ALL  Bravo, bravo.

FIRST FELLOW  The 'Squire has got spunk in him.    35

SECOND FELLOW  I loves to hear him sing, bekeays he never gives us nothing that's low.°

THIRD FELLOW  O damn anything that's *low*, I cannot bear it.

FOURTH FELLOW  The genteel thing is the genteel thing at any time. If so be that a gentleman bees in a concatenation accordingly.°    40

THIRD FELLOW  I like the maxum of it,° Master Muggins. What, though I am obligated to dance a bear,° a man may be a gentleman for all that. May this be my poison if my bear ever dances but to the very genteelest of tunes: 'Water Parted', or the minuet in Ariadne.°    45

SECOND FELLOW  What a pity it is the 'Squire is not come to his own.° It would be well for all the publicans within ten miles round of him.

TONY  Ecod and so it would, Master Slang. I'd then show what it was to keep choice of company.    50

SECOND FELLOW  O he takes after his own father for that. To be sure old 'Squire Lumpkin was the finest gentleman I ever set my eyes on. For winding the straight horn,° or beating a thicket for a hare, or a wench, he never had his fellow.° It was a saying in the place, that he kept the best horses, dogs and girls in the whole    55 county.

TONY  Ecod, and when I'm of age I'll be no bastard° I promise you. I have been thinking of Bett Bouncer and the miller's grey mare to begin with. But come, my boys, drink about and be merry, for you pay no reckoning. Well Stingo, what's the matter?    60

*Enter Landlord*

LANDLORD  There be two gentlemen in a post-chaise at the door. They have lost their way upo' the forest;° and they are talking something about Mr Hardcastle.

TONY  As sure as can be one of them must be the gentleman that's coming down to court my sister. Do they seem to be Londoners?    65

LANDLORD  I believe they may. They look woundily like Frenchmen.

TONY  Then desire them to step this way, and I'll set them right in a twinkling.

*Exit Landlord*

Gentlemen, as they mayn't be good enough company for you, step down for a moment, and I'll be with you in the squeezing of a lemon.°  70

*Exeunt Fellows*

TONY  Father-in-law° has been calling me whelp, and hound, this half year. Now if I pleased, I could be so revenged upon the old grumbletonian.° But then I'm afraid. Afraid of what! I shall soon be worth fifteen hundred a year, and let him frighten me out of *that* if he can.  75

*Enter Landlord, conducting Marlow and Hastings*

MARLOW  What a tedious uncomfortable day have we had of it! We were told it was but forty miles across the country, and we have come above threescore.

HASTINGS  And all, Marlow, from that unaccountable reserve of yours that would not let us enquire more frequently on the way.  80

MARLOW  I own, Hastings, I am unwilling to lay myself under an obligation to everyone I meet, and, often, stand the chance of an unmannerly answer.

HASTINGS  At present, however, we are not likely to receive any answer.  85

TONY  No offence, gentlemen, but I'm told you have been enquiring for one Mr Hardcastle, in these parts. Do you know what part of the country you are in?

HASTINGS  Not in the least sir, but should thank you for information.

TONY  Nor the way you came?  90

HASTINGS  No, sir, but if you can inform us—

TONY  Why, gentlemen, if you know neither the road you are going, nor where you are, nor the road you came, the first thing I have to inform you is, that—You have lost your way.

MARLOW  We wanted no ghost to tell us that.°  95

TONY  Pray, gentlemen, may I be so bold as to ask the place from whence you came?

MARLOW  That's not necessary towards directing us where we are to go.

TONY  No offence; but question for question is all fair, you know. Pray, gentlemen, is not this same Hardcastle a cross-grained, old-fashioned, whimsical fellow, with an ugly face, a daughter, and a pretty son?  100

HASTINGS  We have not seen the gentleman, but he has the family you
mention.

TONY  The daughter, a tall trapesing, trolloping, talkative maypole;° 105
the son, a pretty, well-bred, agreeable youth, that everybody is
fond of.

MARLOW  Our information differs in this. The daughter is said to be
well-bred and beautiful; the son, an awkward booby, reared up, and
spoiled at his mother's apron-string. 110

TONY  He-he-hem. Then, gentlemen, all I have to tell you is, that you
won't reach Mr Hardcastle's house this night, I believe.

HASTINGS  Unfortunate!

TONY  It's a damned long, dark, boggy, dirty, dangerous way. Stingo,
tell the gentlemen the way to Mr Hardcastle's. (*Winking upon the* 115
*landlord*) Mr Hardcastle's, of Quagmire Marsh, you understand
me.

LANDLORD  Master Hardcastle's! Lock-a-daisy, my masters, you're
come a deadly deal wrong! When you came to the bottom of the
hill, you should have crossed down Squash-lane. 120

MARLOW  (*noting it down*)° Cross down Squash-lane!

LANDLORD  Then you were to keep straight forward, 'till you came to
four roads.

MARLOW  (*still noting*)° Come to where four roads meet!

TONY  Ay; but you must be sure to take only one of them. 125

MARLOW  (*who had been noting*)° O sir, you're facetious.

TONY  Then keeping to the right, you are to go sideways till you
come upon Crack-skull common. There you must look sharp for
the track of the wheel, and go forward, 'till you come to farmer
Murrain's barn. Coming to the farmer's barn, you are to turn to 130
the right, and then to the left, and then to the right about again, till
you find out the old mill—

MARLOW  Zounds, man! We could as soon find out the longitude!°

HASTINGS  What's to be done, Marlow?

MARLOW  This house promises but a poor reception, though perhaps 135
the Landlord can accommodate us.

LANDLORD  Alack, master, we have but one spare bed in the whole
house.

TONY  And to my knowledge, that's taken up by three lodgers already.
(*After a pause, in which the rest seem disconcerted*) I have hit it. Don't 140
you think, Stingo, our landlady could accommodate the gentlemen
by the fireside, with—three chairs and a bolster?

HASTINGS  I hate sleeping by the fireside.

MARLOW  And I detest your three chairs and a bolster.

TONY  You do, do you? Then let me see—what—if you go on a mile    145
further, to the Buck's Head, the old Buck's Head on the hill, one of
the best inns in the whole county?

HASTINGS  O ho! So we have escaped an adventure for this night,
however.

LANDLORD  (*apart to Tony*) Sure, you ben't sending them to your    150
father's as an inn,° be you?

TONY  Mum, you fool you. Let *them* find that out. (*To them*) You have
only to keep on straight forward, till you come to a large old house
by the road side. You'll see a pair of large horns over the door.
That's the sign. Drive up the yard, and call stoutly about you.    155

HASTINGS  Sir, we are obliged to you. The servants can't miss the
way?

TONY  No, no. But I tell you though, the landlord is rich, and going
to leave off business, so he wants to be thought a Gentleman, saving
your presence, he! he! he! He'll be for giving you his company, and    160
ecod if you mind him, he'll persuade you that his mother was an
alderman, and his aunt a justice of peace.

LANDLORD  A troublesome old blade to be sure, but a keeps as good
wines and beds as any in the whole country.

MARLOW  Well, if he supplies us with these, we shall want no further    165
connection.° We are to turn to the right, did you say?

TONY  No, no, straight forward. I'll just step myself, and show you a
piece of the way. (*To the landlord*) Mum.

LANDLORD  Ah, bless your heart, for a sweet, pleasant—damned
mischievous son of a whore.°    170

    *Exeunt Tony, Marlow, Hastings and Landlord*

# 2.1

*An old-fashioned house.*

*Enter Hardcastle, followed by three or four awkward servants*

HARDCASTLE  *Well*, I hope you're perfect in the table exercise° I have been teaching you these three days. You all know your posts and your places, and can show that you have been used to good company, without ever stirring from home.

ALL  Ay, ay,                                                                                      5

HARDCASTLE  When company comes, you are not to pop out and stare, and then run in again, like frighted rabbits in a warren.

ALL  No, no.

HARDCASTLE  You, Diggory, whom I have taken from the barn, are to make a show at the side-table, and you, Roger, whom I have      10
advanced from the plough,° are to place yourself behind *my* chair. But you're not to stand so, with your hands in your pockets. Take your hands from your pockets, Roger, and from your head, you blockhead you. See how Diggory carries his hands. They're a little too stiff, indeed, but that's no great matter.                                    15

DIGGORY  Ay, mind how I hold them. I learned to hold my hands this aways,° when I was upon drill for the militia. And so being upon drill—

HARDCASTLE  You must not be so talkative, Diggory. You must be all attention to the guests. You must hear us talk, and not think of      20
talking. You must see us drink, and not think of drinking. You must see us eat, and not think of eating.

DIGGORY  By the laws, your worship, that's parfectly unpossible. Whenever Diggory sees yeating° going forward, ecod he's always wishing for a mouthful himself.                                                       25

HARDCASTLE  Blockhead! Is not a belly-full in the kitchen as good as a belly-full in the parlour? Stay your stomach with that reflection.

DIGGORY  Ecod I thank your worship. I'll make a shift to stay my stomach with a slice of cold beef in the pantry.                              30

HARDCASTLE  Diggory, you are too talkative. Then if I happen to say a good thing, or tell a good story at table, you must not all burst out a-laughing, as if you made part of the company.

DIGGORY  Then, ecod, your worship must not tell the story of Ould Grouse in the gun-room. I can't help laughing at that—he! he!      35 he!—for the soul of me. We have laughed at that these twenty years—ha! ha! ha!

HARDCASTLE Ha! Ha! Ha! The story is a good one. Well, honest Diggory, you may laugh at that—but still remember to be attentive. Suppose one of the company should call for a glass of wine, how will you behave? (*To Diggory*) A glass of wine, sir, if you please. Eh, why don't you move?

DIGGORY Ecod, your worship, I never have courage till I see the eatables and drinkables brought upo' the table, and then I'm as bauld as a lion.

HARDCASTLE What, will nobody move?

FIRST SERVANT I'm not to leave this pleace.

SECOND SERVANT I'm sure it's no pleace of mine.

THIRD SERVANT Nor mine, for sartain.

DIGGORY Wauns,° and I'm sure it canna be mine.

HARDCASTLE You numbskulls! And so while, like your betters, you are quarrelling for places, the guests must be starved. O you dunces! I find I must begin all over again.—But don't I hear a coach drive into the yard? To your posts, you blockheads. I'll go in the meantime and give my old friend's son a hearty reception at the gate.

*Exit Hardcastle*

DIGGORY By the elevens,° my pleace is gone quite out of my head.

ROGER I know that my pleace is to be everywhere.

FIRST SERVANT Where the devil is mine?

SECOND SERVANT My pleace is to be nowhere at all, and so ize go about my business.

*Exeunt servants, running about as if frighted, different ways*

*Enter Servant with candles, showing in Marlow and Hastings*

SERVANT Welcome, gentlemen, very welcome. This way.

HASTINGS After the disappointments of the day, welcome once more, Charles, to the comforts of a clean room and a good fire. Upon my word, a very well-looking house, antique, but creditable.

MARLOW The usual fate of a large mansion. Having first ruined the master by good housekeeping,° it at last comes to levy contributions as an inn.

HASTINGS As you say, we passengers are to be taxed to pay all these fineries. I have often seen a good sideboard, or a marble chimney-piece, though not actually put in the bill, enflame a reckoning° confoundedly.

MARLOW Travellers, George, must pay in all places. The only difference is, that in good inns, you pay dearly for luxuries. In bad inns, you are fleeced and starved.                                                                75

HASTINGS You have lived pretty much among them. In truth, I have been often surprised, that you who have seen so much of the world, with your natural good sense, and your many opportunities, could never yet acquire a requisite share of assurance.

MARLOW The Englishman's malady.° But tell me, George, where         80
could I have learned that assurance you talk of? My life has been chiefly spent in a college, or an inn, in seclusion from that lovely part of the creation that chiefly teach men confidence. I don't know that I was ever familiarly acquainted with a single modest woman, except my mother. But among females of another class you know—   85

HASTINGS Ay, among them you are impudent enough of all conscience.

MARLOW They are of *us* you know.

HASTINGS But in the company of women of reputation I never saw such an idiot, such a trembler. You look for all the world as if you        90
wanted an opportunity of stealing out of the room.

MARLOW Why man that's because I *do* want to steal out of the room. Faith, I have often formed a resolution to break the ice, and rattle° away at any rate. But I don't know how, a single glance from a pair of fine eyes has totally overset my resolution. An impudent fellow       95
may counterfeit modesty, but I'll be hanged if a modest man can ever counterfeit impudence.

HASTINGS If you could but say half the fine things to them that I have heard you lavish upon the barmaid of an inn, or even a college bed-maker—                                                                        100

MARLOW Why, George, I can't say fine things to them. They freeze, they petrify me. They may talk of a comet, or a burning mountain, or some such bagatelle.° But to me, a modest woman, dressed out in all her finery, is the most tremendous object of the whole creation.                                                                              105

HASTINGS Ha! Ha! Ha! At this rate, man, how can you ever expect to marry!

MARLOW Never, unless as among kings and princes, my bride were to be courted by proxy.° If, indeed, like an Eastern bridegroom, one were to be introduced to a wife he never saw before, it might be        110
endured. But to go through all the terrors° of a formal courtship, together with the episode of aunts, grandmothers and cousins, and at last to blurt out the broad staring question, of, 'Madam will you marry me?' No, no, that's a strain much above me I assure you.

HASTINGS I pity you. But how do you intend behaving to the lady you    115
are come down to visit at the request of your father?

MARLOW As I behave to all other ladies. Bow very low. Answer yes, or
no, to all her demands, but for the rest, I don't think I shall venture
to look in her face,° till I see my father's again.

HASTINGS I'm surprised that one who is so warm a friend can be so    120
cool a lover.

MARLOW To be explicit, my dear Hastings, my chief inducement
down was to be instrumental in forwarding your happiness,
not my own. Miss Neville loves you. The family don't know you.
As my friend you are sure of a reception, and let honour do the    125
rest.

HASTINGS My dear Marlow! But I'll suppress the emotion. Were I a
wretch, meanly seeking to carry off a fortune, you should be the last
man in the world I would apply to for assistance. But Miss Neville's
person is all I ask, and that is mine, both from her deceased father's    130
consent, and her own inclination.

MARLOW Happy man! You have talents and art to captivate any
woman. I'm doomed to adore the sex, and yet to converse with the
only part of it I despise. This stammer in my address, and this
awkward professing° visage of mine, can never permit me to soar    135
above the reach of a milliner's 'prentice, or one of the duchesses of
Drury Lane.° Pshaw! This fellow here to interrupt us.

_Enter Hardcastle_

HARDCASTLE Gentlemen, once more you are heartily welcome.
Which is Mr Marlow? Sir, you're heartily welcome. It's not my
way, you see, to receive my friends with my back to the fire. I like to    140
give them a hearty reception in the old style at my gate. I like to see
their horses and trunks taken care of.

MARLOW (_aside_) He has got our names from the servants already.
(_To Hardcastle_) We approve your caution and hospitality, sir. (_To
Hastings_) I have been thinking, George, of changing our travelling    145
dresses in the morning. I am grown confoundedly ashamed of
mine.

HARDCASTLE I beg, Mr Marlow, you'll use no ceremony in this
house.

HASTINGS I fancy, George, you're right. The first blow is half the    150
battle. I intend opening the campaign with the white and gold.°

MR HARDCASTLE Mr Marlow, Mr Hastings, gentlemen. Pray be
under no constraint in this house. This is Liberty Hall,° gentlemen. You may do just as you please here.

MARLOW  Yet, George, if we open the campaign too fiercely at first, we    155
may want ammunition before it is over. I think to reserve the
embroidery to secure a retreat.°

HARDCASTLE  Your talking of a retreat, Mr Marlow, puts me in mind
of the Duke of Marlborough, when we went to besiege Denain.°
He first summoned the garrison—    160

MARLOW  Don't you think the *ventre d'or* waistcoat will do with the
plain brown?

HARDCASTLE  He first summoned the garrison, which might consist
of about five thousand men—

HASTINGS  I think not. Brown and yellow mix but very poorly.    165

HARDCASTLE  I say, gentlemen, as I was telling you, he summoned the
garrison, which might consist of about five thousand men—

MARLOW  The girls like finery.

HARDCASTLE  Which might consist of about five thousand men, well
appointed with stores, ammunition, and other implements of war.    170
Now, says the Duke of Marlborough, to George Brooks, that stood
next to him—You must have heard of George Brooks°—'I'll pawn
my Dukedom', says he, 'but I take that garrison without spilling a
drop of blood'. So—

MARLOW  What, my good friend, if you gave us a glass of punch in the    175
meantime. It would help us to carry on the siege with vigour.

HARDCASTLE  Punch, sir! (*Aside*) This is the most unaccountable kind
of modesty I ever met with.

MARLOW  Yes, sir, punch. A glass of warm punch, after our journey,
will be comfortable. This is Liberty Hall, you know.    180

HARDCASTLE  Here's Cup, sir.

MARLOW  (*aside*) So this fellow, in his Liberty Hall, will only let us
have just what he pleases.

HARDCASTLE  (*taking the Cup*) I hope you'll find it to your mind. I
have prepared it with my own hands, and I believe you'll own the    185
ingredients are tolerable. Will you, be so good as to pledge me,° sir?
Here, Mr Marlow, here is to our better acquaintance. (*Drinks*)

MARLOW  (*aside*) A very impudent fellow, this! But he's a character,
and I'll humour him a little. Sir, my service to you. (*Drinks*)

HASTINGS  (*aside*) I see this fellow wants to give us his company, and    190
forgets that he's an innkeeper, before he has learned to be a
gentleman.

MARLOW  From the excellence of your Cup, my old friend, I suppose
you have a good deal of business in this part of the country. Warm
work, now and then, at elections,° I suppose.    195

HARDCASTLE No, sir, I have long given that work over. Since our betters have hit upon the expedient of electing each other, there's no business *for us that sell ale.*°

HASTINGS So, then you have no turn for politics I find.

HARDCASTLE Not in the least. There was a time, indeed, I fretted    200
myself about the mistakes of government, like other people; but finding myself every day grow more angry, and the government growing no better, I left it to mend itself. Since that, I no more trouble my head about *Hyder Ali*, or *Ali Cawn,*° than about *Ally Croker.*° Sir, my service to you.    205

HASTINGS So that with eating above stairs, and drinking below, with receiving your friends within, and amusing them without, you lead a good pleasant bustling life of it.

HARDCASTLE I do stir about a great deal, that's certain. Half the differences of the parish are adjusted in this very parlour.    210

MARLOW (*after drinking*) And you have an argument in your Cup, old gentleman, better than any in Westminster Hall.°

HARDCASTLE Ay, young gentleman, that, and a little philosophy.

MARLOW (*aside*) Well, this is the first time I ever heard of an innkeeper's philosophy.    215

HASTINGS So then, like an experienced general, you attack them on every quarter. If you find their reason manageable, you attack it with your philosophy. If you find they have no reason, you attack them with this. Here's your health, my philosopher. (*Drinks*)

HARDCASTLE Good, very good, thank you, ha, ha. Your Generalship    220
puts me in mind of Prince Eugene, when he fought the Turks at the battle of Belgrade.° You shall hear—

MARLOW Instead of the battle of Belgrade, I believe it's almost time to talk about supper. What has your philosophy got in the house for supper?    225

HARDCASTLE For supper, sir! (*Aside*) Was ever such a request to a man in his own house!

MARLOW Yes, sir, supper, sir. I begin to feel an appetite. I shall make devilish work tonight in the larder, I promise you.

HARDCASTLE (*aside*) Such a brazen dog sure never my eyes beheld.    230
(*To him*) Why really, sir, as for supper I can't well tell. My Dorothy, and the cook maid, settle these things between them. I leave these kind of things entirely to them.

MARLOW You do, do you?

HARDCASTLE Entirely. By-the-bye, I believe they are in actual con-    235
sultation upon what's for supper this moment in the kitchen.

MARLOW  Then I beg they'll admit *me* as one of their privy council.
It's a way I have got. When I travel, I always choose to regulate my
own supper. Let the cook be called. No offence, I hope, sir.

HARDCASTLE  O no, sir, none in the least, yet I don't know how: our    240
Bridget, the cook maid, is not very communicative upon these occasions. Should we send for her, she might scold us all out of the
house.

HASTINGS  Let's see your list of the larder then. I ask it as a favour. I
always match my appetite to my bill of fare.    245

MARLOW  (*to Hardcastle, who looks at them with surprise*) Sir, he's very
right, and it's my way too.

HARDCASTLE  Sir, you have a right to command here. Here, Roger,
bring us the bill of fare for tonight's supper. I believe it's drawn
out. Your manner, Mr Hastings, puts me in mind of my uncle,    250
Colonel Wallop. It was a saying of his, that no man was sure of his
supper° till he had eaten it.

  *Enter Roger, who gives a bill of fare [to Marlow]*

HASTINGS  (*to Marlow*)  All upon the high ropes!° His uncle a Colonel!
We shall soon hear of his mother being a justice of peace. But let's
hear the bill of fare.    255

MARLOW  (*perusing*)  What's here? For the first course, for the second
course, for the dessert. The devil, sir, do you think we have brought
down the whole Joiners Company, or the Corporation of Bedford,°
to eat up such a supper?° Two or three little things, clean and
comfortable, will do.    260

HASTINGS  But, let's hear it.

MARLOW  (*reading*)  For the first course at the top, a pig, and prune
sauce.

HASTINGS  Damn your pig, I say.

MARLOW  And damn your prune sauce, say I.    265

HARDCASTLE  And yet, gentlemen, to men that are hungry, pig, with
prune sauce, is very good eating.

MARLOW  At the bottom, a calf's tongue and brains.

HASTINGS  Let your brains be knocked out, my good sir. I don't like
them.    270

MARLOW  Or you may clap them on a plate by themselves. I do.

HARDCASTLE  (*aside*)  Their impudence confounds me. (*To them*)
Gentlemen, you are my guests, make what alterations you please.
Is there anything else you wish to retrench or alter, gentlemen?

MARLOW  Item. A pork pie, a boiled rabbit and sausages, a florentine, a    275
shaking pudding, and a dish of tiff-taff-taffety cream!°

HASTINGS Confound your made dishes, I shall be as much at a loss in this house as at a green and yellow dinner° at the French ambassador's table. I'm for plain eating.

HARDCASTLE I'm sorry, gentlemen, that I have nothing you like, but if there be any thing you have a particular fancy to—   280

MARLOW Why, really, sir, your bill of fare is so exquisite, that any one part of it is full as good as another. Send us what you please. So much for supper. And now to see that our beds are aired, and properly taken care of.   285

HARDCASTLE I entreat you'll leave all that to me. You shall not stir a step.

MARLOW Leave that to you! I protest, sir, you must excuse me, I always look to these things myself.

HARDCASTLE I must insist, sir, you'll make yourself easy on that head.   290

MARLOW You see I'm resolved on it. (*Aside*) A very troublesome fellow this, as ever I met with.

HARDCASTLE Well, sir, I'm resolved at least to attend you. (*Aside*) This may be modern modesty, but I never saw any thing look so like old-fashioned impudence.   295

*Exeunt Marlow and Hardcastle[, followed by Roger]*

HASTINGS So I find this fellow's civilities begin to grow troublesome. But who can be angry at those assiduities which are meant to please him? Ha! What do I see? Miss Neville, by all that's happy!

*Enter Miss Neville*

MISS NEVILLE My dear Hastings! To what unexpected good fortune?   300
to what accident am I to ascribe this happy meeting?

HASTINGS Rather let me ask the same question, as I could never have hoped to meet my dearest Constance at an inn.

MISS NEVILLE An inn! Sure you mistake! My aunt, my guardian, lives here. What could induce you to think this house an inn?   305

HASTINGS My friend Mr Marlow, with whom I came down, and I, have been sent here as to an inn, I assure you. A young fellow whom we accidentally met at a house hard by directed us hither.

MISS NEVILLE Certainly it must be one of my hopeful cousin's tricks,° of whom you have heard me talk so often. Ha! Ha! Ha! Ha!   310

HASTINGS He whom your aunt intends for you? He of whom I have such just apprehensions?

MISS NEVILLE You have nothing to fear from him, I assure you. You'd

adore him if you knew how heartily he despises me. My aunt knows    315
it too, and has undertaken to court me for him, and actually begins
to think she has made a conquest.

HASTINGS Thou dear dissembler! You must know, my Constance, I
have just seized this happy opportunity of my friend's visit here to
get admittance into the family. The horses that carried us down are    320
now fatigued with their journey, but they'll soon be refreshed. And
then, if my dearest girl will trust in her faithful Hastings, we shall
soon be landed in France, where even among slaves the laws of
marriage are respected.°

MISS NEVILLE I have often told you, that though ready to obey you,    325
I yet should leave my little fortune behind with reluctance. The
greatest part of it was left me by my uncle, the India Director,° and
chiefly consists in jewels. I have been for some time persuading my
aunt to let me wear them. I fancy I'm very near succeeding. The
instant they are put into my possession, you shall find me ready to    330
make them and myself yours.

HASTINGS Perish the baubles! Your person is all I desire. In the
meantime, my friend Marlow must not be let into his mistake. I
know the strange reserve of his temper is such, that if abruptly
informed of it, he would instantly quit the house before our plan    335
was ripe for execution.

MISS NEVILLE But how shall we keep him in the deception? Miss
Hardcastle is just returned from walking. What if we still continue
to deceive him?—This, this way. (*They confer*)
    *Enter Marlow*

MARLOW The assiduities of these good people tease me beyond    340
bearing. My host seems to think it ill manners to leave me alone,
and so he claps not only himself but his old-fashioned wife on my
back. They talk of coming to sup with us too, and then, I suppose,
we are to run the gauntlet through all the rest of the family. What
have we got here?    345

HASTINGS My dear Charles! Let me congratulate you! The most
fortunate accident! Who do you think is just alighted?

MARLOW Cannot guess.

HASTINGS Our mistresses, boy, Miss Hardcastle and Miss Neville.
Give me leave to introduce Miss Constance Neville to your    350
acquaintance. Happening to dine in the neighbourhood, they
called, on their return to take fresh horses, here. Miss Hardcastle
has just stepped into the next room, and will be back in an instant.
Wasn't it lucky? Eh?

MARLOW (*aside*) I have just been mortified enough of all conscience,  355
and here comes something to complete my embarrassment.

HASTINGS Well! But wasn't it the most fortunate thing in the world?

MARLOW Oh! yes. Very fortunate. A most joyful encounter. But
our dresses, George, you know, are in disorder. What if we should
postpone the happiness 'till tomorrow? Tomorrow at her own  360
house it will be every bit as convenient. And rather more respectful.
Tomorrow let it be. (*Offering to go*)

MISS NEVILLE By no means, sir. Your ceremony will displease her.
The disorder of your dress will show the ardour of your
impatience. Besides, she knows you are in the house, and will per-  365
mit you to see her.

MARLOW O! The devil! How shall I support it? Hem! Hem! Hastings,
you must not go. You are to assist me, you know. I shall be confoundedly ridiculous. Yet, hang it! I'll take courage. Hem!

HASTINGS Pshaw, man! It's but the first plunge, and all's over. She's  370
but a woman, you know.

MARLOW And of all women, she that I dread most to encounter!
*Enter Miss Hardcastle, as returned from walking, wearing a*
*bonnet*

HASTINGS (*introducing them*) Miss Hardcastle, Mr Marlow, I'm proud
of bringing two persons of such merit together, that only want to
know, to esteem each other.

375

MISS HARDCASTLE (*aside*) Now, for meeting my modest gentleman
with a demure face, and quite in his own manner. (*After a pause, in*
*which he appears very uneasy and disconcerted.*) I'm glad of your safe
arrival, sir. I'm told you had some accidents by the way.

MARLOW Only a few madam. Yet, we had some. Yes, madam, a good  380
many accidents, but should be sorry—madam—or rather glad of
any accidents—that are so agreeably concluded. Hem!

HASTING (*to him*) You never spoke better in your whole life. Keep it
up, and I'll ensure you the victory.

MISS HARDCASTLE I'm afraid you flatter, sir. You that have seen so  385
much of the finest company can find little entertainment in an
obscure corner of the country.

MARLOW (*gathering courage*) I have lived, indeed, in the world,
madam, but I have kept very little company. I have been but an
observer upon life, madam, while others were enjoying it.  390

MISS NEVILLE But that, I am told, is the way to enjoy it at last.

HASTINGS (*to him*) Cicero° never spoke better. Once more, and you
are confirmed in assurance for ever.

MARLOW (*to him*) Hem! Stand by me then, and when I'm down,
throw in a word or two to set me up again.                            395

MISS HARDCASTLE An observer, like you, upon life, were, I fear,
disagreeably employed, since you must have had much more to
censure than to approve.

MARLOW Pardon me, madam. I was always willing to be amused.
The folly of most people is rather an object of mirth than     400
uneasiness.

HASTINGS (*to him*) Bravo, bravo. Never spoke so well in your whole
life. Well! Miss Hardcastle, I see that you and Mr Marlow are
going to be very good company. I believe our being here will but
embarrass the interview.                                              405

MARLOW Not in the least, Mr Hastings. We like your company of all
things. (*To him.*) Zounds! George, sure you won't go? How can you
leave us?

HASTINGS Our presence will but spoil conversation, so we'll retire
to the next room. (*To him*) You don't consider, man, that we are to     410
manage a little tête-à-tête of our own.

   *Exeunt Hastings and Miss Neville*

MISS HARDCASTLE (*after a pause*) But you have not been wholly an
observer, I presume, sir. The ladies, I should hope, have employed
some part of your addresses.

MARLOW (*relapsing into timidity*) Pardon me, madam, I—I—I—as yet     415
have studied—only—to—deserve them.

MISS HARDCASTLE And that some say is the very worst way to obtain
them.

MARLOW Perhaps so, madam. But I love to converse only with the
more grave and sensible° part of the sex.—But I'm afraid I grow     420
tiresome.

MISS HARDCASTLE Not at all, sir. There is nothing I like so much as
grave conversation myself. I could hear it forever. Indeed I have
often been surprised how a man of *sentiment*° could ever admire
those light airy pleasures, where nothing reaches the heart.     425

MARLOW It's—a disease—of the mind, madam. In the variety of
tastes there must be some who, wanting a relish—for—um-a-um.

MISS HARDCASTLE I understand you, sir. There must be some, who,
wanting a relish for refined pleasures, pretend to despise what they
are incapable of tasting.                                             430

MARLOW My meaning, madam, but infinitely better expressed. And
I can't help observing—a—

MISS HARDCASTLE (*aside*) Who could ever suppose this fellow

impudent upon some occasions. (*To him*) You were going to
observe, sir—

435

MARLOW I was observing, madam—I protest, madam, I forget what I
was going to observe.

MISS HARDCASTLE (*aside*) I vow and so do I. (*To him*) You were
observing, sir, that in this age of hypocrisy—something about
hypocrisy, sir.

440

MARLOW Yes, madam. In this age of hypocrisy there are few who
upon strict enquiry do not—a—a—a—

MISS HARDCASTLE I understand you perfectly, sir.

MARLOW (*aside*) Egad! And that's more than I do myself.

MISS HARDCASTLE You mean that in this hypocritical age there are
few that do not condemn in public what they practise in private,
and think they pay every debt to virtue when they praise it.

445

MARLOW True, madam. Those who have most virtue in their mouths,
have least of it in their bosoms. But I'm sure I tire you, madam.

MISS HARDCASTLE Not in the least, sir. There's something so agreeable and spirited in your manner, such life and force. Pray, sir, go
on.

450

MARLOW Yes, madam. I was saying—that there are some occasions—
when a total want of courage, madam, destroys all the—and puts
us—upon a—a—a—

455

MISS HARDCASTLE I agree with you entirely, a want of courage upon
some occasions assumes the appearance of ignorance, and betrays
us when we most want to excel. I beg you'll proceed.

MARLOW Yes, madam. Morally speaking, madam—But I see Miss
Neville expecting us in the next room. I would not intrude for the
world.

460

MISS HARDCASTLE I protest, sir, I never was more agreeably entertained in all my life. Pray go on.

MARLOW Yes, madam. I was—But she beckons us to join her.
Madam, shall I do myself the honour to attend you?

465

MISS HARDCASTLE Well then, I'll follow.

MARLOW (*aside*) This pretty smooth dialogue has done for me.
  *Exit Marlow*

MISS HARDCASTLE Ha! Ha! Ha! Was there ever such a sober sentimental interview? I'm certain he scarce looked in my face the whole
time. Yet the fellow, but for his unaccountable bashfulness, is pretty
well too. He has good sense, but then so buried in his fears, that
it fatigues one more than ignorance. If I could teach him a little
confidence, it would be doing somebody that I know of a piece of

470

service. But who is that somebody? That, faith, is a question I can
scarce answer.                                                         475

*Exit Miss Hardcastle.*

*Enter Tony and Miss Neville, followed by Mrs Hardcastle and
Hastings*

TONY What do you follow me for, cousin Con? I wonder you're not
ashamed to be so very engaging.°

MISS NEVILLE I hope, cousin, one may speak to one's own relations,
and not be to blame.

TONY Ay, but I know what sort of a relation you want to make me    480
though. But it won't do. I tell you, cousin Con, it won't do, so I beg
you'll keep your distance. I want no nearer relationship.

*She follows, coqueting him to the back scene*°

MRS HARDCASTLE Well! I vow, Mr Hastings, you are very entertaining. There's nothing in the world I love to talk of so much as
London, and the fashions, though I was never there myself.          485

HASTINGS Never there! You amaze me! From your air and manner,
I concluded you had been bred all your life either at Ranelagh,
St James's, or Tower Wharf.°

MRS HARDCASTLE O! Sir, you're only pleased to say so. We country
persons can have no manner at all. I'm in love with the town, and   490
that serves to raise me above some of our neighbouring rustics.
But who can have a manner, that has never seen the Pantheon, the
Grotto Gardens, the Borough,° and such places where the Nobility
chiefly resort? All I can do, is to enjoy London at second-hand. I
take care to know every tête-à-tête from the Scandalous Magazine,°  495
and have all the fashions, as they come out, in a letter from the two
Miss Rickets of Crooked Lane.° Pray, how do you like this head,°
Mr Hastings?

HASTINGS Extremely elegant and *degagée*, upon my word, madam.
Your *friseur* is a Frenchman, I suppose?                            500

MRS HARDCASTLE I protest I dressed it myself from a print in the
Ladies Memorandum Book° for the last year.

HASTINGS Indeed. Such a head in a side-box,° at the Playhouse,
would draw as many gazers as my Lady Mayoress at a City
Ball.                                                                505

MRS HARDCASTLE I vow, since inoculation began,° there is no
such thing to be seen as a plain woman; so one must dress a little
particular or one may escape in the crowd.

HASTINGS But that can never be your case, madam, in any dress.
(*Bowing*)

MRS HARDCASTLE Yet, what signifies *my* dressing when I have such a     510
piece of antiquity by my side as Mr Hardcastle. All I can say will
never argue down a single button from his clothes.° I have often
wanted him to throw off his great flaxen wig, and where he was
bald, to plaster it over like my Lord Pately, with powder.°

HASTINGS You are right, madam. For, as among the ladies, there are     515
none ugly, so among the men there are none old.

MRS HARDCASTLE But what do you think his answer was? Why, with
his usual Gothic vivacity,° he said I only wanted him to throw off
his wig to convert it into a *tête* for my own wearing.

HASTINGS Intolerable! At your age you may wear what you please,     520
and it must become you.

MRS HARDCASTLE Pray, Mr Hastings, what do you take to be the
most fashionable age about town?

HASTINGS Some time ago, forty was all the mode, but I'm told
the ladies intend to bring up fifty for the ensuing winter.     525

MRS HARDCASTLE Seriously. Then I shall be too young for the
fashion.

HASTINGS No lady begins now to put on jewels 'till she's past forty.
For instance, Miss there, in a polite circle, would be considered as a
child, as a mere maker of samplers.°     530

MRS HARDCASTLE And yet Mrs Niece thinks herself as much a
woman, and is as fond of jewels as the oldest of us all.

HASTINGS Your niece, is she? And that young gentleman, a brother of
yours, I should presume?

MRS HARDCASTLE My son, sir. They are contracted to each other.     535
Observe their little sports. They fall in and out ten times a day, as if
they were man and wife already. (*To them*) Well Tony, child, what
soft things are you saying to your cousin Constance this evening?

TONY I have been saying no soft things; but that it's very hard to be
followed about so. Ecod! I've not a place in the house now that's left     540
to myself but the stable.

MRS HARDCASTLE Never mind him, Con, my dear. He's in another
story behind your back.

MISS NEVILLE There's something generous in my cousin's manner.
He falls out before faces to be forgiven in private.     545

TONY That's a damned confounded—crack.°

MRS HARDCASTLE Ah! He's a sly one. Don't you think they're like
each other about the mouth, Mr Hastings? The Blenkinsop° mouth
to a T. They're of a size too. Back to back, my pretties, that Mr
Hastings may see you. Come Tony.     550

TONY  You had as good not make me, I tell you. (*Measuring*)

MISS NEVILLE  O lud! He has almost cracked my head.

MRS HARDCASTLE  O, the monster! For shame, Tony. You a man, and behave so!

TONY  If I'm a man, let me have my fortin. Ecod! I'll not be made a    555
fool of no longer.

MRS HARDCASTLE  Is this, ungrateful boy, all that I'm to get for the pains I have taken in your education? I, that have rocked you in your cradle, and fed that pretty mouth with a spoon! Did not I work that waistcoat to make you genteel?° Did not I prescribe for    560
you every day, and weep while the receipt° was operating?

TONY  Ecod! You had reason to weep, for you have been dosing me ever since I was born. I have gone through every receipt in the complete huswife° ten times over, and you have thoughts of coursing me through *Quiney*° next spring. But, ecod! I tell you, I'll    565
not be made a fool of no longer.

MRS HARDCASTLE  Wasn't it all for your good, viper? Wasn't it all for your good?

TONY  I wish you'd let me and my good alone then. Snubbing this way when I'm in spirits. If I'm to have any good, let it come of itself, not    570
to keep dinging it, dinging it into one so.

MRS HARDCASTLE  That's false. I never see you when you're in spirits. No, Tony, you then go to the alehouse or kennel. I'm never to be delighted with your agreeable, wild notes,° unfeeling monster!

TONY  Ecod! Mamma, your own notes are the wildest of the two.    575

MRS HARDCASTLE  Was ever the like? But I see he wants to break my heart, I see he does.

HASTINGS  Dear madam, permit me to lecture the young gentleman a little. I'm certain I can persuade him to his duty.

MRS HARDCASTLE  Well! I must retire. Come, Constance, my love.    580
You see, Mr Hastings, the wretchedness of my situation. Was ever poor woman so plagued with a dear, sweet, pretty, provoking, undutiful boy?

*Exeunt Mrs Hardcastle and Miss Neville*

TONY (*singing*) *There was a young man riding by, and fain would have his will. Rang do didlo dee.*    585

Don't mind her. Let her cry. It's the comfort of her heart. I have seen her and sister cry over a book for an hour together, and they said, they liked the book the better the more it made them cry.

HASTINGS  Then you're no friend to the ladies, I find, my pretty young gentleman?    590

TONY  That's as I find 'um.

HASTINGS  Not to her of your mother's choosing, I dare answer? And
  yet she appears to me a pretty, well-tempered girl.

TONY  That's because you don't know her as well as I. Ecod! I know
  every inch about her, and there's not a more bitter cantankerous    595
  toad in all Christendom.

HASTINGS (*aside*) Pretty encouragement this for a lover!

TONY  I have seen her since the height of that. She has as many tricks
  as a hare in a thicket, or a colt the first day's breaking.

HASTINGS  To me she appears sensible and silent!    600

TONY  Ay, before company. But when she's with her playmates she's as
  loud as a hog in a gate.°

HASTINGS  But there is a meek modesty about her that charms me.

TONY  Yes, but curb her never so little, she kicks up, and you're flung
  in a ditch.    605

HASTINGS  Well, but you must allow her a little beauty. Yes, you must
  allow her some beauty.

TONY  Bandbox!° She's all a made-up thing, mun. Ah! Could you but
  see Bet Bouncer of these parts, you might then talk of beauty. Ecod,
  she has two eyes as black as sloes, and cheeks as broad and red as a    610
  pulpit cushion. She'd make two of she.

HASTINGS  Well, what say you to a friend that would take this bitter
  bargain off your hands?

TONY  Anon?°

HASTINGS  Would you thank him that would take Miss Neville and    615
  leave you to happiness and your dear Betsy?

TONY  Ay; but where is there such a friend, for who would take *her*?

HASTINGS  I am he. If you but assist me, I'll engage to whip her off to
  France, and you shall never hear more of her.

TONY  Assist you! Ecod, I will, to the last drop of my blood. I'll clap a    620
  pair of horses to your chaise that shall trundle you off in a twinkling, and maybe get you a part of her fortin beside, in jewels, that
  you little dream of.

HASTINGS  My dear squire, this looks like a lad of spirit.

TONY  Come along then, and you shall see more of my spirit before    625
  you have done with me. (*Singing*). *We are the boys that fears no noise
  where the thundering cannons roar.*
      *Exeunt Tony and Hastings*

      END OF SECOND ACT

# 3.1

*Enter Hardcastle*

HARDCASTLE *What* could my old friend Sir Charles mean by recommending his son as the modestest young man in town? To me he appears the most impudent piece of brass that ever spoke with a tongue. He has taken possession of the easy chair by the fireside already. He took off his boots in the parlour, and desired me to see them taken care of. I'm desirous to know how his impudence affects my daughter. She will certainly be shocked at it.

*Enter Miss Hardcastle, plainly dressed*

HARDCASTLE Well, my Kate, I see you have changed your dress as I bid you, and yet, I believe, there was no great occasion.

MISS HARDCASTLE I find such a pleasure, sir, in obeying your commands, that I take care to observe them without ever debating their propriety.°

HARDCASTLE And yet, Kate, I sometimes give you some cause, particularly when I recommended my *modest* gentleman to you as a lover today.

MISS HARDCASTLE You taught me to expect something extraordinary, and I find the original exceeds the description.

HARDCASTLE I was never so surprised in my life! He has quite confounded all my faculties!

MISS HARDCASTLE I never saw anything like it: And a man of the world too!

HARDCASTLE Ay, he learned it all abroad. What a fool was I, to think a young man could learn modesty by travelling. He might as soon learn wit at a masquerade.°

MISS HARDCASTLE It seems all natural to him.

HARDCASTLE A good deal assisted by bad company and a French dancing-master.

MISS HARDCASTLE Sure you mistake, papa! A French dancing-master could never have taught him that timid look, that awkward address, that bashful manner—

HARDCASTLE Whose look? Whose manner? Child!

MISS HARDCASTLE Mr Marlow's. His *mauvaise honte*,° his timidity, struck me at the first sight.

HARDCASTLE Then your first sight deceived you, for I think him one of the most brazen first sights that ever astonished my senses.

MISS HARDCASTLE Sure, sir, you rally! I never saw any one so modest.

HARDCASTLE And can you be serious! I never saw such a bouncing, swaggering, puppy since I was born. Bully Dawson° was but a fool to him.

MISS HARDCASTLE Surprising! He met me with a respectful bow, a stammering voice, and a look fixed on the ground. 40

HARDCASTLE He met me with a loud voice, a lordly air, and a familiarity that made my blood freeze again.

MISS HARDCASTLE He treated me with diffidence and respect. Censured the manners of the age. Admired the prudence of girls 45 that never laughed. Tired me with apologies for being tiresome. Then left the room with a bow, and, 'Madam, I would not for the world detain you'.

HARDCASTLE He spoke to me as if he knew me all his life before. Asked twenty questions, and never waited for an answer. Inter- 50 rupted my best remarks with some silly pun, and, when I was in my best story of the Duke of Marlborough and Prince Eugene, he asked if I had not a good hand at making punch. Yes, Kate, he asked your father if he was a maker of punch!

MISS HARDCASTLE One of us must certainly be mistaken. 55

HARDCASTLE If he be what he has shown himself, I'm determined he shall never have my consent.

MISS HARDCASTLE And if he be the sullen thing I take him, he shall never have mine.

HARDCASTLE In one thing then we are agreed—to reject him. 60

MISS HARDCASTLE Yes, but upon conditions. For if you should find him less impudent, and I more presuming. If you find him more respectful, and I more importunate—I don't know—the fellow is well enough for a man. Certainly we don't meet many such at a horse race in the country. 65

HARDCASTLE If we should find him so. But that's impossible. The first appearance has done my business. I'm seldom deceived in that.

MISS HARDCASTLE And yet there may be many good qualities under that first appearance.

HARDCASTLE Ay, when a girl finds a fellow's outside to her taste, she 70 then sets about guessing the rest of his furniture.° With her, a smooth face stands for good sense, and a genteel figure for every virtue.

MISS HARDCASTLE I hope, sir, a conversation begun with a com-pliment to my good sense won't end with a sneer at my 75 understanding?

HARDCASTLE Pardon me, Kate. But if young Mr Brazen can find the art of reconciling contradictions, he may please us both, perhaps.

MISS HARDCASTLE And as one of us must be mistaken, what if we go to make further discoveries?                                                  80

HARDCASTLE Agreed. But, depend on't, I'm in the right.

MISS HARDCASTLE And, depend on't, I'm not much in the wrong.

*Exeunt Hardcastle and Miss Hardcastle*

*Enter Tony, running in with a casket*

TONY Ecod! I have got them. Here they are. My Cousin Con's necklaces, bobs and all. My mother shan't cheat the poor souls out of their fortune neither. O! My genus, is that you?                    85

*Enter Hastings*

HASTINGS My dear friend, how have you managed with your mother? I hope you have amused° her with pretending love for your cousin, and that you are willing to be reconciled at last? Our horses will be refreshed in a short time, and we shall soon be ready to set off.                                                                     90

TONY And here's something to bear your charges by the way (*giving the casket*). Your sweetheart's jewels. Keep them, and hang those, I say, that would rob you of one of them.

HASTINGS But how have you procured them from your mother?

TONY Ask me no questions, and I'll tell you no fibs. I procured them    95
by the rule of thumb.° If I had not a key to every drawer in mother's bureau, how could I go to the alehouse so often as I do? An honest man may rob himself of his own at any time.

HASTINGS Thousands do it every day. But to be plain with you: Miss Neville is endeavouring to procure them from her aunt this very   100
instant. If she succeeds, it will be the most delicate way at least of obtaining them.

TONY Well, keep them, till you know how it will be. But I know how it will be well enough. She'd as soon part with the only sound tooth in her head.                                                                    105

HASTINGS But I dread the effects of her resentment, when she finds she has lost them.

TONY Never you mind her resentment, leave *me* to manage that. I don't value her resentment the bounce of a cracker.° Zounds! Here they are. Morrice. Prance.°                                            110

*Exit Hastings*

*Enter Mrs Hardcastle and Miss Neville*

MRS HARDCASTLE Indeed, Constance, you amaze me. Such a girl as

you want jewels? It will be time enough for jewels, my dear, twenty
years hence, when your beauty begins to want repairs.

MISS NEVILLE But what will repair beauty at forty, will certainly
improve it at twenty, madam.                                        115

MRS HARDCASTLE Yours, my dear, can admit of none. That natural
blush is beyond a thousand ornaments. Besides, child, jewels
are quite out at present. Don't you see half the ladies of our
acquaintance, my Lady Kill-Daylight,° and Mrs Crump,° and the
rest of them, carry their jewels to town, and bring nothing but paste   120
and marcasites° back.

MISS NEVILLE But who knows, madam, but somebody that shall
be nameless would like me best with all my little finery about
me?

MRS HARDCASTLE Consult your glass, my dear, and then see, if with    125
such a pair of eyes, you want any better sparklers. What do you
think, Tony, my dear, does your cousin Con want any jewels, in
your eyes, to set off her beauty?

TONY That's as thereafter may be.

MISS NEVILLE My dear aunt, if you knew how it would oblige me.        130

MRS HARDCASTLE A parcel of old-fashioned rose and table-cut
things.° They would make you look like the court of King Solomon
at a puppet-show.° Besides, I believe I can't readily come at them.
They may be missing for aught I know to the contrary.

TONY (aside to Mrs Hardcastle) Then why don't you tell her so at      135
once, as she's so longing for them. Tell her they're lost. It's the only
way to quiet her. Say they're lost, and call me to bear witness.

MRS HARDCASTLE (aside to Tony) You know, my dear, I'm only
keeping them for you. So if I say they're gone, you'll bear me
witness, will you? He! He! He!                                        140

TONY Never fear me. Ecod! I'll say I saw them taken out with my own
eyes.

MISS NEVILLE I desire them but for a day, madam. Just to be permitted to show them as relics,° and then they may be locked up
again.                                                                145

MRS HARDCASTLE To be plain with you, my dear Constance; if I
could find them, you should have them. They're missing, I assure
you. Lost, for aught I know; but we must have patience wherever
they are.

MISS NEVILLE I'll not believe it. This is but a shallow pretence to   150
deny me. I know they're too valuable to be so slightly kept, and as
you are to answer for the loss.

MRS HARDCASTLE Don't be alarmed, Constance. If they be lost, I must restore an equivalent. But my son knows they are missing, and not to be found.    155

TONY That I can bear witness to. They are missing, and not to be found, I'll take my oath on't.

MRS HARDCASTLE You must learn resignation, my dear, for though we lose our fortune, yet we should not lose our patience. See me, how calm I am.    160

MISS NEVILLE Ay, people are generally calm at the misfortunes of others.

MRS HARDCASTLE Now, I wonder a girl of your good sense should waste a thought upon such trumpery. We shall soon find them, and, in the meantime, you shall make use of my garnets till your jewels    165 be found.

MISS NEVILLE I detest garnets.

MRS HARDCASTLE The most becoming things in the world to set off a clear complexion. You have often seen how well they look upon me. You *shall* have them.    170

MISS NEVILLE I dislike them of all things. You shan't stir—
    *Exit Mrs Hardcastle°*
Was ever anything so provoking to mislay my own jewels, and force me to wear her trumpery.

TONY Don't be a fool. If she gives you the garnets, take what you can get. The jewels are your own already. I have stolen them out of her    175 bureau, and she does not know it. Fly to your spark. He'll tell you more of the matter. Leave me to manage *her*.

MISS NEVILLE My dear cousin.

TONY Vanish. She's here, and has missed them already. Zounds! how she fidgets and spits about like a Catharine wheel.°    180
    *Enter Mrs Hardcastle*

MRS HARDCASTLE Confusion! Thieves! Robbers! We are cheated, plundered, broke open, undone.

TONY What's the matter, what's the matter, mamma? I hope nothing has happened to any of the good family!

MRS HARDCASTLE We are robbed. My bureau has been broke open,    185 the jewels taken out, and I'm undone.

TONY Oh! Is that all? Ha, ha, ha. By the laws, I never saw it better acted in my life. Ecod, I thought you was ruined in earnest, ha, ha, ha.

MRS HARDCASTLE Why boy, I *am* ruined in earnest. My bureau has    190 been broke open, and all taken away.

TONY  Stick to that. Ha, ha, ha. Stick to that. I'll bear witness, you know. Call me to bear witness.

MRS HARDCASTLE  I tell you, Tony, by all that's precious, the jewels are gone, and I shall be ruined for ever.    195

TONY  Sure I know they're gone, and I am to say so.

MRS HARDCASTLE  My dearest Tony, but hear me. They're gone, I say.

TONY  By the laws, mamma, you make me for to laugh, ha, ha. I know who took them well enough, ha, ha, ha.    200

MRS HARDCASTLE  Was there ever such a blockhead, that can't tell the difference between jest and earnest. I tell you I'm not in jest, booby.

TONY  That's right, that's right. You must be in a bitter passion, and then nobody will suspect either of us. I'll bear witness that they are    205 gone.

MRS HARDCASTLE  Was there ever such a cross-grained° brute, that won't hear me! Can you bear witness that you're no better than a fool? Was ever poor woman so beset with fools on one hand, and thieves on the other?    210

TONY  I can bear witness to that.

MRS HARDCASTLE  Bear witness again, you blockhead you, and I'll turn you out of the room directly. My poor niece, what will become of *her*! Do you laugh, you unfeeling brute, as if you enjoyed my distress?    215

TONY  I can bear witness to that.

MRS HARDCASTLE  Do you insult me, monster? I'll teach you to vex your mother, I will.

TONY  I can bear witness to that.

*Tony runs off; Mrs Hardcastle follows[, pushing him]*

*Enter Miss Hardcastle and Maid*

MISS HARDCASTLE  What an unaccountable creature is that brother of    220 mine, to send them to the house as an inn, ha, ha. I don't wonder at his impudence.

MAID  But what is more, madam, the young gentleman as you passed by in your present dress, asked me if you were the barmaid? He mistook you for the barmaid, madam.    225

MISS HARDCASTLE  Did he? Then as I live I'm resolved to keep up the delusion. Tell me, Pimple, how do you like my present dress. Don't you think I look something like Cherry in the Beaux Stratagem?°

MAID  It's the dress, madam, that every lady wears in the country, but when she visits or receives company.    230

MISS HARDCASTLE  And are you sure he does not remember my face or person?

MAID  Certain of it.

MISS HARDCASTLE  I vow I thought so, for though we spoke for some time together, yet his fears were such, that he never once looked up 235 during the interview. Indeed, if he had, my bonnet would have kept him from seeing me.

MAID  But what do you hope from keeping him in his mistake?

MISS HARDCASTLE  In the first place, I shall be *seen*, and that is no small advantage to a girl who brings her face to market. Then I shall 240 perhaps make an acquaintance and that's no small victory gained over one who never addresses any but the wildest of her sex. But my chief aim is to take my gentleman off his guard, and like an invisible champion of romance examine the giant's force before I offer to combat. 245

MAID  But are you sure you can act your part, and disguise your voice, so that he may mistake that, as he has already mistaken your person?

MISS HARDCASTLE  Never fear me. I think I have got the true bar cant.—'Did your honour call?'—'Attend the Lion there'.—'Pipes and tobacco for the Angel'.—'The Lamb has been outrageous° this 250 half hour'.

MAID  It will do, madam. But he's here.

     *Exit Maid. Enter Marlow*

MARLOW  What a bawling in every part of the house. I have scarce a moment's repose. If I go to the best room, there I find my host and his story. If I fly to the gallery, there we have my hostess with her 255 curtsy down to the ground. I have at last got a moment to myself, and now for recollection. (*Walks and muses*)

MISS HARDCASTLE  Did you call, sir? Did your honour call?

MARLOW (*musing*)  As for Miss Hardcastle, she's too grave and senti-mental for me. 260

MISS HARDCASTLE  Did your honour call? (*She still places herself before him, he turning away*)

MARLOW  No, child. (*Musing*) Besides from the glimpse I had of her, I think she squints.

MISS HARDCASTLE  I'm sure, sir, I heard the bell ring.

MARLOW  No, No. (*Musing*) I have pleased my father, however, by 265 coming down, and I'll tomorrow please myself by returning. (*Taking out his tablets,° and perusing*)

MISS HARDCASTLE  Perhaps the other gentleman called, sir.

MARLOW I tell you, no.

MISS HARDCASTLE I should be glad to know, sir. We have such a
parcel of servants.                                                    270

MARLOW No, no, I tell you. (*Looks full in her face*) Yes, child, I think
I did call. I wanted—I wanted—I vow, child, you are vastly
handsome.

MISS HARDCASTLE O la, sir, you'll make one ashamed.

MARLOW [*aside*] Never saw a more sprightly malicious eye.—Yes, yes,   275
my dear, I did call. Have you got any of your—a—what d'ye call it
in the house?

MISS HARDCASTLE No, sir, we have been out of that these ten days.

MARLOW One may call in this house, I find, to very little purpose.
Suppose I should call for a taste, just by way of trial, of the nectar  280
of your lips. Perhaps I might be disappointed in that too.°

MISS HARDCASTLE Nectar! Nectar! That's a liquor there's no call for
in these parts. French, I suppose. We keep no French wines here,
sir.

MARLOW Of true English growth, I assure you.                          285

MISS HARDCASTLE Then it's odd I should not know it. We brew all
sorts of wines in this house, and I have lived here these eighteen
years.

MARLOW Eighteen years! Why one would think, child, you kept the
bar before you were born. How old are you?                            290

MISS HARDCASTLE O! Sir, I must not tell my age. They say women
and music should never be dated.

MARLOW To guess at this distance, you can't be much above forty.
(*Approaching*) Yet nearer I don't think so much. (*Approaching*) By
coming close to some women they look younger still, but when we       295
come very close indeed—(*Attempting to kiss her*)

MISS HARDCASTLE Pray, sir, keep your distance. One would think
you wanted to know one's age as they do horses, by mark of
mouth.°

MARLOW I protest, child, you use me extremely ill. If you keep me at   300
this distance, how is it possible you and I can be ever acquainted?

MISS HARDCASTLE And who wants to be acquainted with you? I
want no such acquaintance, not I. I'm sure you did not treat Miss
Hardcastle that was here awhile ago in this obstropalous° manner.
I'll warrant me, before her you looked dashed, and kept bowing to     305
the ground, and talked, for all the world, as if you was before a
justice of peace.

MARLOW (*aside*) Egad! she has hit it, sure enough. (*To her*) In awe of
her, child? Ha! Ha! Ha! A mere, awkward, squinting thing, no, no.
I find you don't know me. I laughed, and rallied her a little, but I    310
was unwilling to be too severe. No, I could not be too severe, *curse
me*!

MISS HARDCASTLE O! Then, sir, you are a favourite, I find, among
the ladies?

MARLOW Yes, my dear, a great favourite. And yet, hang me, I don't    315
see what they find in me to follow. At the Ladies Club° in town, I'm
called their agreeable Rattle.° Rattle, child, is not my real name, but
one I'm known by. My name is Solomons. Mr Solomons, my dear,
at your service. (*Offering to salute her.*)

MISS HARDCASTLE Hold, sir; you were introducing me to your club,    320
not to yourself. And you're so great a favourite there you say?

MARLOW Yes, my dear. There's Mrs Mantrap, Lady Betty Blackleg,
the Countess of Sligo, Mrs Langhorns, old Miss Biddy Buckskin,°
and your humble servant, keep up the spirit of the place.

MISS HARDCASTLE Then it's a very merry place, I suppose.    325

MARLOW Yes, as merry as cards, suppers, wine, and old women can
make us.

MISS HARDCASTLE And their agreeable Rattle, ha! ha! ha!

MARLOW (*aside*) Egad! I don't quite like this chit. She looks knowing,
methinks. You laugh, child!    330

MISS HARDCASTLE I can't but laugh to think what time they all have
for minding their work or their family.

MARLOW (*aside*) All's well, she don't laugh at me. (*To her*) Do *you*
ever work, child?

MISS HARDCASTLE Ay, sure. There's not a screen or a quilt in the    335
whole house but what can bear witness to that.

MARLOW Odso! Then you must show me your embroidery. I
embroider and draw patterns myself a little. If you want a judge of
your work you must apply to me. (*Seizing her hand*)

MISS HARDCASTLE Ay, but the colours don't look well by candlelight.    340
You shall see all in the morning. (*Struggling*)

MARLOW And why not now, my angel? Such beauty fires beyond the
power of resistance.—Pshaw! The father here! My old luck. I never
nicked seven° that I did not throw ames ace° three times following.

    *Exit Marlow*

    *Enter Hardcastle, who stands in surprise*

HARDCASTLE So, madam! So I find *this* is your *modest* lover. This is    345
your humble admirer that kept his eyes fixed on the ground, and

only adored at humble distance. Kate, Kate, art thou not ashamed to deceive your father so?

MISS HARDCASTLE Never trust me, dear papa, but he's still the modest man I first took him for. You'll be convinced of it as well    350
as I.

HARDCASTLE By the hand of my body I believe his impudence is infectious! Didn't I see him seize your hand? Didn't I see him haul you about like a milk maid? And now you talk of his respect and his modesty, forsooth!    355

MISS HARDCASTLE But if I shortly convince you of his modesty, that he has only the faults that will pass off with time, and the virtues that will improve with age, I hope you'll forgive him.

HARDCASTLE The girl would actually make one run mad! I tell you I'll not be convinced. I am convinced. He has scarcely been three    360
hours in the house, and he has already encroached on all my prerogatives. You may like his impudence, and call it modesty, but my son-in-law, madam, must have very different qualifications.

MISS HARDCASTLE Sir, I ask but this night to convince you.

HARDCASTLE You shall not have half the time, for I have thoughts of    365
turning him out this very hour.

MISS HARDCASTLE Give me that hour then, and I hope to satisfy you.

HARDCASTLE Well, an hour let it be then. But I'll have no trifling with your father. All fair and open do you mind me.

MISS HARDCASTLE I hope, sir, you have ever found that I considered    370
your commands as my pride. For your kindness is such, that my duty as yet has been inclination.

*Exeunt Hardcastle and Miss Hardcastle*

END OF THIRD ACT

# 4.1

*Enter Hastings and Miss Neville*

HASTINGS You surprise me! Sir Charles Marlow expected here this
night? Where have you had your information?

MISS NEVILLE You may depend upon it. I just saw his letter to
Mr Hardcastle, in which he tells him he intends setting out a
few hours after his son. 5

HASTINGS Then, my Constance, all must be completed before he
arrives. He knows me, and should he find me here, would discover
my name,° and perhaps my designs, to the rest of the family.

MISS NEVILLE The jewels, I hope, are safe.

HASTINGS Yes, yes. I have sent them to Marlow, who keeps the keys 10
of our baggage. In the meantime, I'll go to prepare matters for
our elopement. I have had the Squire's promise of a fresh pair of
horses, and, if I should not see him again, will write him further
directions.

*Exit Hastings*

MISS NEVILLE Well, success attend you! In the meantime, I'll go 15
amuse my aunt with the old pretence of a violent passion for my
cousin.

*Exit Miss Neville. Enter Marlow, followed by a servant*

MARLOW I wonder what Hastings could mean by sending me so valuable a thing as a casket to keep for him, when he knows the only
place I have is the seat of a post-coach at an inn-door.° Have you 20
deposited the casket with the landlady, as I ordered you? Have you
put it into her own hands?

SERVANT Yes, your honour.

MARLOW She said she'd keep it safe, did she?

SERVANT Yes, she said she'd keep it safe enough. She asked me how I 25
came by it, and she said she had a great mind to make me give an
account of myself.

*Exit Servant*

MARLOW Ha! Ha! Ha! They're safe however. What an unaccountable
set of beings have we got amongst! This little barmaid though runs
in my head most strangely, and drives out the absurdities of all the 30
rest of the family. She's mine, she must be mine, or I'm greatly
mistaken.

*Enter Hastings*

HASTINGS Bless me! I quite forgot to tell her that I intended to prepare at the bottom of the garden. Marlow here, and in spirits too! 35

MARLOW  Give me joy, George! Crown me, shadow me with laurels! Well, George, after all, we modest fellows don't want for success among the women.

HASTINGS  Some women you mean. But what success has your honour's modesty been crowned with now, that it grows so insolent 40 upon us?

MARLOW  Didn't you see the tempting, brisk, lovely, little thing that runs about the house with a bunch of keys to its girdle?°

HASTINGS  Well! And what then?

MARLOW  She's mine, you rogue you. Such fire, such motion, such 45 eyes, such lips—but, egad, she would not let me kiss them though!

HASTINGS  But are you so sure, so very sure of her?

MARLOW  Why man, she talked of showing me her work above-stairs, and I am to improve the pattern.

HASTINGS  But how can *you*, Charles, go about to rob a woman of her 50 honour?

MARLOW  Pshaw! Pshaw! We all know the honour of the barmaid of an inn. I don't intend to *rob* her, take my word for it. There's nothing in this house, I shan't honestly *pay* for.

HASTINGS  I believe the girl has virtue. 55

MARLOW  And if she has, I should be the last man in the world that would attempt to corrupt it.

HASTINGS  You have taken care, I hope, of the casket I sent you to lock up? It's in safety?

MARLOW  Yes, yes. It's safe enough. I have taken care of it. But how 60 could you think the seat of a post-coach at an inn-door a place of safety? Ah! Numbskull! I have taken better precautions for you than you did for yourself.—I have—

HASTINGS  What!

MARLOW  I have sent it to the landlady to keep for you. 65

HASTINGS  To the landlady!

MARLOW  The landlady.

HASTINGS  You did.

MARLOW  I did. She's to be answerable for its forthcoming, you know.

HASTINGS  Yes, she'll bring it forth, with a witness.° 70

MARLOW  Wasn't I right? I believe you'll allow that I acted prudently upon this occasion?

HASTINGS  (*aside*) He must not see my uneasiness.

MARLOW  You seem a little disconcerted though, methinks. Sure nothing has happened? 75

HASTINGS  No, nothing. Never was in better spirits in all my life. And so you left it with the landlady, who, no doubt, very readily undertook the charge?

MARLOW  Rather too readily. For she not only kept the casket, but, through her great precaution, was going to keep the messenger too. Ha! Ha! Ha!          80

HASTINGS  He! He! He! They're safe, however.

MARLOW  As a guinea in a miser's purse.

HASTINGS  (*aside*) So now all hopes of fortune are at an end, and we must set off without it. (*To him*) Well, Charles, I'll leave you to your          85
meditations on the pretty barmaid, and, he! he! he! may you be as successful for yourself as you have been for me.

   *Exit Hastings*

MARLOW  Thank ye, George! I ask no more. Ha! Ha! Ha!

   *Enter Hardcastle*

HARDCASTLE  I no longer know my own house. It's turned all topsy-turvy. His servants have got drunk already. I'll bear it no longer,          90
and yet, from my respect for his father, I'll be calm. (*To him*) Mr Marlow, your servant. I'm your very humble servant. (*Bowing low*)

MARLOW  Sir, your humble servant. (*Aside*) What's to be the wonder now?

HARDCASTLE  I believe, sir, you must be sensible, sir, that no man alive          95
ought to be more welcome than your father's son, sir. I hope you think so?

MARLOW  I do from my soul, sir. I don't want much entreaty. I generally make my father's son welcome wherever he goes.

HARDCASTLE  I believe you do, from my soul, sir. But though I say          100
nothing to your own conduct, that of your servants is insufferable. Their manner of drinking is setting a very bad example in this house, I assure you.

MARLOW  I protest, my very good sir, that's no fault of mine. If they don't drink as they ought *they* are to blame. I ordered them not to          105
spare the cellar. I did, I assure you. (*To the side scene*) Here, let one of my servants come up. (*To him*) My positive directions were, that, as I did not drink myself, they should make up for my deficiencies below.

HARDCASTLE  Then they had your orders for what they do! I'm          110
satisfied!

MARLOW  They had, I assure you. You shall hear from one of themselves.

   *Enter Jeremy, drunk*

You, Jeremy! Come forward, sirrah! What were my orders? Were you not told to drink freely, and call for what you thought fit, for the good of the house? 115

HARDCASTLE (*aside*) I begin to lose my patience.

JEREMY Please your honour, liberty and Fleet Street° for ever! Though I'm but a servant, I'm as good as another man. I'll drink for no man before supper, sir, dammy! Good liquor will sit upon 120 a good supper, but a good supper will not sit upon—hiccup—upon my conscience, sir.

MARLOW You see, my old friend, the fellow is as drunk as he can possibly be. I don't know what you'd have more, unless you'd have the poor devil soused in a beer-barrel. 125

HARDCASTLE Zounds! He'll drive me distracted if I contain myself any longer. Mr Marlow. Sir, I have submitted to your insolence for more than four hours, and I see no likelihood of its coming to an end. I'm now resolved to be master here, sir, and I desire that you and your drunken pack may leave my house directly. 130

MARLOW Leave your house! Sure you jest, my good friend? What, when I'm doing what I can to please you.

HARDCASTLE I tell you, sir, you don't please me, so I desire you'll leave my house.

MARLOW Sure you cannot be serious? At this time o'night, and such 135 a night. You only mean to banter° me?

HARDCASTLE I tell you, sir, I'm serious, and, now that my passions are roused, I say this house is mine, sir. This house is mine, and I command you to leave it directly.

MARLOW Ha! Ha! Ha! A puddle in a storm. I shan't stir a step, I 140 assure you. (*In a serious tone.*) This, your house, fellow! It's my house. This is my house. Mine, while I choose to stay. What right have you to bid me leave this house, sir? I never met with such impudence, curse me, never in my whole life before.

HARDCASTLE Nor I, confound me if ever I did. To come to my 145 house, to call for what he likes, to turn me out of my own chair, to insult the family, to order his servants to get drunk, and then to tell me 'This house is mine, sir'. By all that's impudent it makes me laugh. Ha! Ha! Ha! Pray, sir, (*bantering*)° as you take the house, what think you of taking the rest of the furniture? There's a 150 pair of silver candlesticks, and there's a fire-screen, and here's a pair of brazen-nosed bellows, perhaps you may take a fancy to them?

MARLOW  Bring me your bill, sir, bring me your bill, and let's make no
more words about it.                                                        155

HARDCASTLE  There are a set of prints too. What think you of the
Rake's Progress° for your own apartment?

MARLOW  Bring me your bill, I say, and I'll leave you and your infernal
house directly.

HARDCASTLE  Then there's a mahogany table, that you may see your       160
own face in.

MARLOW  My bill, I say.

HARDCASTLE  I had forgot the great chair, for your own particular
slumbers, after a hearty meal.

MARLOW  Zounds! Bring me my bill, I say, and let's hear no more        165
on't.

HARDCASTLE  Young man, young man, from your father's letter to
me, I was taught to expect a well-bred modest man, as a visitor
here, but now I find him no better than a coxcomb and a bully, but
he will be down here presently, and shall hear more of it.             170
        *Exit Hardcastle*

MARLOW  How's this! Sure I have not mistaken the house! Everything looks like an inn. The servants cry, 'coming'. The attendance
is awkward. The barmaid, too, to attend us. But she's here,
and will further inform me. Whither so fast, child? A word with
you.                                                                   175
        *Enter Miss Hardcastle*

MISS HARDCASTLE  Let it be short then. I'm in a hurry. (*Aside*) (I
believe he begins to find out his mistake, but it's too soon quite to
undeceive him.)

MARLOW  Pray, child, answer me one question. What are you, and
what may your business in this house be?                               180

MISS HARDCASTLE  A relation of the family, sir.

MARLOW  What? A poor relation?

MISS HARDCASTLE  Yes, sir. A poor relation appointed to keep the
keys, and to see that the guests want nothing in my power to give
them.                                                                  185

MARLOW  That is, you act as the barmaid of this inn.

MISS HARDCASTLE  Inn. O law, what brought that in your head? One
of the best families in the county keep an inn. Ha, ha, ha, old Mr
Hardcastle's house, an inn!

MARLOW  Mr Hardcastle's house! Is this house Mr Hardcastle's        190
house, child?

MISS HARDCASTLE  Ay, sure. Whose else should it be?

MARLOW So then all's out, and I have been damnably imposed on.
O, confound my stupid head. I shall be laughed at over the whole
town. I shall be stuck up in *caricatura* in all the print-shops.°     195
The Dullissimo Maccaroni.° To mistake this house of all others
for an inn, and my father's old friend for an inn-keeper! What a
swaggering puppy must he take me for! What a silly puppy do I
find myself! There again, may I be hanged, my dear, but I mistook
you for the barmaid.     200

MISS HARDCASTLE Dear me! Dear me! I'm sure there's nothing in
my *behaviour*° to put me upon a level with one of that stamp.

MARLOW Nothing, my dear, nothing. But I was in for a list of
blunders, and could not help making you a subscriber.° My
stupidity saw everything the wrong way. I mistook your assiduity     205
for assurance, and your simplicity for allurement. But it's over.
This house I no more show *my* face in.

MISS HARDCASTLE I hope, sir, I have done nothing to disoblige you.
I'm sure I should be sorry to affront any gentleman who has been so
polite, and said so many civil things to me. I'm sure I should be     210
sorry (*pretending to cry*) if he left the family upon my account. I'm
sure I should be sorry, people said anything amiss, since I have no
fortune but my character.

MARLOW (*aside*) By heaven, she weeps. This is the first mark of
tenderness I ever had from a modest woman, and it touches me. (*To*     215
*her*) Excuse me, my lovely girl, you are the only part of the family
I leave with reluctance. But to be plain with you, the difference of
our birth, fortune and education, make an honourable connection
impossible, and I can never harbour a thought of seducing
simplicity that trusted in my honour, or bringing ruin upon one,     220
whose only fault was being too lovely.

MISS HARDCASTLE (*aside*) Generous man! I now begin to admire
him. (*To him*) But I'm sure my family is as good as Miss Hardcastle's, and though I'm poor, that's no great misfortune to a contented mind, and, until this moment, I never thought that it was     225
bad to want fortune.

MARLOW And why now, my pretty simplicity?

MISS HARDCASTLE Because it puts me at a distance from one, that if I
had a thousand pound I would give it all to.

MARLOW (*aside*) This simplicity bewitches me, so that if I stay I'm     230
undone. I must make one bold effort, and leave her. (*To her*)
Your partiality in my favour, my dear, touches me most sensibly,
and were I to live for myself alone, I could easily fix my choice. But

I owe too much to the opinion of the world, too much to the authority of a father, so that—I can scarcely speak it—it affects me. Farewell.     235

*Exit Marlow*

MISS HARDCASTLE I never knew half his merit till now. He shall not go. If I have power or art to detain him, I'll still preserve the character in which I stooped to conquer,° but will undeceive my papa, who, perhaps, may laugh him out of his resolution.     240

*Exit Miss Hardcastle. Enter Tony and Miss Neville*

TONY Ay, you may steal for yourselves the next time. I have done my duty. She has got the jewels again, that's a sure thing, but she believes it was all a mistake of the servants.

MISS NEVILLE But, my dear cousin, sure you won't forsake us in this distress. If she in the least suspects that I am going off, I shall     245 certainly be locked up, or sent to my Aunt Pedigree's,° which is ten times worse.

TONY To be sure, aunts of all kinds are damned bad things. But what can I do? I have got you a pair of horses that will fly like Whistlejacket,° and I'm sure you can't say but I have courted     250 you nicely before her face. Here she comes, we must court a bit or two more, for fear she should suspect us. (*They retire, and seem to fondle*)°

*Enter Mrs Hardcastle*

MRS HARDCASTLE Well, I was greatly fluttered, to be sure. But my son tells me it was all a mistake of the servants. I shan't be easy, however, till they are fairly married, and then let her keep her     255 own fortune. But what do I see! Fondling together, as I'm alive. I never saw Tony so sprightly before.—Ah, have I caught you, my pretty doves! What, billing, exchanging stolen glances, and broken murmurs. Ah!

TONY As for murmurs, mother, we grumble a little now and then, to     260 be sure. But there's no love lost between us.

MRS HARDCASTLE A mere sprinkling, Tony, upon the flame, only to make it burn brighter.

MISS NEVILLE Cousin Tony promises to give us more of his company at home. Indeed, he shan't leave us any more. It won't leave us     265 cousin Tony, will it?

TONY O, it's a pretty creature! No, I'd sooner leave my horse in a pound,° than leave you when you smile upon one so. Your laugh makes you so becoming.

MISS NEVILLE Agreeable cousin! Who can help admiring that natural     270

humour,° that pleasant, broad, red, thoughtless—(*patting his cheek*)
ah! it's a bold face.

MRS HARDCASTLE  Pretty innocence.

TONY  I'm sure I always loved cousin Con's hazel eyes, and her pretty
long fingers, that she twists this way and that, over the haspicholls,°    275
like a parcel of bobbins.°

MRS HARDCASTLE  Ah, he would charm the bird from the tree.
I was never so happy before. My boy takes after his father,
poor Mr Lumpkin, exactly. The jewels, my dear Con, shall be
yours incontinently.° You shall have them. Isn't he a sweet boy,    280
my dear? You shall be married tomorrow, and we'll put off the rest
of his education, like Dr. Drowsy's sermons,° to a fitter
opportunity.

*Enter Diggory*

DIGGORY  Where's the 'Squire? I have got a letter for your worship.

TONY  Give it to my mamma. She reads all my letters first.    285

DIGGORY  I had orders to deliver it into your own hands.

TONY  Who does it come from?

DIGGORY  Your worship mun ask that o' the letter itself.

TONY  I could wish to know, though (*turning the letter, and gazing on it*)

MISS NEVILLE  (*aside*) Undone, undone. A letter to him from    290
Hastings. I know the hand. If my aunt sees it, we are ruined for
ever. I'll keep her employed a little if I can. (*To Mrs Hardcastle*)
But I have not told you, madam, of my cousin's smart answer just
now to Mr Marlow. We so laughed—You must know, madam—this
way a little, for he must not hear us. (*They confer*)°    295

TONY  (*still gazing*) A damned cramp piece of penmanship, as ever I
saw in my life. I can read your print-hand° very well. But here there
are such handles, and shanks,° and dashes, that one can scarce tell
the head from the tail. 'To Anthony Lumpkin, Esquire'. It's very
odd, I can read the outside of my letters, where my own name is,    300
well enough. But when I come to open it, it's all—buzz. That's
hard, very hard. For the inside of the letter is always the cream of
the correspondence.

MRS HARDCASTLE  Ha, ha, ha! Very well, very well. And so my son
was too hard for the philosopher.    305

MISS NEVILLE  Yes, madam, but you must hear the rest, madam. A
little more this way, or he may hear us. You'll hear how he puzzled
him again.

MRS HARDCASTLE  He seems strangely puzzled now himself,
methinks.    310

TONY (*still gazing*) A damned up-and-down hand, as if it was disguised in liquor. (*Reading*) 'Dear Sir'. Ay, that's that. Then there's an *M*, and *a T*, and an *S*, but whether the next be an *izzard* or an *R*, confound me, I cannot tell.

MRS HARDCASTLE What's that, my dear. Can I give you any  315
assistance?

MISS NEVILLE Pray, aunt, let me read it. No body reads a cramp hand better than I. (*Twitching*° the letter from her) Do you know who it is from?

TONY Can't tell, except from Dick Ginger the feeder.°  320

MISS NEVILLE Ay, so it is. (*Pretending to read*) 'Dear 'Squire, Hoping that you're in health, as I am at this present. The gentlemen of the Shake bag club has cut the gentlemen of goose-green quite out of feather'. The odds—um—odd battle—um—long fighting—um here, here, it's all about cocks, and fighting. It's of no consequence,  325
here, put it up, put it up. (*Thrusting the crumpled letter upon him*)

TONY But I tell you, Miss, it's of all the consequence in the world. I would not lose the rest of it for a guinea. Here, mother, do you make it out. Of no consequence! (*Giving Mrs Hardcastle the letter*)

MRS HARDCASTLE How's this! (*Reads*) 'Dear 'Squire, I'm now  330
waiting for Miss Neville, with a post-chaise and pair, at the bottom of the garden, but I find my horses yet unable to perform the journey. I expect you'll assist us with a pair of fresh horses, as you promised. Dispatch is necessary, as the *hag*' (ay the hag) 'your mother, will otherwise suspect us. Yours, Hastings'. Grant me  335
patience. I shall run distracted. My rage chokes me.

MISS NEVILLE I hope, madam, you'll suspend your resentment for a few moments, and not impute to me any impertinence, or sinister design that belongs to another.

MRS HARDCASTLE (*curtsying very low*) Fine spoken, madam. You are  340
most miraculously polite and engaging, and quite the very pink of courtesy and circumspection, madam. (*Changing her tone.*) And you, you great ill-fashioned oaf, with scarce sense enough to keep your mouth shut. Were you too joined against me? But I'll defeat all your plots in a moment. As for you, madam, since you have got  345
a pair of fresh horses ready, it would be cruel to disappoint them. So, if you please, instead of running away with your spark, prepare, this very moment, to run off with *me*. Your old aunt Pedigree will keep you secure, I'll warrant me. You too, sir, may mount your horse, and guard us upon the way. Here, Thomas,  350

Roger, Diggory, I'll show you, that I wish you better than you do yourselves.

*Exit Mrs Hardcastle*

MISS NEVILLE  So now I'm completely ruined.

TONY  Ay, that's a sure thing.

MISS NEVILLE  What better could be expected from being connected  355
with such a stupid fool, and after all the nods and signs I made him.

TONY  By the laws, Miss, it was your own cleverness, and not my stupidity, that did your business. You were so nice and so busy with your Shake-bags and Goose-greens,° that I thought you could  360
never be making believe.

*Enter Hastings*

HASTINGS  So, sir, I find by my servant, that you have shown my letter, and betrayed us. Was this well done, young gentleman?

TONY  Here's another. Ask Miss there who betrayed you. Ecod, it was her doing, not mine.  365

*Enter Marlow*

MARLOW  So I have been finely used here among you. Rendered contemptible, driven into ill manners, despised, insulted, laughed at.

TONY  Here's another. We shall have old Bedlam° broke loose presently.  370

MISS NEVILLE  And there, sir, is the gentleman to whom we all owe every obligation.

MARLOW  What can I say to him? A mere boy, an idiot, whose ignorance and age are a protection.

HASTINGS  A poor contemptible booby, that would but disgrace  375
correction.

MISS NEVILLE  Yet with cunning and malice enough to make himself merry with all our embarrassments.

HASTINGS  An insensible cub.

MARLOW  Replete with tricks and mischief.  380

TONY  Baw! Damme, but I'll fight you both one after the other—with baskets.°

MARLOW  As for him, he's below resentment. But your conduct, Mr Hastings, requires an explanation. You knew of my mistakes, yet would not undeceive me.  385

HASTINGS  Tortured as I am with my own disappointments, is this a time for explanations? It is not friendly, Mr Marlow.

MARLOW  But, sir—

MISS NEVILLE  Mr Marlow, we never kept on your mistake, till it was          390
   too late to undeceive you. Be pacified.
   *Enter Servant*
SERVANT  My mistress desires you'll get ready immediately, madam.
   The horses are putting to.° Your hat and things are in the next
   room. We are to go thirty miles before morning.
MISS NEVILLE  Well, well, I'll come presently.
   [*Exit Servant*]°
MARLOW (*to Hastings*)  Was it well done, sir, to assist in rendering me    395
   ridiculous? To hang me out for the scorn of all my acquaintance.
   Depend upon it, sir, I shall expect an explanation.
HASTINGS  Was it well done, sir, if you're upon that subject, to deliver
   what I entrusted to yourself, to the care of another, sir?
MISS NEVILLE  Mr Hastings. Mr Marlow. Why will you increase my           400
   distress by this groundless dispute? I implore, I entreat you.
   *Enter Servant*
FIRST SERVANT  Your cloak, madam. My mistress is impatient.
MISS NEVILLE  I come.
   [*Exit Servant*]°
Pray be pacified. If I leave you thus, I shall die with apprehension.
   *Enter Servant*
SECOND SERVANT  Your fan, muff, and gloves, madam. The horses are       405
   waiting.
MISS NEVILLE  O, Mr Marlow! If you knew what a scene of constraint
   and ill-nature lies before me, I'm sure it would convert your
   resentment into pity.
MARLOW  I'm so distracted with a variety of passions, that I don't         410
   know what I do. Forgive me, madam. George, forgive me. You
   know my hasty temper, and should not exasperate it.
HASTINGS  The torture of my situation is my only excuse.
MISS NEVILLE  Well, my dear Hastings, if you have that esteem for me
   that I think, that I am sure, you have, your constancy for three        415
   years° will but increase the happiness of our future connection.
   If—
MRS HARDCASTLE (*within*)  Miss Neville. Constance, why Constance,
   I say.
MISS NEVILLE  I'm coming. Well, constancy. Remember, constancy is      420
   the word.
   *Exit Miss Neville* [*with Servant*]°
HASTINGS  My heart! How can I support this? To be so near
   happiness, and such happiness.

MARLOW (*to Tony*)  You see now, young gentleman, the effects of your
    folly. What might be amusement to you, is here disappointment,    425
    and even distress.

TONY (*from a reverie*)  Ecod, I have hit it. It's here. Your hands. Yours
    and yours, my poor Sulky. My boots there, ho. [*To Hastings*] Meet
    me two hours hence at the bottom of the garden,° and if you don't
    find Tony Lumpkin a more good-natured fellow than you thought    430
    for, I'll give you leave to take my best horse, and Bet Bouncer into
    the bargain. Come along. My boots, ho !
        *Exeunt Tony, Marlow, and Hastings*

        END OF THE FOURTH ACT

# 5.1

*Scene continues*

*Enter Hastings and Servant*

HASTINGS  You saw the old lady and Miss Neville drive off, you say.

SERVANT  Yes, your honour. They went off in a post coach,° and the young 'Squire went on horseback. They're thirty miles off by this time. 5

HASTINGS  Then all my hopes are over.

SERVANT  Yes, sir. Old Sir Charles is arrived. He and the old gentleman of the house have been laughing at Mr Marlow's mistake this half hour. They are coming this way.

HASTINGS  Then I must not be seen. So now to my fruitless appoint- 10 ment at the bottom of the garden. This is about the time.

*Exeunt Hastings and Servant. Enter Sir Charles and Hardcastle*

HARDCASTLE  Ha, ha, ha! The peremptory tone in which he sent forth his sublime commands.

SIR CHARLES  And the reserve with which I suppose he treated all your advances. 15

HARDCASTLE  And yet he might have seen something in me above a common innkeeper, too.

SIR CHARLES  Yes, Dick, but he mistook you for an uncommon innkeeper, ha, ha, ha.

HARDCASTLE  Well, I'm in too good spirits to think of anything but 20 joy. Yes, my dear friend, this union of our families will make our personal friendships hereditary, and though my daughter's fortune is but small—

SIR CHARLES  Why, Dick, will you talk of fortune to *me*. My son is possessed of more than a competence already, and can want nothing 25 but a good and virtuous girl to share his happiness and increase it. If they like each other, as you say they do—

HARDCASTLE  *If*, man. I tell you they *do* like each other. My daughter as good as told me so.

SIR CHARLES  But girls are apt to flatter themselves, you know. 30

HARDCASTLE  I saw him grasp her hand in the warmest manner myself. And here he comes to put you out of your *ifs*, I warrant him.

*Enter Marlow*

MARLOW I come, sir, once more, to ask pardon for my strange conduct. I can scarce reflect on my insolence without confusion.    35

HARDCASTLE Tut, boy, a trifle. You take it too gravely. An hour or
two's laughing° with my daughter will set all to rights again. She'll
never like you the worse for it.

MARLOW Sir, I shall be always proud of her approbation.

HARDCASTLE Approbation is but a cold word, Mr Marlow. If I am    40
not deceived, you have something more than approbation there-
abouts. You take me.

MARLOW Really, sir, I have not that happiness.

HARDCASTLE Come, boy, I'm an old fellow, and know what's what,
as well as you that are younger. I know what has passed between    45
you. But mum.

MARLOW Sure, sir, nothing has past between us but the most profound respect on my side, and the most distant reserve on hers. You
don't think, sir, that my impudence has been passed upon all the
rest of the family.    50

HARDCASTLE Impudence! No, I don't say that—Not quite impudence—Though girls like to be played with, and rumpled a little
too sometimes. But she has told no tales, I assure you.

MARLOW I never gave her the slightest cause.

HARDCASTLE Well, well, I like modesty in its place well enough. But    55
this is over-acting, young gentleman. You *may* be open. Your father
and I will like you the better for it.

MARLOW May I die, sir, if I ever—

HARDCASTLE I tell you, she don't dislike you; and as I'm sure you like
her—    60

MARLOW Dear sir—I protest, sir—

HARDCASTLE I see no reason why you should not be joined as fast as
the parson can tie you.

MARLOW But hear me, sir—

HARDCASTLE Your father approves the match. I admire it. Every    65
moment's delay will be doing mischief, so—

MARLOW But why won't you hear me? By all that's just and true, I
never gave Miss Hardcastle the slightest mark of my attachment, or
even the most distant hint to suspect me of affection. We had but
one interview, and that was formal, modest and uninteresting.    70

HARDCASTLE (*aside*) This fellow's formal modest impudence is
beyond bearing.

SIR CHARLES And you never grasped her hand, or made any
protestations!

MARLOW As heaven is my witness, I came down in obedience to your 75
commands. I saw the lady without emotion, and parted without
reluctance. I hope you'll exact no further proofs of my duty,
nor prevent me from leaving a house in which I suffer so many
mortifications.

*Exit Marlow*

SIR CHARLES I'm astonished at the air of sincerity with which he 80
parted.

HARDCASTLE And I'm astonished at the deliberate intrepidity of his
assurance.

SIR CHARLES I dare pledge my life and honour upon his truth.

HARDCASTLE Here comes my daughter, and I would stake my 85
happiness upon her veracity.

*Enter Miss Hardcastle*

HARDCASTLE Kate, come hither, child. Answer us sincerely, and
without reserve. Has Mr Marlow made you any professions of love
and affection?

MISS HARDCASTLE The question is very abrupt, sir! But since you 90
require unreserved sincerity, I think he has.

HARDCASTLE (*to Sir Charles*) You see.

SIR CHARLES And pray, madam, have you and my son had more than
one interview?

MISS HARDCASTLE Yes, sir, several. 95

HARDCASTLE (*to Sir Charles*) You see.

SIR CHARLES But did he profess any attachment?

MISS HARDCASTLE A lasting one.

SIR CHARLES Did he talk of love?

MISS HARDCASTLE Much, sir. 100

SIR CHARLES Amazing! And all this formally?

MISS HARDCASTLE Formally.

HARDCASTLE Now, my friend, I hope you are satisfied.

SIR CHARLES And how did he behave, madam?

MISS HARDCASTLE As most professed admirers do. Said some civil 105
things of my face, talked much of his want of merit, and the greatness of mine, mentioned his heart, gave a short tragedy speech, and
ended with pretended rapture.

SIR CHARLES Now I'm perfectly convinced, indeed. I know his
conversation among women to be modest and submissive. This 110
forward canting° ranting manner by no means describes him, and
I am confident, he never sat for the picture.°

MISS HARDCASTLE Then what, sir, if I should convince you to your face of my sincerity? If you and my papa, in about half an hour, will place yourselves behind that screen, you shall hear him declare his passion to me in person. 115

SIR CHARLES Agreed. And if I find him what you describe, all my happiness in him must have an end.

*Exit Sir Charles*

MISS HARDCASTLE And if you don't find him what I describe—I fear my happiness must never have a beginning. 120

*Exeunt Hardcastle and Miss Hardcastle*

## 5.2

*Scene changes to the back of the garden.*

*Enter Hastings*

HASTINGS What an idiot am I, to wait here for a fellow, who probably takes a delight in mortifying me. He never intended to be punctual, and I'll wait no longer. What do I see? It is he, and perhaps with news of my Constance.

*Enter Tony, booted and spattered*

My honest 'Squire! I now find you a man of your word. This looks like friendship. 5

TONY Ay, I'm your friend, and the best friend you have in the world, if you knew but all. This riding by night, by the bye, is cursedly tiresome. It has shook me worse than the basket of a stage-coach.°

HASTINGS But how? Where did you leave your fellow travellers? Are they in safety? Are they housed? 10

TONY Five and twenty miles in two hours and a half is no such bad driving. The poor beasts have smoked for it. Rabbit me, but I'd rather ride forty miles after a fox, than ten with such *varment*.°

HASTINGS Well, but where have you left the ladies? I die with impatience. 15

TONY Left them. Why where should I leave them, but where I found them.

HASTINGS This is a riddle.

TONY Riddle me this then. What's that goes round the house, and round the house, and never touches the house? 20

HASTINGS I'm still astray.

TONY  Why that's it, mon. I have led them astray. By jingo, there's not
a pond or slough° within five miles of the place but they can tell the
taste of.                                                                    25

HASTINGS  Ha, ha, ha, I understand. You took them in a round, while
they supposed themselves going forward. And so you have at last
brought them home again.

TONY  You shall hear. I first took them down Feather Bed Lane,
where we stuck fast in the mud. I then rattled them crack over          30
the stones of Up-and-Down Hill. I then introduced them to
the gibbet on Heavy Tree Heath, and from that, with a circumbendibus, I fairly lodged them in the horse-pond at the bottom of
the garden.

HASTINGS  But no accident, I hope.                                            35

TONY  No, no. Only mother is confoundedly frightened. She thinks
herself forty miles off. She's sick of the journey, and the cattle°
can scarce crawl. So if your own horses be ready, you may whip off
with cousin, and I'll be bound that no soul here can budge a foot to
follow you.                                                                   40

HASTINGS  My dear friend, how can I be grateful?

TONY  Ay, now it's dear friend, noble 'Squire. Just now, it was all idiot,
cub, and run me through the guts. Damn *your* way of fighting, I say.
After we take a knock in this part of the country, we kiss and be
friends. But if you had run me through the guts, then I should be     45
dead, and you might go kiss the hangman.

HASTINGS  The rebuke is just. But I must hasten to relieve Miss
Neville. If you keep the old lady employed, I promise to take care of
the young one.

TONY  Never fear me. Here she comes. Vanish. [*Exit Hastings*] She's    50
got from the pond, and draggled up to the waist like a mermaid.
        *Enter Mrs Hardcastle*

MRS HARDCASTLE  Oh, Tony, I'm killed. Shook. Battered to death. I
shall never survive it. That last jolt that laid us against the quickset
hedge° has done my business.

TONY  Alack, mama, it was all your own fault. You would be for          55
running away by night, without knowing one inch of the way.

MRS HARDCASTLE  I wish we were at home again. I never met so
many accidents in so short a journey. Drenched in the mud, over-
turned in a ditch, stuck fast in a slough, jolted to a jelly, and at last
to lose our way. Whereabouts do you think we are, Tony?                 60

TONY  By my guess we should be upon Crackskull Common, about
forty miles from home.

MRS HARDCASTLE O lud! O lud! The most notorious spot in all the country. We only want a robbery to make a complete night on't.

TONY Don't be afraid, mama, don't be afraid. Two of the five that kept here° are hanged, and the other three may not find us. Don't be afraid. Is that a man that's galloping behind us? No, it's only a tree. Don't be afraid.

MRS HARDCASTLE The fright will certainly kill me.

TONY Do you see anything like a black hat moving behind the thicket?

MRS HARDCASTLE O death!

TONY No, it's only a cow. Don't be afraid, mama. Don't be afraid.

MRS HARDCASTLE As I'm alive, Tony, I see a man coming towards us. Ah! I'm sure on't. If he perceives us we are undone.

TONY (aside) Father-in-law,° by all that's unlucky, come to take one of his night walks. (To her) Ah, it's a highwayman, with pistols as long as my arm. A damned ill-looking fellow.

MRS HARDCASTLE Good heaven defend us! He approaches.

TONY Do you hide yourself in that thicket, and leave me to manage him. If there be any danger I'll cough and cry hem.° When I cough be sure to keep close.°

> Mrs Hardcastle hides behind a tree in the back scene.° Enter Hardcastle.°

HARDCASTLE I'm mistaken, or I heard voices of people in want of help. Oh, Tony, is that you. I did not expect you so soon back. Are your mother and her charge in safety?

TONY Very safe, sir, at my aunt Pedigree's. Hem.

MRS HARDCASTLE (from behind) Ah death! I find there's danger.

HARDCASTLE Forty miles in three hours. Sure, that's too much, my youngster.

TONY Stout horses and willing minds make short journeys, as they say. Hem.

MRS HARDCASTLE (from behind) Sure he'll do the dear boy no harm.

HARDCASTLE But I heard a voice here. I should be glad to know from whence it came?

TONY It was I, sir, talking to myself, sir. I was saying that forty miles in four hours was very good going. Hem. As to be sure it was. Hem. I have got a sort of cold by being out in the air. We'll go in, if you please. Hem.

HARDCASTLE But if you talked to yourself, you did not answer yourself. I am certain I heard two voices, and am resolved (raising his voice) to find the other out.

MRS HARDCASTLE (from behind) Oh, he's coming to find me out! Oh!

TONY  What need you go, sir, if I tell you. Hem. I'll lay down my life for the truth.° Hem. I'll tell you all, sir. (*Detaining him*)

HARDCASTLE  I tell you, I will not be detained. I insist on seeing. It's in vain to expect I'll believe you.                                          105

MRS HARDCASTLE (*running forward from behind*) O lud, he'll murder my poor boy, my darling. Here, good gentleman, whet your rage upon me. Take my money, my life, but spare that young gentleman. Spare my child, if you have any mercy.

HARDCASTLE  My wife! As I'm a Christian. From whence can she    110
come, or what does she mean?

MRS HARDCASTLE (*kneeling*) Take compassion on us, good Mr Highwayman. Take our money, our watches, all we have, but spare our lives. We will never bring you to justice, indeed we won't, good Mr Highwayman.                                                 115

HARDCASTLE  I believe the woman's out of her senses. What, Dorothy, don't you know *me*?

MRS HARDCASTLE  Mr Hardcastle, as I'm alive! My fears blinded me. But who, my dear, could have expected to meet you here, in this frightful place, so far from home? What has brought you to follow   120
us?

HARDCASTLE  Sure, Dorothy, you have not lost your wits. So far from home, when you are within forty yards of your own door. (*To him*) This is one of your old tricks, you graceless rogue, you. (*To her*) Don't you know the gate, and the mulberry-tree. And don't you   125
remember the horsepond, my dear?

MRS HARDCASTLE  Yes, I shall remember the horsepond as long as I live. I have caught my death in it. (*To Tony*) And is it to you, you graceless varlet, I owe all this. I'll teach you to abuse your mother, I will.                                                       130

TONY  Ecod, mother, all the parish says you have spoiled me, and so you may take the fruits on't.

MRS HARDCASTLE  I'll spoil you, I will.

*Exeunt Mrs Hardcastle and Tony, she driving him off the stage*

HARDCASTLE  There's morality, however, in his reply.

*Exit Hardcastle. Enter Hastings and Miss Neville*

HASTINGS  My dear Constance, why will you deliberate thus? If we   135
delay a moment, all is lost forever. Pluck up a little resolution, and we shall soon be out of the reach of her malignity.

MISS NEVILLE  I find it impossible. My spirits are so sunk with the agitations I have suffered, that I am unable to face any new danger. Two or three years' patience will at last crown us with happiness.   140

HASTINGS Such a tedious delay is worse than inconstancy. Let us fly, my charmer. Let us date our happiness from this very moment. Perish fortune. Love and content will increase what we possess beyond a monarch's revenue. Let me prevail.

MISS NEVILLE No, Mr Hastings. No. Prudence once more comes to 145
my relief, and I will obey its dictates. In the moment of passion, fortune may be despised, but it ever produces a lasting repentance. I'm resolved to apply to Mr Hardcastle's compassion and justice for redress.

HASTINGS But though he had the will, he has not the power to relieve 150
you.

MISS NEVILLE But he has influence, and upon that I am resolved to rely.

HASTINGS I have no hopes. But since you persist, I must reluctantly obey you. 155

*Exeunt Hastings and Miss Neville*


# 5.3

*Scene changes [to Hardcastle's house].*

*Enter Sir Charles and Miss Hardcastle*

SIR CHARLES What a situation am I in? If what you say appears, I shall then find a guilty son. If what he says be true, I shall then lose one that, of all others, I most wished for a daughter.

MISS HARDCASTLE I am proud of your approbation, and to show I merit it, if you place yourselves as I directed, you shall hear his 5
explicit declaration. But he comes.

SIR CHARLES I'll to your father, and keep him to the appointment.

*Exit Sir Charles. Enter Marlow*

MARLOW Though prepared for setting out, I come once more to take leave, nor did I, till this moment, know the pain I feel in the separation. 10

MISS HARDCASTLE (*in her own natural manner*) I believe these sufferings cannot be very great, sir, which you can so easily remove. A day or two longer, perhaps, might lessen your uneasiness, by showing the little value of what you now think proper to regret.

MARLOW (*aside*) This girl every moment improves upon me. (*To her*) 15
It must not be, madam. I have already trifled too long with my heart. My very pride begins to submit to my passion. The disparity

of education and fortune, the anger of a parent, and the contempt
of my equals, begin to lose their weight; and nothing can restore me
to myself, but this painful effort of resolution.                          20

MISS HARDCASTLE  Then go, sir. I'll urge nothing more to detain you.
Though my family be as good as hers you came down to visit,
and my education, I hope, not inferior, what are these advantages
without equal affluence? I must remain contented with the slight
approbation of imputed merit.° I must have only the mockery of      25
your addresses, while all your serious aims are fixed on fortune.

    *Enter Hardcastle and Sir Charles from behind*°

SIR CHARLES  Here, behind this screen.

HARDCASTLE  Ay, ay, make no noise. I'll engage my Kate covers him
with confusion at last.

MARLOW  By heavens, madam, fortune was ever my smallest con-        30
sideration. Your beauty at first caught my eye, for who could see
that without emotion. But every moment that I converse with
you, steals in some new grace, heightens the picture, and gives it
stronger expression. What at first seemed rustic plainness, now
appears refined simplicity.° What seemed forward assurance, now   35
strikes me as the result of courageous innocence, and conscious
virtue.

SIR CHARLES  What can it mean? He amazes me!

HARDCASTLE  I told you how it would be. Hush!

MARLOW  I am now determined to stay, madam, and I have too good    40
an opinion of my father's discernment, when he sees you, to doubt
his approbation.

MISS HARDCASTLE  No, Mr Marlow, I will not, cannot detain you. Do
you think I could suffer a connection, in which there is the smallest
room for repentance? Do you think I would take the mean           45
advantage of a transient passion, to load you with confusion? Do
you think I could ever relish that happiness, which was acquired by
lessening yours?

MARLOW  By all that's good, I can have no happiness but what's in
your power to grant me. Nor shall I ever feel repentance, but in not  50
having seen your merits before. I will stay, even contrary to your
wishes, and though you should persist to shun me, I will make my
respectful assiduities atone for the levity of my past conduct.

MISS HARDCASTLE  Sir, I must entreat you'll desist. As our acquaintance began, so let it end, in indifference. I might have given an hour  55
or two to levity, but, seriously, Mr Marlow, do you think I could
ever submit to a connection, where *I* must appear mercenary, and

*you* imprudent? Do you think I could ever catch at° the confident addresses of a secure admirer?

MARLOW (*kneeling*) Does this look like security? Does this look like 60 confidence? No, madam, every moment that shows me your merit only serves to increase my diffidence and confusion. Here let me continue—

SIR CHARLES [*coming forward*] I can hold it no longer. Charles, Charles, how hast thou deceived me! Is this your indifference, your 65 uninteresting° conversation!

HARDCASTLE Your cold contempt; your formal interview. What have you to say now?

MARLOW That I'm all amazement! What can it mean!

HARDCASTLE It means that you can say and unsay things at pleasure. 70 That you can address a lady in private, and deny it in public. That you have one story for us, and another for my daughter.

MARLOW Daughter! This lady your daughter!

HARDCASTLE Yes, sir, my only daughter. My Kate, whose else should she be? 75

MARLOW Oh, the devil.

MISS HARDCASTLE Yes, sir, that very identical tall squinting lady you were pleased to take me for. (*Curtsying*) She that you addressed as the mild, modest, sentimental man of gravity,° and the bold forward agreeable rattle of the ladies club, ha, ha, ha! 80

MARLOW Zounds, there's no bearing this. It's worse than death.

MISS HARDCASTLE In which of your characters, sir, will you give us leave to address you? As the faltering gentleman, with looks on the ground, that speaks just to be heard, and hates hypocrisy, or the loud confident creature, that keeps it up with Mrs Mantrap, and 85 old Miss Biddy Buckskin, till three in the morning, ha, ha, ha!

MARLOW O, curse on my noisy head. I never attempted to be impudent yet, that I was not taken down. I must be gone.

HARDCASTLE By the hand of my body, but you shall not. I see it was all a mistake, and I am rejoiced to find it. You shall not, sir, I tell 90 you. I know she'll forgive you. Won't you forgive him, Kate? We'll all forgive you. Take courage, man. (*They retire, she tormenting him to the back scene*)

    *Enter Mrs Hardcastle and Tony*

MRS HARDCASTLE So, so, they're gone off. Let them go, I care not.

HARDCASTLE Who gone?

MRS HARDCASTLE My dutiful niece and her gentleman, Mr Hastings, 95 from town. He who came down with our modest visitor here.

SIR CHARLES  Who, my honest George Hastings? As worthy a fellow
as lives, and the girl could not have made a more prudent
choice.

HARDCASTLE  Then, by the hand of my body, I'm proud of the    100
connection.

MRS HARDCASTLE  Well, if he has taken away the lady, he has not
taken her fortune. That remains in this family to console us for her
loss.

HARDCASTLE  Sure, Dorothy, you would not be so mercenary?    105

MRS HARDCASTLE  Ay, that's my affair, not yours.

HARDCASTLE°  But you know if your son, when of age,° refuses to
marry his cousin, her whole fortune is then at her own disposal.

MRS HARDCASTLE°  Ay, but he's not of age, and she has not thought
proper to wait for his refusal.    110

   *Enter Hastings and Miss Neville*

(*Aside*) What? Returned so soon? I begin not to like it.

HASTINGS (*to Hardcastle*)  For my late attempt to fly off with your
niece, let my present confusion be my punishment. We are now
come back, to appeal from your justice to your humanity. By her
father's consent, I first paid her my addresses, and our passions    115
were first founded in duty.

MISS NEVILLE  Since his death, I have been obliged to stoop to dissimulation to avoid oppression. In an hour of levity, I was ready
even to give up my fortune to secure my choice. But I'm now
recovered from the delusion, and hope from your tenderness what    120
is denied me from a nearer connection.

MRS HARDCASTLE  Pshaw, pshaw. This is all but the whining end of a
modern novel.°

HARDCASTLE  Be it what it will, I'm glad they're come back to reclaim
their due. Come hither, Tony boy. Do you refuse this lady's hand    125
whom I now offer you?

TONY  What signifies my refusing? You know I can't refuse her till I'm
of age, father.

HARDCASTLE  While I thought concealing your age, boy, was likely to
conduce to your improvement, I concurred with your mother's    130
desire to keep it secret. But since I find she turns it to a wrong use,
I must now declare, you have been of age these three months.

TONY  Of age! Am I of age, father?

HARDCASTLE  Above three months.

TONY  Then you'll see the first use I'll make of my liberty. (*Taking*    135
*Miss Neville's hand*) Witness all men by these presents, that I,

Anthony Lumpkin, Esquire, of *blank* place, refuse you, Constantia Neville, spinster, of no place at all, for my true and lawful wife. So Constance Neville may marry whom she pleases, and Tony Lumpkin is his own man again. 140

SIR CHARLES O brave 'Squire.

HASTINGS My worthy friend.

MRS HARDCASTLE My undutiful offspring.

MARLOW Joy, my dear George, I give you joy sincerely. And could I prevail upon my little tyrant here to be less arbitrary, I should be 145 the happiest man alive, if you would return me the favour.

HASTINGS (*to Miss Hardcastle*) Come, madam, you are now driven to the very last scene of all your contrivances. I know you like him, I'm sure he loves you, and you must and shall have him.

HARDCASTLE (*joining their hands*) And I say so too. And Mr Marlow, if 150 she makes as good a wife as she has a daughter, I don't believe you'll ever repent your bargain. So now to supper. Tomorrow we shall gather all the poor of the parish about us, and the Mistakes of the Night shall be crowned with a merry morning. So, boy take her, and, as you have been mistaken in the mistress, my wish is, that you 155 may never be mistaken in the wife.

## FINIS

# Epilogue

## By Dr. Goldsmith°

Well, having stooped to conquer with success,
And gained a husband without aid from dress,
Still as a barmaid, I could wish it too,
As I have conquered him to conquer you:
And let me say, for all your resolution,                           5
That pretty barmaids have done execution.°
Our life is all a play, composed to please,
'We have our exits and our entrances.'°
The first act shows the simple country maid,
Harmless and young, of ev'ry thing afraid;                        10
Blushes when hired, and with unmeaning action,
I hopes as how to give you satisfaction.
Her second act displays a livelier scene,—
Th' unblushing barmaid of a country inn.
Who whisks about the house, at market caters,°                    15
Talks loud, coquets the guests, and scolds the waiters.°
Next the scene shifts to town, and there she soars,
The chop house toast of ogling connoisseurs.°
On 'Squires and Cits she there displays her arts,°
And on the gridiron broils her lover's hearts—                    20
And as she smiles, her triumphs to complete,
Even Common Councilmen forget to eat.°
The fourth act shows her wedded to the 'Squire,
And madam now begins to hold it higher;
Pretends to taste, at Operas cries caro,°                         25
And quits her Nancy Dawson, for Che Faro.°
Dotes upon dancing, and in all her pride,
Swims round the room, the Heinel of Cheapside:°
Ogles and leers with artificial skill,
Till having lost in age the power to kill,                        30
She sits all night at cards, and ogles at spadille,
Such, through our lives, the eventful history—
The fifth and last act still remains for me.
The barmaid now for your protection prays,
Turns Female Barrister, and pleads for Bayes.°                    35

# Epilogue

To be Spoken in the Character of Tony Lumpkin.
By J. Craddock, Esq.

Well—now all's ended—and my comrades gone,
Pray what becomes of mother's nonly son?°
A hopeful blade!—in town I'll fix my station,°
And try to make a bluster in the nation.
As for my cousin Neville, I renounce her,                    5
Off—in a crack—I'll carry big Bet Bouncer.

Why should not I in the great world appear?
I soon shall have a thousand pounds a year;
No matter what a man may here inherit,
In London—'gad, they've some regard to spirit.             10
I see the horses prancing up the streets,
And big Bet Bouncer, bobs to all she meets;
Then hoikes to jigs and pastimes ev'ry night—°
Not to the plays—they say it ain't polite,
To Sadler's-Wells perhaps, or Operas go,°                  15
And once by chance, to the roratorio.°
Thus here and there, for ever up and down,
We'll set the fashions too, to half the town;
And then at auctions—money ne'er regard,
Buy pictures like the great, ten pounds a yard;            20
Zounds, we shall make these London gentry say,
We know what's damned genteel, as well as they.

 * *This came too late to be spoken*°

# THE COMEDY OF WILD OATS

## or,

## The Strolling Gentlemen

BY

## JOHN O'KEEFFE

# THE CHARACTERS OF THE PLAY

### MEN

| | |
|---|---|
| Sir George Thunder | Mr Quick |
| Rover | Mr Lewis |
| Harry | Mr Holman |
| John Dory | Mr Wilson |
| Banks | Mr Hill |
| Gammon | Mr Cubit |
| Ephraim Smooth | Mr Munden |
| Sim | Mr Blanchard |
| Twitch | Mr Rock |
| Lamp | Mr C. Powell |
| Trap | Mr Evatt |
| Zachariah | Mr Rees |
| Three Ruffians | Messrs Farley, Thompson, and Milbourne |
| Landlord | Mr Powel |

### WOMEN

| | |
|---|---|
| Lady Amaranth | Mrs Pope |
| Amelia | Miss Chapman |
| Jane | Mrs Wells |

# Prologue

Written by John Taylor, Esq.,
and spoken by Mr Holman

What can we now invite you to partake,
When realms have been exhausted for your sake,
And ample Nature travers'd o'er and o'er,
'Till all her beaten haunts will yield no more?
From climes where Phoebus pours his brightest ray          5
To where scarce faintly gleams the twilight day,
The dauntless Bard has urg'd his venturous aim,
To greet you still with fresh Dramatic game.
One noble Hunter, of the Thespian train,
Rush'd from his Avon's side o'er earth's domain,          10
And brought with happy Magic, more than toil,
The motley tribes of ev'ry varying foil;°
While his quick eye so widely could explore
That Time himself, shall ne'er discover more:
Nay, in the track of his sublime career,                 15
We pass the bounds of Nature's humble sphere;
And zealous after all our search has found,
Through radiant wilds of Fancy's fairy ground;°
Once more the arduous chase we dare pursue,
And fondly hope we've started something new.             20
    Our Hero, for so far we may discover,
Is a young Actor, and of course a lover!
But, what, perhaps, will raise no slight surprize!
Though used to various shapes, above disguise.
Fictitious language, of a borrow'd part,                 25
Sports from his tongue, indeed, but not his heart!
For Nature's warm and absolute control
Guides ev'ry impulse of his generous soul.°
Sure such a part your favour must engage,
And though a stranger on the mimic stage,                30
Yet may the Scenic band, with honest pride!
Howe'er, by formal Prejudice decry'd,
Boast as fair patterns of domestic worth,
As that our present Drama pictures forth!

Let then the Bard, who vindicates our cause,       35
Obtain the sanction of your warm applause!
So may we prove, in spite of prudish Spleen!
Actors can feel beyond the passing scene;
And long, too harshly deem'd a thoughtless kind,
Live to the friendly model he design'd.       40

# 1.1

*SCENE.—A Parlour in Lady Aramanth's.*

*Enter John Dory*

JOHN DORY  Fine cruizing° this! Without flip or biscuit! Don't know
who's the governor of this here fort, but if he can victual us a few—
how hollow my bread-room sounds! (*Striking his sides*) I'm as empty
as a stoved keg,° and as tired as an old Dutchman°—my obstinate
master, Sir George, to tow my old hulk—aboard the house. Ha,    5
hoy!

SIR GEORGE (*without*)  John! John Dory!

JOHN DORY (*sits*)  I'm at anchor.

*Enter Sir George Thunder*

SIR GEORGE  I don't know whose house we've got into here, John, but
I think, when he knows me, we may hope for some refreshment.    10
Eh! (*Looking at John Dory*) Was not I not your captain?

JOHN DORY  Yes, and I was your boatswain. And what of all that?

SIR GEORGE  Then how dare you sit in my presence, you bluff head?°

JOHN DORY  Why, for the matter of that I don't mind, but had I been
your captain, and you my boatswain, the man that stood by me at    15
sea, should be welcome to sit before me at land. (*Rising*)

SIR GEORGE  That's true, my dear John. Offer to stand up, and,
damme, if I don't knock you down. Zounds, I'm as dry as a powder
match, and to sail at the rate of ten knots an hour, over fallow and
stubble° from my own house, but half a league on this side of    20
Gosport,° and not catch these deserters!

JOHN DORY  In this here chase, you wanted the ballast° of wisdom.

SIR GEORGE  How sirrah! Hasn't my dear old friend, Dick Broadside,
got the command of the ship I so often fought myself.° To man it
for him with expedition, didn't I out of my own pocket offer two    25
guineas over the King's bounty° to every seaman that would enter
on board her? Haven't these three scoundrels fingered the shot,°
then ran, and didn't I do right to run after them? Damn the money!
I no more mind that than a piece of clinker,° but 'twas the pride of
my heart to see my beloved ship (the Eagle) well-manned, when my    30
old friend is the commander.

JOHN DORY  But since you've laid yourself up in ordinary,° retired to
live in quiet, on your own estate, and had done with all sea affairs—

SIR GEORGE  John, John, a man should forget his own convenience for

his country's good. Though Broadside's letter said these fellows    35
were lurking about this part of Hampshire, yet still it's all hide and
seek.

JOHN DORY  Your ill luck.

SIR GEORGE  Mine, you swab?°

JOHN DORY  Ah, you've money and gold, but grace and good fortune    40
have shook hands with you these nineteen years, for that rogue's
trick you played poor Miss Amelia, by deceiving her with a sham
marriage, when you passed yourself for Captain Seymour, and then
putting off to sea, leaving her to break her poor heart, and since
marrying another lady.    45

SIR GEORGE  Wasn't I forced to it by my father?

JOHN DORY  Ay, because she had a great fortune. Her death too was a
judgement upon you.

SIR GEORGE  Why, you impudent dog-fish!° Upbraid me for running
into false bay,° when you were my pilot? Wasn't it you even brought    50
me the mock clergyman that performed the sham marriage with
Amelia?

JOHN DORY  (aside) Yes, you think so, but I took care to bring you a real
clergyman.

SIR GEORGE  But is this a time or place for your lecture? At home,    55
abroad, sea or land, you will still badger me! Mention my Wild
Oats again, and—you scoundrel, since the night my bed-curtains
took fire, aboard the Eagle, you've got me quite into leading-strings.
You snatched me upon deck, and tossed me into the sea to save me
from being burnt. I was almost drowned.    60

JOHN DORY  You would, but for me.

SIR GEORGE  Yes, you dragged me out by the ear, like a water-dog,°
and because applauded for that, ever since you're so cursed careful
of me, that only lifting my leg to step aboard a boat, you whip me
up, and chuck me into it. Last week, because you found the tenth    65
bottle uncorked, you rushed in among my friends, and ran away
with me, and, next morning, Captain O'Shanaghan sends me a
challenge, for slinking off when he was toastmaster. So, to save me
from a headache, you'd like to have got my brains blown out.

JOHN DORY  Oh, very well. Be burnt in your bed, and tumble in the    70
water by jumping into boats, like a tight fellow as you are, and
poison yourself with sloe juice.° See if John cares a piece of mouldy
biscuit about it, but I wish you hadn't made me your valet de
Shamber. No sooner was I got on shore, after five years dashing
among rocks, shoals, and breakers, then you sets me on a high-    75

trotting cart-horse, which knocked me up and down like an old
bomb-boat° in the Bay of Biscay. And here's nothing to drink after
all! Because at home you keep open house, you think every body
else does the same.

SIR GEORGE Why, by sailing into this strange port we may be more    80
free than welcome.

JOHN DORY Holloa! I'll never cease piping till it calls up a drop to wet
my whistle.

    *Exit John Dory*

SIR GEORGE Yes, as John Dory remarks, I fear my trip through life
will be attended with heavy squalls and foul weather. When my    85
conduct to poor Amelia comes athwart my mind, it's a hurricane
for that day, and, turn in at night, the ballad of 'William and
Margaret'° rings in my ear. (*Sings*) 'In glided Margaret's grimly
ghost'. Oh, zounds, the dismals° are coming upon me, and can't get
a cheering glass to—Holloa!    90

    *Enter Ephraim Smooth*

EPHRAIM Friend, what would'st thou have?

SIR GEORGE Grog.

EPHRAIM Neither man nor woman of that name abideth here.

SIR GEORGE Ha, ha, ha! Man and woman! Then if you'll bring me
Mr Brandy and Mrs Water, we'll couple them, and the first child    95
probably will be Master Grog.

EPHRAIM Thou dost speak in parables,° which I understand not.

SIR GEORGE Sheer off with your sanctified poop,° and send the
gentleman of the house.

EPHRAIM The owner of this mansion is a maiden and she    100
approacheth.

    *Enter Lady Amaranth*

LADY AMARANTH Friend, Ephraim Smooth, did'st thou—(*Turns,
sees Sir George*) Do I behold? It is! How dost thou, uncle?

SIR GEORGE Is it possible you can be my niece Lady Maria Amaranth
Thunder?    105

LADY AMARANTH I am the daughter of thy deceased brother, Loftus,
called Earl Thunder, but no Lady. My name is Mary.

SIR GEORGE But, how is all this? Eh, unexpectedly find you in a
strange house, of which old Sly here tells me you're mistress,
turned Quaker, and disclaim your title!    110

LADY AMARANTH Title is vanity.

SIR GEORGE Why certainly I drop my Lord by courtesy for my Sir
Knighthood acquired by my own merit, girl.

LADY AMARANTH  Thou knowest the relation to whose care my father left me?  115

SIR GEORGE  Well! I know our cousin, old Dovehouse, was a Quaker, but I didn't suspect he would have made you one.

LADY AMARANTH  Being now gathered to his fathers, he did bequeath unto me his worldly goods, among them this mansion, and the lands around it.  120

EPHRAIM  So thou becomest and continue one of the faithful. I am executor of his will, and, by it, cannot give thee, Mary, possession of these goods but on these conditions.

SIR GEORGE  Tell me of your thees and thous, Quaker's wills, and mansions! I say, girl, though on the death of your father, my eldest  125 brother, Loftus, Earl Thunder, from your being a female, his title devolved to his next brother, Robert, though as a woman, you can't be an Earl, nor as a woman you can't make laws for your sex and our sex, yet, as the daughter of a peer, you are, and, by heaven, shall be called Lady Maria Amaranth Thunder.  130

EPHRAIM  Thou makest too much noise, friend.

SIR GEORGE  Call me friend, and I'll bump your block against the capstan.

EPHRAIM  Yea, this is a man of danger, and I'll leave Mary to abide it.
*Exit Ephraim Smooth*

SIR GEORGE  S'fire, my Lady.  135
*Enter Zachariah*

ZACHARIAH.  Shall thy cook, this day, roast certain birds of the air, called woodcocks, and ribs of the oxen likewise?

LADY AMARANTH  All. My uncle sojourneth with me peradventure,° and my meal shall be a feast, friend Zachariah.

ZACHARIAH  My tongue shall say so, friend Mary.  140

SIR GEORGE  Sir George Thunder bids thee remember to call your mistress, Lady Amaranth. (*Strikes him*)

ZACHARIAH  Verily, George.

SIR GEORGE  George, sirrah! Though a younger brother, the honour of knighthood was my reward for placing the British flag over that  145 of a daring enemy. Therefore address me with respect.

ZACHARAIAH  Yea, I do, good George.
*Exit Zachariah*

SIR GEORGE  George and Mary! Here's levelling!° Here's abolition of title with a vengeance! In this house, they think no more of an English Knight, than a French Duke.°  150

LADY AMARANTH  Kinsman, be patient. Thou, and thy son, my

cousin Henry, whom I have not beheld, I think, these twelve years, shall be welcome to my dwelling. Where now abideth the youth?

SIR GEORGE  At the Naval Academy, at Portsmouth.

LADY AMARANTH  May I not see the young man?    155

SIR GEORGE  What, to make a Quaker of him? No, no. (*Aside*) But hold, as she's now a wealthy heiress, her marrying my son, Harry, will keep up and preserve her title in our own family too. Would'st thou really be glad to see him? Thou shalt, Mary. Ha, ha, ha! (*Calling*) John Dory!—Here comes my valet de chambre.    160
    *Enter John Dory*

JOHN DORY  Why, sir, such a breeze sprung up?

SIR GEORGE  Avast, old man of war! You must instantly convoy my son from Portsmouth.

JOHN DORY  Then I must first convoy him to Portsmouth, for he happens to be out of dock already.    165

SIR GEORGE  What wind now?

JOHN DORY  You know, on our quitting harbour—

SIR GEORGE  Damn your sea jaw, you marvellous dolphin, give the contents of your log-book° in plain English.

JOHN DORY  The young squire has cut and run.    170

SIR GEORGE  What!

JOHN DORY  Got leave to come to you, and master didn't find out before yesterday, that, instead of making for home, he had sheered off towards London, directly sent notice to you, and Sam has traced us all the way here to bring you the news.    175

SIR GEORGE  What, a boy of mine quits his guns? I'll grapple him. Come, John, come along.

LADY AMARANTH  Order the carriage for mine uncle.

SIR GEORGE  No, thank ye, my Lady. Let your equipage keep up your own dignity. I've horses here, but I won't knock 'em up.° Next    180 village is the channel for the stage.° My Lady, I'll bring the dog to you by the bowsprit. Weigh anchor! Crowd sail, and after him!
    *Exit Sir George and John Dory. Enter Ephraim Smooth*

EPHRAIM  The man of noise doth not tarry. Then my spirit is glad.

LADY AMARANTH  Let Sarah prepare chambers for my kinsman, and hire the maiden for me that thou didst mention.    185

EPHRAIM  I will, for this damsel is passing fair, and hath found grace in mine eyes. Mary, as thou art yet a stranger in this land, and have just taken possession of this estate, the laws of society command thee to be on terms of amity with thy wealthy neighbours.

LADY AMARANTH  Yea, but while I entertain the rich, the hearts of the    190 poor shall also rejoice. I myself will now go forth into the adjacent hamlet, and invite all to hearty cheer.

EPHRAIM  Yea. I will distribute among the poor, the good books thou didst desire me.

LADY AMARANTH  And meat and drink too, friend Ephraim. In the     195
fulness of plenty they shall join in thanksgiving for those gifts which I overabundantly possess.

*Exit Lady Amaranth and Ephraim Smooth*


# 1.2

*Scene—A road*

*Enter Harry and Muz*

MUZ  (*to Harry*)  I say, Dick Buskin! Harkee, my lad.

HARRY  what keeps Rover?

MUZ  I'm sure I don't know. As you desired, I paid for our breakfast. But the devil's in that fellow. Every inn we stop at he will always hang behind, chattering to the bar-maid or chamber-maid.     5

HARRY  Or any, or no maid. But he's a worthy lad, and I love him better, I think, than my own brother, had I one.

MUZ  Oh, but Dick, mind, my boy—

HARRY  Stop, Muz. Though 'twas my orders, when I set out on this scamper° with the players, (the better to conceal my quality) for     10
you, before people to treat me as your companion, yet, at the same time, you should have had discretion enough to remember, when we're alone, that I am still your master, and son to Sir George Thunder.

MUZ  Sir, I ask your pardon. But by making yourself my equal, I've got     15
so used to familiarity, that I find it hard to shake it off.

HARRY  Well, sir, pray mind that familiarity is all over now. My frolic's out. I now throw off the player, and shall directly return. My father must by this time have heard of my departure from the academy at Portsmouth, and, though I was deluded away by my rage for a little     20
acting, yet 'twas wrong of me to give the gay old fellow any cause for uneasiness.

MUZ  And, sir, shall you and I never act another scene together? Shall I never again play Colonel Standard for my own benefit? Never again have the pleasure of caning your honour in the character of Tom     25
Errand?°

HARRY In future, act the part of a smart hat and coat-brusher,° or I shall have the honour of kicking you in the character of an idle puppy. You were a good servant, but I find, by letting you crack your jokes and sit in my company, you're grown quite a lounging rascal. 30

MUZ Yes, sir, I was a modest well-behaved lad, but evil communication° corrupts good manners.

HARRY Begone, sir, 'till I call for you.

*Exit Muz*

Well, if my father but forgives me—This three months excursion 35 has shown me some life, and a devilish deal of fun. For one circumstance, I shall ever remember it with delight: it's bringing me acquainted with Jack Rover. How long he stays! (*Calls*) Jack! In this forlorn stroller I have discovered qualities that honour human nature, and accomplishments that might grace a prince. I don't 40 know a pleasanter fellow, except when he gets to his abominable habit of quotation.° I hope he won't find the purse I've hid in his coat-pocket before we part. I dread the moment, but it's come.

ROVER (*without*) 'The brisk li-li-lightning I'.°

HARRY Aye, here's the rattle. Hurried on by the impetuous flow of his 45 own volatile spirits, his life is a rapid stream of extravagant whim, and, while the serious voice of humanity prompts his heart to the best actions, his features shine in laugh and levity. Studying Bayes,° eh, Jack?

*Enter Rover*

ROVER 'I am the bold Thunder'.° 50

HARRY (*aside*) I am if he knew but all. Keep one standing in the road—

ROVER Beg your pardon, my dear Dick, but all the fault of—Plague on't, that a man can't sleep and breakfast at an inn, then return up to his bedchamber for his gloves that he'd forgot, but there 55 he must find chambermaids thumping feathers and knocking pillows about. And keep one, when one has affairs and business! 'Pon my soul these girls' conduct to us is intolerable. The very thought brings the blood into my face, and whenever they attempt to serve, provoke me so. Dam'me but I will, I will! Aren't I right 60 Dick?

HARRY 'No, all in the wrong'.°

ROVER No matter, that's the universal play 'all round the wreken'.° But you're so conceited because, by this company you're going to join at Winchester, you are engaged for high tragedy. 65

HARRY  And you for Rangers, Plumes, and Foppingtons.°

ROVER  Our first play is Lear. I was devilish imperfect in Edgar t'other
night at Lymington. I must look it over (*Takes out a book*) 'Away!
the foul fiend follows me!'°—Hollo! Stop a moment. We shall have
the whole county after us.                                                            70

HARRY  What now?

ROVER  That rosy-face[d] chambermaid put me in such a passion,
that, by heaven, I walked out of the house and forgot to pay our bill.

HARRY  Never mind, Rover. It's paid.

ROVER  Paid! Why, neither you nor Muz had money enough. No,          75
really!

HARRY  Ha, ha, ha! I tell you. It is.

ROVER  You paid? Oh, very well! Every honest fellow should be a stock
purse.° Come then, let's push on now. Ten miles to Winchester. We
shall be there by eleven.                                                            80

HARRY  Our trunks are booked at the inn for the Winchester coach.

ROVER  'Ay, to foreign climates my old trunk I bear'.° But I prefer
walking to the car of Thespis.°

HARRY  Which is the way?

ROVER  (*pointing off*)  Here.                                                        85

HARRY  (*pointing opposite*)  Then I go there.

ROVER  Eh?

HARRY  My dear boy, on this spot, and at this moment, we must part.

ROVER  Part!

HARRY  Rover, you wish me well.                                                       90

ROVER  Well, and suppose so. Part, eh? What mystery and grand?°
What are you at? Do you forget, you, Muz, and I are engaged to
Truncheon, the manager, and that the bills are already up with our
names tonight to play at Winchester?

HARRY  Jack, you and I have often met on a stage, in assumed char-         95
acters. If it's your wish we should ever meet again in our real ones,
of sincere friends, without asking whither I go, or my motives for
leaving you, when I walk up this road, do you turn down that.

ROVER  Joke!

HARRY  I'm serious. Goodbye.                                                         100

ROVER  If you repent your engagement with Truncheon, I'll break off
too, and go with you wherever you will. (*Takes him under the arm*)

HARRY  Attempt to follow me, and even our acquaintance ends.°

ROVER  Eh?

HARRY  Don't think of my reasons; only that it must be.                        105

ROVER Have I done anything to—Dick Buskin, leave me? (*Turns and puts his handkerchief to his eyes*)

HARRY I'm as much concerned as you. Goodbye.

ROVER I can't even bid him goodbye. I won't neither. If any cause could have given—Farewell.

HARRY Bless my poor fellow! Adieu. (*Silently weeps*)    110
    *Exeunt Rover and Harry, severally*

# 2.1

*A village; a farmhouse, and near it, a cottage.*

*Enter Farmer Gammon and Ephraim Smooth*

GAMMON Well, Master Ephraim, I may depend on thee, as you Quakers never breaks your words.

EPHRAIM I have spoken to Mary, and she, at my request, consenteth to take thy daughter, Jane, as her handmaid.

GAMMON Very good of you.                                                    5

EPHRAIM (*aside*) Goodness I do like, and also—comely Jane. The maiden, I will prefer for the sake of—myself.

GAMMON I intended to make a present to the person that did me such a piece of service, but I shan't affront you with it.

EPHRRAIM I am meek and humble, and must take affronts.          10

GAMMON Then here's a guinea, Master Ephraim.

EPHRAIM I expected not this, but there's no harm in a guinea.

*Exit Ephraim Smooth*

GAMMON So, I shall get my children off my hands. My son, Sim, robbing me day and night, giving away my corn and what not among the poor. My daughter, Jane, to prevent me from killing the  15
fowls, buys eggs, and tells me they are still laying them. Besides, when girls have nought to do, this love-mischief creeps into their heads (*Calling*) Sim!

*Enter Sim*

SIM Yes, feyther.

GAMMON Call your sister.                                                   20

SIM [*calls*] Jane, feyther wants you.

*Enter Jane, from the house*

JANE Did you call me?

GAMMON I often told you both, but it's now settled. You must go out into the world and work for your bread.

SIM Well, feyther, whatever you think right must be so, and I am  25
content.

JANE And I'm sure, feyther, I'm willing to do as you'd have me.

GAMMON There's ingratitude! When my wife died, I brought you both up from the shell,° and now, you want to fly off and forsake me.                                                                     30

SIM Why, no, I'm willing to live with you all my days.

JANE And I'm sure, feyther, if it's your desire, I'll never part from you.

GAMMON  What, you want to hang upon me like a couple of leeches, aye, to strip my branches, and leave me a withered hawthorn!° See who's yon.                                                                        35

    *Exit Sim*

Jane, Ephraim Smooth has hired you for Lady Amaranth.

JANE  O lack! Then I shall live in the great house.

GAMMON  Aye, and mayhap come in for her cast-off clothes.

JANE  But she's a Quaker, and I'm sure, every Sunday for church, I dress much finer than her ladyship.                                                      40

GAMMON  (*opens a book*) She has sent us all presents of good books, to read a chapter in, now and then. 'The Economy of Human Life'.° Ah, I like economy. Read that. When a man's in a passion, this may give him patience. There, Jane. (*Gives her the book*)

JANE  Thank her good ladyship.                                                              45

GAMMON  My being encumbered with you both is the cause why old Banks won't give me his sister.

JANE  That's a pity; if we must have a step-mother, madam Amelia would make us a very good one. But I wonder how she can refuse you, feyther, for I'm sure she must think you a very portly° man, in      50 your scarlet coat and new scratch.° You can't think how parsonable you'd look, if you'd only shave twice a week, and put sixpence in the poor-box on a Sunday. (*Retires reading*)

GAMMON  However, if Banks still refuses, I have him in my power. I'll turn them both out of their cottage yonder, and the bailiff shall      55 provide them with a lodging.

    *Enter Banks [from the cottage]*

Well, neighbour Banks, once for all, am I to marry your sister?

BANKS  That she best knows.

GAMMON  Aye, but she says she won't.

BANKS  Then I dare say she won't. For, though a woman, I never knew      60 her to speak what she didn't think.

GAMMON  Then she won't have me? A fine thing this, that you and she, who are little better than paupers, dare be so saucy!

BANKS  Why, farmer, I confess we are poor. But while that's the worst our enemies can say of us, we're content.                                             65

GAMMON  [*aside*] Od, dom it! I wish I had now a good, fair occasion to quarrel with him. I'd make him content with a devil. I'd knock 'en down, send him to a jail, and—But I'll be up with him!°

    *Enter Sim*

SIM  Oh, feyther, here's one Mr Lamp, a ringleader° of showfolks

come from Andover, to act in our village. He wants a barn to play    70
in, if you'll hire him yourn.

GAMMON Surely, boy, I'll never refuse money. But, lest he should
engage the great room in the inn, run thou and tell him—Stop, I'll
go myself. A short cut through that garden—

    *Going through the cottage garden, Banks stops him*

BANKS Why, you, or any neighbour is welcome to walk in it, or to    75
partake of what it produces, but making it a common thoroughfare
is—

GAMMON Here, Sim, kick open that gate.

BANKS What!

GAMMON Does the lad hear?    80

SIM Why, yes, yes.

GAMMON Does the fool understand?

SIM I'm as yet young, but if understanding teaches me how to wrong
my neighbour, may I never live to years of discretion.

GAMMON What, you cur, do you disobey your feyther? Burst open    85
the garden gate, as I command you.

SIM Feyther, he that made both you and the garden, commands me
not to injure the unfortunate.

GAMMON Here's an ungracious rogue! Then I must do it myself.
(*Advances*)

BANKS (*stands before it*) Hold, neighbour! Small as this spot is, it's    90
now my only possession, and the man shall first take my life, who
sets a foot in it against my will.

GAMMON I'm in such a passion.

JANE ([*coming*] *forward*) Feyther, if you're in a passion, read 'The
Economy of Human Life'. (*Offers book*)    95

GAMMON Plague of the wench! But, you hussy I'll,—and you, you
unlucky bird!

    *Exeunt Sim and Jane.*

    *A Shower of rain*

    *Enter Rover, hastily*

ROVER Here's a pelting shower, and no shelter! 'Poor Tom's a-cold'.°
I'm wet through. O, here's a fair promising house (*going to
Gammon's*).

GAMMON (*stops him*) Hold, my lad. Can't let folks in till I know who    100
they be. There's a public house° not above a mile on.

BANKS Step in here, young man. My fire is small, but it shall cheer
you with a hearty welcome.

ROVER (*to Banks*) The poor cottager! (*To Gammon*) And the substantial farmer! (*Kneels*) 'Hear nature, dear goddess, hear! If ever you   105
designed to make his cornfields fruitful, change thy purpose; that,
from the blighted ear no grain may fall to fat his stubble goose. And
when to town he drives his hogs, so like himself, oh, let him feel the
soaking rain. Then may he curse his crime too late, and know how
sharper than a serpent's tooth it is'.°—Damme, but I'm spouting in   110
the rain all this time.
       *Rises and runs into Banks's [cottage]*
GAMMON Ah, neighbour, you'll soon rise from a beggar's bed, if you
harbour every mad vagrant. This may be one of the footpads that,
it seems, have got about the country. But I'll have an execution and
seize on thy goods, this day, my charitable neighbour! Eh, the sun   115
strikes out, quite cleared up.
       *Enter Jane*
JANE La! Feyther if there isn't coming down the village—
GAMMON Ah, thou hussy!
JANE Bless me, feyther! No time for anger now. Here's Lady
Amaranth's chariot, drawn by her new grand, long-tailed horses!   120
La, it stops!
GAMMON Her ladyship is coming out and walks this way. She may
wish to rest herself in my house. Jane, we must always make rich
folks welcome.
JANE Dear me, I'll run in and set things to rights. But, feyther, your   125
cravat and wig are all got so rumplified° with your cross-grained
tantarums! I'll tie your neck-cloth in a big bow, and, for your wig, if
there is any flour in the drudging-box—
       *Adjusts them and runs into house. Enter Twitch*
TWITCH Well, master Gammon, as you desired, I am come to serve
this here warrant of yours, and arrest master Banks. Where   130
is he?
GAMMON Yes! Now I be's determined on't. He's—Stand aside, I'll
speak to you anon. (*Looking out*)
       *Enter Lady Amaranth, Zachariah following*
LADY AMARANTH Friend Jane, whom I have taken to be my hand-
maid, is thy daughter?   135
GAMMON Aye, so her mother said, an't please your ladyship.
LADY AMARANTH Ephraim Smooth acquainteth me thou art a
wealthy yeoman.
GAMMON Why, my lady, I pay my rent.
LADY AMARANTH Being yet a stranger on my estate around here, I   140

have passed through thy hamlet to behold, with mine own eyes, the distresses of my poor tenants. I wish to relieve their wants.

GAMMON Right, your ladyship, for charity hides a deal of sins.° How good of you to think of the poor! That's so like me. I'm always contriving how to relieve my neighbours. (*Aside to Twitch*) You must lay Banks in jail tonight. 145

*Enter Jane*

JANE A'nt please you, will your ladyship enter our humble dwelling and rest your ladyship in feyther's great cane-bottomed elbow chair with a high back? (*Curtsies*)

GAMMON Do my lady. To receive so great a body from her own chariot is an honour, I dreamt not of. Though, for the hungry and weary-foot traveller, my doors are always open, and my morsel ready. (*Aside to Twitch*) Knock. When he comes out, touch him.° 150

LADY AMARANTH Thou art benevolent, and I will enter thy dwelling with satisfaction. 155

JANE O, precious! This way, my lady.

*Exeunt Jane, Lady Amaranth, Zachariah and Gammon*
*[into Gammon's house]*

TWITCH Eh, where's the warrant? (*Feels his pocket, and knocks at Banks's door*)

*Enter Banks*

BANKS Master Twitch, what's your business with me?

TWITCH Only a little affair here against you.

BANKS Me! 160

TWITCH Yes! Farmer Gammon has bought up a thirty pound note of hand° of yours.

BANKS Indeed, I didn't think his malice could have stretched so far. I thought the love he professed for my sister might—Why it's true, master Twitch. To lend our indigent cottagers small sums, when they've been unable to pay their rents, I got lawyer Quirk to procure me this money, and hoped their industry would have put it in my power to take up my note before now. However, I'll go round and try what they can do, then call on you and settle it. 165

TWITCH No, no, you must go with me. 170

ROVER (*without*) Old gentleman come quick, or I'll open another bottle of your currant wine.

TWITCH (*to Banks*) You'd best not make a noise, but come.

*Enter Rover*

ROVER Oh, you're here? Rain over. Quite fine. I'll take a sniff of the open air, too. Eh! What's the matter? 175

TWITCH  What's that to you?

ROVER  What's that to me? Why you're very unmannerly—

TWITCH  Oh, here's a rescue!

BANKS  Nay, my dear sir, I'd wish you not to bring yourself into trouble about me.                                                    180

TWITCH  Now, since you don't know what's civil. If the debt's not paid directly, to jail you go.

ROVER  My kind, hospitable, good old man, to jail! What's the amount, you scoundrel?

TWITCH  Better words, or I'll—                                       185

ROVER  Stop! (*In a low tone*) Utter you a word, good or bad, except to tell me what's your demand upon this gentleman, and I'll give you the greatest beating you ever got since the hour you commenced rascal.

TWITCH  Why, master, I don't want to quarrel with you, because—     190

ROVER  You'll get nothing by it. Do you know, you villain, that I am this moment the greatest man living.

TWITCH  Who, pray?

ROVER  'I am the bold Thunder!'.° Sirrah, know that I carry my purse of gold in my coat-pocket, (*aside, and takes it out*) though damme   195
if I know how a purse came there. There's twenty pictures of his Majesty.° Therefore, in the King's name, I free his liege subject, (*takes Banks away*) and now who am I? Ah, ah!

TWITCH  Ten pieces short, my master. But if you're a housekeeper,° I'll take this and your bail.                                       200

ROVER  Then for bail you must have a housekeeper? What's to be done?
    *Enter Gammon*
Oh, here's little Hospitality! I know you've a house, though your fire-side was too warm for me. Lookye, here's some rapacious, griping rascal has had this worthy gentleman arrested. Now, a certain   205
good-for-nothing, rattling fellow has paid twenty guineas of the debt. You pass your word for the other nine, we'll step back into the old gentleman's friendly house, and over his currant wine, our first toast shall be, liberty to the honest debtor, and confusion to the hard-hearted creditor.                                              210

GAMMON  Shan't.

ROVER  Shan't? Pray, an't your name Mr Shylock?°

GAMMON  No, my name's Gammon.

ROVER  Gammon! You're the Hampshire hog.°
    *Exit Gammon*

'Sdeath! How shall I do to extricate—?                                    215
    *Enter Lady Amaranth, from Gammon's*
LADY AMARANTH What tumult's this?
ROVER A lady! (*Bows*) Ma'am, your most obedient humble servant.
    (*Aside*) A Quaker too! They are generally kind and humane, and
    that face is the prologue to a play of a thousand good acts. Maybe,
    she'd help us here.—Ma'am you must know that—that I—no—       220
    this gentleman—I mean this gentleman and I—He got a little
    behindhand, as any honest, well-principled, man often may, from
    bad harvests and rains, lodging corn, and his cattle from murrain
    and rot—and rot the murrain! (*To Banks*) You know this is the
    way all this affair happened, and then up steps this gentleman (*to*   225
    *Twitch*) with a—a tip° in his way—madam, you understand? And
    then in steps I—with my a—In short, madam, I am the worst
    story-teller in the world, when myself is the hero of the tale.
TWITCH In plain English, Mr Banks has been arrested for thirty
    pounds, and this gentleman has paid twenty guineas of the debt.      230
BANKS My litigious neighbour to expose me thus!
LADY AMARANTH The young man and maiden within have spoken
    well of thy sister, and pictured thee as a man of irreproachable
    morals, though unfortunate.
ROVER Madam, he's the honestest fellow. I've known him above forty    235
    years. He has the best hand at stirring a fire.° If you were only to
    taste his currant wine.
BANKS Madam, I never aspired to an enviable rank in life, but
    hitherto pride and prudence kept me above the reach of pity. But
    obligations from a stranger—                                         240
LADY AMARANTH He really a stranger, and attempt to free thee? But
    friend, (*to Rover*) thou hast assumed a right which here belongeth
    alone to me. As I enjoy the blessing which these lands produce,
    I own also the heart-delighting privilege of dispensing those
    blessings to the wretched. Thou mad'st thyself my worldly banker,    245
    and no cash of mine in thine hands, (*takes a note from a pocket-book*)
    but thus I balance our account. (*Offers it*)
ROVER 'Madam, my master pays me, nor can I take money from
    another hand without injuring his honour, or disobeying his
    commands'.°                                                          250
            'Run, run, Orlando, carve on ev'ry tree,
            The fair, the chaste, the inexpressive she'.°
        *Rover runs off*

BANKS (*to Twitch*)  But, sir, I insist you'll return him his money. Stop! (*Going*)

TWITCH  Aye, stop! (*Holds the skirt of Banks's coat*)

LADY AMARANTH  Where dwelleth he?                                                    255

BANKS  I fancy, where he can, madam. I understand, from his discourse, that he was on his way to join a company of actors in the next town.

LADY AMARANTH  A profane stage player° with such a gentle, generous heart, yet so whimsically wild, like the unconscious rose,    260 modestly shrinking from the recollection of its own grace and sweetness!

    *Enter Jane, from the house, dressed*

JANE  Now, my lady, I'm fit to attend your ladyship. [*Aside*] I look so genteelish mayhap her ladyship may take me home with her.

LADY AMARANTH (*aside*)  This maiden may find out for me whither    265 he goeth. (*To Twitch*) Call on my steward, and thy legal demands shall be satisfied.

    [*Exit Twitch*]

JANE (*calls off*)  Here, coachman, drive up my lady's chariot nearer to our door. (*Aside*) If she'd take me with her, la, how all the folks will stare. Madam, though the roads are so very dusty, I'll walk all the    270 way on foot to your ladyship's house, aye, though I should spoil my bran new° petticoat.

LADY AMARANTH  Rather than sully thy garment, thou shalt be seated by me.

JANE  Oh, your ladyship! (*Aside*) He, he, he! If I didn't think so—    275

    *Enter Sim*

Here you Sim, order the chariot for us.

SIM  Us! Come, come, Jane, I've the little tax cart° to carry you.

JANE  Cart!

LADY AMARANTH  Friend, be cheerful. Thine, and thy sister's, sorrows shall be but an April shower.    280

    *Exeunt Lady Amaranth, Jane, Banks and Sim severally*

## 2.2

*Before an inn*
*Enter Rover and Waiter*

ROVER  Hillo! Friend, when does the coach set out for London?

WAITER  In about an hour, sir.

ROVER  Has the Winchester coach passed yet?

WAITER  No, sir.
    *Exit Waiter*

ROVER  That's lucky! Then, my trunk is here still. Go I will not. Since    5
I've lost the fellowship of my friend Dick, I'll travel no more. I'll
try a London audience. Who knows, but I may get an engagement.
This celestial lady Quaker! She must be rich, and ridiculous for
such a poor dog as I, even to think of her. How Dick would laugh at
me, if he knew. I dare say by this she has released my kind host from    10
the gripe of that rascal. I should like to be certain, though.
    *Enter Landlord*

LANDLORD  You'll dine here, sir? I'm honest Bob Johnston, have kept
the Sun these twenty years. Excellent dinner on table at two.

ROVER  'Yet my love indeed is appetite. I'm as hungry as the sea, and
can digest as much.'°    15

LANDLORD  Then you won't do for my shilling ordinary, sir. There's
a very good ordinary at the Saracen's Head at the end of the town.
Shouldn't have thought, indeed, hungry foot-travellers to eat like
aldermen.°—[*calls off*] Coming, sir.
    [*Exit Landlord*]

ROVER  I'll not join this company at Winchester. No, I'll not stay in the    20
country, hopeless even to expect a look (except of scorn), from this
lady. I'll take a touch at a London theatre. The public there are
candid and generous and, before my merit, can have time to create
enemies. I'll save money, and 'a fig for the sultan and sophy.'°
    *Enter Jane at the back, and Sim, watching her*

JANE  Aye, that's he!    25

ROVER  But if I fall, by heavens I'll overwhelm the manager, his
empire, and 'himself, in one prodigious ruin.'°

JANE  O, lord! (*Runs back*)

SIM  What can you expect, when you follow young men. I've dodged
you all the way.    30

JANE  Well, wasn't I sent?

SIM  O, yes, you were sent, very likely. Who sent you?

JANE  It was—(*Aside*) I won't tell it's my lady, 'cause she bid me not.

SIM  I'll keep you from sheame. A fine life I should have in the parish, rare fleering, if a sister of moine should stand some Sunday at church, in a white sheet,° and to all their flouts, what could I say? 35

ROVER  Thus, 'I say my sister's wronged, my sister Blowsabella, born as high and noble as the attorney. Do her justice, or, by the gods, I'll lay a scene of blood shall make this haymow horrible to beedles.'° 'Say that, Chamont'.° 40

SIM  I believe it's full moon. [*To Jane*] You go hoame to your place, and moind your business.

JANE  My lady will be so pleased I found him! I don't wonder at it. He's a fine- spoken man. 45

SIM  Dang it! Will you stand here grinning at the wild bucks? You saucy slut, to keep me and the cart waiting for you at the end of the lane!

JANE  Never mind him, sir. It's because my lady gave me a ride in her coach that makes the boy so angry. 50

ROVER  'Then you are Kastrill, the angry boy?'°

SIM  So was the prime minister 'till he got himself shaved.°

JANE  Perhaps the gentleman might wish to send her ladyship a compliment. An't please you, sir, if it's even a kiss between us two, it shall go safe. For though you should give it me, brother Sim then can take it to my lady. 55

ROVER  'I kiss'd thee ere I kill'd thee'.

JANE  Kill me!

ROVER  'No way but this killing myself to die upon a kiss!'° (*Advancing*)

SIM  (*interposing*) And you walk home, my forward miss. (*Mimicks*) 60

ROVER  'I've heard of your painting, too. You gig, you lisp, you amble, and nickname God's creatures.'°

SIM  Why, who told you she called me an ass?

ROVER  'Oh, that the town clerk was here, to write thee down an ass! But though not written down in black and white, remember, thou art an ass.'° 65

JANE  Yes, sir. I'll remember it.

SIM  (*to Jane, puts her out*)  Go!

ROVER  'Aye, to a nunnery, go.'° I'm cursedly out of spirits, but hang sorrow, I may as well divert myself. ''Tis meat and drink for me to see a clown'.° 'Shepherd, was't ever at court?'.° 70

SIM  Not I.

ROVER  'Then thou are damn'd.'°

SIM  Eh!

ROVER  Aye! 'Like an ill-roasted egg, all on one side'.° Little Hospi-    75
tality! (*Looking out*)

     *Enter Gammon*

GAMMON  Eh, where's the showman that wants to hire my barn? So,
madame Jane, I place her out to sarvice, and, instead of attending
her mistress, she gets galloping all about the village. How's this,
son?    80

ROVER  'Your son? Young Clodpate, take him to your wheat-stack, and
there teach him manners.'°

GAMMON  Ah, thou'rt the fellow that would bolt out of the dirty roads
into people's houses. Ho, ho, ho! Sim's schooling is mightily
thrown away, if he hasn't more manners than thou.    85

SIM  Why, feyther, it is! Gadzooks, he be one of the play! Acted Tom
Fool, in King Larry, at Lymington t'other night. I thought I
know'd the face, thof he had a straw cap and blanket about'n. Ho,
ho, how comical that was when you said—

ROVER  'Pillicock sat upon Pillicock-hill, pil—i-loo, loo!'°    90

SIM  That's it! That's it! He's at it! (*Claps*) Laugh, feyther, laugh.

GAMMON  Hold your tongue, boy! I believe he's no better than he
should be. The moment I saw him, says I to myself, you are a rogue.

ROVER  There you spoke truth for once in your life.

GAMMON  I'm glad to hear you confess it. But her ladyship shall have    95
the vagrants whipped out of the country.

ROVER  Vagrant! 'Thou wretch! Despite overwhelm thee!'° 'Only
squint, and by heaven I'll beat thy blown body 'till it rebounds like a
tennis ball.'°

SIM  Beat my feyther! No, no. Thou must first beat me. (*Puts himself in    100
a posture of defence*)

ROVER  (*with feeling*) 'Though love cool, friendship fall off, brothers
divide, subjects rebel, oh, never let the sacred bond be crackt 'twixt
son and father!'° I never knew a father's protection, never had a
father to protect. (*Puts his handkerchief to his eyes*)

SIM  He's not acting now!    105

     *Enter Landlord, with a book, pen, and ink*

GAMMON  Landlord, is this Mr Lamp here?

LANDLORD  I've just opened a bottle for him and the other gentleman
in the parlour.

ROVER 'Go, father, with thy son, give him a livery more guarded than his fellows.'° ¹¹⁰

SIM Livery! Why, I be no sarvant man, though sister Jane is. (*To Rover*) Gi's thy hand. I don't how 'tis, but I think I could lose my life for thee, but mustn't let feyther be beat though. No, no! (*Going, turns and looks at Rover*) Ecod, I never shall forget Pillicock upon a hill! ¹¹⁵

    *Exeunt Gammon and Sim*

ROVER 'Thou art an honest reptile!'° I'll make my entree on the London boards in Bayes.° Yes, I shall have no comparison against me. 'Egad, it's very hard that a gentleman and an author can't come to teach them, but he must break his nose, and—and—all that—but—so the players are gone to dinner'.° ¹²⁰

LANDLORD No such people frequent the Sun, I assure you.

ROVER 'Sun, moon, and stars!' Now mind the eclipse, Mr Johnston.

LANDLORD I heard nothing of it, sir.

ROVER 'There's the sun between the earth and moon, There's the moon between the earth and the sun, tol, lol, lol! Dance the hay! ¹²⁵ Luna means to show her tail!'°

    *Enter Waiter*

WAITER [*to Rover*] Two gentlemen in the parlour would speak with you, sir.

ROVER 'I attend them, were they twenty times our mother'.°

    *Exit Waiter*

LANDLORD Sir, you go in the stage.° As we book the passengers, what ¹³⁰ name?

ROVER 'I am the bold Thunder'.°

LANDLORD (*writing*) Mr Thunder.

    *Exit Rover. Enter John Dory*

JOHN DORY I want two places in the stage coach, because I and another gentleman are going a voyage. ¹³⁵

LANDLORD Just two vacant. What name?

JOHN DORY Avast, I go aloft. But let's see who'll be my master's messmates in the cabin: (*reads*) 'Captain. Muccolah, Counsellor Fazacherly, Miss Gosling, Mr Thunder' What's this? Speak, man! Is there one of that name going? ¹⁴⁰

LANDLORD Booked him this minute.

JOHN DORY If our voyage should be at an end before we begin it? If this Mr Thunder should be my master's son! What rate is this vessel?°

LANDLORD Rate?

JOHN DORY What sort of a gentleman is he?

LANDLORD Oh! A rum sort of a gentleman. I suspect he's one of the players.

JOHN DORY True. Sam said it was some players' people coaxed him from Portsmouth school. It must be the 'squire. Show me where 150 he's moored, my old purser.

*Exeunt John Dory, singing, and Landlord, following*


# 2.3

*A room in the Inn*

*Lamp and Trap, discovered drinking*

TRAP This same Farmer Gammon seems a surly spark.

LAMP No matter. His barn will hold a good thirty pounds,° and, if I can but engage this young fellow, this Rover, he'll cram it every night he plays. He's certainly a devilish good actor. Now, Trap, you must enquire out a good carpenter, and be brisk about the building. 5 I think we shall have smart business, as we stand so well for pretty women° too. Oh, here is Mr Rover!

TRAP Snap him at any terms.°

*Enter Rover*

ROVER Gentlemen, your most obedient. The waiter told me—

LAMP Sir, to our better acquaintance. (*Fills*)                    10

ROVER I don't recollect having the honour of knowing you.

LAMP Mr Rover, though I am a stranger to you, your merit is known to me.

ROVER Sir! (*Bows*)

LAMP My name is Lamp. I am manager of the company of comedians 15 that's come down here, and Mr Trap is my treasurer, engages performers, sticks bills, finds properties, keeps box-book, prompts plays and takes the towns.°

TRAP (*aside to Rover*) The most reputable company, and charming money-getting circuit.                                          20

ROVER I haven't a doubt, sir.

LAMP Only suffer me to put up your name to play with us for six nights, and twelve guineas are yours.

ROVER Sir, I thank you, and must confess your offer is liberal, but my

friends have flattered me into a sort of opinion that encourages me    25
to take a touch at the capital.

LAMP   Ah, my dear Mr Rover, a London theatre is dangerous ground.

ROVER   Why, I may fail, and gods may groan, and ladies drawl, 'La,
what an awkward creature!', but should I top my part,° then shall
gods applaud, and ladies sigh, 'the charming fellow!', and managers    30
take me by the hand, and treasurers smile upon me, as they count
the shining guineas!

LAMP   But, suppose—

ROVER   Ah, suppose the contrary. I have a certain friend here in my
coat pocket. (*Puts his hand in his pocket*) Eh? Where is—[*aside*] Oh,    35
the devil! I gave it to discharge my kind host. Going to London,
and not master of five shillings! Then I must engage here. 'Sir, to
return to the twenty pounds'.°

LAMP   Twenty pounds! Well, let it be so.

ROVER   I engage with you. Call a rehearsal when and where you please.    40
I'll attend.

LAMP   I'll step for the cast-book,° and you shall choose your
characters.

TRAP   And, sir, I'll write out the play-bills directly.
        *Exeunt Lamp and Trap*

ROVER   Since I must remain here some time, and I've not the most    45
distant hope of ever speaking to this goddess again, I wish I
had enquired her name, that I might know how to keep out of her
way.
        *Enter John Dory and Landlord*

LANDLORD   There's the gentleman.

JOHN DORY   Very well.
        *Exit Landlord*    50
What cheer, ho, master Squire!

ROVER   What cheer, my hearty?

JOHN DORY   The very face of his father! And ain't you ashamed of
yourself?

ROVER   Why, yes, I am sometimes.    55

JOHN DORY   Do you know, if I had you at the gangway, I'd give you a
neater dozen° than ever you got from your schoolmaster's cat-o-
nine-tails?

ROVER   You wouldn't, sure.

JOHN DORY   I would, sure.    60

ROVER   Indeed? Pleasant enough! Who is this genius?

JOHN DORY   I've dispatched a shallop° to tell Lady Amaranth you're here.

ROVER   You haven't?

JOHN DORY   I have.                                                                        65

ROVER   Now, who the devil's Lady Amaranth?

JOHN DORY   I expect her chariot every moment, and, when it comes, you'll get into it, and I'll get into it, and I'll set you down genteelly at her house. Then I'll have obeyed my orders, and I hope your father will be satisfied.                                          70

ROVER   My father! Who's he, pray?

JOHN DORY   Pshaw! Leave off your fun, and prepare to ask his pardon.

ROVER   Ha, ha, ha! Why, my worthy friend, you're totally wrong in this affair. Upon my word, I'm not the person you take me for.    75 (*Going*)

JOHN DORY   You don't go, though you've got your name down in the stagecoach book, Mr Thunder.

ROVER   Mr Thunder! Stagecoach book! (*Pauses*) Ha, ha, ha! This must be some curious blunder!

JOHN DORY   Oh! My lad, your father, Sir George, will change your      80 note.

ROVER   He must give me one first, Sir George! Then my father is a knight, it seems. Ha, ha, ha! Very good, faith! I am not the gentleman you think me.

JOHN DORY   I ought not to think you any gentleman for giving your      85 honour in a falsehood. Oh! Them play-actors you went amongst have quite spoiled you. I wish only one of 'em would come in my way. I'd teach 'em to bring a gentleman's son tramboozing about the country.

*Enter Stage Coachman*

COACH   Any passengers here for the balloon coach?                        90

ROVER   I was going, 'but by the care of standers by, prevented was'.°

JOHN DORY   Aye, that was my care. I don't sail either, so you may weigh anchor without us.

*Exit Stage Coachman. Enter Waiter*

WAITER   Her ladyship's carriage is at the door, and [*to John Dory*] I fancy it's you, sir, the coachman wants.                               95

JOHN DORY   Yes, it's me. I attend her honour.

[*Exit Waiter*]

ROVER   Then you insist on it that I am—

JOHN DORY   I insist on nothing. Only you shall come.

ROVER  Indeed! Shall! 'Hear you this tritons of the minnows? Mark
you his absolute Shall?'° Shall is a word that does not sound over-    100
agreeable to my ears.

JOHN DORY  Does a pretty girl sound well to your ear?

ROVER  'More music in the clink of her horse's hoofs than twenty
hautboys.'° Why, is this Lady thing-o-me pretty?

JOHN DORY  Beautiful as a mermaid, and stately as a ship under sail.    105

ROVER  A beautiful woman! 'Oh, such a sight! Talk of a coronation.'°

JOHN DORY  Coronation! Zounds! What are you thinking of?

ROVER  'I was thinking of a side-saddle.'°

JOHN DORY  Side-saddle! Why, we go in a coach!

ROVER  (aside) I've a mind to humour the frolic. Well, well, I'll see    110
your mermaid. But then on the instant of my appearance the
mistake must be discovered. Hearky, is this father of mine you talk
of at this lady's?

JOHN DORY  No. Your father's in chase of the deserters. (Aside) I find
he's afraid to face the old one, so, if I tell him, he won't go with me.    115
No, no, we shan't see him in a hurry.

ROVER  Then I'll venture. Has the lady ever seen me?

JOHN DORY  Pshaw! None of your jokes, man. You know that her
ladyship, no more than myself, has set eyes upon you since you
were the bigness of a Rumbo Canakin.°    120

ROVER  The choice is made. I've my Ranger's dress° in my trunk.
'Cousin of Buckingham, thou sage grave man'.°

JOHN DORY  What?

ROVER  'Since you will buckle fortune on my back, to bear her bur-
then, whether I will or no, I must have patience to endure the load.    125
But, if black scandal, or foul-fac'd'° —

JOHN DORY  Black! My foul face was as fair as yours before I went to
sea.

ROVER  'Your mere enforcement shall acquittance me'.°

JOHN DORY  Man, don't stand preaching parson Palmer.° Come to    130
the chariot.

ROVER  'Aye, to the chariot! Bear me, Bucephalus among the billows.
Hey, for the Tigris!'°

    *Exeunt Rover and John Dory*

# 3.1

*Lady Amaranth's House*

*Enter Lady Amaranth and Ephraim Smooth*

LADY AMARANTH Though thou hast settled that distressed gentleman's debt, let his sister come unto me, and remit a quarter's rent
unto all my tenants.

EPHRAIM As thou biddest, I have discharged from the pound,° the
widow's cattle, but shall I let the lawsuit drop against the farmer's          5
son, who did shoot the pheasant?

LADY AMARANTH Yea, but instantly turn from my service the game-
keeper's man that did kill the fawn while it was eating from his
hand. We should hate guile, though we may love venison.

EPHRAIM (*aside*) I love a young doe.—Since the death of friend          10
Dovehouse, who, though one of the faithful, was an active magistrate, this part of the country is infested with covetous men,
called robbers, and I have, in thy name, said unto the people,
whoever apprehendeth one of these, I will reward, yea, with thirty
pieces of gold. (*A loud knocking without*). That beating of one brass°          15
against another at thy door, proclaimeth the approach of vanity
whose pride of heart swelleth at an empty sound.

*Exit Ephraim Smooth*

LADY AMARANTH But my heart is possessed with the idea of that
wandering youth, whose benevolence induced him to part with
(perhaps) his all, to free the unhappy debtor. His person is amiable.          20
His addresses (according to worldly modes) formed to pleasure,
to delight. But he's poor. Is that a crime? Perhaps meanly born, but
one good act is an illustrious pedigree. I feel I love him, and in that
word are contained birth, fame, and riches.

*Enter Jane*

JANE Madam, my lady, an't please you.          25

LADY AMARANTH Did'st thou find the young man, that I may return
him the money he paid for my tenant?

JANE I found him, ma'am, and—I found him, and he talked of—what
he said.

LADY AMARANTH What did he say?          30

JANE He saw me ma'am, and called me Blowsabella, and said he
would—I'll be hanged, ma'am, if he didn't say he would—Now,
think of that—but if he hadn't gone to London in the stagecoach.

LADY AMARANTH  Is he gone? (*With emotion*)
    *Enter John Dory*

JOHN DORY  Oh, my lady, mayhap John Dory is not the man to be sent   35
  after young gentlemen that scamper from school, and run about
  the country a play-acting. (*Calls off*) Pray walk upstairs, Master
  Thunder.

LADY AMARANTH  Hast thou brought my kinsman hither?

JOHN DORY  Well, I haven't then.   40

JANE  If you haven't, why do you make such a talk about it?

JOHN DORY  Don't give me your palaver. [*Calls off*] Will you only walk
  up, if you please, Master Harry?

JANE  [*calls off*] Will you walk up, if you please, Master Harry?

LADY AMARANTH (*aside*)  Friendship requireth, yet I am not disposed   45
  to commune with company.

JANE  Oh, bless me, ma'am, if it isn't—
    *Enter Rover, dressed°*

ROVER  ' 'Tis I, Hamlet, the Dane !'° 'Thus far into the bowels of the
  land have we march'd on.'° 'John, that bloody and devouring
  boar.'°   50

JOHN DORY  He called me bull° in the coach.

ROVER  This the Lady Amaranth! By heavens, the very angel Quaker!

LADY AMARANTH (*turns*)  The dear, generous youth, my cousin
  Harry!

JOHN DORY  There, he's for you, and make the most of him.   55
    [*Rover crosses over to Lady Amaranth. John whispers him on
    left-hand side*]

JANE  Oh, how happy my lady is! He looks so charming now he's fine.

JOHN DORY (*aside, to Rover*)  Harky! She's as rich as a Spanish
  India-man,° and I tell you, your father wishes you'd grapple her by
  the heart. Court her, you mad devil. (*To Jane*) There's an engagement to be between these two vessels, but little Cupid's the only   60
  man that's to take minutes,° so come.

JANE  Ma'am, an't I to wait on you?

JOHN DORY  No, my lass, you're to wait on me.

JANE  Wait on this great sea-bull! Am I, ma'am?

JOHN DORY (*aside*)  By this, Sir George is come to the inn. Without   65
  letting the younker° know, I'll go bring him here, and smuggle both
  father and son into a joyful meeting. (*To Jane*) Come now, usher
  me down like a lady.

JANE  This way, Mr Sailor Gentleman.
    *Exeunt John Dory and Jane*

ROVER (*aside*) By heavens, a most delectable woman!                    70

LADY AMARANTH Cousin, when I saw thee in the village free the
    sheep from the wolf, why didst thou not tell me then thou wert son
    to my uncle, Sir George?

ROVER Because, my lady, then I—(*aside*) didn't know it myself.

LADY AMARANTH Why would'st thou vex thy father, and quit thy        75
    school?

ROVER 'A truant disposition, good my lady brought me from
    Wirtemburg'.°

LADY AMARANTH Thy father designs thee for his dangerous pro-
    fession, but is thy inclination turned to the voice of trumpets and   80
    smites of mighty slaughter?

ROVER 'Why, ma'am, as for old Boreas, my dad, when the blast of war
    blows in his ears, he's a tiger in his fierce resentment.'° But for me:
    "I think it a pity, and so it is, that villainous saltpetre should be
    digged out of the bowels of the harmless earth, which many a good    85
    tall fellow has destroyed, with wounds and guns, and drums,
    heaven save the mark!"°

LADY AMARANTH Indeed, thou art tall, my cousin, and grown of
    comely stature. Our families have long been separated.

ROVER They have. (*Aside*) Since Adam, I believe.—'Then, lady, let   90
    that sweet bud of love now ripen to a beauteous flower.'°

LADY AMARANTH Love!

ROVER 'Excellent lady! Perdition catch my soul, but I do love thee,
    and, when I love thee not, chaos is come again.'°

LADY AMARANTH Thou art of a happy disposition.                        95

ROVER 'If I were now to die, 'twere now to be most happy!' 'Let our
    senses dance in concert to the joyful minutes, and this, and this, the
    only discord make."° (*Kisses her hand*)
          *Enter Jane, with cake and wine*

JANE Ma'am, an't please you, Mr Zachariah bid me—

ROVER 'Why, you fancy yourself Cardinal Wolsey in this family'.°      100

JANE No, sir, I'm not a Cardinal. I'm only my lady's maid here. Jenny
    Gammon, at your service.

ROVER 'A bowl of cream for your Catholic Majesty'.°

JANE Cream? La, sir, it's wine and water.

ROVER 'You get no water. Take the wine, great Potentate'.° (*Presents a*   105
    *glass to Lady Amaranth*)

JANE Madam, my father begs leave—

ROVER 'Go, go, thou shallow Pomona'.°

*Puts her out. [Exit Jane]*

Eh, s'death! My manager!

*Enter Gammon and Lamp*

GAMMON (*aside*) I hope her ladyship hasn't found out 'twas I had Banks arrested. Would your ladyship give leave for this here honest    110
man and his comrade to act a few plays in the town, 'cause I have let 'n my barn. 'Twill be some little help to me, my lady.

ROVER I understand more of these affairs than ladies do. Leave me to settle 'em, madam.

LADY AMARANTH True. These are delusions, as a woman, I under-    115
stand not. But by my cousin's advice I will abide. Ask his consent.

GAMMON (*aside*) So, I must pay my respects to the young 'Squire.—
An't please your honour, if a poor man like me (*bows*) dare offer my humble duty?    120

ROVER 'Can'st thou bow to a vagrant.'° Eh, Little Hospitality?

*Gammon looks at him and sneaks off. Exit Gammon*

LAMP Please your honour, if I may presume to hope, you'll be graciously pleased to take our little squad under your honour's protection.

ROVER Ha!    125

LADY AMARANTH What say'st thou, Henry?

ROVER (*aside*) Aye, where's Henry? True, that's me. Strange I should already forget my name, and not half an hour since I was christened!—Hark! Do you play yourself? Eh! (*Vapouring*) Ha! Hem! Fellow?    130

LAMP Yes, sir, and, sir, I have just now engaged a new actor, one Mr Rover. Such an actor! But, I dare say, sir, you've heard of Mr Rover?

ROVER Eh? What! You've engaged that—what's his name, Rover? If such is your best actor, you shan't have my permission. My dear madam, the worst fellow in the world. Get along out of the town, or    135
I'll have all of you, man, woman, child, rag and fiddlestick,° clapped into the whirligig.°

LADY AMARANTH Good man, abide not here.

ROVER Eh! What, my friend? Now, indeed, if this new actor you brag of, this crack of your company, was anything like a gentleman—    140

LAMP (*surprised*) It isn't!

ROVER It is. My good friend, if I was really the unfortunate, poor strolling dog you thought me, I should tread your four boards, and crow the cock of your barn-door fowl,° but, as fate has ordained

that I'm a gentleman, and son to Sir—Sir (*aside*) what the devil's    145
my father's name?—You must be content to murder Shakespeare
without making me an accomplice.

LAMP  But, my most gentle sir, I, and my treasurer, Trap, have trum-
peted your fame ten miles round the country. The bills are posted,
the stage built, the candles booked, fiddles engaged:° all on the tip-    150
top of expectation. We should have, tomorrow night, an overflow,°
ay, thirty pounds. Dear worthy sir, you wouldn't go to ruin a
whole community and their families, that now depend only on the
exertion of your brilliant talents.

ROVER  Eh! I never was uniform but in one maxim, that is, though I do    155
little good, to hurt nobody but myself.

LADY AMARANTH  Since thou hast promised, much as I prize the
adherence to those customs in which I was brought up, thou shalt
not sully thy honour by a breach of thy word. For truth is more
shining than beaten gold. Play, if it can bring good to these people.    160

ROVER  Shall I?

LADY AMARANTH  This falleth out well, for I have bidden all the
wealthy people round unto my housewarming,° and these
pleasantries may afford them a cheerful and innocent entertainment.    165

ROVER  True, my lady. Your guests an't Quakers, though you are, and,
when we ask people to our house, we study to please them, not
ourselves. But if we do furnish up a play or two, the muses
shan't honour that churlish fellow's barn. The God that illumines
the soul of genius should never visit the iron door of inhumanity.    170
No Gammon's barn for me!

LADY AMARANTH  Barn! That gallery shall be thy, theatre, and, in
spite of the grave doctrines of Ephraim Smooth, my friends and
I will behold and rejoice in thy pranks, my pleasant cousin.

ROVER  My kind, my charming lady! Hey, brighten up, bully° Lamp.    175
Carpenters, tailor, manager, distribute your box-tickets for my
lady's gallery. 'Come, gentle coz.'
          'The actors are at hand, and by their show
          You shall know all
          That you are like to know'.°    180
    *Exeunt Rover, Lady Amaranth and Lamp*

# 3.2

*The inn*

*Enter Harry, in a riding dress, and Muz, in a livery°*

HARRY Though I went back to Portsmouth Academy with a contrite
heart to resume my studies, yet, from my father's angry letter, I
dread a woeful storm at our first meeting. I fancy the people at this
inn don't recollect me. It reminds me of my pleasant friend, poor
Jack Rover. I wonder where he is now.                                      5

MUZ And it brings to my memory a certain stray-vaguing acquaintance of mine, poor Dick Buskin.

HARRY Ha, ha, ha! Then I desire, sir, you'll turn Dick Buskin again
out of your memory.

MUZ Can't, sir. The dear, good-natured, wicked—beg your honour's     10
pardon.

HARRY Oh, but Muz, you must, soon as I'm dressed, step out and
inquire whose house is this my father's at. I did not think he
had any acquaintance in this part of the country. Sound what
humour he's in, and how the land lies before I venture into his     15
presence.

*Enter Waiter*

WAITER Sir, the room is ready for you to dress.

*Exit Waiter*

HARRY I shall only throw off my boots, and you'll shake a little powder in my hair.

MUZ Then, hey puff, I shoulder my curling irons.°                         20

*Exeunt Muz and Harry. Enter Sir George and Landlord*

SIR GEORGE I can hear nothing of these deserters, yet, by my first
intelligence, they'll not venture up to London. They must still be
lurking about the country. Landlord, have any suspicious looking
persons put in at your house?

LANDLORD Yes, sir, now and then.                                          25

SIR GEORGE What do you do with them?

LANDLORD Why, sir, when a man calls for liquor, that I think has no
money, I make him pay beforehand.

SIR GEORGE Damn your liquor, you self-interested porpoise! Chatter
your own private concerns, when the public good, or fear of general   30
calamity, should be the only compass. These fellows that I'm in
pursuit of, have run from their ships. If our navy's unmanned, what
becomes of you and your house, you cormorant?

LANDLORD (*aside*) This is a very abusive sort of a gentleman, but he has a full pocket, or he wouldn't be so saucy.    35

*Exit Landlord*

SIR GEORGE This rascal, I believe, doesn't know I'm Sir George Thunder. Winds still variable blow my affairs right athwart each other. To know what's become of my runagate° son Harry, and there my rich lady niece, pressing and squeezing up the noble plumage of our illustrious family in her little mean Quaker    40
bonnet—but I must up to town after. 'Sblood, when I catch my son Harry!—Oh, here's John Dory.

*Enter John Dory*

Have you taken the places in the London coach for me?

JOHN DORY Hahoy! Your honour, is that yourself?

SIR GEORGE No, I'm besides myself. Heard anything of my son?    45

JOHN DORY What's o'clock?

SIR GEORGE What do you talk of clocks or timepieces? All glasses reckoning and log-line are run wild with me.°

JOHN DORY If it's two, your son is at this moment walking with Lady Amaranth in her garden.    50

SIR GEORGE With Lady Amaranth!

JOHN DORY If half after, they're cast anchor to rest themselves amongst the posies. If three, they're got up again. If four, they're picking a bit of crammed° fowl, and if half after, they're cracking walnuts over a bottle of Calcavella.°    55

SIR GEORGE My son! My dear friend, where did you find him?

JOHN DORY Why, I found him where he was, and I left him where he is.

SIR GEORGE What, and he came to Lady Amaranth's?

JOHN DORY No. But I brought him there from this house, in her    60
ladyship's chariot. (*Aside*) I won't tell him master Harry went amongst the players, or he'd never forgive him.—Oh, such a merry, civil, crazy crack-brain. The very picture of your honour.

SIR GEORGE (*joyfully*) Ha, ha, ha! What, he's in high spirits? Ha, ha, ha! The dog! But I hope he had discretion enough though to throw    65
a little gravity over his mad humour before his prudent cousin.

JOHN DORY He threw himself on his knees before her, and that did quite as well.

SIR GEORGE Ha, ha, ha! Made love to her already! Oh, the impudent, the cunning villain! What, and may be he—    70

JOHN DORY Indeed he did give her a smack.

SIR GEORGE Me! Ha, ha, ha!

JOHN DORY  Oh, he's yours! A chip of the old block.

SIR GEORGE  He is! Ha, ha, ha !

JOHN DORY  Oh, he threw his arms around her as eager as I would to    75
catch a falling decanter of Madeira.°

SIR GEORGE  Huzza! Victoria! Here will be a junction of two bouncing
estates! But, confound the money! John, you shall have a bowl for
a jolly boat to swim in. Roll in here a puncheon of rum, a hogshead
of sugar, shake an orchard of oranges, and let the landlord drain his    80
fishpond yonder. (*Sings*) 'A bumper, a bumper of good liquor!'°

JOHN  Then, my good master, Sir George, I'll order a bowl in, since
you are in the humour for it. 'We'll dance a little and sing a little'°
        *Exit John Dory, singing*

SIR GEORGE  And so the wild rogue is, this instant, rattling up° her
prim ladyship? Eh, isn't this he? Left her already!    85
        *Enter Harry, dressed*°

HARRY  I must have forgot my cane in this room. My father!

SIR GEORGE  (*looks at his watch*) Just half after four! Why, Harry,
you've made great haste in cracking your walnuts.

HARRY  Yes. (*Aside*) He's heard of my frolics with the players.—Dear
father, if you'll but forgive—    90

SIR GEORGE  Why, indeed, Harry, your running away was not well.
I've heard all. You've acted very bad.

HARRY  Sir, it should be considered I was but a novice.

SIR GEORGE  However, I shall think of nothing now but your benefit.

HARRY  (*aside*) Very odd his approving of—I suppose he means to let    95
me have my frolic out. I thank you, sir, but if agreeable to you, I've
done with benefits.°

SIR GEORGE  If I wasn't the best of fathers, you might indeed hope for
none, but, no matter, if you can get but the Fair Quaker.°

HARRY  Or The Humours of the Navy,° sir?    100

SIR GEORGE  What! How dare you reflect on the humours of the navy?
The navy has very good humours, or I'd never see your dog's face
again, you villain! But I'm cool. Eh, boy, a snug easy chariot?

HARRY  I'll order it. (*Calls off*) Desire my father's carriage to draw up.

SIR GEORGE  Mine, you rogue? I've none here. I mean Lady    105
Amaranth's.

HARRY  Yes, sir. (*Calling off*) Lady Amaranth's chariot!

SIR GEORGE  What are you at? I mean that which you left this house
in.

HARRY  Chariot! Sir, I left this house on foot.    110

SIR GEORGE  What, with John Dory?

HARRY  No, sir, with Jack Rover.

SIR GEORGE  Why, John has been a rover to be sure, but now he's settled since I've made him my valet de chambre.

HARRY  Made him your valet! Why, sir, where did you meet with him? 115

SIR GEORGE  I met him on board, and I met him on shore, the cabin, steerage, gallery and forecastle. He sailed round the world with me.

HARRY  Strange this, sir! I understood he had been in the East Indies, but he never told me he even knew you. But, indeed, he knew me 120 only by the name of Dick Buskin.

SIR GEORGE  Then how came he to bring you to Lady Amaranth's?

HARRY  Bring me where, sir?

SIR GEORGE  Answer me. Are not you now come from her ladyship's?

HARRY  Me? Not I. 125

SIR GEORGE  Ha! This is a lie of John's to enhance his own services. Then, you have not been there?

HARRY  There! I don't know where you mean, sir.

SIR GEORGE  Yes, 'tis all a brag of John's, but I'll—

*Enter John Dory*

JOHN DORY  The rum and sugar is ready, but as for the fishpond— 130

SIR GEORGE  I'll kick you into it, you thirsty old grampus.°

JOHN DORY  Will you? Then I'll make a comical roasted orange.°

SIR GEORGE  How dare you say you brought my son to Lady Amaranth's?

JOHN DORY  And who says I did not? 135

SIR GEORGE  (*ironically*) He that best should know: only Dick Buskin here.

JOHN DORY  Then Dick Buskin might find some other amusement than shooting off his guns here.

SIR GEORGE  Did you bring my son to Lady Amaranth's in her 140 chariot?

JOHN DORY  And to be sure I did.

SIR GEORGE  There, what do you say to that?

HARRY  I say it's false.

JOHN DORY  False! Shiver my hulk, Mr Buckskin, if you wore a lion's 145 skin I'd curry you for this.°

*Exit John Dory in a rage*

SIR GEORGE  No, no, John's honest. I see through it now. The puppy has seen her. Perhaps he has the impudence not to like her and so blows up this confusion and perplexity only to break off a marriage that I've set my heart on. 150

HARRY  What does he mean?—Sir, I'll assure you—
SIR GEORGE  Damn your assurance, you disobedient, ungrateful—I'll
  not part with you 'till I confront you with Lady Amaranth herself,
  face to face, and, if I prove you've been deceiving me, I'll launch
  you into the wide ocean of life without rudder, compass, grog, or    155
  tobacco.

    *Exeunt Sir George and Harry*

# 4.1

*Lady Amaranth's House*

*Enter Lady Amaranth, reading*

LADY AMARANTH  The fanciful flights of my pleasant cousin enchant
my senses. This book he gave me to read containeth good morals.
The man Shakespeare, that did write it, they call immortal.° He
must indeed have been filled with a divine spirit. I understand,
from my cousin, the origin of plays were religious mysteries, that,      5
freed from the superstition of early, and grossness of, latter ages,
the stage is now the vehicle of delight and morality.° If so, to hear
a good play, is taking the wholesome draught of precept from a
golden cup, embossed with gems, yet, my giving countenance to
have one in my house, and even to act in it myself, proves the      10
ascendancy that my dear Harry hath over my heart. Ephraim
Smooth is much scandalised at these doings.

*Enter Ephraim Smooth*

EPHRAIM  This mansion is now become the tabernacle of Baal.°

LADY AMARANTH  Then abide not in it.

EPHRAIM  'Tis full of the wicked ones.      15

LADY AMARANTH  Stay not among the wicked ones.

*Loud laughing without*

EPHRAIM  I must shut my ears.

LADY AMARANTH  And thy mouth also, good Ephraim. I have
bidden my cousin Henry to my house, and I will not set
bounds to his mirth to gratify thy spleen, and show my own      20
inhospitality.

EPHRAIM  Why dost thou suffer him to put into the hands of thy
servants books of tragedies, and books of comedies, prelude, inter-
lude, yea, all lewd. My spirit doth wax wrath. I say unto thee, a
playhouse is the school for the old dragon,° and a playbook the      25
primer of Belzebub.°

LADY AMARANTH  This is one. Mark: (*reads*) 'Not the king's crown,
nor the deputed sword, the marshal's truncheon, nor the judge's
robe, become them with one half so good a grace as mercy doth.
Oh! Think on that, and mercy then will breathe within your lips      30
like man new made!'° Doth Belzebub speak such words?

EPHRAIM  Thy kinsman hath made all the servants actors.

LADY AMARANTH  To act well is good service.

EPHRAIM (*aside*) Here cometh the damsel, for whom my heart
    yearneth.                                                                                          35
        *Enter Jane, reading a paper, joyfully*
JANE Oh, ma'am! His honour, the 'Squire, says the play's to be 'As
    You Like It'.
EPHRAIM I like it not.
JANE He's given me my character. I'm to be Miss Audrey, and brother
    Sim's to be William of the Forest,° as it were. But how am I to get          40
    my part by heart?
LADY AMARANTH By often reading it.
JANE Well, I don't know but that's as good a way as any. But I must
    study it. 'The gods give us joy'.°
        *Exit Jane*
EPHRAIM Thy maidens skip like young kids.                                              45
LADY AMARANTH Then, do thou go skip with them.
EPHRAIM Mary, thou should'st be obeyed in thine own house, and
    I will do thy bidding.
LADY AMARANTH Ah, thou hypocrite! To obey is easy when the heart
    commands.                                                                                    50
        *Enter Rover*
ROVER Oh, my charming cousin, how agree you and Rosalind?°
    Are you almost perfect? 'Eh, what, all a-mort, old Clytus?' 'Why,
    you're like any angry fiend broke in amongst the laughing Gods.'°
    Come, come, I'll have nothing here but 'quips and cranks, and
    wreathed smiles, such as dwell on Hebe's cheek.'° (*Looking at Lady*          55
    *Amaranth*)
LADY AMARANTH He says we mustn't have this amusement.
ROVER 'But I'm a voice potential, double as the Duke's, and I say we
    must.'°
EPHRAIM Nay.
ROVER Yea! 'By Jupiter, I swear. Aye.'°                                                  60
        *Music without*
EPHRAIM I must shut my ears. The man of sin rubbeth the hair of the
    horse to the bowels of the cat.
        *Enter Lamp, with a violin*
LAMP Now, if agreeable to your ladyship, we'll go over your
    song.
EPHRAIM I will go over it. (*Snatches the book from Lady Amaranth,*          65
    *throws it on the ground and steps on it*)
ROVER Trample on Shakespeare! 'A sacrilegious thief, that, from a
    shelf the precious diadem stole, and put it in his pocket!'° (*Takes up*

*the book and presents it to Lady Amaranth*) Silence, 'thou owl of
Crete',° and hear the 'Cuckoo's song'.°

LADY AMARANTH To practice it, I'm content.                                        70
          *Lamp begins to play. Ephraim jostles him, and puts him out of
          tune*

LAMP Why, what's that for, my dear sir?

EPHRAIM Friend, this is a land of freedom, and I've as much right to
move my elbows, as thou hast to move thine.
          *Rover pushes him*
Why dost thou so, friend?

ROVER 'Friend, this is a land of freedom, and I have as much right to      75
move my elbows as thou hast to move thine.' (*Pushes him*)
          [*Exit Ephraim Smooth*]
'Verily, I could smite that Amalekite 'till the going down of the sun.'°

LADY AMARANTH But, Harry, do your people of fashion act these
follies themselves?

ROVER Aye, and scramble for the top parts as eager as for star,            80
ribband, place or pension,° and no wonder, for a good part in a play
is the first good character some of them ever had. Lamp, decorate
the seats out smart and theatrical, and drill the servants that I've
given the small parts to.
          *Exit Lamp*

LADY AMARANTH I wished for some entertainment (in which gay          85
people now take delight) to please those I have invited, but we'll
convert these follies into a charitable purpose. Tickets for this day
shall be delivered unto my friends gratis, but money to their
amount, I will (after rewarding our assistants) distribute amongst
the indigent of the village. Thus, while we please ourselves, and      90
perhaps amuse our friends, we shall make the poor happy.
          *Exit Lady Amaranth*

ROVER An angel! If Sir George doesn't soon arrive to blow me,° I
may, I think, marry her angelic ladyship. But will that be honest?
She's nobly born, though I suspect I had ancestors too, if I knew
who they were. I entered this house the poorest wight° in England,       95
and what must she imagine when I'm discovered? That I am a
scoundrel, and, consequently, though I should possess her hand
and fortune, instead of loving, she'll despise me. (*Sits*) I want a
friend now to consult. Deceive her I will not. Poor Dick Buskin
wants money more than myself, yet this is a measure I'm sure he'd      100
scorn. No, no, I must not.

*Enter Harry*

HARRY Now, I hope my passionate father will be convinced that this is the first time I was ever under this roof. Eh, what beau is here? Astonishing! My old strolling friend! (*Unperceived, sits by Rover*)

ROVER Heigho! I don't know what to do.                                105

HARRY (*in the same tone*) 'Nor what to say'.°

ROVER (*turns*) Dick Buskin! My dear fellow! Ha, ha, ha! Talk of the devil, and—I was just thinking of you. 'Pon my soul, Dick, I'm so happy to see you.

*Shakes hands cordially*

HARRY But, Jack, eh, perhaps you found me out?                         110

ROVER Found you! I'm sure I wonder how the deuce you found me out. Ah, the news of my intended play has brought you.

HARRY (*aside*) He doesn't know as yet who I am, so I'll carry it on.— Then you too have broke your engagement with Truncheon, at Winchester? Figuring it away° in your stage clothes too. Really, tell   115
us what you are at here, Jack.

ROVER Will you be quiet with your Jacking? I'm now 'Squire Harry.

HARRY What?

ROVER I've been pressed into this service by an old man of war, who found me at the inn, and, insisting I'm son to a Sir George   120
Thunder, here, in that character, I flatter myself I have won the heart of the charming lady of this house.

HARRY (*aside*) Now the mystery's out.—Then it's my friend Jack has been brought here for me.—Do you know the young man they take you for?                                                                  125

ROVER No, but I'm proud to say he is honoured in his representative.

HARRY Upon my soul, Jack, you're a very high fellow.° Ha, ha, ha!

ROVER I am, now I can put some pounds in your pocket. You shall be employed. We're getting up 'As You Like It'. Let's see, in the cast, have I a part for you? I'll take Touchstone from Lamp. You shall   130
have it, my boy. I'd resign Orlando° to you with any other Rosalind, but the lady of the mansion plays it herself.

HARRY (*aside*) The very lady my father intended for me.—Do you love her, Jack?

ROVER To distraction, but I'll not have her.                           135

HARRY No! Why?

ROVER She thinks me a gentleman, and I'll not convince her I'm a rascal. I'll go on with our play, as the produce is appropriated to

a good purpose, and then lay down my 'Squireship, bid adieu to
my heavenly Rosalind, and exit for ever from her house, poor Jack   140
Rover.

HARRY (*aside*) The generous fellow I ever thought him, and he shan't
lose by it. If I could make him believe—(*Pauses*) Ha, ha, ha! Well,
this is the most whimsical affair! You've anticipated, superseded
me, ha, ha, ha! You'll scarce believe that I'm come here too   145
(purposely, though) to pass myself for this young Harry.

ROVER No!

HARRY I am.

SIR GEORGE (*without*) Harry, where are you?

ROVER Eh, who's that?   150

HARRY Ha, ha, ha! (*Aside*) I'll try it. My father will be cursedly vexed,
but no other way.

ROVER Somebody called Harry. 'If the real Simon Pure'° should be
arrived, I'm in a fine way.

HARRY Be quiet. That's my confederate.   155

ROVER Eh!

HARRY He's to personate the father, Sir George Thunder. He started
the scheme, having heard a union was intended, and Sir George
not immediately expected. Our plan is, if I can, before his arrival,
flourish myself into the lady's good graces, and whip her up,° as   160
she's an heiress.

ROVER But who is this comrade?

HARRY One of my former company, a devilish good actor in the old
men.

ROVER So, you're turned fortune hunter! O ho, then 'twas on this plan   165
you parted with me on the road, standing like a finger-post. 'You
walk up that way, and I walk down this.' Why, Dick, I didn't know
you were half so capital a rogue.

HARRY I didn't know my forte lay that way, 'till persuaded by this
experienced stager.   170

ROVER He must be an impudent old scoundrel. Who is he? Do I know
him?

HARRY (*aside*) Why, no. I hope not.

ROVER I'll step downstairs, and have the honour of—I'll kick him.

HARRY No, I wouldn't have him hurt, either.   175

ROVER What's his name?

HARRY His name is—is—Abrawang.

ROVER Abrawang! I never heard of him, but, Dick, why would you let
him persuade you to such a scandalous affair?

HARRY Why, faith, I would have been off it, but when once he takes       180
a project into his head, the devil himself can't drive him out of it.

ROVER Yes, but the constables may drive him into Winchester gaol.

HARRY Eh! Your opinion of our intended exploit has made me
ashamed of myself. Ha, ha, ha! Harkey, Jack, to frighten and
punish my adviser, do you still keep your character of young Squire       185
Thunder. You can easily do that, as he, no more than myself, has
ever seen the young gentleman.

ROVER But, by heavens, I'll—'Quoit him down, Bardolph.'°

HARRY Yes, but Jack, if you can marry her, her fortune is a snug thing.
Besides, if you love each other—I tell you—                              190

ROVER Hang her fortune! 'My love more noble than the world, prizes
not quantity of dirty lands'° Oh, Dick, she's the most lovely—but
you shall see her. She is female beauty in its genuine decoration.

    *Exit Rover*

HARRY Ha, ha, ha! This is the drollest—Rover little suspects that I
am the identical 'Squire Thunder that he personates. I'll lend him       195
my character a little longer. Yes, this offers a most excellent
opportunity of making my poor friend's fortune, without injuring
anybody. If possible, he shall have her. I can't regret the loss of
charms I never knew, and, as for an estate, my father's is competent
to all my wishes.° Lady Amaranth, by marrying Jack Rover, will          200
gain a man of honour, which she might miss in an Earl. It may tease
my father a little at first, but he's a good old fellow in the main, and,
I think, when he comes to know my motive—Eh! This must be
she—an elegant woman, faith! Now for a little finesse, to continue
her in the belief that Jack is the man she thinks him.                    205

    *Enter Lady Amaranth*

(*Bowing*) Madam, a word if you please.

LADY AMARANTH Who art thou, friend?

HARRY I've scarce time to warn you against the danger you are in, of
being imposed upon by your uncle, Sir George.

LADY AMARANTH How?                                                        210

HARRY He has heard of your ladyship's partiality for his son, but is
so incensed at the irregularity of his conduct, that he intends, if
possible, to disinherit him, and to prevent your honouring him with
your hand, has engaged and brought me hither, to pass me on you
for him, designing to treat the poor young gentleman himself as an       215
impostor, in hopes you'll banish him from your heart and house.

LADY AMARANTH Is Sir George such a parent? I thank thee for thy
caution. What is thy name?

HARRY Richard Buskin, ma'am. The stage is my profession. In the young 'Squire's late excursion we contracted an intimacy, and I saw 220 so many good qualities in him, that I could not think of being the instrument of his ruin, nor deprive your ladyship of so good a husband as I am certain he'll make you.

LADY AMARANTH Then Sir George intends to disown him?

HARRY Yes ma'am. I've this moment told the young gentleman of 225 it, and he's determined, for a jest, to return the compliment, by seeming to treat Sir George himself as an impostor.

LADY AMARANTH 'Twill be a just retaliation, and indeed what my uncle deserveth for his cruel intentions both to his son and me.

SIR GEORGE (*without*) What, has he run away again?   230

LADY AMARANTH That's mine uncle.

HARRY (*aside*) Yes here is my father, and my standing out° that I'm not his son, will rouse him into the heat of battle, ha, ha, ha! Here he is, madam. Now, mind how he'll dub me a 'Squire.

LADY AMARANTH It's well I'm prepared, or I might have believed 235 him.

> *Enter Sir George*

SIR GEORGE Well, my lady, wasn't it my wild rogue set you to all the Calcavella capers you've been cutting in the garden? You see here I have brought him into the line of battle again.—You villain, why do you drop astern° there? Throw a salute-shot, buss her bob-stays,° 240 bring to, and come down straight as a mast,° you dog.

LADY AMARANTH Uncle, who is this?

SIR GEORGE Who is he?—Ha, ha, ha! That's an odd question to the fellow that has been three hours with you cracking walnuts.

LADY AMARANTH He is bad at his lesson.   245

SIR GEORGE Certainly, when he ran from school—why don't you speak, you lubber? You're cursed modest, now. Before I came, 'twas all down among the posies.—Here, my lady, take from a father's hand, Harry Thunder.

LADY AMARANTH That is what I may not.   250

SIR GEORGE There, I thought you'd disgust her, you flat fish!

> *Enter Rover*

LADY AMARANTH (*taking Rover's hand*) Here, Uncle, take from my hand Harry Thunder.

SIR GEORGE Eh! (*Staring at Rover*)

ROVER (*aside to Harry*) Oh, this is our sham Sir George?   255

HARRY (*aside to Rover*) Yes, I've been telling the lady, and she'll seem to humour him.

ROVER (*to Harry*) I shan't, though.—How do you do, Abrawang?

SIR GEORGE Abrawang!

ROVER You look like a good actor. Aye, that's very well indeed. Never    260
lose sight of your character. You know Sir George Thunder is a
noisy, turbulent, wicked old seaman.—Angry! bravo! Pout your
underlip, purse your brows. Very well! But, dem it, Abrawang, you
should have put a little red upon your nose. Mind a rule: ever play
an angry man with a red nose. That's right! Strut about on your    265
little pegs.

SIR GEORGE I'm in such a fury!

ROVER We know that. Your figure is the most happy comedy squab°
I ever saw. Why, only show yourself, and you set the audience in a
roar.    270

SIR GEORGE S'blood and fire!

ROVER 'Keep it up. I like fun.'°

LADY AMARANTH (*to Sir George, pointing to Rover*) Who is this?

SIR GEORGE Some puppy unknown.

LADY AMARANTH (*to Rover, pointing to Sir George*) And you don't    275
know this gentleman?

ROVER Excellently well! 'He's a fishmonger.'°

SIR GEORGE A what?

LADY AMARANTH Yes, father and son are determined not to know
each other.    280

ROVER Come, Dick, give the lady a specimen of your talents.
'Motley's your only wear. Ha, ha, ha! I met a fool in the forest.'°
    *Enter Jane*

HARRY Here comes Audrey. 'Salutation and greeting to you all. Trip,
trip apace, good Audrey'.° (*Takes Jane's arm under his. They trip
round, then go up to Sir George*)

JANE (*to Sir George*) 'La! Warrants. What features!'°    285

SIR GEORGE 'Sblood! what's this?

HARRY 'A homely thing, sir, but she's my own.'°

SIR GEORGE Yours? Oh, you most audacious—What, this slut?

JANE 'I thank the Gods for my sluttishness'.°

LADY AMARANTH (*to Rover, pointing to Harry*) You know this youth?    290

ROVER 'My friend, Horatio.'° 'I wear him in my heart's core, yea, in
my heart of hearts,'° as I do thee. (*Kisses her hand*)

SIR GEORGE Such freedom with my niece before my face! Do you
know that lady? Do you know my son, sir?

ROVER Be quiet. 'Jaffier has discovered the plot, and you can't deceive    295
the senate'.°

HARRY  Yes, my conscience wouldn't let me carry it through.

ROVER  'Aye, his conscience hanging about the neck of his heart, says, good Launcelot, and good Gobbo, as aforesaid, good Launcelot Gobbo, take to thy heels and run.'°   300

SIR GEORGE  Why, my lady! Explain, scoundrel and puppy unknown!

LADY AMARANTH  Uncle, I've heard thy father was kind to thee. Return that kindness to thy child. If the lamb in wanton play doth fall among the waters, the shepherd taketh him out, instead of plunging him deeper till he dieth. Though thy hairs now be grey,   305
I'm told they were once flaxen. In short, he is too old in folly, who cannot excuse it in youth.

 *Exit Lady Amaranth*

SIR GEORGE  I'm an old fool! Well, that's civil of you, Madam Niece, and I'm a grey shepherd. With her visions and her vines and her lambs in a ditch! But as for you, young Mr Goat, I'll butt you—   310

ROVER  My dear Abrawang, give up the game. Her ladyship, in seeming to take you for her uncle, has been only humming° you!— What the devil, don't you think the fine creature knows her own true-born uncle?

SIR GEORGE  Certainly, to be sure she knows me.   315

ROVER  Will you have done? Zounds, man, my honoured father was here himself today. Her ladyship knows his person.

SIR GEORGE  Your honoured father! And who's your honoured self?

ROVER  'Now, by my father's son, and that's myself, it shall be sun,   320
moon, or a Cheshire Cheese before I budge. Still crossed and crossed!'°

SIR GEORGE  What do you bawl out to me about Cheshire cheeses, I say—

ROVER  'And I say, as the saying is.'° Your friend, Dick, has told me all,   325
but to convince you of my forgiveness, in our play, as you're a rough and tough, I'll cast you Charles the wrestler.° I do Orlando. I'll trip up your heels° before the whole court.

SIR GEORGE  Trip up my heels! Why, dam'me, I'll—and you, you undutiful chick of an old pelican!° (*Lifting up his cane to strike*   330
*Harry*)

 *Enter John Dory, who receives the blow*

JOHN DORY  What are you at here, cudgelling the people about? But, Mr Buckskin,° I've a word to say to you in private.

SIR GEORGE  Buckskin!

 *Enter Lamp and Trap, and two female servants*

LAMP 'All the world's a stage, and all men and women—'°

SIR GEORGE The men are rogues, and the women hussies. I'll    335
make a clear stage. (*Beats them off, and, amongst the rest, strikes
Rover*)

      *Exeunt Sir George, Harry, John Dory, Lamp and the servants*

ROVER 'A blow, Essex, a blow!'° An old rascally impostor stigmatise
me with a blow? No, I must not put up with it. Zounds! I shall be
tweaked by the nose all round the country. 'Strike me! So may this
arm dash him to the earth like a dead dog despised. Blindness and    340
leprosy, lameness and lunacy, pride, shame, and the name of villain
light on me, if I don't—'° bang Mr Abrawang.

      *Exit Rover*

## 4.2

      *Another apartment*

      *Enter Lady Amaranth and Banks*

BANKS Madam, I could have paid the rent of my little cottage, but
I dare say it was without your ladyship's knowledge that your
steward has turned me out and put my neighbour in possession.

LADY AMARANTH My steward oppress the poor! I did not know it
indeed, friend.    5

BANKS The pangs of adversity I could bear, but the innocent partner
of my misfortunes, my unhappy sister—

LADY AMARANTH I did desire Ephraim to send for thy sister. Did she
dwell with thee, and both now without a home? Let her come to
mine.    10

BANKS The hand of misery has struck us beneath your notice!

LADY AMARANTH Thou dost mistake. To need my assistance is the
highest claim to my attention. Let me see her.

      *Exit Banks*

I could chide myself that these pastimes have turned mine eyes
from the house of woe. Ah, think ye proud and happy affluent! How    15
many in your dancing moments, pine in want, drink the salt tear.
Their morsel, the bread of misery, whilst shrinking from the cold
blast into their cheerless hovels!

      *Enter Banks, leading in Amelia*

BANKS Madam, my sister. (*Bows and retires*)

      *Exit Banks*

LADY AMARANTH Friend, thou art welcome. I feel myself interested    20
in thy concerns.

AMELIA Madam!

LADY AMARANTH I judge thou wert not always unhappy. Tell me
thy condition. Then I shall better know how to serve thee. Is thy
brother thy sole kindred?    25

AMELIA I had a husband and a son.

LADY AMARANTH A widow! If it recall not images, thou wouldst
forget, impart to me thy story. 'Tis rumoured in the village thy
brother is a clergyman. Tell me.

AMELIA Madam, he was, but he has lost his early patron, and is now    30
poor and unbeneficed.

LADY AMARANTH But thy husband—

AMELIA By this brother's advice, now twenty years since, I was prevailed on to listen to the addresses of a young sea officer (my
brother was then chaplain in the navy), but, to our surprise and    35
mortification, we discovered, by the honesty of a sailor in whom
he put confidence, that the Captain's design was only to decoy
me into a seeming marriage, he having ordered him to procure a
counterfeit clergyman. Our humble friend, instead of us, put the
deceit upon his master, by concealing from him that my brother    40
was in orders. He, flattered with the hopes of procuring me an
establishment,° gave into the supposed imposture, and performed
the ceremony.

LADY AMARANTH Duplicity, even with a good intent, is ill.

AMELIA Madam, the event has justified your censure, for my hus-    45
band, not knowing himself bound by any legal tie, abandoned me.
I followed him to the Indies, distracted, still seeking him. I left my
infant at one of our settlements, but, after a fruitless pursuit, on my
return, I found the friend to whose care I had committed my child,
[who] was compelled to retire from the ravages of war, but where I    50
could not learn. Rent with agonising pangs, now without child or
husband, I again saw England, and my brother, who, wounded with
remorse for being the cause of my misfortunes, secluded himself
from the joys of social life, and invited me to partake the repose of
solitude in that humble asylum, from whence we've both just now    55
been driven.

LADY AMARANTH My pity can do thee no good, yet I pity thee. But as
resignation to what must be, may restore peace, if my means can
procure thee comfort, they are at thy pleasure. Come, let thy griefs

subside. Instead of thy cottage, accept thou and thy brother every    60
convenience that my mansion can afford.

AMELIA Madam, I can only thank you with—(*Weeps*)

LADY AMARANTH My thanks are here. Thou shalt be cheerful. I will
introduce thee to my sprightly cousin Harry, and his father, my
humorous uncle. We have delights going forward that may amuse    65
thee.

AMELIA Kind lady!

LADY AMARANTH Come, smile. Though a Quaker, thou seest I am
merry. The sweetest joy of wealth and power is to cheer one
another's drooping heart, and wipe from the pallid cheek the tear of    70
sorrow.

    *Exeunt Lady Amaranth and Amelia*

## 5.1

*A road.*

*Enter three ruffians, dressed as sailors*

FIRST RUFFIAN Well, now, what's to be done?

SECOND RUFFIAN Why, we've been long upon our shifts,° and after all our tricks, twists, and turns, as London was then too hot for us, our tramp to Portsmouth was a hit.°

THIRD RUFFIAN Aye, but since the cash we touched, upon pretending 5 to be able-bodied seamen, is now come to the last shilling, [and] as we deserted, means of a fresh supply to take us back to London must be thought on.

SECOND RUFFIAN How to recruit the pocket without hazarding the neck. 10

FIRST RUFFIAN By an advertisement posted on the stocks° yonder, there are highwaymen upon this road. Thirty guineas are offered by the Quaker lady, owner of the estate round here, to him, who shall apprehend one of these collectors. I wish we could snap up any straggler to bring before her. A Quaker will only require yea for 15 an oath. We might sack° these thirty guineas.

SECOND RUFFIAN Yes, but we must take care, if we fall into the hands of this gentleman that's in pursuit of us. 'Sdeath, isn't this his man, the old boatswain?

FIRST RUFFIAN Don't run, I think we three are a match for him. 20 Instantly, put on your characters of sailors. We may get something out of him. A pitiful story makes such an impression on the soft heart of a true tar, that he'll open his hard hand and drop you his last guinea. If we can but make him believe we were pressed, we have him, only mind me. 25

*Enter John Dory*

JOHN DORY To rattle my lantern! Sir George's temper now always blows a hurricane.

SECOND RUFFIAN (*to John Dory*) What cheer?

JOHN DORY Ha, boy!

THIRD RUFFIAN Bob up with your speaking trumpet. 30

SECOND RUFFIAN Do you see, brother, this is the thing—

*Enter Sir George at the back, unperceived*

SIR GEORGE (*aside*) If these should be my deserters.

FIRST RUFFIAN We three hands, just come home after a long voyage, were pressed in the river,° and, without letting us see our friends, brought round to Portsmouth, and then we entered freely. 'Cause why? We had no choice. Then we run. We hear some gentleman is in chase of us, so, as the shot is all out, we'll surrender.

JOHN DORY  Surrender! Oh, then you've no shot left, indeed. Let's see. (*Feels his pocket*) I haven't the loading of a gun about me now, and this same Monsieur Poverty is a bitter bad enemy.

SIR GEORGE (*aside*)  They are the deserters I've been after!

JOHN DORY  Meet me in an hour's time in the little wood yonder. I'll raise a wind to blow you into a safe latitude. Keep out to sea.° My master's the rock you'll certainly split upon.

SECOND RUFFIAN  This is the first time we ever saw you, but we'll steer by your chart, for I never knew one seaman to betray another.
    *Exeunt Ruffians*

SIR GEORGE (*aside*)  Then they have been pressed. I can't blame them so much for running away.

JOHN DORY  Yes, Sir George would certainly hang 'em.

SIR GEORGE (*advancing*)  I wouldn't. They shall eat beef and drink the King's health. Run and tell them so. Stop. I'll tell them myself.

JOHN DORY  Why, now you are yourself, and a kind, good gentleman, as you used to be.

SIR GEORGE  Since these idle rogues are inclined to return to their duty, they shan't want sea-store.° Take them this money—but, hold! I'll meet them myself, and advise them as I would my children.
    *Exeunt Sir George and John Dory, severally*


# 5.2

*A wood*

*Enter Rover, in his first clothes, with pistols*

ROVER (*agitated*)  Which way did Mr Abrawang take? Dick Buskin, I think, has no suspicion of my intentions. Such a choleric spark will fight, I dare say. If I fall, or even survive this affair, I leave the field of love and the fair prize to the young gentleman I've personated, for I'm determined to see Lady Amaranth no more. Oh, here comes Abrawang. [*Puts up the pistols*]
    *Enter Sir George*

SIR GEORGE Now to relieve these foolish seagulls. They must be
 hovering about this coast.—Ha, puppy unknown!

ROVER You, sir, are the very man I was seeking. You are not ignorant,    10
 Mr Abrawang—

SIR GEORGE Mr What?

ROVER You will not resign your title, ha, ha, ha! Oh, very well, I'll
 indulge you. Sir George Thunder, you honoured me with a blow.

SIR GEORGE Did it hurt you?

ROVER 'Sdeath, sir, as it's my pride to reject even favours, no man    15
 shall offer me an injury.

SIR GEORGE Eh!

ROVER In rank we're equal.

SIR GEORGE Are we, faith? The English of all this is, we're to fight.

ROVER Sir, you've marked on me an indelible stain, only to be washed    20
 out by blood.

SIR GEORGE Why, I've only one objection to fighting you.

ROVER What's that, sir?

SIR GEORGE That you're too brave a lad to be killed.

ROVER Brave! No, sir. At present, I wear the stigma of a coward.    25

SIR GEORGE Zounds! I like a bit of fighting, haven't had a morsel a
 long time. Don't know when I've smelt gunpowder, but to bring
 down a woodcock.

ROVER Take your ground.

SIR GEORGE Yes, but are we to thrust with bullrushes, like two frogs,    30
 or, like two squirrels, pelt one another with nut-shells? For I see no
 other weapons here.

ROVER Oh, yes, sir, here are weapons. (*Gives a pistol*)

SIR GEORGE Well, this is bold work for a privateer° to give battle to a
 King's ship!    35

ROVER Try your charge,° sir, and take your ground.

SIR GEORGE I would not wish to sink, burn, or destroy what I think
 was built for good service. But damme if I don't wing you, to teach
 you better manners.

　　　*Enter the three ruffians, not perceiving Rover*

THIRD RUFFIAN (*looking at Sir George*) Ah, here's the honest fellow    40
 has brought us some cash.

SECOND RUFFIAN We're betrayed. It's the very man that's in pursuit
 of us, and this promise was only a decoy to throw us into his power.
 (*Aside, and pointing to it*) The pistol! We'll secure you! (*Seizes and
 wrenches the pistol from Sir George*)

SIR GEORGE Ah, boys!    45

SECOND RUFFIAN You'd have our lives. Now, we'll have yours. (*Presents the piece° at Sir George*)
>> *Rover advances, and knocks it out of his hand. The ruffians exit, running*

ROVER Rascals! (*Pursues them*)

SIR GEORGE (*takes up the other pistol*) My brave lad! I'll—(*going*)
>> *Enter John Dory*

JOHN DORY No, you shan't. (*Holding him*)

SIR GEORGE The rogues will—

JOHN DORY Never mind the rogues—                                    50
>> *Noise of fighting without. A shot fired.*

SIR GEORGE 'S'blood, must I see my preserver perish? (*Struggling*)

JOHN DORY Well, I know I'm your preserver, and I will perish, but I'll bring you out of harm's way. (*Still holding him*)

SIR GEORGE Though he'd fight me myself—

JOHN DORY Sure, we all know you'd fight the devil.                  55

SIR GEORGE He saved my life.

JOHN DORY I'll save your life. (*Takes him in his arms*) So, hey, haul up,° my noble little crab-walk!°
>> *Exeunt John Dory, carrying Sir George off*

# 5.3

*A room in Banks's cottage*

*Enter Gammon, Banks, and Sim, writing and crying*

GAMMON Boy, go on with the inventory.

SIM (*aside*) How unlucky! Feyther to lay hold of me, when I wanted to practice my part.

BANKS This proceeding is very severe, to lay an execution° on my wretched trifling goods.

GAMMON Aye, you know you've gone up to the big house with your       5
complaint. Her ladyship's steward, to be sure, has made me give back your cottage and farm, but your goods I seized for my rent.

BANKS Only leave me a very few necessaries. By the goodness of my neighbours, I may soon redeem what the law has put into your       10
hands.

GAMMON The affair is now in my lawyer's hands, and plaintiff and defendant chattering about it is all smoke.

SIM Feyther, don't be so cruel to Mr Banks.

GAMMON  I'll mark what I may want for myself. (*To Sim*) Stay here   15
and see that not a pin's worth be removed without my knowledge.
    *Exit Gammon*

SIM  I'll be dom'd if I'll be your watch-dog to bite the poor, that I
won't. Mr Banks, as feyther intends to put up your goods at
auction, if you could but get a friend to buy the choice of them for
you again. Sister Jane has got steward to advance her a quarter's   20
wages, and when I've gone to sell corn for feyther, besides presents,
I've made a market penny° now and then. (*Takes out a small leather
purse, and offers it to Banks*) Here, it's not much, but every little
helps.

BANKS  I thank you, my good-natured boy, but keep your money.   25

SIM  Last summer, you saved me from being drowned in Black Pool.
If you'll not take this, ecod, in there I'll directly fling it, and let old
Nick save it from being drowned, an' he can. Take it. Now, do take
it. Take it—take it. (*Weeps*)

BANKS  My kind lad, then I'll not hurt your feelings by opposing your   30
liberality. (*Takes it*)

SIM  He, he, he! You've now given my heart such a pleasure as I never
felt, nor I'm sure feyther afore me.

BANKS  But, Sim, whatever may be his opinion of worldly prudence,
still remember he's your parent.   35
    [*Exit Banks*]

SIM  I will. 'One elbow chair, one claw-table'.
    *Exit Sim, writing. Enter Amelia*

AMELIA  The confusion into which Lady Amaranth's family is thrown
by the sudden departure and apprehended danger of her young
cousin, must have prevented her ladyship from giving that
attention to our affairs that I'm sure was her inclination. If I can   40
but prevail on my brother, too, to accept her protection—I can't
enjoy the delights of her ladyship's hospitable mansion, and leave
him here still subject to the insults of the churlish farmer. Heavens,
who's this?
    *Enter Rover, hastily, his hair and dress disordered*

ROVER  What a race! I've at last got from the bloodhounds! Ah, if old   45
Abrawang had but followed and backed me, we'd have 'tickled their
catastrophes',° but, when they got me alone, three upon one were
odds, so safe's the word.° What did they want with my life? If
printed, it wouldn't sell for sixpence. Whose house is this I've
dashed into? Eh! The friendly cottage of my old gentleman. (*Calls*)   50
Are you at home? Gadso, I had a hard struggle for it. Murder was

their intent, so it was well for me I was born without brains. I'm quite weak, faint! (*Leans against the wall*)

AMELIA (*advancing, with concern*)  Sir, are not you well?

ROVER  Madam, I ask pardon. Hem, yes, ma'am, very well. I thank  55
you—now exceeding well—got into an affray there, a kind of
hobble° with some worthy gentlemen, only simple, honest farmers.
I fancy they mistook me for a sheaf of barley, for they down with
me, and then threshed so heartily, gad, their flails flew merrily
about my ears, but I got up, and when I could no longer fight like a  60
mastiff, why, I ran like a greyhound. But, dear ma'am, pray excuse
me. This is very rude, faith.

AMELIA  You seem disturbed. Sir, will you take any refreshment?

ROVER  Madam, you're very good. Only a little of your currant wine,
if you please. If I don't forget, it stands—(*points*)  65

> *Amelia brings a decanter from a beaufet. Rover takes it and fills*

Madam, I've the honour of drinking your health. (*Drinks*)

AMELIA  I hope you're not hurt, sir.

ROVER  'A little better, but very faint still.'° I had a sample of this
before, and liked it so much that. Madam, 'won't you take
another'?°  70

AMELIA  Sir! (*Takes a glass, and lays it by*)

ROVER  Madam, 'if you'd been fighting as I have', you'd—well, well.
(*Fills and drinks*) Now I'm as well as any man—'in Illyria.'° Got a
few hard knocks though.

AMELIA  You'd better repose a little. You seemed much disordered  75
coming in.

ROVER (*places chairs and both sit*)  Why, ma'am, you must know, thus it
was—

> *Enter Sheriff's Officer*

OFFICER  Come ma'am. Mr Gammon says this chair is wanted to
make up the half dozen above.  80

> *Lays hold of Amelia's chair. She rises terrified*

ROVER  Why, what's all this?

OFFICER  Why, the furniture's seized on execution, and a man must
do his duty.

ROVER  Then, scoundrel, know, a man's first duty is civility and tenderness to a woman.  85

AMELIA  Heavens! Where's my brother? This gentleman will bring
himself into trouble.

OFFICER  Master, d'ye see, I'm representative for his honour the High
Sheriff.

ROVER  Every High Sheriff should be a gentleman, and, when he's    90
    represented by a rascal, he's dishonoured. Damn it, I might as well
    live about Covent Garden and every night get beating the watch,°
    for here, among groves and meadows, I'm always squabbling with
    constables.

    *Takes up a stick from a corner of the room, and holds it behind
    him*

OFFICER  Come, come, I must.    95

ROVER  'As you say, sir, last Wednesday, so it was.'° Sir, your most
    obedient humble servant. (*Bows, with great ceremony*) Pray, sir, may
    I take the liberty to know, were you ever astonished?

OFFICER  What?

ROVER  Because, sir, I intend to astonish you. (*Takes his hand and*    100
    *strikes him*) Now, sir, you are astonished.

OFFICER  Yes, but see if I don't suit you with an action.°

ROVER  'Right, suit the action to the word, the word to the action. See
    if the gentlewoman be not affrighted.'° 'Michael, I'll make thee an
    example.'°    105

OFFICER  Yes, fine example when goods are seized here by the law,
    and—

ROVER  'Thou worm and maggot of the law!'° 'Hop me over every
    kennel, or you shall hop without my custom.'°

OFFICER  I don't value your custom.    110

ROVER  You are astonished. Now, I'll amaze you.

OFFICER  No, I won't be amazed, but see if I don't.

ROVER  Hop.

    *Exit Officer, muttering and frightened*

    Stop, ma'am. These sort of gentry are unpleasant company for a
    lady, so I'll just see him to the door, and then I'll see him outside the    115
    door. Ma'am, I'm your most obedient humble servant.

    *Rover bows respectfully and exits hastily*

AMELIA  I feel a strange kind of curiosity to know who this young
    gentleman is. He must have known the house by the freedom,° but
    then his gaiety (without familiar rudeness), native elegance of
    manners and good breeding, seem to make him at home every-    120
    where. My brother, I think must know—

    *Enter Banks hastily, and agitated*

BANKS  Amelia, did you see the young man that was here? Some
    ruffians and a posse of the country people have bound and dragged
    him from the door, on the allegation of three men who mean

to swear he has robbed them. They have taken him to Lady   125
Amaranth's.

AMELIA How! He did enter in confusion as if pursued, but I'll stake
my life on his innocence.

BANKS The freedom of his censures on Farmer Gammon's conduct,
and the friendly office he did me, have brought the sordid churl's   130
malice on him, and he has encouraged these ruffians, in hopes
of the reward offered by Ephraim Smooth, for apprehending
footpads,° to drag the young fellow up to Lady Amaranth's, where
the farmer says, he has already appeared in a feigned character.

AMELIA I'll speak to Lady Amaranth, and, in spite of calumny, he   135
shall have justice. He would not let me be insulted, because he saw
me an unprotected woman, without a husband or a son, and shall
he want an advocate? Brother, come.

*Exeunt Amelia and Banks*

## 5.4

*A dressing-room in Lady Amaranth's*

*Enter Jane, with a light*

JANE I believe there's not a soul in the house but myself. My lady has
sent all the folks round the country to search after the young
'squire. She'll certainly break her heart if anything happens to him.
I don't wonder, for surely he's a dear sweet gentleman. The pity of
it is, his going spoils all our fine play, and I had just got my part   5
quite by heart. However, I must do the room up for Mr Banks's
sister, that my lady has invited here. (*Adjusts the toilet*)°

*Enter Ephraim Smooth*

EPHRAIM The man John Dory has carried the man George hither in
his arms and has locked him up. Coming into the house, they did
look to me like a blue lobster with a shrimp in his claws. Oh, here is   10
the damsel I love, and alone.

JANE They say when folks look in the glass, at night, they see the
black gentleman.°

*As she's looking in the glass, Jane sees Ephraim over her shoulder
and screams*

EPHRAIM Thou art employed in vanity.

JANE Well, who want's you?   15

EPHRAIM  It's natural for woman to love man.

JANE  Yea, but not such ugly men as you. Why would you come in to frighten me, when you know there's nobody here but ourselves?

EPHRAIM  [aside] I am glad of that.—I am the elm, and thou the honeysuckle. Let thy arms entwine me.                                    20

JANE  (aside) Oh, what a rogue is here! But yonder comes my lady, and I'll show him off to her in his true colours.

EPHRAIM  Clasp me round.

JANE  Well, I will, if you'll take off your hat and make me a fine, low bow.                                                          25

EPHRAIM  I cannot bend my knee, nor take off my beaver.

JANE  Then you're very impudent. Go along.

EPHRAIM  (takes off his hat and bows) But to win thy favour.

JANE  Now kneel down to me.

EPHRAIM  I cannot, but one lovely smile may smile me down.            30
        *She smiles; he kneels*

JANE  Well now, read me a speech out of that fine playbook.

EPHRAIM  I read a play? A-bo-mi-na-tion! But, Jane, wilt thou kiss me?

JANE  I kiss a man! A-bo-mi-na-ti-on! But you may take my hand.

EPHRAIM  Oh, 'tis comfort to the lip of the faithful! (*Kisses her hand*)   35
        *Enter Lady Amaranth*

LADY AMARANTH  How! (*Taps him on the shoulder*) Ah, thou sly and deceitful hypocrite!

JANE  There, ma'am is the demure, holy man that would prevent our play.

LADY AMARANTH  So severely censure others, and put fetters on me,     40
which now I'm determined to break!

EPHRAIM  Verily Mary, I was buffeted by Satan in the shape of a damsel.

LADY AMARANTH  Go!

EPHRAIM  My spirit is sad though my feet move so nimble.              45
        *Exit Ephraim Smooth slowly*

LADY AMARANTH  But, oh heavens, no tidings of my dearest Henry! Jane, let them renew their search.

JANE  Here's Madam Amelia. You see I've got her room ready, my lady, but I'll go make brother Sim look for the young 'squire.
        *Exit Jane. Enter Amelia*

AMELIA  Oh, madam, might I implore your influence with—             50

LADY AMARANTH  Friend, thou art ill accommodated here, but I hope thou wilt excuse. My mind is a sea of trouble, my peace shipwrecked. Oh, friend, had'st thou seen my cousin Harry, thou too, all who knew him, must be anxious for his safety! How unlucky this servant to prevent Sir George from giving him that assistance, which paternal care and, indeed, gratitude demanded, for it was filial affection which led him to pursue those wicked men. 55

JOHN DORY (*without*) Heave ahead.°

*Enter John Dory and Sir George*

SIR GEORGE Rascal! Whip me up like a pound of tea!° Dance me about like a young bear! Make me quit the preserver of my life! Yes, 60 puppy unknown will think me a poltroon, and that I was afraid to follow and second him.

JOHN DORY Well, you may as well turn into your hammock, for this night out you shall not budge. (*Sees Amelia*) Oh, mercy of heaven. Isn't it? Only give one look. 65

AMELIA (*seeing Sir George*) My husband! (*Swoons; Lady Amaranth supports her*)

SIR GEORGE 'Tis my Amelia!

JOHN DORY (*stopping Sir George and looking attentively at Amelia*) Reef the foresail!° First, you cracked her heart by sheering off, and now you'll overset her by bringing to.°

LADY AMARANTH Hold! Soft! She recovers! 70

AMELIA Are you at length returned to me, my Seymour?

LADY AMARANTH Seymour! Her mind is disturbed. This is mine uncle, Sir George Thunder.

JOHN DORY No, no, my lady, she knows what she's saying very well.

SIR GEORGE Niece, I have been a villain to this lady, I confess. But, 75 my dear Amelia, Providence has done you justice in part. From the first month I quitted you, I have never entered one happy hour on my journal. Hearing that you foundered, and considering myself the cause, the worm of remorse has since gnawed my timbers. 80

AMELIA You're not still offended with me?

SIR GEORGE Me! Can you forgive my offence, and condescend to take my hand as an atonement?

AMELIA Your hand! Do you forget that we are already married?

SIR GEORGE Aye, there was my rascality. 85

JOHN DORY You may say that.

SIR GEORGE That marriage, my dear, I'm ashamed to own it—but it was—

JOHN DORY As good as you had been lashed together by the Chaplain of the Eagle. 90

SIR GEORGE Hold your tongue, you impudent crimp,° you pandar, you bad adviser! I'll strike my false colours!° I now acknowledge the chaplain you provided was—

JOHN DORY Was a good man, and a greater honour to his black, than your honour has been to your blue cloth. Eh, by the word of a    95
seaman, here he is himself.

*Enter Banks*

SIR GEORGE Your brother?

BANKS Captain Seymour!

SIR GEORGE My dear Banks, I'll make every reparation. Amelia shall really be my wife.    100

BANKS That, sir, my sister is already, for when I performed the marriage ceremony, which you took only as the cloak of your deception, I was actually in orders.

JOHN DORY Now who's the crimp and the pandar? I never told you this since because I thought a man's own reflections were the best    105
punishment for betraying an innocent woman.

SIR GEORGE You shall be a post-captain,° sink me, if you shan't. (*Shakes hands with John Dory*)

LADY AMARANTH Madam, my inmost soul partaketh of thy gladness and joy for thy reformation, (*to Sir George*) but thy prior marriage to this lady annuls the subsequent, and my cousin Harry is not now    110
thy heir.

SIR GEORGE So much the better. He's an unnatural cub, but, Amelia, I flatter myself I have an heir—my infant boy.

AMELIA Ha, husband, you had.

SIR GEORGE Gone! Well, well, I see I have been a miserable scoundrel.    115
Eh, I will, yes, if my son Harry proceeds in his unworthy disobedience, I'll adopt that brave, kind, lad, that wouldn't let anybody kill me but himself. He shall have my estate, that's my own acquisition. My lady, marry him. Puppy Unknown's a fine fellow! Amelia, only for him, you would never have found your husband,    120
Captain Seymour in Sir George Thunder.

AMELIA How!

BANKS Are you Sir George Thunder?

JOHN DORY Oh, I didn't tell you that at the time because you might be for finding him out too soon and upstall.    125

*Enter Landlord, followed by Ephraim Smooth*

LANDLORD Please you, madam, they've got a footpad in custody.

EPHRAIM I am come to sit in judgement, for there is a bad man in thy house, Mary.

JOHN DORY  Then why don't you get out of it?

EPHRAIM  Bring him before me.    130

SIR GEORGE  Before you, old Squintibus! And, perhaps you don't know I'm a magistrate?

EPHRAIM  I'll examine him.

SIR GEORGE  You be damned. I'll examine him myself. (*Shoves Ephraim*) Tow him in here. I'll give him a passport to Winchester    135
bilboes.°

AMELIA (*kneels to Sir George*)  Oh, sir, as you hope for mercy, extend it to this youth. But even should he be guilty, which from our knowledge of his benevolent and noble nature, I think next to an impossibility, let the services he has rendered to us—he protected,    140
relieved your forsaken wife, and her unhappy brother, in the hour of want and sorrow.

SIR GEORGE  What, Amelia plead for a robber! Consider, my love, justice is above bias or partiality. If my son violated the laws of his country, I'd deliver him up a public victim to disgrace and    145
punishment.

LADY AMARANTH  Ah, my impartial uncle, had thy country any laws to punish him, who, instead of paltry gold, would rob the artless virgin of her dearest treasure, in the rigid judge I should now behold the trembling criminal.    150

> *Enter Twitch, with Rover bound, who keeps his face averted*
> *behind his hat, and two of the Ruffians*

EPHRAIM (*advances*)  Speak thou!

SIR GEORGE  Hold thy clapper,° thou! Who are the prosecutors?

EPHRAIM  Call in—

SIR GEORGE  Will nobody stop his mouth?

> *John Dory pushes him against the wall*

Who are the prosecutors?    155

TWITCH  There, tell his worship, the justice.

SECOND RUFFIAN  A justice! Oh, the devil! (*Aside*) I thought we should have nothing but quakers to deal with.

SIR GEORGE  Come, how did this fellow rob you?

SECOND RUFFIAN (*in a feigned country voice*)  Why, your honour, I    160
swear—

SIR GEORGE (*looking at them*)  Oh, ho!

SECOND RUFFIAN  Zounds, we're wrong! This is the very—

SIR GEORGE  Clap down the hatches, secure these sharks.

ROVER  I thought I should find you here, Abrawang, and that you had    165
some knowledge of these fellows.

LADY AMARANTH (*aside*)  Heavens, my cousin Harry!

SIR GEORGE  The devil! Isn't this my spear and shield?°

JOHN DORY (*advances*)  My young master, oh, what have you been at  170
here? (*Unbinds him*) This rope may yet be wanted.

> *Enter Harry*

HARRY  My dear fellow, are you safe?

ROVER  Yes, Dick. I was brought in here very safe, I assure you.

HARRY  A confederate in custody below has made a confession of
their villainy: that they concerted° this plan to accuse him of a
robbery, first, for revenge, then, in hopes to share the reward  175
for apprehending him. He also owns they are not sailors, though
they fraudulently took the bounty,° but depredators° on the
public.

SIR GEORGE  Keep them safe in limbo.°

> *The Ruffians [are] taken off°*

SIR GEORGE  Not knowing that the Justice of Peace whom they've  180
brought the lad now here before, is the very man they attacked, ha,
ha, ha! The rogues have fallen into their own snare.

ROVER  What, now you're a Justice of the Peace? Well said, Abrawang!

AMELIA  Then, Sir George, you know him too?

SIR GEORGE  Know puppy unknown? To be sure!  185

ROVER  Still, Sir George! What, then, you will not resign your
Knighthood? (*To Amelia*) Madam, I am happy to see you again.
(*Shakes hands with Banks*) Ah, how do you do, my kind host?

LADY AMARANTH  I rejoice at thy safety. (*To Sir George*) Be reconciled
to him.  190

SIR GEORGE  Reconciled? If I don't love, respect and honour him, I
should be unworthy of the life he rescued. But who is he?

HARRY  Sir, he is—

ROVER  Dick, I thank you for your good wishes, but I am determined
not to impose on this lady. Madam, as I at first told that well-  195
meaning tar, when he forced me to your house, I am not the son of
Sir George Thunder.

JOHN DORY  No! Then I wish you were the son of an admiral, and I
your father.

HARRY  You refuse the lady! To punish you, I've a mind to take her  200
myself. My dear cousin—

ROVER  Stop Dick. If I who adore her won't, you shall not. No, no,
madam, never mind what this fellow says, he's as poor as myself,
isn't he, Abrawang?

HARRY Then my dear Rover, since you are so obstinately dis-   205
interested,° I'll no longer tease my father, whom you here see,
and in your strolling friend, his very truant Harry, that ran from
Portsmouth school and joined you and fellow comedians.

ROVER Indeed!

HARRY (to Lady Amaranth) Dear cousin forgive me, if through my   210
zeal for the happiness of my friend, I endeavoured to promote
yours, by giving you a husband more worthy than myself.

ROVER Am I to believe? Madam, is your uncle, Sir George Thunder,
in this room?

LADY AMARANTH He is. (Looking at Sir George)   215

ROVER 'Tis so! Then you are in reality, what I've had the impudence
to assume, and have perplexed your father with my ridiculous
effrontery! (Turns to John Dory, angrily) I told you, I insisted, I
wasn't the person you took me for, but you would thrust me into
your chariot, and drag me hither! I am ashamed and mortified.   220
Madam, I take my leave.

EPHRAIM Thou art welcome to go.

ROVER (aside) Sir George, as the father of my friend, I cannot lift my
hand against you, but I hope, sir, you'll apologise to me.

SIR GEORGE Aye, with pleasure, my noble splinter. Now tell me from   225
what dock you were launched, my heart of oak?

ROVER I've heard, in England, sir, but from my earliest knowledge, till
within a very few years, I've been in the East Indies.

SIR GEORGE Beyond seas? Well, and how?

ROVER It seems I was committed an infant to the care of a lady, who   230
was herself obliged by the gentle Hyder Ally° to strike her toilet,°
and decamp without beat of drum, leaving me a chubby little
fellow, squatted on a carpet. A sergeant's wife alone returned, and
snatched me off triumphant, through fire, smoke, cannon, cries,
and carnage.   235

LADY AMARANTH (to Amelia) Dost thou mark?

AMELIA Sir, can you recollect the name of the town where—

ROVER Yes, ma'am, the town was Negapatnam.°

AMELIA I thank you, sir. (Gazes with delight and earnestness on Rover)

ROVER An officer, who'd much rather act Scrub on the stage than   240
Hotspur° in the field, brought me up behind the scenes on the
Calcutta theatre. I was rolled on the boards, acted myself into
favour of a colonel, promised a pair of colours,° but, impatient to
find my parents, hid myself in the steerage of an homeward-bound

ship, assumed the name of Rover, from the uncertainty of my fate, 245
and having murdered more poets than Rajahs,° stepped on English
ground, unencumbered with rupees or pagodas.° Ha, ha, ha!
Would'st thou come home so, little Ephraim?

EPHRAIM  I would bring myself home with some money.

AMELIA  Excuse my curiosity, sir, what was the lady's name in whose 250
care you were left?

ROVER  Oh, ma'am, she was the lady of a Major Linstock, but I heard
my mother's name was Seymour?

SIR GEORGE  Why, Amelia!

AMELIA  My son! 255

ROVER  Madam!

AMELIA  It is my Charles! (*Embraces him*)

SIR GEORGE  Eh!

LADY AMARANTH  Thou seest he is my gay, gallant, generous cousin!

JOHN DORY (*sings and capers; Claps Ephraim on the shoulder*) Tol lol 260
lol! Though I never heard it before, my heart told me he was a chip
of the old block.

AMELIA (*to Rover, pointing to Sir George*) Your father!

ROVER  Can it? Heaven! Then have I attempted to raise my impious
hand against a parent's life! 265

SIR GEORGE  My dear, brave boy! My son with spirit to fight me as a
stranger, yet defend me as a father!

AMELIA  And knowing her only as a woman wronged, to protect his
helpless mother!

BANKS  By relieving the stranger, Charles, you little thought 'twas an 270
uncle you snatched from a prison.

LADY AMARANTH  Nor that thou by that benign action, did first
engage the esteem of thy fond cousin. (*Takes him by the hand*)
Uncle, you'll recollect 'twas I, who first introduced a son to thee.

SIR GEORGE  And I hope you will next introduce a grandson to me, 275
young slyboots. Harry, you've lost your fortune.

HARRY  Yes, sir, but I've gained a brother, whose friendship (before I
knew him to be such) I prized above any fortune in England.

ROVER  My dearest Rosalind!

AMELIA (*To Lady Amaranth*) Then, will you take our Charles?° 280

LADY AMARANTH  Yes, but only on condition thou bestowest thy
fortune on his friend and brother. Mine is sufficient for us, is
it not?

ROVER  Angelic creature! To think of my generous friend! But now for
*As You Like It*—Where's Lamp and Trap? I shall ever love a play. 285

A spark from Shakespeare's muse of fire was the star that guided
me through my desolate and bewildered maze of life, and brought
me to these unexpected blessings.

> To merit friends so good, so sweet a wife,
> The tender husband be my part for life.
> My Wild Oats sown, let candid Thespian laws°
> Decree that glorious harvest—your applause.

290

## FINIS

# Epilogue

Written by George Colman, junior, Esq.

And spoken by Mrs Pope

'Twas Epilogue's tame talk in ancient days,
With trembling step advanced, to court your praise,
And mercy beg for guilty Poets' lays—
Good lack! how she is chang'd! long used to speak,
She scorns to bear her faculties so meek,                    5
Like a spoilt Miss, vain, pert, and forward grown,
She chatters—on all business but her own.
The Play, the Poet, Actors, all forgot,
Epilogue prates about she knows not what;
Lugs head and shoulders in, a jumble all!                    10
Box-lobby Bobbies, Lady Mayoress's Ball,°
Thick neck-cloths, city frumps, cork-rumps, and hops at
    Pewterer's Hall.°

Thus would-be Wits, whate'er has been expressed,
Foist in their oar—they have but one smart jest,°
Start bluntly from the subject, that's before ye,            15
To tell their frothy, threadbare, only story.

Let us for once, however, Fashion sway,
Speak somewhat of the Poet and his Play,
How like ye our wild Drama, wou'd ye know,
A certain sower, who came forth to sow,                      20
Sprinkling his Oats—that's character—his Quakers,
His Sailors, Players, o'er five acts—that's Acres!
Or rather here his field—'tis you who nourish
The seeds of Genius, and make merit flourish.
Hence springs the harvest of the labourers toil,            25
From hence, this genial air, this generous foil.
Here humble worth securely strikes the root,
While favour fans the plant, and bids it shoot:
No spleen to bite the blossoms as they ope,
No malice breathes, to mildew—modest hope.                  30

If such the land, secure our Poet then;
Safe his *Wild Oats*; secure his *Strolling Gentlemen*;
And let no Stroller, who our Drama sees,
For Strollers now there are of all degrees,
Think we mean satire, when we mean to please;               35
We wou'd not wring their withers, whose sad curse°
It is, in barns, to bellow forth blank verse;
Where hungry Richard deals forth death and grief,
And stakes a kingdom, for a steak of beef:°
Where crook'd-back'd Glos'ter plays the bloody glutton,°      40
And cuts up Kings; but never cuts up mutton.
Where Romeo too, that billing Turtle Dove,
Feeds with his Juliet upon airy Love;
While Hamlet vainly fights for boil'd and roast,
'Till Hamlet's self appears like Hamlet's Ghost.             45
Where Denmark's King, his murd'rous ends fulfilling,
Soon gains a crown—the Actor not a shilling!
These wou'd we not offend, our Bard reveres,
Our strolling Actors, and out acting Peers.
Nor would he glance, like some invidious elves,             50
At those who act to entertain themselves,
He is not one of those same trait'rous fellows
To vex Right Honourable, tame Othello's.
If our wise Commons, in a sapient mood,
Act Plays thro' Christmas for their country's good;°         55
If Pierre plans treason, thro' a black December,
And votes at last—an honest Country Member:
If fashionable Jaffier rants, whose life°
In private proves the love he bears his wife;
If four-foot Lords, will gay Lothario roar,                 60
And round, squat, Lady Betties, act Jane Shore.°
If this be true as holy Writ or Bible,
Tho' 'tis a truth, our Author means no Libel.
His mark is life, should his sketch give you pleasure,
The grateful Bard is happy beyond measure.                  65

# EXPLANATORY NOTES

## Abbreviations

Citations are usually to the first edition unless otherwise indicated. Shakespeare quotations are from *William Shakespeare: The Complete Works*, ed. Stanley Wells, Gary Taylor, John Jowett, and William Montgomery (Oxford, 1986).

| | |
|---|---|
| *CH* | *Henry Fielding: The Critical Heritage*, ed. Ronald Paulson and Thomas Lockwood (London, 1969) |
| *Chevalier* | *The Clandestine Marriage*, ed. Noel Chevalier (Peterborough, Ont., 1995) |
| *Cotton* | *The Compleat English Gamester* (London, 1674) |
| *Davis* | *She Stoops to Conquer*, ed. Tom Davis (London, 1979) |
| *Garrick Letters* | *The Letters of David Garrick*, ed. David M. Little and George M. Kahrl, 3 vols. (London, 1963) |
| *Goldsmith Letters* | *The Collected Letters of Oliver Goldsmith*, ed. Katharine C. Balderston (Cambridge, 1928) |
| *Hunt and Willis* | John Dixon Hunt and Peter Willis, *The Genius of the Place: The English Landscape Garden, 1620–1820* (London, 1975) |
| *Joseph Andrews* | Fielding, *Joseph Andrews*, ed. M. C. Battestin (Oxford, 1967) |
| *Life of Johnson* | *The Life of Samuel Johnson*, ed. G. B. Hill, rev. L. F. Powell, 6 vols. (Oxford, 1934–64), |
| *Mikhail* | *Goldsmith: Interviews and Recollections*, ed. E. H. Mikhail (Basingstoke, 1993) |
| *Miscellanies* | Fielding, *Miscellanies*, vol. i, ed. H. K. Miller (Oxford, 1972) |
| *OED* | *Oxford English Dictionary* |
| *Ogden* | *She Stoops to Conquer*, ed. James Ogden (London, 2001) |
| *Paulson* | Ronald Paulson, *Hogarth*, 3 vols (New Brunswick, NJ, 1991–3) |
| *Pedicord and Bergmann* | *The Plays of David Garrick. A Complete Collection of the Social Satires, French Adaptations, Pantomimes, Christmas and Musical Plays, Preludes, Interludes, and Burlesques, to which is added the Alterations and Adaptations of the Plays of Shakespeare and Other Dramatists from the Sixteenth to the Eighteenth Centuries*, ed. Harry William Pedicord and Frederick Louis Bergmann, 7 vols. (Carbondale, Ill., 1980–2) |

| | |
|---|---|
| *Plays* | *Henry Fielding: Plays (Volume One, 1728–1731)*, ed. Thomas Lockwood (Oxford, 2004). |
| *Rousseau* | *Goldsmith: The Critical Heritage*, ed. G. S. Rousseau (London, 1974) |
| *SJ* | *A Dictionary of the English Language*, compiled by Samuel Johnson, 1st ed., (London, 1755). |
| *The Alchemist and Other Plays* | ed. Gordon Campbell (Oxford, 1998) |
| *The Recruiting Officer and Other Plays* | ed. William Myers (Oxford, 1995) |
| *Tom Jones* | Fielding, *Tom Jones*, ed. Martin C. Battestin; text ed. by Fredson Bowers, 2 vols. (Oxford, 1974) |
| *Wood* | *Plays by David Garrick and George Coleman the Elder*, ed. E. R. Wood (Cambridge, 1982) |
| *Works (Johnson)* | *The Yale Edition of the Works of Samuel Johnson*, general editorship of Allen T. Hazen, later John H. Middendorf (New Haven, 1958– ) |
| *Works* | *The Collected Works of Oliver Goldsmith*, ed. Arthur Friedman, 5 vols. (Oxford, 1966) |
| *WW* | *The Way of the World*, ed. Brian Gibbons (London, 1971) |

# The Modern Husband

### EPIGRAPH

*Haec ego non credam . . .*: lines 51–2, 55–7 of Juvenal's First Satire (trans. Niall Rudd, *Juvenal: The Satires* (Oxford, 1992), 4):

> Am I not right to think this calls for Venusina's lamp?
> am I not right to attack it ? . . .
> when a pimp, if his wife is barred from benefit, coolly pockets
> the gifts brought by her lover, trained to stare at the ceiling,
> trained to snore in his cups through a nose that's wide awake . . .

Its relevance to the Moderns is clear. The whole passage supplies Juvenal's motives for writing satire. Lines 52 to 54 have the poet refusing to turn to the writing of epics or epic episodes of Hercules or Diomedes because of a more pressing need to focus on widespread immorality nearer to hand.

### DEDICATION

*Sir Robert Walpole*: see Introduction, pp. xv–xvii. As Prime Minister since 1720, he had attracted staunch opposition to his style of government (self-aggrandizing and monopolistic) from various commentators. For example, Viscount Bolingbroke's opposition paper, *The Craftsman*, persistently claimed that he had used Treasury funds to bribe electors in the 1727 election; see Isaac Kramnick, *Bolingbroke and his Circle: The Politics of Nostalgia in the Age of Walpole* (Cambridge, Mass., 1968), 111–15, 121–4 and Bertrand Goldgar, *Walpole and the Wits: The Relation of Politics to Literature, 1722–1742* (Lincoln, Neb., 1976), 65–86. There is no clear indication in the Dedication that Fielding's praise is ironic. He was certainly capable of applying to the powerful for favour; see his verse epistle, 'To the Right Honourable Sir Robert Walpole' (1730) wherein he petitions for some form of government sinecure. On the other hand, Fielding had recently attacked Walpole for (*a*) his own personal profiteering (in the anonymous ballad, 'The Norfolk Lanthorn', published in *The Craftsman* during the summer of 1728) and (*b*) on his screening himself and friends from the law, the implicit comment of his play, *Rape upon Rape* (1730). In 1731, his thinly disguised ridicule of both the Prime Minister and the royal family had so concerned the Haymarket company that they obliged Fielding to withdraw his *The Grub-Street Opera* from production. It is probable that Fielding could praise Walpole in a Dedication, whilst depending on *The Modern Husband*'s clear distaste for the Great, in the person of Lord Richly, to tell a quite different story in production.

2 *peace of Europe*: Walpole had skilfully isolated France commercially and diplomatically in the second Treaty of Vienna (July 1731); see J. H. Plumb, *Sir Robert Walpole*, 2 vols. (London, 1956), I. 228–32.

29 *your enemies at home*: see above. Bolingbroke's satires on the administration in the pages of *The Craftsman* (principally 1726–35) were the most consistent source of opposition, but there were several literary sources that exposed the nepotism and financial double-dealing supposed to be characteristic of Walpole's government, e.g. Alexander Pope's *Dunciad* (1728; rev. as *The Dunciad Variorum* (1729)), especially Book III, and Jonathan Swift's *Gulliver's Travels* (1726), especially Book I. The most trenchant satires were street ballads, such as 'Robin will be out at last' (collected in *Political Ballads illustrating the Administration of Sir Robert Walpole*, ed. Milton Percival (Oxford, 1916), 15–16):

> Each Post he hath fill'd
> With Wretches unskill'd,
> In all other Arts except Fobbing;
> For no Man of Sense
> Would ever commence
> Such prostitute Creatures of *Robin*.
>
> (p. 15)

PROLOGUE

8 *killed a ghost*: in his *Tom Thumb, A Tragedy* (1730), revised as *The Tragedy of Tragedies: or The Life and Death of Tom Thumb the Great* (1731), Fielding has Tom Thumb, on the point of marriage to Huncamunca, swallowed by a cow. This does not prevent his being killed a second time, but this time as a Ghost, by Lord Grizzle.

10 *'gainst the cause of sense*: Nearest in meaning to Johnson's 'Meaning; import' (sense 10). This was very much a debate Fielding was ready to have with several current popular forms of entertainment, even if his own work proved vulnerable to the argument. His own Epilogue to Theobald's *Orestes: A Dramatic Opera* (1731) had claimed that his recent success with *Tom Thumb* was questionable:

> Once in an Age, at least, your Smiles dispense
> To *English* Sounds, and Tragedy that's Sense.
> These are Variety to you, who come
> From the *Italian Opera*, and *Tom Thumb*.
> (ll. 35–8, p. 79)

The realist, Witmore, in *The Author's Farce* (1730), educates Harry Luckless in the ways of the London audiences in 2.9, and bewails the scarcity of dramatic *ethos:* 'I have heard Sense run down, and seen Idiotism, downright Idiotism triumph so often, that I cou'd almost think of Wit and Folly as Mr *Hobbes* does of Moral Good and Evil, that there are no such things' (*Plays*, 253). cf. Lord Richly and Gaywit's exchange on the taste of the town at 2.1.200–28.

20 *the Temple*: a renowned law college in Fleet Street, once the residence of the Knights Templars in Britain. Harry Wilding is a libertine law student, the eponymous rake of *The Temple Beau* (1730).

34 *comedy to farce debase*: the main contention of *The Author's Farce*, probably written to emphasize the debased choices made by managers Colley Cibber and Robert Wilks for the Drury Lane season of 1730. They had been so lukewarm in supporting at the theatre Fielding's first attempt at a five-act comedy, *Love in Several Masques* (1728), that he was immediately obliged to have his next 'regular' play, *The Temple Beau*, staged at the far less fashionable Goodman's Fields in January 1730. Luckless, as Master of his own Puppet Show, in *The Author's Farce*, reacts to the Player's objection that such 'art' is 'below the Dignity of the Stage' by attempting a pragmatic defence of that 'low' form: 'That may be, so is all Farce, and yet you see a Farce brings more Company to a House than the best Play that ever was writ, . . . who would not then rather Eat by his Nonsense than Starve by his Wit?' (3.1; *Plays*, 256).

38 *sinking honour of the stage*: as Fielding had had to endure much recent denigration for his unsparing descriptions of immorality, this reads as an ironic reversal of the critical current. Worse was to come; see 'Prosaicus',

on *The Covent Garden Tragedy*, in *The Grub-Street Journal* (no. 127), 8 June 1732: 'The success of the Piece will determine whether the age is fallen to the lowest ebb; for I should entertain but a bad opinion of the intellects of that Man, or chastity of that Woman, who would give the least encouragement to the most dull obscene Piece, that, I may venture to say, ever appeared on any public stage' (*CH*, 43). In the 'Preface' to *The Tragedy of Tragedies* (1731), Fielding, as 'H. Scriblerus Secundus', his affectionate homage to the composite *nom de plume* of Swift, Pope, Gay, and other early-century wits made great play with the mock-heroic possibilities of the writer: 'He is very rarely within sight through the whole Play, either rising higher than the Eye of your understanding can soar, or sinking lower than it careth to stoop' (*Plays*, 546).

1.1.4 *maam*: dialectal form of address to female superior.

22 *tomorrow se'ennight*: a week tomorrow.

30 *Lady Matadore's*: in certain card games, such as Quadrille or Ombre, Matadores were the principal cards. Cotton calls them the 'killing cards' (*Cotton*, 70).

60 *Quadrille rings*: no technical term. Mrs Modern refers to jewellery won at Quadrille.

70 *Sans-prendre-vole*: a game where one player wins all the tricks without the benefit of having first discarded and picked up substitute cards.

76 *Did I not know the other company*: there may be some irony at Mrs Modern's expense in this comment. Her confidence in 'knowing' the other players stops short of her actually winning any of their money.

77 *cheat without a partner*: as in the more familiar card game, Bridge, Quadrille was played with a partner, and, even when you are dealt a particularly powerful hand, individual success depends on an understanding with at least one other player.

83 *jail the next morning*: an inability to redeem a debt led to immediate imprisonment.

93 *if he will not pay the music*: i.e. if he will not pay his way in recompensing the Moderns for Mrs Modern's company. A version of the more prevalent phrase, 'he who pays the piper, calls the tune'.

102 *as charity in the next*: an allusion to 1 Peter 4: 8: 'For charity shall cover a multitude of sins', but proverbial from the early seventeenth century onwards. The Moderns typically approach charity as an investment or moral cleansing agent; cf. note to 3.2.6.

104 *all the scandal falls on the husband*: in that it is he who would suffer the worse shame, as a cuckold.

118 *Reputation is the soul of virtue*: an enduring ironic inversion in Fielding's work. His entry for both 'Virtue' and 'Vice' in his 'Modern Glossary' was 'Subjects of discourse' (*The Covent-Garden Journal*, no. 4 (14 January

1752), in *The Covent-Garden Journal and a Plan of the Universal Register-Office*, ed. Bertrand A. Goldgar (Oxford, 1988), 38). There is here a prefiguring of Lord Richly's values; see 3.1.19–20: 'There are as few women who have not the reputation of virtue, as that have the thing itself'.

129  *losses in the South Sea*: the South Sea Company, founded in 1711, provided the government of the day with a quick solution to a shortage of funds when waging the War of the Spanish Succession. Holders of *c.* £9 million of government bonds were offered in exchange South Sea stock (with 6 per cent interest). In return, the Company won the exclusive right to trade in the South Seas and South America. Investment opportunities, at best risky, were encouraged by the Company's grandiose claims and a decision, in 1720, to assume responsibility for all of the national debt. A fever of speculation saw the price of Company stock shoot up from £128 in January to £1,000 in August. This 'bubble' burst in September when banks found that they could not collect loans on inflated stock. Jonathan Swift captured this mood of desperate hope in his poem, 'Upon the South Sea Project' (1721):

> . . . the deluded bankrupt raves,
>   Puts all upon a desperate bet;
> Then plunges in the Southern waves,
>   Dipped over head and ears—in debt.
> (ll. 21–4)

Fielding's own father lost a considerable amount in this general calamity.

153  *Grand Signior*: the Sultan of Turkey.

161  *generous*: cf. 2.2.33, 5.1.80, 5.4.40–1, and 5.4.69. The forgoing of an advantage over others stands in stark contrast to the 'modern' ethics of a Richly.

1.2.3  *levee*: the formal and ritualistic rising from bed of a noble or other dignitary. This inset scene is deliberately thematic rather than expository, and a levee summed up for Fielding the parade of 'greatness' in society as well as belittling sycophancy. In his poem, 'To the Rt. Hon. Sir Robert Walpole' (1731), collected in his *Miscellanies* (1743; ed. Henry Knight Miller (Oxford, 1972), 59), the topos has a particularly relevant and contemporary application:

> Great Sir, as on each Levee Day
> I still attend you—still you say
> I'm busy now, To-morrow come;
> To-morrow, Sir, you're not at Home.
> So says your Porter, and dare I
> Give such a Man as him the Lie?
> (ll. 1–6)

# NOTES TO PAGES 10–11

From the upper rooms of a house leased by his father on the east side of Dover Street, in Mayfair, London, Fielding could look down daily on the procession of placemen and supplicants outside Walpole's house on Arlington Street. As the Prime Minister was besieged thus, the poet-narrator is similarly imprisoned—but by bailiffs and creditors. In *Eurydice Hiss'd* (1737), Pillage, the compromised playwright that surely derives from an aspect of Fielding himself, was to liken the literary farce on stage to the farce off it, as crowds of impecunious actors apply to him for work in a strange 'lower' levee:

> Who'd wish to be the Author of a Farce,
> Surrounded daily by a Croud of Actors,
> Gaping for Parts, and never to be satisfied;
> Yet, say the Wise, in loftier Seats of Life,
> Solicitation is the chief Reward;
> And *Wolsey's* self, that mighty Minister,
> In the full Height and Zenith of his Power,
> Amid a Croud of Sycophants and Slaves,
> Was but perhaps the Author of a Farce.

There then follows a burlesqued levee, '*to a ridiculous Tune*' (pp. 32–3). This relative identification of rank figures also in the depiction of the 'whole Ladder of Dependance' during a levee in *Joseph Andrews* (1742), Book 2, ch. 13. The temptation would be to trace burlesque, too, in this scene, yet the very reverse is the case. The allusion to Shakespeare's Timon and the petitioning at his gates, framed by the Painter and Poet's commentary, is indirect; Thomas Shadwell's adaptation, *Timon of Athens; or the Man-Hater* (1678), was the only version in production at the time. There were new editions in 1688 and 1696. In 1694, Henry Purcell added a masque at the end of Act 2, complete with Aegipanes, Bacchus, and Cupid, attended by shepherds and nymphs. Demetrius, Timon's steward, introduces us to his master, who is too generous for his own good—the polar opposite to Richly's egotistical avarice. This version had been in the Drury Lane repertoire throughout the 1730–1 and 1731–2 seasons. The January 1732 production preceded Fielding's afterpiece, *The Lottery*.

24 *mounted a breach . . . file of the enemy*: defended a gap in a fortification against an armed line of enemy infantry.

31 *great man*: a being significant in terms of magnitude or riches rather than moral or intellectual worth. 'Greatness' is a heavily ironic term in Fielding's vocabulary, connoting its opposite. The association of this form of greatness with riches (Lord Richly?) is evident at the close of Air VIII of *The Author's Farce*, 3.1 (1730), where:

> Would you have Men to flatter?
> To be Rich is the Matter;

303

> When you cry he is Rich, you cry a Great Man.
>
> *(Plays,* 272)

In his *Tragedy of Tragedies* (1731), Tom Thumb is dubbed 'the Great', and Fielding toys with the association of Walpole and 'greatness' as early as the 'Ode to the Right Honourable Sir Robert Walpole' (1730), ll. 5–16; *Miscellanies,* 56).

59 *the levee is begun by this*: i.e. there are signs that the levee has commenced.

61 *the vanity of that leviathan*: 'Leviathan' has a biblical lineage (Job 41, or Psalm 74: 14) and is taken variously to refer to a sea monster, either a crocodile or whale. Fielding may be more precisely associating this 'great rogue' with Thomas Hobbes's infamous study of the all-engrossing state in his study of 1651.

1.3.14 *breach of privilege*: 'privilege', in this context, is a form of protection against the legal process (especially in the case of possible defamation) for those in parliamentary debate. Lord Richly would appear to be upholding the married rights of ownership, yet 'privilege', in the sense of an unearned right, might be taken to encourage a 'breach'.

25 *parcel of toupet coxcombs*: group of perhaps effeminate and/or foolish beaux fond of sporting a crest of artificial hair as a topknot.

58 *liquorish dog . . . first snap*: a greedy (lascivious?) animal who desires to have the first turn, as, perhaps, a dog at a feeding bowl. Here, the barely submerged association of Woodall with one who 'desires everything' comes to the fore.

67, 70 *fox-hunter*: a type of the backwoods Tory, wedded to country pursuits rather than general moral awareness. Fielding named one of his brainless political candidates in *Pasquin* (1736) Sir Henry Fox-Chace.

71 *Modern, your servant*: Modern must have been on the periphery of this free banter, and here just manages to introduce himself successfully for the first time.

90 *lost his cause*: failed in his legal suit.

97 *Constant Husband*: i.e. faithful and attentive. It is typical of Richly to regard this impulse as a type only, divorced from actual behaviour. Whilst Fielding had had a prolific amorous life in early years, this accompanied a steadfast abhorrence of adultery. Although the episode where Mrs Tow-wouse discovers Betty, the maid, in bed with her spouse (*Joseph Andrews* (1742), 1.17) is chiefly mock-tragic, Fielding's closing reflection reclaims it for a serious purpose, as a 'Catastrophe, common enough, and comical enough too, perhaps in modern History, yet often fatal to the Repose and Well-being of Families, and the Subject of many Tragedies, both in Life and on the Stage'. It is telling that *The Modern Husband* does not actually portray any Constant Husband.

110 s.d. *aside*: this edn.; *om. 1732* (1) and (2). Richly is obviously stepping outside the frame of the preceding action to supply this statement.

*chimerical devils . . . return for them*: the syntax is a little convoluted here. The supplicants resemble, in Richly's opinion, a legion of the damned chasing goals that are in reality fantastic and illusory. Favours are sought and yet Richly expects no normal recompense ('return') for them as those attending the levee will never thrive enough by them. The crucial qualification in the above is 'normal'; Modern and Bellamant can pay in other ways.

114 *paradise of fools*: inspired by Ariosto's Limbo of Vanity in Book 34 of *Orlando Furioso*, Milton has Satan pass by a 'Paradise of Fools' in Book 3 of *Paradise Lost*. It is seen as 'a limbo large and broad' (l. 495), filled with predominantly Catholic detritus:

> Cowls, hoods and habits with their wearers tossed
> And fluttered into rags; then relics, beads,
> Indulgences, dispenses, pardons, bulls,
> The sport of winds: all these upwhirled aloft
> Fly o'er the backside of the world . . .
>
> (ll. 490–4)

Pope, in his note to Book 5, l. 517 of his translation of *The Iliad* (1715), noted this as one of Milton's few 'Gayeties', a descent into the 'ludicrous' akin to Homer, but Johnson, in his 'Life of Milton' (*Lives of the Poets* (1779–81)), was to find this unbecoming for an epic poet: 'a fiction not in itself ill-imagined, but too ludicrous for its place' (in *Samuel Johnson*, ed. Donald Greene (Oxford, 1984), 713). Richly sees the hopeful supplicants at his levee as deluded and vain.

2.1.2 *ramble*: 'wandering irregular excursion' (*SJ*).

21 *mother-in-law*: in this case, stepmother.

26 *his picture in my eyes*: exhibit an obvious fascination with.

44 *run over*: inspected minutely and critically.

45 *Mrs Termagant*: clearly, a forceful scold; 'a brawling, turbulent woman' (*SJ*).

50 *plain-dealing*: truthful, but with an association of satiric accuracy. In *The Temple Beau* (1730), Lady Gravely admonishes Lady Lucy Pedant for her aversion to 'Plain-dealing', where 'to [be] put . . . in Mind of Faults' might be the 'truest sign of Friendship' (1.1; *Plays*, 114). Mrs Modern finds Lord Richly a plain-dealer at 2.2.199.

61 *bank note*: a promissory note given by a banker; an earlier version of today's currency.

91 *embroidery*: the art of ornamenting by way of needlework, especially raised patterns or figures; here the reference is probably to fine waistcoats. Fielding associated the wearing of any garment so highly decorated as decadent. The worthy Mr Wilson, when in debt in *Joseph Andrews*, describes a levee much like that experienced by Merit and Bravemore in

1.2: 'Many a Morning have I waited Hours in the cold Parlours of Men of Quality, where, after seeing the lowest Rascals in Lace and Embroidery, the Pimps and Buffoons in Fashion admitted, I have been sometimes told, on sending in my Name, that my Lord could not possibly see me this Morning' (3.3).

114 ... *a man look like a monkey*: probably associating a monkey's grinning and chattering with the behaviour of a would-be courtier. Shaftesbury illustrated the proposition that a deity who presided over humanity only by a system of rewards or punishments might not reform the heart or character: 'There is no more of *Rectitude. Piety*, or *Sanctity* in a Creature thus reform'd, than there is ... *Innocence* or *Sobriety* in a Monkey under the Discipline of the Whip' (Book 1, Part 3, Sect. 2, Treatise 4, *Characteristicks of Men, Manners, Opinions, Times* (1711). The comparison was explicit in Fielding's poem to 'Celia, On her Wishing to have a Lilliputian to Play With' (*c.*1730; 1st.pub., 1743), where, in order to please her, a 'Monkey Beau' would wish to be a 'Monkey quite' (ll. 3–4). The uncanny resemblance of humankind with monkeys was a common Scriblerian *topos*; see John Gay's *Fable XIV*, 'The Monkey Who Had Seen the World' (1st. series, 1727), and Jonathan Swift's adaptation of it in his 'Tim and the Fables' (*Intelligencer*, no. 10, 1728) plus Alexander Pope's 'Fourth Satire of John Donne' (1736), ll. 246–8.

132 *son-in-law*: in this case, stepson.

173 *cause*: the expensive case that Bellamant brought unsuccessfully before the House of Lords.

190 *properest*: a profoundly ambivalent description, veering from the unimpeachably acceptable (*OED*, sense II 5 b: '... of good character ...') to the less so (sense A I i 'Belonging to oneself...' or 11 a: '... in conformity with social ethics'). Gaywit leaves open the possibility that he may simply be complimenting Richly on his economic self-sufficiency and his blending in with social norms.

205 *Mr Crambo*: Crambo was a game in which each player had to provide a rhyme to the word suggested by others. It was loosely associated with simple word-play. Joseph Spence, in his *Essay on Pope's Odyssey* (1726–7), had his Antiphaus declaim against this overly ingenious tendency in dramatic verse, wherein, especially in tragedies, 'all the Actors to me seem rather to be *playing at Crambo* with one another, than endeavouring in the least to affect the audience' ('Evening the Third', 118–19). Crambo is obviously a fashionable author; see 3.2.103–8. In an unkind reflection upon Fielding's difficulties in 1733 as one of the authors most closely linked to the ailing Theatre Royal at Drury Lane, Edward Phillips portrayed him as Crambo in his mercilessly opportunistic *The Stage-Mutineers: or, A Play-House to be Lett* (1733).

207 *Humours of Bedlam*: Bethlehem Royal Hospital had been situated in

Moorfields in the east of London since 1675–6. It housed the mentally disturbed, and these patients were chained in caged cells for visits by the public. Crambo's play does not seem to be a text of much social concern. Although the primary meanings of 'Humour' indicate simply a cast of mind, the context here is probably nearer Johnson's sense 6: 'diseased or morbid disposition'.

213 *The design . . . who can laugh at sense*: Fielding would have hoped that this was not universally the case. The 'Prologue' to the play hopes for an audience that can trace 'true nature' and the difference between 'Comedy' and 'Farce':

> If modern vice detestable be shown,
> And, vicious as it is, he draws the town;
> Though no loud laugh applaud the serious page,
> Restore the sinking honour of the stage ! . . .
>
> (ll. 33–8)

This is a consistent aesthetic principle of Fielding's. The clearest exposition of it can be found in Bookweight's distinction between an 'Acting' and a 'Reading' play in *The Author's Farce* (1730): 'Why, Sir, your Acting Play is entirely supported by the Merit of the Actor, without any Regard to the Author at all:—In this Case, it signifies very little whether there be any Sense in it or no. Now your Reading Play is of a different Stamp, and must have Wit and Meaning in it—These latter I call your Substantive, as being able to support themselves. The former are your Adjective, as what require the Buffoonery and Gestures of an Actor to be joined to them, to shew their Signification' (1.6, *Plays*, 237). This is exactly the aim of the attack on 'this *Gothick* Leaden Age' in his poem, 'Of True Greatness' (*c.*1740):

> When Wit is banish'd from the Press and Stage,
> When Fools to greater Folly make Pretence,
> And those who have it, seem asham'd of Sense.
>
> (ll. 187, 188–90—*Miscellanies*, 26)

220 *. . . tumblers and ballad-singers*: a reflection on the rage for ballad operas and pantomimes principally fostered by John Rich at Lincoln's Inn Fields theatre, the rival house. There is also perhaps a determination on his own behalf to turn away from the writing of operas of his own, such as *The Grub-Street Opera* (1731).

228 *. . . as empty as the galleries in St James's*: not St James's Palace, but rather St James, Piccadilly, a church first consecrated in 1684 that had proved a fashionable place to worship. Fielding attended when in London. Lord Foppington, in Sir John Vanbrugh's *The Relapse* (1696), claimed that it drew 'the best company' (2.1.269–70; *The Relapse and Other Plays*, ed. Brean Hammond (Oxford, 2004), 29), although he also testified to his own wandering attention during sermons. 'Galleries' in theatres,

accommodated 'the meaner people' in seats just above the Pit, but in Restoration churches they were upper storeys, usually accommodating latecomers or any overspill on popular occasions.

233 *the only age that has scorned a pretence to religion*: the quarrel between Valentine and Veromil in *The Temple Beau* (1730) helps illustrate the depth of Fielding's concern at bare-faced irreligion:

*Val* Preach not Religion to me—Oh! it well becomes the Mouth of Hypocrisy to thunder Gospel Tenets to the World, while there is no Spark of Honour in the Soul.

*Ver* You speak the Meaning of a Libertine Age; the Heart that throws off the Face of Religion, wears but the Mask of Honour.

*Val* Rather, he that has not Honour, wears but the Mask of Piety. (4.10, *Plays*, 159)

In the character of Parson Abraham Adams, in *Joseph Andrews*, Fielding portrayed a sincere belief in the essential goodness of humanity, marked by the Parson's determination to act out his beliefs rather than mouth them. It was to be one of the first reflections upon that hypocrite, Blifil, in *Tom Jones*, that there 'was a great Appearance of Religion' in him (1.1.10). However, even a rhetoric of belief was preferable to no pretence at all.

235 . . . *hypocrisy is the only religion it wants*: in both *1732 (1)* and *(2)*: . . . hypocrisy is the only hypocrisy it wants.

258 *Party and prejudice have the same dominion over us*: Richly's view of the world as ultimately ruled by 'favour' and 'partiality' at least draws an implicit warning from Bellamant as far as his wife is concerned. The view of Britain as consumed by the rage of 'party' would have been a more likely perspective on a previous generation's failings, such as in the election campaigns of 1715 and 1722. The reference is more likely to be a reflection upon the enforced withdrawal from the Little Haymarket schedules of Fielding's revision of his *The Welsh Opera: The Grub-Street Opera* (1730–1).

311 *It is a stock-jobbing age*: according to Johnson, a stockjobber was 'a low wretch who gets money by buying and selling shares in the funds' (*SJ*). Fielding was not alone in regarding the stock market as an institutionalized game of chance—akin to apparently recreational diversions such as dice or quadrille.

312 *Marriage is traffic*: . . . i.e. a commercial activity. There is a strong personal ingredient from Fielding in this, and it is in the unsparing depiction of the consequences of infidelity that the play most resembles his last novel, *Amelia* (1751), wherein Booth bitterly regrets his liaison with Fanny Mathews. Squire Allworthy, in conversation with Blifil in *Tom Jones* (1749), offers some of the most heartfelt sentiments when considering a situation where that 'most holy Ceremony' is profaned,

converting 'this most sacred Institution into a wicked Sacrifice to Lust, or Avarice: And what better can be said of those Matches to which Men are induced merely by the Consideration of a beautiful Person, or a great Fortune !' (1.1.12).

329 *encumbered . . . cut off the entail*: literally, for an estate to come with encumbrances is for it to be saddled with debt. Gaywit considers Lady Charlotte in that light, given his affection for Emilia. Bellamant is surprised that Richly could have the power to bar Gaywit from his rightful inheritance, yet the marriage is a firm condition in its 'entail'.

2.2.13 *fourteen more*: i.e. 14 hundreds (1,400 pounds) more than he regards a woman's honour is worth.

22 *enow*: enough.

33 *Generous creature*: the precise sense in which the virtue of generosity pervades several scenes in the play is illustrated in the note to 1.1.161.

44 *note*: the bank note of £100 first mentioned at 2.1.61.

50 *opera*: it is not surprising that Lady Charlotte should be drawn to this fashionable art form of the moment. George Frederick Handel was the foremost exponent of *opera seria*, and, from *Rinaldo* (1711) onwards, London became its most prominent venue. Fielding was not alone in distrusting its influence, principally at the Queen's Theatre and Haymarket. John Dennis, in his *Essay on the Operas after the Italian Manner* (1706) provided the first warning against the 'soft and effeminate Measures of the Italian Opéra' that were 'below the Dignity' of the British (see Roger Fiske, *English Theatre Music in the Eighteenth Century* (London, 1973), 49). Lady Matchless probably summed up Fielding's view in *Love in Several Masques* (1728) when she found 'three absolute Farces' to be wit found in a lover, good music in an English opera, and 'common Sense in an *Italian* one' (2.11, *Plays*, 47).

71 *varnished over a windmill ten several times*: the windmill is part of the design that Emilia is attempting to protect (or embellish?) ten or so times.

88 *hazard*: a very popular game of dice, invariably involving extensive wagers. Its addictive qualities were proverbial, and Charles Cotton claimed that the game 'speedily makes a Man or undoes him; in the twinkling of an Eye either a Man or a Mouse' (*Cotton*, 119). It was also the most 'bewitching Game that is play'd on the Dice', leaving those caught never knowing when to 'leave off' (p. 123).

114 *allay*: the mixture of a baser metal within one of a superior kind, i.e. some addition that reduces the intrinsic quality.

142 *Victoria*: cry of victory.

143 *Stripped, by Jupiter*: defeated, and thus 'stripped' of money. The oath is heavily ironic, as Jupiter was normally associated with the spoils of victory.

309

144 *Eleven mains*: in competition with others, the throwing of a 'Main' is in response to that thrown by the 'Caster', whose first numbers constitute a 'Chance'. The exact number of the 'Chance' determines what will be the successful 'Mains'. To win eleven straight 'Mains' is lucky indeed.

147 *nine thousand mains in one hand, and won all the world*: wild hyperbole, probably showing Lady Charlotte's ignorance of the actual scoring.

149 *Surprising today, upon my word*: Richly seems suspicious, yet there is no hint that the dice were loaded; it is rather that, as one of the few to know of Mrs Modern's full plight, he notes how opportune the luck has been.

164 *Madcap*: a reckless buffoon.

189 *let Piquet be the word*: Piquet is a two-handed card game. Mrs Modern appears to be suggesting a game where she might be lucky enough to redeem herself financially by winning off Richly. He, however, is no games player.

199 *plain-dealing*: a perhaps too truthful proffering of advice. See 2.1.50, 3.2.32 and 3.2.69 for further uses of the term. Ever since Manly in William Wycherley's *The Plain Dealer* (1677), the association of plain-dealing was not straightforward; he has to learn how to trust society. The irony here is that Richly is the least deluded of the play's characters, yet that is not all. Emilia finds that plain-dealers show their 'wit at the expense of . . . breeding' (3.2.69–70).

205 *glass*: mirror. Mrs Modern blames her lack of skill at cards on bad luck with as much accuracy as if one were to blame a lack of beauty on a faulty mirror.

3.1.5 *repiqued from forty, when I played but for five*: in the card-game of picquet, the pack consists of thirty-two cards, with nothing lower than a seven. The object of the game is to outscore your opponent in terms of points awarded both for certain combinations of cards and for tricks taken. After the opportunity to exchange up to five cards from the pack so as to strengthen the hand, there follows a process of declarations. Before moving to playing for tricks, points are gained by obtaining the most cards in a single suit ('points') or by a sequence of cards within one suit or the most cards of the same rank. At this point it is possible for one player to gain thirty points on the declaration alone whilst her/his opponent scores none; this is rewarded by raising the points tally from thirty to sixty and is called a repique. Mrs Modern seems to be bemoaning her luck in having exchanged fully five cards and yet still ending up as the victim of a repique.

24 *civility*: the basic meaning of 'civility' ('Freedom from barbarity; the state of being civilized'—*SJ* 1) could, in a purely social sense, simply signify politeness, or, in Johnson's sense 2, 'elegance of behaviour'. There are several references to this virtue throughout the play but rarely where truly civilized behaviour is either expected or celebrated. Mrs Modern,

especially, cannot use the term without highlighting how inappropriate it is in a 'modern' society (1.1.19, 1.1.65, 2.1.67, and 2.2.57). There is the distinct possibility that Fielding wished to gesture to a wider consequence of its disappearance. Locke's 'Essay Concerning the True Original, Extent and End of Civil Government' from his *Two Treatises of Government* (1690) had attempted to define the word in terms of a self-legislating social responsibility (in opposition to absolute rule): 'Wherever . . . any number of men so unite into one society as to quit every one his executive power of the law of Nature, and to resign it to the public, there and there only is a political or civil society' (2.7.89). Shaftesbury, in his generally optimistic *Characteristicks* (1711), celebrated the ingredients of what might compose the '*Publick Weal* and the *Common Interest*' and found it lay in a 'love of the *Community* or *Society*, Natural Affection, Humanity, Obligingness, or that sort of *Civility* which rises from a just *Sense* of the *Common Rights* of Mankind, and the *natural Equality* there is amongst those of the same Species' (Treatise II, Part III, sect. I, p. 104). Richly's *hauteur* is an example of the powerful forces that rob society of this level of trust.

35 *laid this passion . . . abated that for you*: Richly is claiming that this passion for Mrs Bellamant has temporarily resulted in a lack of feeling for Mrs Modern, but that once he has allayed this urge, they could return to previous ways.

51 *no more dogs in St James's parish, than there are lions at the tower*: Wren's St James Piccadilly was one of the most fashionable places to worship, placed in St James's Fields, only recently developed (1662 onwards) by Henry Jermyn, Earl of St Albans, into the smartest suburban district. The menagerie, located since 1603 at the west gatehouse of the Tower of London, was a popular visitors' attraction, and the phrase 'going to see the lions' had become proverbial for venturing forth to see the sights. It had become so customary that the polite tended to regard it as a low form of entertainment. Sir Richard Steele, in his *Tatler*, no. 30 (16 June 1709, pub. June 18), had reluctantly taken visitors to see the lions as well as Bedlam, and regarded it as an 'Entertainment to raw Minds' (in *The Tatler*, ed. Donald F. Bond (Oxford, 1987), 3 vols., 224). Richly is claiming that the appearance of 'real' dogs in St James's parish might be on a par with such curiosities. Daniel Hahn gives a full account of this curiosity in his *The Tower Menagerie: The Amazing 600-Year History of the Royal Collection of Wild and Ferocious Beasts Kept at the Tower of London* (2003), 117–41.

65, 66 *La Dovi's . . . la Fama*: these are no real divas of the newly fashionable Italianate opera, but fabricated in a sham conversation to exclude Mr Modern. 'Dovi' might suggest a dove and 'fama' one of some celebrity (from the Italian, *fama*).

81 *like the fool in a play*: probably referring to the witty fools, such as Feste

in Shakespeare's *Twelfth Night* or the Fool in *King Lear*, that were often regarded as expedients to air an author's wit. Trapwit, in Fielding's *Pasquin* (1736), probably speaks for the author, when he sets 'witty' modern comedies (where 'three or four Gentlemen' are introduced merely to 'talk wit') against those wherein there is 'Humour, Nature and Simplicity' in the spirit of Molière (1.1, p.5). He has deliberately written in a Fool's part in his comedy 'to set off the rest' (p. 6).

102 *Machiavil*: the traditional description of a conniving, ill-natured, individual. Niccolo Machiavelli's *The Prince* (1532) explored the possibilities in an amoral and skilful manipulation of position to maintain and enhance power.

3.2.6 *To which ... it is the greatest*: the primary meaning of 'charity' for Fielding was less a giving of alms to those less fortunate than a sense of universal benevolence, derived from the Latin, *caritas*. He consistently regarded the virtue as an active one (see *Joseph Andrews*, 1.12 (a version of the parable of the Good Samaritan) and 3.13 (Parson Adams and Peter Pounce's disagreement on the term)) and *Tom Jones*, 1.2.5, where Blifil cannot accept Allworthy's emphasis on generosity when defining the word). It is, however, likely that Gaywit's instinctive irony includes an allusion to 1 Peter 4: 8: 'For charity shall cover the multitude of sins.' At 1.1.101–2, Mr Modern notes that gold 'covers as many sins, as charity in the next'—another instance of a debased moral vocabulary.

38 *where did you get that lace*: Lady Charlotte indicates any lacework. It is clear that such adornment was regarded by Fielding as suspect and as a rather spurious indication of worth. Mr Bellamant regards his son as a 'dressed-up daw' and one of the ingredients of this is a 'coat covered with lace' (2.1.102–3). Mr Modern's servant, John, is rather innocently impressed by lace on the livery of his rival, Tom Brisk (4.1.307–9). The question indicates more the presumption of Lady Charlotte than any actual finery worn by Emilia.

54 *one only goes to see the company*: i.e. the audience and certainly not the cast of the play. Fielding was ambivalent about an audience's capacity to absorb complex material. His Trapwit, in *Pasquin* (1736), is determined to start on his plot in earnest as late as the fourth act, as he is 'not willing to burden either the Audience's Memory, or [his] own; for they may forget all that has hitherto past, and know full, as much of the Plot as if they remember'd it' (2.1, p. 23). His poem on the Haymarket theatre world, 'The Masquerade' (1728), treats an audience as an exotic menagerie:

> In wild confusion huddled lies
> A heap of inconsistencies:
> So here in one confusion hurl'd,
> Seem all the nations of the world; ...
>
> (ll. 65–8)

Perhaps Lady Charlotte's distraction is excusable if that is her destination.

55 *sent to me*: sent a message.

57 *first payment*: not a financial transaction, but rather the paying of respects to mark the commencement of the social season.

71 *truth*: not an accusation of untruthfulness, but rather of breaking some sort of promise or troth.

77 *voucher*: 'one who gives witness to any thing' (*SJ*).

87 *as a Spaniard's is a game at chess*: the equation of Lady Charlotte's desire to have her life one long party playing Quadrille with a Spaniard playing chess is not immediately clear. The proverbial sense of a Spaniard as a close, proud, and covetous individual was one that Fielding recognized, even if he did not endorse it in himself. Merital, in *Love in Several Masques* (1728), finds a similarity between a 'jealous *Spaniard* [keeping] his wife' under close scrutiny and a 'City-Usurer his Treasure' (1.1, *Plays*, p. 26). Captain Bellamant would appear to be charitable to Lady Charlotte in this exchange, so, in this remark, he is probably drawing attention to the suitability both of partying with the game of Quadrille and also a Spaniard's introspection and the virtues necessary to win at chess.

91 *votaries*: devotees with almost religious fervour. This is one further suggestion of modern alternative (and debased) systems of belief.

94 *none should have . . . weather in their mouths*: i.e. those who deal only in small talk, as in commenting on the state of the weather incessantly.

96 *[re]public of wit*: all printed texts omit the prefix. Mrs Bellamant is careful not to claim that the vogue for gaming will actually affect the republic of letters, or literary world.

107 *Bedlam on the stage*: a reference back to the 'Humours of Bedlam', Mr Crambo's new opera, according to Lord Richly (2.1.204–9). The characterization of post-restoration drama as one where 'Bedlam Heroes' prospered is George Granville, Lord Lansdowne's, in his 'Concerning Unnatural Flights in Poetry' (1701), but he chiefly had Dryden's Heroic dramas in mind, where there was 'scarce . . . one reasonable Word' (ll.99–100). At least there was energy and some profligate inspiration in the rant; Charles Gildon, in his *A New Rehearsal, or, Bays the Younger* (1714) had his Freeman note this passage of Granville's in a review of modern theatre, and regretted that one would now be 'puzled to find one good line in many Plays of our most taking Authors' (1.1, p. 4).

112 *the Kings, and the Queens*: the habit of viewing lunatics at the Bethlehem Royal Hospital in Moorfields was long established. Chained in a gallery of small cells, the most spectacularly deranged were paraded for a small fee. Lady Charlotte has encountered several who believed they were royal. There is a tacit assumption here, however, that it was not clear that

there was a division between this type of 'theatre' and the 'Bedlam Heroes' of the most extreme Heroic Tragedies, noted above.

121 *filthy he-creature*: the fastidiousness of this description (plus Gaywit's aside at ll. 122–3) tells us as much about Lady Charlotte's innocence as much as any effeminacy in Captain Bellamant. As part of the hopeful set of marriages that conclude the play, this union might have some saving graces if she projects this garrulous delicacy as a protection, and he sports his modern sartorial fashions simply as a means to disconcert his father.

133 *Piquet*: the card-game is a complex two-hander where experience is often decisive.

136 *I'll give you what points you please*: the game is scored by reckoning up in three ways: (*a*) the *point* is gained by the player who has the most cards in one suit, (*b*) the *sequence* (usually the greatest number of consecutive cards), and (*c*) the *quatorze* or *trio*, collections of four or three kinds of card. Richly would appear to be allowing Mrs Bellamant certain points' start so as to handicap himself as the better player.

137 *one party*: six deals make up a 'party' or game.

3.3.10 *this first slip*: an obvious fiction to intensify Bellamant's feelings of guilt.

45 *fly to execute your commands*: a suddenly poetic phrase, probably ironic.

52 *flies with wings of lead*: a laboured punning reference to the leaden plummet of a clock.

53 *on golden wings*: the phrase is addressed to the departing Bellamant and offers him the image of an elevated quest—undercut once Mrs Modern is alone.

3.4.1 *six parties successively*: an unlikely sequence of victories, perhaps testifying to a certain skill in not winning.

2 *fortune will change . . . not blind*: proverbially portrayed as blind, Fortune is the presiding spirit over all games of chance.

6 *five points place the odds on my side*: thus indicating that she has five cards of the same suit which would be a powerful hand.

7 *change this note*: i.e. provide change so that the winnings are paid exactly. Richly knows that Mrs Bellamant is unlikely to possess that amount of money, so he contrives to leave the debt on her side by pressing a high-denomination note on her. As the real skill of Picquet lies in knowing just when, and what cards, to discard, he is here displaying a similar skill in a 'discard' of another order.

50 *it is equal to me*: i.e. I am indifferent.

98 *should I have discovered the truth*: Richly's stratagem is effective in that Mrs Bellamant is keeping secrets from her husband already.

**4.1.2** *drive a separate trade at my expense*: set up in business on your own account when you should be working for others.

3 *bought it lawfully in the church*: included in the 'chattel interests' of the marriage settlement, a wife and her 'portion' or dowry could literally be bought within marriage according to common law. The only independent possession usually allowed the wife were 'paraphenalia', i.e. jewels and dress suitable to keeping up her social status. Sometimes more watchful parents could set up trustees to administer a wife's dowry, but that was an exception. The most succinct account is probably that by Alan Macfarlane, in *Marriage and Love in England: Modes of Reproduction, 1300–1840* (New York, 1986), 263–90. Fielding regarded this arrangement as a bar to a lasting and deep relationship, and rehearsed its dangers in *Love in Several Masques* (1728), where Merital, the penniless suitor of the well-born Helena, is initially thwarted by her guardian, Sir Positive Trap. Helena objects to being 'put up at Auction! to be disposed, as a piece of Goods, by way of Bargain and Sale' (2.5, *Plays*, 41). Wisemore, a learned commentator on the marriage market, similarly refuses to allow his heart to be 'a Place of mercenary Entertainment' (4.2, *Plays*, 66). This predicament is also represented in *The Temple Beau* (1730), where Veromil aspires to Bellaria, who is intended by her uncle, Sir Avarice Pedant, for his son.

36 *golden fruit*: in Modern's imagination, the fruit is financial, but there is a distinct mock-heroic allusion to the golden apples in the west guarded by the Hesperides and obtained by Hercules as his eleventh labour.

37 *women sprung from the earth, as some philosophers think*: the association of the feminine with primal matter is less a philosophy than a basic myth, derived from the *anima mundi*, or the animating soul of the world. For example, Demeter, in Greek mythology, produced Plutus (the world's wealth) from her liaison with Iasion.

38 *clay of Egypt, not the sands of Peru*: the belief that, *ex nihilo*, matter could be produced out of inorganic material was proverbially 'confirmed' by the observation that crocodiles emerged out of the fertile mud of the Nile delta. The ooze actually sheltered the eggs, laid long before. Modern draws a distinction between the natural riches of Egypt and the mined and so more precious wealth of Peru.

41 *ten plagues*: the plagues visited on Egypt as a punishment for oppressing the Israelites, as described in Exodus.

43 *had I not been born a Turk . . . that I might have sold her*: the reference is to the Turkish harem and to the widespread assumption that a Chinese husband could trade in a wife in an actual market.

55 *my horns in . . . wear them in public*: if Modern is to be publicly regarded as a cuckold, then he hopes that it will be lucrative for him. The sentiment is shared by the corrupt Justice Squeezum in *Rape upon Rape*:

'It is not enough that a Man knows himself to be a Cuckold, the World must know it too. He that will keep his Horns in his Pocket, must keep his Wife in his Bosom' (4.1, p. 47).

59 *One good discovery in Westminster Hall*: a testimony in the High Court at Westminster Hall that 'criminal conversation' (adultery) had taken place would extort expensive damages for the wronged party, in this case, Modern.

66 *in that name*: i.e. the country.

74 *I cannot resolve*: Mrs Modern seems genuinely to be in a quandry. The possibility in performance that she might be portrayed as a part-victim of social amorality might emerge from moments such as these.

113 *threw away six parties*: see note to 3.4.1.

117 *a double fee, or a court-priest a plurality*: the main sense of 'double fee' is simply an excessive charge for services rendered to their clients by ambitious lawyers and physicians, but, in the case of the legal profession, there was another possibility: that some would take fees from both sides in a case by passing information to the other side. A 'plurality' was a state wherein a priest oversaw the care of souls in more than one living or parish. Inevitably, this led to absenteeism, especially if one had taken up a position at court as well.

126 *by virtue of my mortgage*: i.e. Richly would aim to redeem this pledge (paying back any change owing from the large-denomination bill) by taking sexual favours from the unfortunate (or spendthrift) woman.

127 *generous*: see note to and 2.2.33.

135 *like the ghost . . . nowhere at all*: Barnado, Marcellus, and Horatio all try to pursue the Ghost of the elder Hamlet, yet strike at air:

Barn.            'Tis here
Hor.                             'Tis here. *Exit the Ghost*
Mar. 'Tis gone.
        We do it wrong, being so majestical,
        To offer it the show of violence,
        For it is as the air invulnerable, . . . (I.I.122–6)

Hamlet uses the Latin tag, '*Hic et ubique*' (here and everywhere), to describe the spirit's existence at 1.5.158.

158 *So that your fools . . . by a shadow*: the allusion is probably to Aesop's Fable no. 185 ('The Dog Who Carried the Meat'), where a dog, carrying a piece of meat in his jaws across a river, catches sight of his reflection in the water and what he takes to be a larger piece. Forsaking his own meat, he leaps into the current in search of the 'shadow', the larger piece, and ends up losing both.

198 *make interest*: usually the use of financial metaphors in the play signals the reduction of affection and morality to the cash nexus, so it is significant

that this phrase should be Bellamant's. He here believes that his wife will yield monetary interest (as on a loan) to none of her admirers but himself.

200 '*It is the curse . . . Altamont's*': the phrase is the villain Lothario's, in Nicholas Rowe's *The Fair Penitent* (1703):

> *Hor.* You blast the Fair with Lies because they scorn you,
> Hate you like Age, like Ugliness and Impotence:
> Rather than make you blest they wou'd die Virgins,
> And stop the Propagation of Mankind.

> *Loth.* It is the Curse of Fools to be secure;
> And that be thine and *Altamont*'s: Dream on,
> Not think upon my Vengeance 'till thou feel'st it.

> (4.2, pp. 21–2).

Mrs Bellamant has an equivalent in Altamont's virtuous, though tragically compromised, wife, Calista.

216 *Affirm*: 'To declare; to tell confidently' (*SJ*). Bellamant is still assessing the truth of Mrs Modern's assertion, whilst she has progressed to consider the advisability of publicizing the supposed misdemeanour.

224 *I'll never discover it*: i.e. she will not reveal it—expecting that to be the focus of Bellamant's perturbation.

242 *demur*: 'To doubt; to have scruples or difficulties; to deliberate' (*SJ*).

247 *citron-water*: '*Aqua vitae*, distilled with the rind of citrons' (*SJ*)—a common restorative.

255 *cinnamon-water . . . plague-water*: Mrs Modern wants any tonic. Cinnamon—and aniseed-water are flavoured, and supposed to aid digestion; surfeit-water cured a feeling of satiety or bloatedness, and plague-water was an infusion of various herbs and roots, distilled in fortified wine, supposed to prevent the plague—in this instance, any vexation.

265 *she seems to walk . . . miracle of St Dennis*: Mrs Modern seems to have in mind the myth associated with St Dionysius or Denys, the bishop of Paris, beheaded in *c.*250 at Montmartre ('The Martyrs' Hill'), that he carried his own head to a place of burial, the abbey church of Saint-Denys.

289 *support for a tiring woman*: tolerate as a dresser or chambermaid.

293 *puss*: a generalized term of mild contempt, usually connoting slyness.

330 *double perjury*: lying under oath twice—once in obedience to his master, testifying to his being a cuckold, the other, breaking a vow of secrecy that he would not disclose the fact.

343 *dram*: 'such a quantity of distilled spirits as is usually drunk at once' (*SJ*).

4.2.9 *plains of Arcadia*: geographically, the mountainous region in the centre of the Peloponnese, in Greece. The primary reference here is to the mythical pastoral setting for Virgil's *Eclogues*, a place of lyricism and innocent complaint or celebration. Its fictive qualities were parodied by Fielding in *Tom Jones* (5.12): 'The reader may remember, that in our description of this grove, we mentioned a murmuring brook, which brook did not come there, as such gentle streams flow through vulgar romances, with no other purpose than to murmur. No; Fortune had decreed to enoble this little brook with a higher honour than any of those which wash the plains of Arcadia, ever deserved' (i.e. his description of Tom's battle with both Blifil and Thwackum).

25 *do for you*: act on your behalf.

26 *given over*: desisted—presumably, is no longer in the running for the place (occupation or position) in which Richly supposes Bellamant is interested.

77 *many a woman . . . husband's coach*: provide the economic means by which her husband appears to such good effect in a coach. Richly's perspective is here refuted by Mrs Bellamant's resistance.

86 *What do I see*: a more complex scene than might at first appear. At this point, Mrs Bellamant notes only that Mr Modern has discovered his wife's infidelity. Richly's sudden departure and his mention of two husbands who may be seeking redress suggests that he fears being caught with Mrs Bellamant, as part of a prearranged plan. Bellamant's appearance with Mrs Modern incriminates him in some way, and this is confirmed when Modern involves Bellamant in his accusation at lines 99–101. Presumably, Modern enters with both his wife and Bellamant restrained by servants.

87 *masterpiece*: main excellence. Given especially the need for Bellamant's repentance so soon after this entrance, this comment must surely be ironic—and at his own expense.

93 *Thou hast a forehead . . . on my forehead*: modern claims that his wife has a sufficiently brazen exterior, or front, to survive any objection to her reputation—a slur that marks him out as a cuckold.

112 *truth*: faithfulness to one's word.

149 *it obliges you*: an awkward construction, where probably 'it' refers to the necessity of their parting.

152 *take back this . . . thou hast given me*: the most likely result in performance is an increasingly fond contact, culminating in an embrace.

154 *Ha*: again, the text merely suggests stage action, probably signifying surprise and joy at forgiveness.

161 *Oh! let me press . . . for their father's crime*: the sentimental qualities of this scene are underlined in this speech, yet, strategically, this is a little less than reassuring as the rapid attainment of reconciliation is usually the gesture of the final action, not that of the fourth act. Fielding goes on to

depict vices in the Moderns and Richly in the fifth that may be displayed for all to see but they persist after the close of the play and are probably irredeemable.

**5.1.4** *wait upon her up*: show her up to Emilia's private apartment.

**20** *Lady Pinup's*: a character summoned up only by the minutiae of the dressmaker's craft. A pin was also an item of very little worth. Lady Charlotte is quick to note the cost of Lady Pinup's dress.

**25** *these things*: a significant euphemism, referring to the events of the previous night, namely, Emilia's parents' apparent disgrace.

**39** *these fifty years*: an obvious hyperbole. Lady Charlotte presumably has such a fashionably busy social calendar that it keeps her up so late that early calls are beyond her.

**65** *Very fine, indeed*: Emilia's comment is not a judgement on Lady Charlotte's countenance so much as on Captain Bellamant's finely turned compliment—and one not to be taken unironically.

**81** *Didst thou know ... more on mine*: the first clear declaration of affection for Gaywit by Emilia. It is precisely a quality of generosity that is chosen to represent his virtues: a sensitivity to the feelings of others as well as an instinctive magnanimity. The play points to the scarcity of this impulse in contemporary society at several points, either by praise (see 1.1.161–2, 5.4.38 (Mrs Modern on Bellamant), 5.4.40–1 (Gaywit on Bellamant), 5.1.109–10 (Emilia on Gaywit), and 5.4.40 (Gaywit on Mrs Bellamant), or by implicit censure (2.2.33 and 4.1.127, both where it is plain that Mrs Modern is claiming the opposite of Richly)).

**96** *be of any date*: have lasted any time.

**5.2.9** S.D. *gives him a bank-bill*: the bill Richly gave Mrs Bellamant to settle his picquet debt at 3.4.13–14.

**27** *venal*: 'mercenary; prostitute' *SJ*.

**38** *Where grandeur can give licence ... liberty they please*: far more the presiding idea of the play than any contained in the last two scenes. Fielding's concern at the erosion of a people's liberties should here be set against the apparently contradictory opinion contained in the Dedication, where Robert Walpole appears as the defender of the nation's liberties. In his poem 'Liberty' (drafted *c.*1736; pub. in volume one of the *Miscellanies* (1743)), the sense of liberty within a nation civilizes it:

> Did God, who Freedom to these Creatures gave,
> Form his own Image, Man, to be a Slave ?
> But Men, it seems, to Laws of Compact yield;
> While Nature only governs in the Field.
> Curse on all Laws which Liberty subdue,
> And make the Many wretched for the Few.
>
> (ll. 25–30—*Miscellanies*, p. 57)

Heavily influenced by James Thomson's poem of the same title (1735–6), Fielding's version does set greater store by a theory of contract, in line with the interests of the poem's dedicatee (and his most consistent patron), George Lyttleton. The latter's *Letters from a Persian in England* (1735) illustrated, in Letters X–XXI, the miserable fate of those who acquiesced in a corrupt 'state of government'. Fielding was well aware of the misuse of the word in slogans such as that used by the drunken Mayor in *Pasquin* (1736): 'Liberty, property and no excise' (2.1; p. xx). The salient ingredient here is the protection offered the poor and weak by a class of wise guardians ('Liberty', ll. 42–61), probably suggested here by Locke's *Two Treatises of Government* (1690), 2.7.

47 *House of Lords ... Westminster Hall*: Richly is here referring to the expensive (and unsuccessful) suit with which Bellamant is currently involved. It has failed in the House of Lords and an appeal is presumably about to be heard in the Law Courts in Westminster Hall.

96 *instrument*: '3. A writing containing any contract or order' (*SJ*).

106 *I must always be your slave*: a part-reference back to lines 37–8, although the slavery here is deserved. He repeats the term at line 106. The position that now seems destined for Modern has not been mentioned before, but could be a reward for his wife's mediation with Mrs Bellamant. Both Richly and Modern react as if morally outraged, yet the concern with honour is simply an imitation and an exercise in polite superficiality.

127 *damages*: the financial rewards for discovering a spouse in 'criminal conversation' with another were enough to offset the sense of disgrace when it was made public. The writ was actually served for trespass, and, as Lawrence Stone puts it, the common law was now invoked to award 'financial damages not merely for financial losses but also for emotional pain and suffering' (*Uncertain Unions and Broken Lives* (Oxford, 1995), 45). It is probable that Fielding had in mind the notoriety of the *Abergavenny* v. *Lyddell* case of 1730, where the former had set up his wife to be discovered in adultery and gained damages of some £10,000. Widely regarded as an abuse of the system, the case provoked widespread adverse comment just at the time that Fielding was drafting the play.

135 *set you down*: finish the interview.

5.3.30 *the thing*: Captain Bellamant, or rather the fact that he may be 'agreeable'.

33 *Well, he has ... in my life*: it appears that this might be an aside, yet Captain Bellamant's reflection at line 26 implies that he has heard all. If so, this contributes to the archness of Lady Charlotte's character.

36 *A propos*: on that subject.

38 *scheme of matrimony*: in reference to marriage contracts, this applied more to a Restoration reality than a contemporary one. By the turn of the

century, private, verbal, or even written contracts had become discredited in law (see Lawrence Stone, *Uncertain Unions & Broken Lives: Intimate and Revealing Accounts of Marriage and Divorce in England* (Oxford, 1995), 24–35, and Alan Macfarlane, *Marriage and Love in England: Modes of Reproduction, 1300–1840* (Oxford, 1985), 123–47); Lady Charlotte's 'scheme' is, however, congruent with a general sense that the marriage partners' drawing up of pre-nuptial articles might be a safeguard of choice against strong family interests. This is the idea of modernity espoused by Mirabell and Millamant in William Congreve's *The Way of the World* (1700), (4.1.146–250; *WW*), where the identification of marriage 'provisos' emerges out of dialogue, not a formal legal contract. Mrs Western's opposition, in *Tom Jones*, to the view that a marriage might arise out of a 'romantic Scheme of Happiness' leads her to the most mercenary of conclusions: that it was rather 'a Fund in which prudent Women deposit their Fortunes to the best Advantage' (3.7.3).

52 *Then I will . . . one of those articles*: reminiscent of Millamant's stance noted above. 'I'll never marry, unless I am first made sure of my will and pleasure' (4.1.151–2).

126 *Billet doux*: love letters. Lady Charlotte imagines that the note is from Lady Betty Shuttlecock. It is more likely, given Captain Bellamant's aside from lines 123–5, that it is simply a ruse to raise her jealousy.

147 *hartshorn*: usually diluted, it was a common smelling salt.

5.4.6 *passions . . . before yours set*: female passion rarely reaches its peak (or noon) to coincide with male desire, whose sun is apt to set just before.

9 *the sun . . . a moon to shine in it*: carrying on the planetary theme, Gaywit imagines himself much like the sun inevitably leaving one side of the earth or hemisphere, yet allowing the moon to rise as a faint reminder of past heat.

26 *I always take . . . gives you his purse*: Gaywit's harshness is a complex ingredient, as its rationale could be regarded as similar to Richly's: that a woman's 'person' is equivalent to her whole being, and owning one engages the other. Mrs Modern's distress does not at all appear synthetic, and she appears trapped by the needs of an arranged marriage.

45 *blast my fame*: harm her reputation.

48 *s.d. and Capt. Merit*: the appearance of Merit seems a narrative excrescence. He is given just two lines and appears to have just the thinnest relation to the Modern/Bellamant circle, the briefest mention of his visits to the Bellamants occurring at 1.2.57–8. There is a distinct possibility that Fielding wanted to suggest a more capacious, even allegorical, closing action, where Merit is brought in to witness the discomfiture of one who appeared so unassailable in the first act.

66 *in another place*: cited under a charge of criminal conversation, the disclosure could be particularly public, potentially as high as the House of Lords.

74 *Newgate's levee*: Gaywit indicates Richly as one who is more in keeping with a prison environment than an aristocratic one. In fact, the keeper of Newgate prison could be an 'aristocrat' of a lower world, running his petty realm much like an independent state, charging the inmates for a wide variety of services. See Fielding's own portrayal of this in *Amelia*, especially 1.1–6 and in *Jonathan Wild*, 4.3.

95 *at law we shall dare to defy you*: the reference to law is not incidental. Fielding has the potential threat to Richly emerging from legal redress.

96 *voluntary cuckold*: he who gives himself up to being cuckolded for monetary gain.

122 *mogul*: originally, a reference to the Great Mogul, a European title for the emperor of Delhi, whose authority extended throughout Hindustan; by the eighteenth century, it had come simply to designate any autocratic ruler.

125 *My estate . . . I must hate*: a rare admission of weakness from Richly: with Lady Charlotte, his inheritance will pass to the Bellamant line.

133 *We had no . . . very short date*: the lack of affectation in Lady Charlotte's speeches is significant here. Just as Mrs Modern is given scope in this scene for problematic and conflicting emotions (see the note to 5.4.26), there is some textual evidence to suppose that Lady Charlotte also gains in seriousness. Gaywit identifies her 'good nature and good sense' at 5.4.158.

136 *bated*: held back from giving.

162 *whimsical*: 'freakish; capricious; oddly fanciful' (*SJ*).

173 *libertines*: although its Latin root, *libertinus*, meant simply a freed man, the French version, *libertin*, had, by the mid-sixteenth century, taken on a more precise set of connotations derived from antinomian sects. Johnson's definitions recognized the libertarian aspects, yet also found 'one who pays no regard to the precepts of religion' (meaning 3).

EPILOGUE [1]

2 *at the tree*: on the scaffold.

21 *Gay Masquerades*: see note to 3.2.54. Mrs Bellamant is no frequenter of masquerades; see 2.1.42–3.

23 *No Ring, no Mall*: Both fashionable places of resort. The Ring was a circuit for carriages and other equestrian display in Hyde Park, and the Mall was a newly popular area of St James's Park. It was an alley of about half a mile long, lined with a double row of trees on either side; the

fashionable would promenade there, but at night it would transform itself into a less savoury area, where prostitutes and thieves were numerous. This was recognized by Alexander Pope in his *Sober Advice from Horace* (1734): 'Some feel no Flames but at the *Court* or *Ball*, | And others hunt white Aprons in the *Mall*' (ll. 37–8).

24 *All-Fours*: a two-handed card-game, renowned for rewarding the deft and quick-witted. This also earned it a dubious reputation. Whilst mock-heroic overall, Gyles Smith specifically chose the game as 'big with all the Evils that the *Beast* can bring upon the Earth' (*Serious Reflections on the Dangerous Tendency of the Common Playing: Especially of the Game of All-Fours* (London, 1755), 23).

### EPILOGUE [2]

11 *cuckold's corporation*: a corporation was any legal association, authorized by royal charter to possess its own seal. 'Mrs Modern' here notes the formal organization of cuckolding in a modern age.

13 *directors*: members of a board appointed to oversee a commercial concern.

19 *Long's*: a popular gaming club in London.

22 *embroidered trader*: typically speaking, near to an oxymoron. The adjective also calls to mind Bellamant's distaste at the excesses of his son's dress at 2.1.89–92.

27 *an estate*: according to the damages one could gain by discovering a wife in criminal conversation with another.

29 *A wife with gold . . . get your money*: a wife who comes with a large dowry is like poison within the sweetest honey; here, the money you gain through damages is at the cost of a wife, in that the marriage will have to be annulled.

## The Clandestine Marriage

### EPIGRAPH

From Ovid, *Amores*, 2.13, 15–16: 'Turn your face this way, and, in sparing one spare both; | Let her live, and let us both be parent to the same one!' 2.14 runs, '*nam vitam dominae tu dabis, illa mihi*' ('for you will thus give life to my mistress and she to me'). The speaker is a distressed girl who has just attempted an abortion and severely injured herself. She calls on Isis to save her. The relevance to Lovewell and Fanny's own predicament is clear, even if the tenor of the sentiments is far more tragic.

ADVERTISEMENT

1 *Hogarth's Marriage à la Mode*: William Hogarth worked on his *Marriage à la Mode* series from 1743 to 1744. Prints were on the market in 1745. They depict an ill-matched pair enduring an arranged marriage. The self-obsessed Viscount Squanderfield marries a socially ambitious Alderman's daughter with disastrous consequences: she and her lover, Silvertongue, are eventually caught in each other's company and, in the ensuing skirmish, the Viscount is mortally wounded. Silvertongue is executed and the Countess poisons herself with laudanum, leaving a diseased child as the only legacy of the alliance and a probable sequestration of the estate the result of the pragmatic motives of both the aristocrats and the bourgeoisie.

Hogarth was himself alluding to John Dryden's play of the same name, published in 1671, that also depicts the unlearned affectations of the middle class in Melantha in an arrangement of convenience with the naïve courtier, Palamede. Colley Cibber had recently revived the play in his own adaptation, *The Comical Lovers* (1707).

3 *The Marriage Act*: John Shebbeare's two-volume novel (1745) shares several themes with Garrick and Colman's play. Barter and his wife attempt to ennoble their family by marrying off their all-too-willing daughter, Molly, to Lord Sapplin, the son of an impoverished nobleman, Lord Wormeaton, who thinks to raise much-needed capital from the union. The younger daughter, Eliza Barter, meanwhile is much in love with a poor, but well-meaning clerk, William Worthy. In the early drafts of the play, the name, 'Lord Sapplin' was used by the authors instead of Sir John Melvil.

9 *publication of the piece*: there had been a serious disagreement between the authors in late 1765 as to the degree each had contributed to the play and as to the authorship of favourite passages. Garrick, on returning from an extensive European tour, refused to take the part of Lord Ogleby. Colman took this as a breach of trust. See *Letters*, i. 209–12, and Ian McIntyre, *Garrick* (Harmondsworth, 1999), 373–6.

13 *In justice to . . . of the Clandestine Marriage*: some friends, and some enemies, have endeavoured to allot distinct portions of this play to each of the authors. Each, however, considers himself as responsible for the whole; and though they have, on other occasions, been separately honored with the indulgence of the public, it is with peculiar pleasure that they now make their joint acknowledgements for the very favourable reception of *The Clandestine Marriage 1777*.

THE CHARACTERS OF THE PLAY

*Mrs [Abington]*: Frances Abington was so dismayed at the minor and 'low' part offered her (that of Betty) that she insisted that her name be omitted from all playbills and the first printings. It was only included from *1777* on.

PROLOGUE

8   *matchless Hogarth ... pictured morals and mankind*: the close identity between Hogarth's moral purpose and his graphic realism was often lauded. Garrick opened his 'Epitaph on William Hogarth in Chiswick Church-Yard' (*c.*1771) with praise of the

> great Painter of Mankind
> Who reached the noblest point of art,
> Whose pictured morals claim the mind
> And through the eye correct the heart!

Cf. Samuel Johnson's 'Epitaph on William Hogarth' (1771), where the painter is capable of seeing 'the manners in the face'. Christopher Smart even went so far as to claim that Hogarth was 'the Garrick of his Art' (*The Hilliad* (1753), i. 257).

13   *cits*: 'Pert, low townsmen; pragmatical traders' (*SJ*).

15   *trade from interest*: both a distraction from commerce—and self-interest.

19   *struts his hour upon the stage*: cf. *Macbeth*, 5.5.24.

24   *Jack Falstaff's grave and Juliet's bier*: roles that James Quin and Susannah Cibber (see below) had both made their own.

30   *Quins and Cibbers of their own*: James Quin (March) and Susannah Cibber (January 1766) had recently died, and Arthur Murphy felt that this passage was 'a handsome funeral eulogium' on the pair (*Life of Johnson*, ii. 36)). It is also proof either that the Prologue was revised to include Quin's elegy (the play's première was a month before Quin's demise) or that the Prologue was included after its first run.

1.1.35   *qualms*: 'A sudden fit of sickness; a sudden seizure of sickly languor' (*SJ*).

45   *tide-waiter's place*: post as a customs officer who boarded ships on arrival at port so as to ensure the payment of duties and the observance of customs house regulations.

123   *Quality*: of high social rank.

163   *fast*: firmly, irrevocably.

177   *Stuff*: an idiomatic term for anything material—and perhaps gross. Sterling regards the term as signifying the most substantial part of any suitor.

224   *'Change*: the Royal Exchange, situated on Threadneedle Street, was at the hub of London's commercial activity. Sterling is anxious about his foreign investments.

325

225 *Nothing material*: the primary sense is probably 'nothing significant, or to the point', but Lovewell may perhaps be using the term knowingly, implying that Sterling's curiosity might only be sharpened by the materialistic.

232 *good news from America*: the Stamp Act, passed the previous year, had imposed a much more swingeing tax burden on the colonies. Sterling was not alone in hoping that it had finally been accepted. Two days after the play's première the Act was repealed.

249 *They shall eat gold, and drink gold, and lie in gold*: cf. Sir Epicure Mammon's dreams of the luxurious courting of Doll Common in Ben Jonson's *The Alchemist* (1610): 'She shall feel gold, taste gold, hear gold, sleep gold' (*The Alchemist and other Plays*, 4.1.29).

252 *the great man*: a heavily discredited term by 1766. It had become the ironic appellation of Sir Robert Walpole, First Lord of the Treasury (nearest to our term, Prime Minister) from 1721 to 1742, and, in Fielding's *Jonathan Wild* (1743), denoted Wild himself and any notorious criminal.

259 *an English merchant ... in the universe*: a sentiment codified in Daniel Defoe's *The Complete English Tradesman* (1725), but not a particularly Whig view by 1766. Colman was at the time drafting his play, *The English Merchant* (1767) in which Freeport, the plain and forthright trader of the title, is the hero, and who well deserves Mrs Goodman's commendation, that he 'is not a man of compliment' and 'does the most essential service in less time, than others take in making protestations' (Act 3, p. 40). Colman probably alluded to Joseph Addison's Sir Andrew Freeport from his *Spectator* series (see especially nos. 69 (19 May 1711) and 549 (29 November 1712)), a similarly dynamic, yet unshowy, social catalyst. Richard Cumberland's *The Fashionable Lover* (1772) was soon to be consistently popular over several seasons. Aubrey, in Act 5, castigates Bridgemore for his financial irregularities, hoping that 'integrity [might] for ever remain the inseparable characteristic of an English Merchant' (p. 60).

261 *Nabob*: originally the title for a deputy governor in the provinces of the Mogul empire; now a less specific term for anyone with great wealth.

1.2.17 *romantick*: the archaic spelling is retained to capture the contemporary understanding of the word as 'quixotic; not practical'.

18 *Love and a cottage*: a common phrase to denote unambitious contentment. Booth regrets not having heeded Amelia's advice (in Fielding's *Amelia* (1751), 3.4), when aboard for Gibraltar on military service, 'and preferred love and a cottage to all the dazzling charms of honour'. Frances Brooke has her heroine in *Emily Montague* (1769) confess to John Temple from Quebec how attractive to her would now be 'love, content and a cottage' (vol. i, letter 51).

42 *Polly . . . kept mistress*: the part of Polly Peachum in John Gay's *The Beggar's Opera* (1728) was played by an unknown, Lavinia Fenton, who so captivated the Duke of Bolton that he eventually lured her away from the stage to be his kept mistress, thereafter to be his wife, in 1751. Their first encounter is portrayed in Hogarth's series on the *Opera* (1729). The affair was the stuff of scandal and admiration in equal measure; Gay, himself, was amused at Fenton's sudden elevation, noting that the Duke had 'run away with Polly Peachum, having settled £400 a year upon her during pleasure, and upon disagreement £200 a year' (Letter to Jonathan Swift, July 1728, in *The Letters of John Gay* ed. C. F. Burgess (Oxford, 1966), 76). Miss Sterling may, inadvertently, be bracketing herself with a similar romantic transformation. The association with Gay is confirmed by the allusion to his own dramatic satire, *The What D'Ye Call It* (1715).

45 *Joseph Lutestring's*: lutestring was a dress of glossy silk fabric. It perhaps paints the Lutestrings as rather meretricious, though fashionable.

50 *city-knights*: those wealthy merchants who had only recently been elevated.

52 *crown-whist at Haberdasher's-Hall*: crown-whist was a popularly polite card-game. Haberdasher's Hall was the main hall of the haberdashers' guild in the city (Gresham Street, EC2), one of the twelve great city livery companies. Designed by Wren and finally open in 1668, the Hall was the epitome of *arriviste* glamour. Lady Lutestring may be dressed well, but her pastimes belie her noble airs and graces.

56 *like a bad shilling*: a slightly elevated version of the proverbial assumption that a bad penny always turns up (e.g. in your change). Sir Joseph is similarly steadfast at his tradesman's post.

59 *Temple Bar*: running from Fleet Street to the Strand, the Bar marked the western gate of the City.

62 *Grosvenor-Square*: next to Lincoln's Inn Fields, the largest square in London and one of its finest, set in the newly fashionable district of Mayfair, just south of Oxford Street.

63 *Aldersgate . . . Without and Within*: typical City addresses. Aldersgate stood near Smithfield meat market; Cheap is a contraction of Cheapside, a wide and bustling commercial thoroughfare; Candlewick Street is now named Cannon Street and runs parallel to Cheapside; Farringdon Without and Within are situated at the edge of Holborn, to the west of Smithfield Market.

70 *Arthur's*: Robert Arthur had reopened the once particularly notorious White's Chocolate House (burned down in 1733) as Arthur's in 1755. Pedicord and Bergmann note that it now signified aristocratic and conservative tastes.

74 *Carlisle House*: once the property of the Earls of Carlisle, the House in Soho had become a newly fashionable venue for assemblies and balls.

84 *front-box at a benefit play*: authors, usually from the third night's performance of their work, were given the proceeds of the take. Prices were occasionally reduced on such occasions, so obtaining a 'Front Box' might only have been possible at Benefits.

86 *Tunbridge*: Tunbridge Wells, although given royal patronage, was a Kent spa town that was fast becoming faded and a place of little style. Betsey associates it now with 'citizens', and imagines that it would be one of the few places to which Fanny and her husband could aspire.

115 *Unpaper the curtains*: paper was used as a protection against fading for curtains in rooms not in current use.

134 *nataral*: a profound pun. Mrs Heidelberg means that love robs Fanny of her wits, but the play poses the question as to just where 'nature' lies.

169 *land-carriage mackerel*: an expensive method of procurement, implying that the fish would have been hand-picked at the port and brought fresh straight to Sterling's estate.

2.1 S.D. *cups of chocolate*: the original stage direction indicates just 'chocolate'. The full ceremony surrounding the drinking of chocolate is probably indicated—an implicit parody of the servants' social aspirations.

2 *positive*: 'Dogmatical; ready to lay down notions with confidence; stubborn in opinion' (*SJ*, sense III).

19 *qualms*: 'A sudden fit of sickness; a sudden seizure of sickly languor' (*SJ*).

38 *comes from Italy*: traditionally, England's chocolate trade was via its own routes from the East Indies; a provision from Italy implies the very height of quality.

53 *Saturn*: an ancient Roman God, originally identified with Cronos, the Greek father of Time and thus associated with the Golden Age. Perhaps Miss Sterling has adopted Mrs Heidelberg's pride in apparent tradition and quality.

67 *Abigails*: derived from the name for King David's handmaid, then a generic word for female servants.

76 *Advertise ... Gazette, de Gazette de Chronique*: the probable journals are *the Public Advertiser, the Gazetteer and New Daily Advertiser* and *the St James's Chronicle; or, The British Evening-Post*. Lord Ogleby wishes to keep up with both court and city news.

78 *Anti-Sejanus*: the pseudonym for Dr James Scott, who, throughout 1765–6 in the *London Magazine* and *Public Advertiser*, wrote several lengthy diatribes against the recently resigned Prime Minister, Lord Bute. His increasing influence on George III threatened the potency of the American Stamp Act, a tax on the Colonies to help meet the costs of the American campaign.

103  *palsy-drops*: infusion to help a (non-specific) disease of the nervous system, usually involving a numbness and eventual paralysis of one or more limbs.

129  *surfeit-water*: any liquid that aided indigestion due to overindulgence. Johnson defined a surfeit as 'Sickness or satiety caused by overfulness' (*SJ*).

135  *Blackfriars*: an area just south of Fleet Street that comprised the open sewer of Fleet Ditch and Bridewell Prison.

136  *Borachio*: originally the Spanish term for a wine bag or container. *Pedicord and Bergmann*, and *Chevalier* conjecture that the reference might be to the wine trade, but it is more likely a generalized term of abuse. There is a character by that name (who is drunk in one scene) in Shakespeare's *Much Ado about Nothing* as well as in Tourneur's *The Atheist's Tragedy*.

149  *is it*: Chevalier adopts 'it is' in the face of all textual authority in that it 'seems' here to be 'more of a statement than a question' (p. 218).

163  *game of romps*: boisterous and rough frolics.

185  *clumps*: a cluster of trees or shrubs, here indicating their strategic placement. William Chambers, in his *Designs of Chinese Buildings, Furniture, Dresses, Machines, and Utensils* (1757), admired the Chinese method of using 'clumps' sparingly: 'They never fill a whole piece of ground with clumps; they consider a plantation as painters do a picture, and groupe their trees in the same manner as these do their figures . . .' (p. 18).

199  *go to the Grand Tower*: For a fuller consideration of contemporary garden design, see Introduction, pp. xxii–xxiii. Sterling's Tower would seem to stand out too prominently as an obvious 'feature' against the surrounding landscape, a consideration of the part at the expense of the whole.

214  *island of Love*: associated with Cythera, an island off the south coast of Laconia in the Peloponnese. According to Hesiod (*Theogony*, 195–8), Aphrodite was supposed to have landed there immediately after her birth from the sea. The phrase, 'What news from the Island of Love ?', was often used to compliment (sometimes ironically) another's good fortune in affairs of the heart, e.g. Vizard to Sir Harry Wildair in Farquhar's *The Constant Couple* (1699), 2.3.96; Harry Hunter to Grigg in Charles Coffey's *The Beggar's Wedding* (1729), p. 20.

2.2.38  *Great Improvements*: for a fuller discussion of the various debates about Improvement, see Alastair M. Duckworth, *The Improvement of the Estate: A Study of Jane Austen's Novels* (1971), 2–34, and *Hunt and Willis*, 30–46.

42  *man at Hyde-Park Corner*: not a particularly stylish individual; Hyde Park Corner was rapidly becoming a particularly busy concourse that had attracted several temporary vendors, especially for the sale of plaster statuary.

48  *smack-smooth*: perfectly level—thus allowing no respite from either sun or wind.

52  *turned many a thousand of my money*: made use of commercially. Sterling is obviously now an investor in overseas trade as well as a direct participant.

57  *flip*: carrying on the nautical theme, a drink often associated with seafaring: a warm and sweet mixture of beer and spirits.

63  *gothic dairy*: although Walpole had just published *The Castle of Otranto: A Gothic Story* (1765), the aura of romantic medievalism in the dairy may have been secondary to a sense merely of a cultivated 'rustic'. For Shaftesbury, in his *Characteristicks* (1727–1.3.217), the Gothic suggested a brutal and unmannered proceeding, redolent of the 'harsh Discord of jingling Rhyme'. Squire Western is upbraided by Mrs Western for his 'more than Gothic ignorance' in Fielding's *Tom Jones* (1749–7.3).

72  *close walks*: covered avenues, with the added sense of secret, even 'confined; stagnant; without ventilation' (*SJ*, sense 3 for *close*, adj.) *Chevalier* notes that the details we receive of Sterling's landscaped grounds show a mistaken taste for 'bourgeois reductions of the kind of vast estate conceived by the landed gentry', where 'space-saving' substitutes for 'aristocratic spaciousness' (p. 20).

73  *serpentine*: the term had been rescued from its primary (and pejorative) meaning, 'snake-like', by William Hogarth in his *The Analysis of Beauty* (1753), who found it the line of beauty in its sinuous and varied movement: 'The eye hath this sort of enjoyment in winding walks, and serpentine rivers, and all sorts of objects, whose forms . . . are composed principally of what, I call, the *waving* and *serpentine* lines . . . Intricacy in form . . . I shall define to be that peculiarity in the lines, which compose it, that *leads the eye a wanton kind of chase*, and from the pleasure that gives the mind, intitles it to the name of beautiful' (p. 25). To its detractors, this theory was unduly formulaic (see *Paulson*, iii.121–5, 132–51), although the term achieved a currency in garden design. As early as Francis Coventry's contribution to *The World* (no. 15, 1753), however, the taste for the serpentine was associated with *nouveau riche* villas: 'Nothing on earth, at least, can please out of that model; and there is reason to believe that paradise itself would have no charms for one of these gentlemen, unless its walks be disposed into labyrinth and maeander' (*Hunt and Willis*, 275). For a more affectionate parody, see Sterne's comments in vol. vi, ch. 29 of his *Tristram Shandy* (1761). Sterling's adoption of this maxim has perhaps led him into an overinvolved intricacy.

76  *crinkum-crankum*: composed of twists and turns.

82  *Gracechurch-Street*: Sterling's City address is suitably a few yards from the Royal Exchange.

# NOTES TO PAGES 103–111

95 *beaupot*: a large decorated vase for cut flowers.

100 *my ruins*: in William Shenstone's 'Unconnected Thoughts on Gardening' (1764), ruins were effective triggers of the imagination: 'A ruin, for instance, may be neither new to us, nor majestick, nor beautiful, yet afford that pleasing melancholy which proceeds from a reflection on decayed magnificence' (*Works in Verse and Prose*, 2 vols. (1764), ii.77).

108 *Chinese bridge*: Sterling is all for catching novelty on the wing. If his own variety of *chinoiserie* was copied from William Chambers's model, then Lord Ogleby is in for an adventure in inspecting the cascades: 'They frequently throw rough wooden bridges from one rock to another, over the steepest part of the cataract; and often intercept it's passage by trees and heaps of stones, that seem to have been brought down by the violence of the torrent' (*Designs of Chinese Buildings*, 17).

118 *terminate the prospect*: provide a focal point for, yet the termination could be too final. Alexander Pope (in his *Epistle to Burlington* (1731)), mocks the garden design around Timon's villa:

> His *Gardens* next your Admiration call,
> On ev'ry side you look, behold the Wall!
> No pleasing Intricacies intervene,
> No artful Wilderness to perplex the Scene: . . .
>
> (ll. 113–16)

Pope's friend, Joseph Spence, assembled, in his Letter to the Revd Mr Wheeler (1751), a checklist of the principles of his landscaping. No. 8 advises the gardener, 'to conceal the bounds of your grounds everywhere, if possible. This is done by grove-works, sunk fences . . . and what they call invisible fences, as being but little discernible to the eye' (*Hunt and Willis*, 270).

196 *Cheapside . . . Whitechapel*: both are City sites, and associated with the newly emergent trading interest. Whitechapel was also proverbially a centre for organized crime.

330 *particular*: odd, of a singular nature.

338 *sentimental*: open to the higher, more exquisite, feelings.

3.1 S.D. *Sergeant*: '3. A lawyer of the highest rank under a judge' (*SJ*).

6 *two*: three *1766 (1)*, *1766 (3)*, *1768*, *1774*. only two other legal visitors are noted in the texts, but there must have been an impulse to create an impression of weighty legal might whenever the payroll permitted.

15 *settling these marriage articles*: framing and defining the legal conditions for marriage.

16 *circuits*: a set journey (usually twice a year) whereby a judge presided over the assizes in a particular area.

21 *commission-day*: the opening day of the assizes, when the commission entitling the court to take place is formally read.

331

22 *cause in the paper*: case in the printed schedule.

25 *tack opinions to them*: formulate (usually written) items of legal advice.

26 *currente calamo*: literally, with a swift or running pen; to set to or get down to work.

30 *devise of an estate*: the right to property given in a will.

31 *in fee or in tail*: in 'fee-simple', i.e. with absolute possession or by reference to the rights of a superior, whereby (usually) the possession would revert to the donor's descendants.

34 *nisi prius*: *Chevalier* suggests this term amounts to 'civil suits', i.e. cases tried outside London—or the Court of Westminster.

*crown side*: acting on behalf of the crown, in prosecution, and usually in the capital.

39 *gaol-delivery*: a set of cases involving defendants already imprisoned as they have been refused bail.

41 *alibi*: a plea that one was elsewhere when the crime took place.

43 *our identity*: positively identify the defendant as the wrong-doer.

47 *crim. con.*: criminal conversation, i.e. adultery. Damages could be claimed from the adulterer by the wronged husband.

56 *luce clarius*: clearly and obviously.

61 *commission, the cause will come on before him*: as he is empowered to try the case, 'brother Puzzle' will stand instead.

79 *Will his tackle hold*: primarily, 'tackle' meant the rigging of a ship; in this context, Sterling is enquiring as to whether 'old Ferret' is up to the job and if he has constructed a watertight set of binding legal conditions.

83 *business out of hand*: complete his business competently.

87 *encumbrances*: burdens (here, financial limitations).

92 *Down on the nail*: straightaway.

93 *India-bonds*: in modern parlance a debenture, or acknowledgement of indebtedness, by the thriving East India Company.

99 *recovery*: the gaining possession of property by way of a legal verdict.

100 *the entail of the Ogleby estate*: Sir John has now established himself and his heirs as the rightful possessors.

115 *long-robe*: idiomatic phrase for the legal profession.

*pudding-sleeves*: a physician, implying one who will attend the birth of the first child–and so aid Sterling's purchase of nobility for his blood-line.

148 *bill after acceptance*: the recognition of financial liability when a bill of exchange falls due.

178 *statute-fair*: annual fair held in a small town or village principally for the hiring of servants.

180 *Grand Signior*: the Sultan of Turkey, known for his omnipotence and an absolute power over his harem.

182 *African slave-trade*: in 1766, the ethical debates surrounding slavery were muted. Blackstone's *Commentaries on the Laws of England* (1765) had offered the view that, once a slave had set foot in England, he became free (i. 411–12). Davis claims that, by the 1760s, there were 'at least twenty thousand blacks' in Britain, and that, apart from a few Quaker tracts (see the summary on pp. 107–12) and the earliest writings of Granville Sharp, the general view was that it was a 'progressive' venture (David Brion Davis, *Slavery and Human Progress* (Oxford, 1984), 79–82; see also Edward Lascelles, *Granville Sharp and the Freedom of Slaves in England* (London, 1928)). There is little that is progressive about Sterling's opinion—but, similarly, little that would have been widely seen as reprehensible.

221 *éclat*: conspicuous social brilliance.

278 *uncertain as the stocks*: a common concern as, compared to the relative stability of land prices, it was always believed that investment in shares or stocks was 'uncertain'. Sterling does not here refer to any particular disturbance.

280 *whirligig man*: a whirligig was a child's top; Sterling's comment is eloquent about his general distrust of 'fashion' as well as superior class.

281 *china orange*: 'the sweet-orange; supposed originally of China' (*SJ*).

3.2.55 *caballins*: furtive intrigues.

161 *common-council-man*: member of a common council, probably in London. Rather an anticlimax in the list coming after a knight and an MP.

194 *Plum*: in City 'cant' according to Johnson, £100,000 (*SJ*).

198 *three per cents*: government securities, that, in 1751, had been consolidated to form a single stock, yielding 3 per cent interest.

199 *South-Sea annuities*: a yearly allowance from South Sea Company shares.

221 *not upon the figures*: does not add up.

4.1.5 *Positively*: 'With assurance or confident assertion' (*OED*, sense 1).

9 *incendaries*: incendiaries could indicate, quite literally, persons who set fire to buildings as well as those who might just inflame the passions. There is a clear irony in assigning that quality to Fanny rather than either the speaker or Miss Sterling.

23 *post-shay*: a hired carriage, indicating either one taken for a specific journey or drawn by hired horses.

27 *in your hand*: approximate to a plea that Sterling takes his daughter 'in hand', i.e. supervises her closely.

39 *absolute . . . make us absolute*: the first reference means 'positive, certain, without any hesitation' (*SJ*, sense 5), the latter, 'not limited; as, *absolute*

power' (*SJ*, sense 4). Sterling realizes only too well the only bargaining tool his family possesses.

4.2.3 *Je ne sais pas*: 'I do not know'.

7 *very abstract of 'Change-Alley*: a true epitome of the commercial spirit. 'Change Alley, now Cornhill, was named so after the Royal Exchange nearby. Although now noted for its banking, it was then more a mixture of smaller-scale stock-jobbers or -dealers who frequented its various coffee-houses, such as Jonathan's and Garraway's. Although past its first peak of activity, reduced by legislation in the wake of the South Sea Bubble crash of 1720, there were still similar, persistent, forms of dealing, or gambling, in market trends (see Stephen Inwood's *A History of London* (1998), 349–54).

10 *la petite Fanchon*: a Gallic form of 'Fanny', and derived from the character of little, or dear, Fanny regularly found in folk-songs.

12 *sympatie entre vous*: 'sympathy—fellow-feeling—between you'.

14 *Goths and Vandals*: a fear repeated in the Epilogue by Lord Minum, in reference to 'nasty Plays' (ll. 27–8). See note to 2.2.63 for the possible associations of the 'Gothic' at this time.

17 *object*: 'objection'.

21 *My eyes are involuntarily attracted by beautiful objects*: Ogleby, whilst not obviously interested in aesthetics, aligns himself here with a rather progressive view: that beauty is less a consciously defined property than an 'involuntary' reflex, and part of a subjective investment on the part of the spectator. This view was popularized by Joseph Addison in his *Spectator* papers on the Pleasures of the Imagination (1711–12), where the associations that accrue to fertile objects of contemplation surprisingly unlock a relay of impressions: 'any single Circumstance of what we have formerly seen often raises up a whole Scene of Imagery, and awakens numberless Ideas that before slept in the Imagination ... Our Imagination takes the Hint, and leads us unexpectedly into Cities or Theatres, Plains or Meadows' (no. 417, 28 June 1712; *The Spectator*, ed. Donald F. Bond (London, 1965), 5 vols., iii. 562). This associationist theory might be more familiar to the audience via Edmund Burke's *Philosophical Enquiry into the Origin of Ideas of the Sublime and the Beautiful* (1757), especially in the fifth part, where he claimed that 'we yield to sympathy, what we refuse to description' (5.7, *Philosophical Enquiry*, ed. J. T. Boulton (London, 1958), 175). At the very least, there is a deft contrast here between the sympathies of the responsive viewer and Sterling's mechanical deployment of mere wealth.

25 *Vous êtes un sot*: 'You are an idiot'.

27 *prode*: proud.

42 s.d. *looking with a glass*: a perspective glass, held up against the eye to bring distant objects into sharper contrast, or simply a field-glass.

45 *I am monkeé, I am ole*: a wry joke; Canton claims that, although he lacks in certain particulars (*manquer*), he is still 'whole' now and again and in some details.

47 *Taisez-vous bête*: 'shut up, you beast'.

48 *Elle vous attend*: 'She is waiting for you'.

52 *crinkum-crankum*: see note to 2.2.76.

55 S.D. *Another part of the garden: Wood* creates a third scene at this point, but I follow *Chevalier* and *Pedicord/Bergmann* in continuing the second; there is no complete change of location, and it resembles 2.2 in construction.

63 *Do you open the whole affair*: broach the subject of the marriage.

91 *satire upon mankind*: Ogleby probably means that Fanny on her own seems like a reproach upon men who should be vying to be her companion. The link to John Wilmot, Earl of Rochester's 'A Satyr against Mankind' (written, 1675–6) is distant, but, in that it indicates the need to learn humility from experience, it could reflect upon Ogleby's self-deception:

> Then Old Age and Experience, hand in hand,
> Lead him to death, and make him understand,
> After a search so painful and so long,
> That all his life he has been in the wrong.
>
> (ll. 25–8)

103 *Allez-vous en!*: Go on then!

128 *sentiments*: nearer to 'notions' or 'attitudes', but Johnson's second sense, 'the sense considered distinctly from the language or things' (*SJ*), conveys a sense of depth and conviction, too.

131 *Venus forbid*: a rather formulaic oath, laying claim to the necessity of following love's promptings. When Palamede is willingly coaxed by Doralice into a place of assignation in Dryden's *Marriage a la Mode* (1673; 3.2.11–13, *Dramatic Works*, vol. xi, ed. John Loftis, David Stuart Rodes, and Vinton A. Dearing (Berkeley, 1978)), he utters the oath as a rather empty gesture towards decorum: '*Venus* forbid that I should harbour so unreasonable a thought of a fair young Lady, that you should lead me hither into temptation'.

143 *my duty to my father*: the issue of how far to adhere to filial devotion is one of the comic questions of the play. Fanny pretends to an obedience she has clearly not maintained.

168 *Fort bien*: very well.

203 *sacrifice the whole sex to her*: abandon the pursuit of any other woman for her.

204 *open the matter*: see note to 4.2.63.

216 *apostasy*: 'departure from what a man has professed' (*SJ*).

238 *sensibility*: strength of feeling. Ogleby has been transformed in this scene into a 'man of feeling', more aware of his emotions than most and certainly less capable of disciplining them. Through plays such as George Lillo's *The London Merchant* (1731) and Edward Moore's *The Gamester* (1753), the drama of bourgeois sensibility had become acceptable on the London stage.

252 *omnium*: the whole sum of what one values. *OED* sense 1 gives a precise monetary meaning: 'the aggregate amount (at market price) of the parcels of different stocks and other considerations, formerly offered by Government, in raising a loan, for each unit of capital (i.e. every hundred pounds) subscribed'. It is typical of Sterling that his desires should be expressed in commercial terms.

278 *demon Interest*: both self-interest and cash raised on a loan.

287 *father to an Earl instead of a Baronet*: Ogleby notes the difference between his own rank and that of Sir John. In terms of feudal rank, an earl stands just above a viscount and just below a marquis, and was equivalent to the continental 'count'. A baronet is the lowest rank that is still hereditary, and could be awarded to a commoner.

303 *than the post in his warehouse*: a guard of the stock in a warehouse. Proverbially, this implied an improbable venture, likely to end in disappointment. There is some evidence here that Garrick worked on Act IV. This phrase is given to Cob by Ben Jonson in his *Every Man in his Humour* (*The Alchemist and other Plays*, 3.3.36), and is adopted by Garrick in his own adaptation of the play (1752): 'Then am I a Vagabond, and fitter for Bridewell, than your Worship's Company, if I saw any body to be kiss'd, unless they wou'd have kiss'd the Post in the middle of the Warehouse' (p. 34).

312 *first conceived*: in this context, first struck with a mature emotion.

346 *Who pleads her cause . . . finds a full redress*: 'Then plead your cause with never-failing Beauty, | Speak all your griefs, and find a full redress' (Nicholas Rowe, *The Tragedy of Jane Shore* (1714), 2.1, p. 18).

395 *city-philosophy*: an easy target for Garrick. *Chevalier* is accurate when he describes Sterling's landscaping as a form of bourgeois control: 'The central meaning of Sterling's garden is not nature, but property, or nature commodified . . . Sterling, as a man of business, wants to make his garden busy. The land itself functions as a sign of conspicuous consumption' (p. 19).

405 *auxiliary*: an accomplice or assistant.

444 *ferae naturae*: literally, wild animals, over which Man should establish strenuous dominance, if Virgil is to be followed (see *Georgic 1*, l. 328). It

is probable that Ogleby's conceit is derived from Dryden in his *An Evening's Love* (1671), where Bellamy claims that 'Women are not compris'd in our Laws of friendship: they are *ferae naturae*; our common game, like Hare and Partridge: every man has equal right to them, as he has to the Sun and Elements' (4.1.419–22; *Dramatic Works*, vol. x, ed. Maximilian E. Novak and George Robert Guffey (Berkeley, 1970)).

451 *Allons donc*: 'Let's go then'.

453 *Suivons l'amour*: 'Let's follow where love leads'.

5.1.31 *maintaining*: providing for.

40 *waiting*: waiting for.

89 *carrater*: character. In this context, more probably a character-reference that would help with future employment.

108 *the wrong sow by the ear*: mistaken the situation.

5.2 S.D. *night-cap*: a general term for any headdress worn in bed or informally.

3 *fly-cap*: a cap generally worn by the elderly, with raised side-flaps. The delicacy felt by Mrs Heidelberg that she swap a simple night-cap for this is surely fastidious.

5 *perdigus disconcarted*: not a regular legal term nor recognizable Latin. 'Perdigus' is nearest 'perditus' ('lost, abandoned, ruined'), but could simply be a corruption of 'prodigious'.

10 *flustrated*: a jocular or vulgar form of 'flustered'.

18 *'Change-broker*: a dealer in stocks at the Royal Exchange.

24 *interested*: biased or easily swayed.

42 *dalimma*: dilemma.

59 *asp*: aspen tree, like a small poplar, the leaves of which always seem to tremble.

63 *impurence*: impudence.

79 *whimsical*: 'freakish; capricious; oddly fanciful' (*SJ*).

82 *spider-brusher*: i.e. one who clears curtains and other surfaces of spiders' webs; a maid.

95 *Miss Jezabel*: a free and perhaps shameless woman, derived from the biblical account at 1 Kings 16: 31, 19: 1, 2, and 21 and 2 Kings 9: 30–7 of the impure wife of Ahab, king of Israel.

169 *rancounter*: a jumble between 'encounter' and the French, *rencontrer*, to meet.

184 *peach*: inform on, as a contraction of 'impeach', usually used in connection with the apprehending of criminals.

199 *insure privately*: the advantage of taking out 'private' insurance was that you did not have to disclose the actual worth (according to external

valuation) of your goods. Sterling wishes to keep matters as secret as possible.

203 *Unnatural fathers make unnatural children*: i.e. the sins of the father will be visited on the children. In this case, Miss Sterling claims that her father should not be surprised if she takes after his example—of unreasonable behaviour.

218 *twenty per cent. for our money*: it is typical for Sterling to compute the gains of an aristocratic association. He imagines that his investments would yield enhanced, gilt-edged, dividends.

221 *'Change-Alley spirit*: see note to 4.2.7.

244 *circuit-time*: a period for a set journey undertaken by a judge in a particular district to hear cases.

270 *on the scamper to Scotland*: more precisely Gretna Green, just over the Scottish border from England, where the 1753 Marriage Act did not apply.

307 *luce clarius*: see note to 3.1.56.

348 *magnanimity*: 'Greatness of mind; bravery; elevation of soul' (*SJ*).

373 *never strike a balance without errors excepted*: to strike a balance was to ascertain where a financial account did not add up and, tacitly, rectify it. To do this 'with errors excepted' was to excuse oneself for minor inaccuracies. Ogleby is pointing out that city morals always allowed for some measure of condonement of potentially underhand, or at least inadvertent, dealings.

382 *Young ladies with minds . . . serve to deter them*: this is near to the closing comments of Shebbeare's novel, *The Marriage Act*, where the legislation was regarded as a charter for family interference: 'How many snares will be laid for the Open-hearted and Honest, to circumvent them, by artful relations, to induce them to illegal Marriages, and thus possess their Estates?' (Ch. 69, ii. 324).

411 *sensibility*: '1. Quickness of sensation' or '2. Quickness of perception' (*SJ*). Sir John's primary sense is here nearer to 'acuteness of sensation'.

### EPILOGUE

15 *two by Honours*: equivalent of declaring an intention to win at least two tricks in the trump suit.

18 *Spadille*: in Ombre and Quadrille, the Ace of Spades.

21 *And dwell such daring Souls in little Men*: an allusion to lines 11–12 of Canto 1 of Alexander Pope's *The Rape of the Lock* (1712): 'And dwells such rage in softest bosoms then, | And lodge such daring souls in little men?' Thereafter, the lines were altered to 'In tasks so bold, can little

NOTES TO PAGES 153–154

men engage, | And in soft bosoms dwells such mighty rage?' The earlier reading was perpetuated in Pope's own note in his 1736 *Works*.

27 *Handel's*: George Friedrich Handel's operas and devotional works were unshunnable in fashionable London at this time. Since his death in 1759, and his interment in Westminster Abbey, his work had continued to be performed often at Covent Garden. Mrs Quaver's aversion to his work (and to 'nasty Plays' (l. 28)) is surely part of a questionable taste.

31 *the Pool*: the sum of stakes wagered at the table.

38 *Jonas*: there are two contenders for this reference, one that is more likely than the other. There is a Captain Jonas, from Thomas D'Urfey's *The Royalist* (1682), according to the *Dramatis Personae*, 'a Seditious Rascal that disturbs the People with News and Lyes, to Promote his own Interest' and one who is more given to trickery and japes than the 'Jonas' in William Wycherley's *Love in a Wood* (1672), the assumed name (and lower-life character) of Sir Simon Addleplot in his pursuit of Mistress Martha's favour. Trill is more likely to know the Wycherley character. *Love in a Wood* was revived at Drury Lane in 1718; there were texts of the play published in 1711 and then again 1733, and Wycherley's plays were collected in 1725 and 1731. Garrick must have also been preoccupied with Wycherley, or, at least his *The Country Wife*; his adaptation, *The Country Girl*, was to appear at Drury Lane in October 1766.

39 *Comus*: in Milton's masque (1637), the eponymous 'false traitor' (according to the Lady at l. 690) had been indulged during a varied stage history. Regularly more recently an excuse to introduce extravagant musical set pieces, the 'joy and feast | Midnight shout and revelry' (ll. 102–3) summoned whenever the character takes the stage became more the trademark of the piece than his dubious materialism. To a large extent, this was a consequence of John Dalton's influential adaptation of 1738 (with music by Thomas Arne) that interpolated lines from *L'Allegro* and introduced a new character, Euphrosyne, to lighten the mood. It was to this version that Garrick spoke Samuel Johnson's *A New Prologue, Spoken at the Representation of Comus*, at Drury Lane on 5 April 1750. Colman was to adapt the masque in 1772, and, in the Prologue, he admired its 'poetical beauties' at the same time as fearing its tendency to produce a certain 'coldness and languor in the audience'. His abridgement tried to remedy this, and yet it did so whilst acknowledging that it hitherto 'only maintained its place on the theatre chiefly by the assistance of Musick'.

44 *King Lare*: the 'touching' power of *King Lear* was no doubt enhanced by the almost total adoption of Nahum Tate's version (1681) during the period. This was the '*Lear*' that Garrick attempted in just his first full professional season (in March 1742). It lacked a Fool, supplied a love interest between Edgar and Cordelia, dispenses with Lear and Cordelia's

deaths, and then had Albany restore land to Lear that the old man passes over as a delayed dowry to his daughter.

45 *Ould ... 'To be, or not to be'*: the appearance of the ghost of Hamlet's father had a potent effect on contemporary audiences. The novice play-goer, Partridge, in Fielding's *Tom Jones* (1749), is left with a 'violent fit of trembling that his knees knocked against each other' when the Ghost first appears (16.5). G. C. Lichtenberg, in 1775, remembered the effect of this apparition on Garrick's Hamlet: 'so expressive of horror is his mien that a shudder seized me again and again even before he began to speak' ('Briefe aus England' in *Works* (1867), iii. 214). The 'To be or not to be' passage (3.1.58 ff.) was as well known as it is now. Lichtenberg describes Garrick's appearance when delivering it: with his 'hair all in disorder, locks of it hanging down over one shoulder, one of his black stockings [had] fallen down.'

46 *Othello's roar*: Sir Patrick has possibly read Thomas Rymer's unsympathetic account of the play, and Othello's part in particular, in his *A Short View of Tragedy* (1692). Emphasizing Othello's disintegration in 4.2, he finds the spectacle too degraded for tragedy: 'Some Drayman or drunken Tinker might possibly treat his drab at this sort of rate, and mean no harm by it,' yet the 'volly of scoundrel filthy Language' Shakespeare gives to his hero is really just an 'absurd Maggot' (p. 134).

49 *What, when ... calls her whore*: as Othello does repeatedly in 4.2 (at lines 22, 74, 89, and 92).

50 *King Richard calls his horse*: at 5.7.7 of *Richard III*, the king calls for any horse to help him return to the battle at Bosworth Field. Again, a signifi-cant passage that became an indication of how Garrick approached the part. One of his very first professional appearances (October 1742) was as Richard in Colley Cibber's adaptation (1700). Arthur Murphy, in his *Life* of Garrick (2 vols., 1801), noted the ferocity of Garrick's Richard at this point: 'in spite of all the terrors of Conscience, his courage mounted to a blaze'. He found that 'all was rage, fury, and almost reality' (i. 16).

53 *that's invisible*: Macbeth imagines he sees the dagger with which he intends to murder Duncan (2.1.34–41). He concludes that it is a 'fatal vision', a 'false creation, | Proceeding from the heat-oppressed brain' (ll. 36, 38–9). In the anonymously published pamphlet, *An Essay on Acting: In which will be considered The Mimical behaviour of a Certain fashionable faulty Actor, and the Laudableness of such unmannerly, as well as inhumane Proceedings. To which will be added, A short Criticism on his Acting Macbeth* (1744), this scene was regarded as a test case for a new style of acting. Now widely regarded as authored by Garrick, it contrasts the declamatory approach of James Quin with the more naturalistic manner of the new master, Garrick, who had first attempted the part on 7 January that same year. When imagining the dagger, the advice was that the actor 'should not rivet his Eyes to an imaginary Object, as if it *really*

were there, but should show an *unsettled Motion* in his Eye, like one not quite awak'd from some disordering Dream; his *Hands* and *Fingers* should not be *immoveable*, but *restless*' (sigs. D1$^{r-v}$).

59 *they have ta'en away*: for the 1765–6 season at Drury Lane, Garrick and James Lacy had introduced a radical lighting scheme, first introduced in France. Where before there were predominantly naked overhead lights, the stage was now lit by reflectors on foot- and side-wing lights. Jean Louis Monnet, the Director of Paris's L'Opéra Comique, was Garrick's mentor in introducing this more indirect and flexible illumination. In a letter dated 15 June 1765, he drew Garrick's attention to two types of reflectors: 'some are of earthenware, and in biscuit form; they have six or eight wicks, and you put oil in them; the others are of tin, in the shape of a candle, with a spring, and you put candles in them' (*The Private Correspondence of David Garrick with the most Celebrated Persons of his Time*, ed. James Boaden, 2 vols. (1831), ii. 441). *The Public Advertiser* announced that the managers seemed by this change to have 'created an Artificial Day' and 'brought down the Milky Way to the Bottom of the Stage' (25 September 1765).

61 *Put out the light, and then*: cf. 'Put out the light, and then put out the light' (*Othello*, 5.2.7). Othello is about to extinguish his chamber lamp and then another far more significant light, his wife, Desdemona. As with the allusions above, this scene had often been the highlight of an Othello's performance. Henry Fielding, in the journey to Elysium in his *Journey from This World to the Next* (1743), ch. 8, has Booth and Betterton both lay claim to excellence in the delivery of this speech and the whole scene.

68 *push*: throng or immoderate crowd. Sir Patrick would tolerate a throng of people to see a little Shakespeare.

74 *Capuchin*: 'A female garment, consisting of a cloak and hood, made in imitation of the dress of capuchin monks' (*SJ*).

87 *Guildhall Giants*: the statues of Gog and Magog, carved by Richard Saunders in 1708, and then placed over the steps leading to the Mayor's Court. The statues were 14.5 feet high and placed on 2 octagonal pedestals, the one holding a 'Pole Ax', the other a 'Halbert', according to Edward Hatton in his *New View of London* (1708, ii. 608). They were removed in 1815 and placed by the Great West Window.

107 *ten lawyers*: Miss Crotchet's recollection is accurate enough until this detail. At the most there would appear to be just three principal lawyers unless the first production used several extras in 3.1 busying themselves with silent legal calculations.

122 *de tout mon coeur—I've one in petto*: with all my heart—I have one [a song] off by heart.

# She Stoops to Conquer

*Title:* The Novel—*L.* A last-minute choice over the play's eventual subtitle. It necessitated a further change at 4.1.238–9, where Kate is to 'preserve the character in which I stooped to conquer' (*1773a*) in place of the character 'in which I conquered' (*L*)). *Ogden* traces a possible source in John Dryden's *Amphitryon* (1690), where Jupiter, in pursuit of Alcmena, utters the closing couplet of Act 3 (ll. 609–10): 'Th'offending Lover, when he lowest lies, | Submits, to conquer; and but kneels, to rise' (*Works*, vol. xv, ed. Earl Miner, George G. Guffey, and Franklin B. Zimmerman (Berkeley, 1976), 284). The play would have been better known in Dr John Hawkesworth's adaptation (1756) that was staged at Drury Lane on 26 October 1771, and 25 February 1773 and, at Covent Garden, as a benefit for Henry Woodward, the original choice for Tony Lumpkin, on 20 March 1773.

*Dedication: om. L.* Printed separately in the *St James's Chronicle* for 27 March 1773.

4 *lived many years in intimacy with you*: Goldsmith was first introduced to Johnson, possibly by Tobias Smollett, in 1759, and became a consistent member of the (dining and debating) Club that congregated around him from 1763 onwards. He rescued Goldsmith (as he was prone to do) by buying the MS of *The Vicar of Wakefield* in 1762, probably influenced Newbery to print it eventually in 1766 and added nine lines to the conclusion to his poem, *The Traveller* (1764). Sorely disappointed at the delay in staging the play, Goldsmith was glad of Johnson's influence with Colman, 'who [Johnson believed] was prevailed on at last by much solicitation, nay, a kind of force' to put it on (*Life of Johnson*, iii. 321, 25 April 1778)). The first night was graced by the attendance not only by Johnson, but also Burke and Reynolds.

7 *unaffected piety*: not a quality much appreciated by Johnson himself. Boswell quotes him (10 June 1784) as claiming that even 'a wicked fellow is the most pious when he takes to it. He'll beat you all at piety' (*Life of Johnson*, iv. 289). Piety alone just meant a staunch belief, but this could be manufactured by circumstance, not conviction. Especially recently (see Walter Jackson Bate, *Samuel Johnson* (London, 1984), 248–61), he believed that true faith entailed struggle and self-examination: 'Trust in God . . . is to be obtained only by repentance, obedience, and supplication, not by nourishing in our hearts a confused idea of the goodness of God, or a firm persuasion that we are in a state of grace'. The state of being in a certain religious torment signalled not a weakness of faith, but a real 'piety, and a sincere and fervent desire of pleasing God' (Sermon 14, in *Works* (*Johnson*), xiv. 156–7).

9 *sentimental*: see Introduction (pp. xxvii–xxix) for Goldsmith's views on Sentimental Comedy. The word had become overused to denote a giving

in to polite emotion, the enjoyment of being moved. See *OED*, sense 1, where the movement from being affected by the higher emotions was gradually supplanted by an 'indulgence in superficial emotion'. The Prologue of George Colman's 'dramatick novel', *Polly Honeycombe* (1760), has the term characterize an excessively decorous style:

> So chaste, yet so bewitching all the while!
> Plot, and elopement, passion, rape, and rapture,
> The total sum of ev'ry dear—dear—Chapter.

(p. xiv)

10 *Mr Colman*: George Colman, manager of Covent Garden since 1767, had delayed giving a judgement on the play, having it in his hands probably since early 1772. Goldsmith is appealing to his judgement as late as January of 1773, betraying a fear that the situation would be as protracted as with his earlier play, *The Good Natur'd Man*, in 1768: 'I entreat you'l relieve me from that state of suspense in which I have been kept for a long time. Whatever objections you have made or shall make to my play I will endeavour to remove and not argue about them' (*Letters*, 116). After a short interview between them on 23 March, Colman feared some form of retribution in the printed Dedication, and wrote to Goldsmith (perhaps mock-) imploringly: 'Let me beseech you to put me out of my pain one way or other—Either take me off the rack of the Newspapers, or give me the *Coup de Grace*' (*Letters*, p. xlix). In the event, Goldsmith was merciful.

13 *till late in the season*: the first night was in mid-March. The Covent Garden season ended in May.

## PROLOGUE

s.d. *Mr Woodward*: Henry Woodward, an established comic actor in the company, had been first choice for the part of Tony Lumpkin. Nearly 60, he would certainly have tested an audience's suspension of disbelief in the part. Thomas Davies, in his *Memoirs* of Garrick (1780), recorded the impact of this Prologue: 'Woodward spoke this whimsical address in mourning, and lamented pathetically over poor dying Comedy' (in *Rousseau*, 195).

4 *'Tis not alone . . . I've that within*: cf. Hamlet 1.2.77, 85.

11 *sweet maid*: i.e. the Comic Muse.

12 *Shuter*: Edward Shuter (?1728–76), a distinguished comic actor who had also recently developed a line in older, 'character', roles. Zoffany's portrait (?1766) of Shuter as Justice Woodcock in a scene from Bickerstaffe's *Love in a Village* (with John Beard as Hawthorn and John Dunstall as Hodge) portrays him as a genial, if still serious, presence, perhaps a suitable counterpart to Mr Hardcastle. His gravitas is helped by the

introduction of a painting of the Judgement of Solomon over the fire-place. Over the last few Covent Garden seasons, he had been a memorable Fluellen in *Henry V* (last appearing on 6 January 1773), the Clown in *All's Well That Ends Well*, Corbaccio in Jonson's *Volpone*, and Launcelot Gobbo in *The Merchant of Venice*, but he had also provided a Peachum in Gay's *The Beggar's Opera*, a most unclownlike role.

13 *mawkish drab of spurious breed*: thus indicating Sentimental Comedy's lack of classical credentials.

18 *take down a hearty cup*: Shuter, especially, was known for taking to the stage in his cups.

20 *They'll turn us out, and no one else will take us*: as *Davis* notes, this is an allusion, with no clear motive, to Buckingham's *The Rehearsal* (1671), 2.4, p. 17: 'they'll turn us out, and nobody else will take us'.

24 *Faces are blocks, in sentimental scenes*: wooden and humourless, resembling a head for a wig.

30 *All is not gold that glitters . . . if she tumble*: this and the following proverbial saws are supposed to illustrate Sentimental Comedy's overt moralizing—and its lack of originality.

34 *A doctor*: Garrick is here toying with Goldsmith as well as the audience, as he knows that the author had practised medicine—though perhaps without a full degree, cf. line 43.

36 *five draughts prepared*: the five acts of the comedy.

1.1.10 *basket*: in the baggage rack on the outside of the coach.

13 *rambling*: rumbling *1733*; unevenly planned, perhaps in the manner of an inn. 'Rumbling' would have conveyed an additional sense of commotion and noise.

17 *and all our entertainment . . . Duke of Marlborough*: Prince Eugene, as leader of the Austrian forces, was Britain's staunchest ally in the War of the Spanish Succession (1701–14). The Duke of Marlborough won his most famous victories at Blenheim (1704), Ramillies (1706), and Oudenarde (1708). It is therefore unlikely that Hardcastle would have been present in person.

23 *You may be a Darby, but I'll be no Joan*: Darby and Joan were proverbial examples of the old yet still devoted couple.

25 *make money of that*: make what you can of that.

30 *and he's not come to years of discretion yet*: in a literal sense, a minor was able to exercise discretion on reaching 14 years of age, but the Hardcastles obviously have in mind the legal recognition of a coming of age at 21, and would wish to conceal the fact that Tony has now reached it, as Hardcastle claims, to 'conduce to [his] improvement' (5.3.130).

38 *Humour, my dear, nothing but humour*: *SJ*, sense 9 for Humour is 'Caprice; whim; predominant inclination'.

40 *horse-pond*: both for watering and washing horses and also for ducking minor miscreants.

46 *The poor boy . . . to do any good*: John Quick was no 'consumptive', to be sure, but also not noticeably stout. The fond claim that her child still needed mothering tells us as much about Mrs Hardcastle as Tony.

49 *A cat and fiddle*: an unlikely combination.

59 *like a speaking trumpet*: as if using a megaphone.

60 S.D. *Tony hallooing behind the scenes*: calling as if to urge on hounds when hunting.

    S.D. *scenes*: stage-scenery.

61 S.D. *Enter Tony, crossing the stage*: Ogden places the entry before Hardcastle's comment on his 'consumptive figure', thus heightening its 'sarcasm'.

69 *A low, paltry set of fellows*: the first of a set of references to 'low' subject-matter (cf. 1.1.70; 1.2.37–8) designed not to suit an audience expecting Sentimental politeness. See Introduction, pp. xxvii–xxix.

70 *exciseman*: *SJ*: 'An officer who inspects commodities, and rates their excise [i.e. taxable value]'.

71 *horse doctor*: i.e. with no certified medical or veterinary knowledge. George Carey has his Mrs Buzby declare of Pittem in *The Inoculator* (1766), Act 3: 'What a ridiculous Lyar he is! he knows no more of Medicine than a Rat-catcher; about four Years ago he was nothing but a Horse-doctor, or a Cow-leech' (p. 25).

72 *the music box*: a barrel organ.

    *Dick Muggins . . . pewter platter*: Tony does not register the low associations attached to the naming of his drinking companions. A muggins is a gullible fool; slang is likely to connote nonsense rather than coarse language; Aminadab is likely to be a Jew, summoning several stock prejudices about underhand financial dealings, and Tom Twist is unlikely to be a straightforward individual.

    *spins the pewter platter*: i.e. juggles with spinning plates. Although not quite contemporary, in Sir Walter Scott's *Kenilworth* (1821), on the way to Kenilworth in conversation with the Countess of Leicester, the 'good dame' likens her capacity to pirouette neatly to 'a juggler [who can] spin a pewter platter on the point of a needle' (2.7.125).

85 *gauze*: a finely-spun transparent silk.

88 *indigent*: the Vicar of Wakefield admonishes his family that walking in finery to church is a form of vanity: 'I don't know whether such flouncing and shredding is becoming even in the rich, if we consider, upon a moderate calculation, that the nakedness of the indigent world may be cloathed from the trimmings of the vain' (*Works*, iv: 34). Friedman

identifies the original sentiment as from William Penn's *Some Fruits of Solitude* (*c.* 1693; 7th edn., 1718), part I, no. 73 (p. 32).

92 *housewife's dress*: plain and serviceable apparel.

112 *generous*: this quality is a pre-eminent virtue for Goldsmith, and both Tony Lumpkin (2.1.544) and Marlow (eventually, at 4.1.222–3) are praised for generous attitudes. Whilst Goldsmith regarded it as cheaply available in Sentimental Comedies (see his distrust of works in the *Essay on the Theatre* where 'all the Characters are good, and exceedingly generous' (*Works*, iii: 212)), its rarer appearance is in characters who exhibit an openness of heart and magnanimity that is truly noble.

136 *set my cap to some newer fashion*: try to gain the affection of a new conquest.

139 *muster*: *SJ*: 'review of a body of forces'. Hardcastle is used to military metaphors when expressing himself.

153 *among the canary birds . . . been too moving*: Miss Hardcastle is obviously agitated, enough for a jibe at her expense, as Miss Neville imagines that she appears to be abnormally concerned about the health of domestic pets—or too given over to sentimental excess at the reading of a modish new novel.

170 *trust to occurrences*: believe in chance and circumstances.

174 *setting off*: presenting favourably

175 *pink*: *SJ*: 3, 'any thing supremely excellent'.

190 *improvements*: alterations (to a modern design) of landscape gardens or architecture. *Ogden* points out that such work must surely have been according to Mrs Hardcastle's taste, and not her husband's.

*Allons*: Fr. Let's go.

*Courage is necessary . . . affairs are critical*: no direct source found, but the mock-heroic register is noticeable.

19 *Would it were bedtime . . . were well*: cf. Falstaff's fear before the battle of Shrewsbury in 1 *Henry IV* (5.1.125): 'I would 'twere bed-time, Hal, and all well.'

1.2.3 *knock himself down for a song*: using his mallet, Tony is to gain silence for his song.

10 *genus*: dialectal form of 'genius'.

12 *Lethes, . . . Styxes, and Stygians*: Lethe and Styx were rivers in the Underworld. Lethe's waters were drunk by souls just before they were reincarnated, so as to bring about the forgetfulness of a previous existence. Styx was the principal river. Stygians lived along its banks.

13 *Quis . . . Quaes . . . Quods*: in Latin, the nominative forms of the relative pronoun.

16 *Methodist preachers*: Goldsmith was struck by the power of such forcible oratory. In his comments 'On Eloquence' in *The Bee* (no. 7—17 Nov. [1759]), he marvelled at 'how seldom they [Methodist preachers] are endued with common sense, and yet how often they affect their hearers' (*Works*, i: 481–2). Lien Chi Altangi, his *nom de plume* for one of the letter-writers in *The Citizen of the World*, classed them amongst a body of 'Enthusiasts', who 'weep for their amusement', and whose 'voluntary affliction makes up all the merit they can boast of' (Letter CXI; *Works*, ii: 430). This perspective is consistent with a distrust of Sentimentality.

37 *he never gives us nothing that's low*: see Introduction for Goldsmith's deliberate portrayal of apparently 'low' subjects to dissociate his drama from Sentimentality. In his *An Enquiry into the Present State of Polite Learning in Europe* (1759), he bridled against an excess of politeness in critical judgements: 'Does the poet paint the absurdities of the vulgar; then he is *low*; does he exaggerate the features of folly, to render it more thoroughly ridiculous, then he is then very *low*. In short, they have pro-scribed the comic or satyrical muse from every walk but high life, which, though abounding in fools as well as the humblest station, is by no means so fruitful in absurdity' (*Works*, i: 320).

40 *bees in a concatenation accordingly*: is in full agreement.

41 *I like the maxum of it*: i.e. I note your idea. 'Maxum' is a dialectal form of 'maxim', a basic axiom.

42 *dance a bear*: keep a dancing bear for the profit.

45 *'Water Parted', or the minuet in Ariadne*: perhaps excessively polite musical entertainments. 'Water Parted' was an aria from Thomas Arne's opera *Artaxerxes* (1762); *Ariadne* is probably a reference to Handel's opera *Arianna in Creta* (1734), that contained a popular minuet in its overture.

47 *not come to his own*: i.e. not able to claim his inheritance.

53 *winding the straight horn*: blowing the hunting-horn.

54 *he never had his fellow*: there was none who matched him.

57 *bastard*: Tony is asserting that he will take after his father.

62 *They have lost their way upo' the forest*: either on account of attempting to pick their way through a forest or near one.

70 *in the squeezing of a lemon*: in a trice.

71 *Father-in-law*: stepfather, i.e. Mr Hardcastle.

73 *grumbletonian*: habitual grumbler; at the turn of the century, the Country party had been dubbed grumbletonians by the Court faction.

95 *wanted no ghost to tell us that*: did not want any body *L*; the revision for the printed edition makes the allusion to *Hamlet* more secure: 'There needs no ghost, my lord, come from the grave, | To tell us this'

(1.5.128-9), Horatio's puzzled response to Hamlet's strange statements after first seeing the ghost of his father.

105 *tall, trapesing, trolloping, talkative maypole*: this account has Kate Hardcastle 'tall' (perhaps for alliteration's sake), yet she is regarded by Marlow as a 'chit' at 3.1.329, a 'little barmaid' at 4.1.29, as 'brisk' and a 'little thing' at 4.1.42 and as a 'little tyrant' at 5.3.145. 'Trapesing' and 'trolloping' imply an ungainly and slovenly gait—surely also part of Tony's invention.

121-6 S.D. *Ogden* omits these, noting that, as they were not in *1773*, or subsequent printed editions, such as Bell (1791), Inchbald (1806) or Cooke (1817), they were presumably 'found awkward'. I do not regard the directions quite as intrusive and have introduced them, as they provide some evidence of authorial intention.

121 S.D. *noting it down*: L; om *1773*.

124 S.D. *still noting*: L; om *1773*.

126 S.D. *who had been noting*: L; om *1773*.

133 *find out the longitude*: an almost proverbially impossible task. A government reward of £20,000 for its discovery had been offered in 1713. Goldsmith regarded the search as on a par with alchemy: 'We may not find the Philosopher's stone, but we shall probably hit upon new inventions in pursuing it. We shall, perhaps, never be able to discover the longitude, yet, perhaps we may arrive at new truths in the investigation' ('The Characteristics of Greatness', in *The Bee* (29 October 1759), *Works*, i: 429). Just three months after the play's opening night, it was in fact discovered by John Harrison.

151 *to your father's as an inn*: the assumption that this mistake was in fact once Goldsmith's own is based on his sister, Mrs Hodson's, anecdote about his days preparing for college under the tuition of the Revd. Pat Hughes of 'Edgworths Town' in Longford, some twenty miles distant from home. When passing by Ardagh, Goldsmith enquired as to where 'the best house in Town' might be. After having his horse catered for by what he took to be the inn's ostler, he entered the parlour and demanded attention and food. It was only the morning after, and his attempt to settle the bill, that the misconception became clear, and payment was refused, his host proud that it was in his 'power to entertain Mr Goldsmith son his dear Old friend & neighbour' (*Goldsmith Letters*, 166-8). Sir James Prior's view is a sceptical one in his *Life* (1837), claiming it merely 'sufficient for the purposes of the dramatist' (*Rousseau*, 299).

166 *connection*: close relationship.

170 *damned mischievous son of a whore*: this sudden intensity of opinion was doubtless calculated to shock, as part of Goldsmith's toying with Sentimental ideas. Its vehemence is probably not intended also to pass authentic judgement on Tony or Mrs Hardcastle.

**2.1.1** *table exercise*: presumably, how to wait at table.

11 *advanced from the plough*: Ogden traces a classical allusion, to Cincinnatus, who, according to Goldsmith himself in his *The Roman History from the Foundation of the City of Rome to the Destruction of the Roman Empire* (1769), was 'a man who had, for some time, given up all views of ambition, and retired to his little farm, where the deputies of the senate found him holding the plough, and dressed in the mean attire of a labouring husband-man'. He thereby showed that he 'preferred the charms of a country retirement, to the fatiguing splendours of office' (ch. 11).

17 *aways*: this is the one instance in this exchange where the more dialectal form is not represented in the printed texts, so I have adopted the Larpent reading.

24 *yeating*: dialectal for 'eating'.

50 *Wauns*: derived from the oath, 'by God's wounds'.

57 *By the elevens*: Davis points out that this phrase only occurs here, and conjectures—as does Ogden—that it could be derived from the 'heavens'.

67 *good housekeeping*: not, as today's primary meaning, domestic prudence, but rather generous hospitality.

71 *enflame a reckoning*: increase the bill by obliging the guest to cover exorbitant costs.

80 *The Englishman's malady*: Goldsmith frequently returned to the contradictory elements that made up the English character. On the positive side, he admired their tendency to analyse, as 'a reasoning philosophical people', but his Lien Chi Altangi also traced an 'inconstancy and irresolution' (Letter CXXI, *The Citizen of the World* (1762), *Works*, ii. 468). From a French perspective, the Abbé Le Blanc's, in his *Letters on the English and French Nations* (adapted by Goldsmith as *The Sentiments of a Frenchman on the Temper of the English* (in *The Bee*, 17 November 1759)), this could appear to be a 'gloomy reserve': 'One may assert, without wronging them, that they [the English] do not study the method of going through life with pleasure and tranquility, like the French' (*Works*, i. 490–1). Ogden locates a probable source in George Cheyne's *The English Malady* (1733), where the condition involves 'Distempers, Spleen, Vapours, and Lowness of Spirits' (p. i).

93 *rattle*: 'To speak eagerly and noisily' (*SJ*, sense 2), i.e. the very reverse of his temper before 'a pair of fine eyes' (l. 78).

103 *bagatelle*: 'A trifle; a thing of no importance' (*SJ*).

109 *courted by proxy*: therefore, an arranged marriage.

111 *terrors*: in Letter LXXII of *The Citizen of the World* (first published in the *Public Ledger* (10 September 1760)), Goldsmith's highly ironic treatment of those opposing the 1753 Marriage Act (see Introduction,

pp. xix–xxii), his Chinese visitor, Lien Chi Altangi, is amazed at the obstacles recently placed in the way of marriage: 'I should never find courage to run through all the adventures prescribed by the law. I could submit to court my mistress herself upon reasonable terms, but to court her father, her mother, and a long tribe of cousins, aunts and relations, and then stand the butt of a whole country church: I would as soon turn tail and make love to her grandmother' (*Works*, ii. 302).

119 *look in her face*: together with the bonnet worn by Kate Hardcastle at ll. 373 ff., a crucial factor in rendering Marlow's deception plausible.

135 *professing*: L; prepossessing *1773a*. One of the few obvious mistakes in the printed texts. 'Prepossessing' ('fill[ed] with an opinion unexamined; to [be] prejudice[d]', *SJ*), though favoured by *Ogden*, seems not to fit the context quite so well as 'professing' (*Profess*: 'to declare openly', sense 1. *SJ*), implying a tendency to give the self away, perhaps by blushing.

137 *duchesses of Drury Lane*: Drury Lane, in the heart of London's theatre district, had long been notorious for prostitution. John Gay, in his walker's tour through London, advised the uninitiated to avoid its precincts:

> O! may thy virtue guard thee through the roads
> Of *Drury's* mazy courts, and dark abodes,
> The harlot's guileful paths, who nightly stand,
> Where *Katharine-street* descends into the *Strand*.

(*Trivia; or the Art of Walking the Streets of London* (1716), Book 3, ll. 259–62). Aubrey L. Williams claims that Drury Lane's prostitutes at that time often assumed noble titles (*Review of English Studies*, 4 (1953), 359–61).

151 *white and gold*: presumably wearing a white coat and embroidered waistcoat, cf. ll. 151, 161.

153 *Liberty Hall*: Goldsmith's phrase, first introduced here. It is likely that the political controversies surrounding the expulsions of John Wilkes from his Middlesex seat after three elections at which he had gained the popular vote (1768–9) were uppermost in an audience's minds in 1773. Wilkes's watchword, liberty, was used to berate the Court and peers in general (see Peter D. G. Thomas, *John Wilkes: A Friend to Liberty* (Oxford, 1996), 141–58 and H. G. Dickinson, *Liberty and Property: Political Ideology in Eighteenth-Century Britain* (London, 1977), 197–205). Goldsmith often reflected upon an Englishman's fondness for liberty with some detachment, the clearest instance being Letter IV from *The Citizen of the World* (*The Public Ledger*, 31 January 1760), where 'Liberty' is 'ecchoed in all their assemblies, and thousands might be found ready to offer up their lives for the sound, though perhaps not one of all the number understands its meaning' (*Works*, ii. 27–8). His own distrust of political action *tout court* is best exemplified in the closing

passage of *The Traveller, or a Prospect of Society* (1764), where the 'weary search' to 'find | That bliss which only centres in the mind' merely disturbs 'pleasure and repose' and leads to an ignorance of the basic 'good' that 'each government bestows' (ll. 423–6).

157 *reserve the embroidery to secure a retreat*: Marlow suggests appearing in embroidered finery when in the process of extricating himself from an awkward and probably amorous affair. *L* then immediately includes a speech by Hastings: 'And the Spring velvet brings up mine'. As Hardcastle then includes his own sense of a retreat at l. 158, this line was obviously clumsy.

159 *besiege Denain*: Goldsmith's own account of this event from the War of the Spanish Succession can be found in his *History of England* (1771), iv. 166, 178. It is therefore significant that its inaccuracy reflects more on Hardcastle than Goldsmith. The Dutch, not Marlborough, participated in the siege (1712) and, unless Mr Hardcastle is in advanced old age, neither did he. As Mrs Hardcastle notes, it is quite likely that it amounts to no more than 'old-fashioned trumpery' (1.1.17).

172 *George Brooks . . . George Brooks*: another fiction in Hardcastle's reminiscences. No George Brooks makes it to any historical record.

186 *pledge me*: join me in a toast.

195 *elections*: a probable reference to an inn's staging of hustings where candidates curried favour with their potential electors with free drink. Electoral practices at this time often involved violent confrontations, especially so as votes were rarely cast secretly. Lien Chi Altangi, Goldsmith's fictional visitor to England in *The Citizen of the World*, was alarmed at the bustle and antagonism at election time. Written in the wake of the dissolution of Parliament on 20 March 1761, Letter CXII notes the feasting and drinking that had become characteristic of the English electoral process: 'In short, an election-hall seems to be a theatre where every passion is seen without disguise; a school where fools may readily become worse, and where philosophers may gather wisdom' (*The Public Ledger* (3 April 1761), *Works*, ii. 435).

198 *Since our betters . . . that sell ale*: in *L*, this sentence is crossed out with two clear 'X's. The imputation that the electoral system was rigged must have seemed something of a risk. *1773* has 'for us that sell ale' italicized and is here adopted. Hardcastle unwittingly furnishes further 'proof' that he may be an innkeeper.

204 *about Hyder Ally, or Ali Cawn*: Hyder Ali and Mahomed Ali Khan ruled Mysore and Bengal respectively during the early years of Clive and Hastings's imposition of British rule in India. The principles behind Hyder Ali's stand against British forces are summarized in his *The Manifesto or Remonstrance of Hyder Ally Cawn, to the Rajahs and Princes of India; in a Letter to Sir Richard S(utton), on the Bengal Petitions* (London,

1781). See H. V. Bown, *Revenue and Reform: The Indian Problem in British Politics, 1751–1773* (Cambridge, 1991), 69–78, and Mark Bence-Jones, *Clive of India* (London, 1974), 258–9.

*Ally Croker*: a sincere and artless character from a popular Irish ballad.

212 *Westminster Hall*: site of the main London law courts.

222 *battle of Belgrade*: the siege, not battle, of Belgrade took place in 1717. Goldsmith was present when General Oglethorpe recounted the events to Boswell and Johnson, 'pouring a little wine upon the table' and tracing troop movements 'with a wet finger' (*Life of Johnson*, 10 April 1772, ii. 181), so this is another instance of a deliberate inaccuracy.

252, 259 *supper*: the last meal of the day, usually served after 10.00 p.m. *Davis* acutely observes that the ensuing action multiplies the confusion of the occasion: a supper at an inn would usually consist of a cold collation, yet Hardcastle provides fare that was 'much more formal and sumptuous' than expected, and thus provokes a measure of condescension from his visitors.

253 *All upon the high ropes*: acting in a superior fashion.

258 *Joiners Company, or the Corporation of Bedford*: a 'Joiner' for Johnson was 'One whose trade is to make utensils of wood joined' (*SJ*). Examples of municipal feasting were proverbial, and here there is an example of both a trade guild and local government body conforming to type.

276 *a florentine, a shaking pudding, and a dish of tiff-taff-taffety cream*: a Florentine could denote both a savoury dish, a meat pie usually with spinach, and a dessert, a fruit cheesecake. Its position in the Bill of Fare does not help us decide which. A shaking pudding was any jelly or blancmange and the dish of taffety cream was silky (as in the texture of taffeta) and seasoned with spices and refined sugar. Marlow is presumably stuttering, taken aback by the quantity of food on offer.

278 *made dishes . . . green and yellow dinner*: Peter Dixon's gloss is helpful ('Goldsmith's "Green and Yellow" Dinner', *Notes and Queries*, 42 (1995), 70–1), in indicating the immediate context of Hastings's speech. The distrust of 'made dishes', i.e. those comprising several ingredients, displays a preference for plain Anglo-Saxon fare: unadorned meat, probably roast beef, and vegetables. This extends by Goldsmith to fancy vegetarian alternatives, associated by Goldsmith with French cuisine in Letter LXXVIII of *The Citizen of the World* (in *The Public Ledger* for 26 September 1760). Here the French are ingenious as 'they can dress you out five different dishes from a nettle top, seven from a dock-leaf, and twice as many from a frog's haunches' (*Works*, ii. 322). The green indicates salad, the yellow the hind-legs of a frog. The British distrust of French cuisine is summarized succinctly by Ben Rogers in his *Beef and Liberty* (London, 2003), 31–4, 40–3.

310 *hopeful cousin's tricks*: Tony is 'hopeful' in that he always anticipates

NOTES TO PAGES 182–186

success, akin to Johnson's meaning 1: 'Full of qualities which produce hope; promising; likely to obtain success' (*SJ*).

324 *even among slaves, the laws of marriage are respected*: it was proverbial to compare French subjection with English freedoms (see the dialogues in *The Vicar of Wakefield*, in *Works*, ii. 28, 464). The recent private marriages of two of the brothers of George III (the Dukes of Cumberland and Gloucester) had provoked a widely unpopular Royal Marriage Act (1772), forbidding such free choice. At the play's first performance, it was noted that William Henry, the Duke of Gloucester, was present, provoking general applause in his direction. Friedman is dubious that this gesture points to Goldsmith's full intention, and quotes Boswell's conversation with the author and General Paoli to that effect (*Life of Johnson*, 15 April 1773, ii. 224).

327 *India Director*: a Director of the East India Company.

393 *Cicero*: Cicero's oratory and his rules for excellence in his 'De Oratore' (55 BC) were a recognized authority for all public speakers. His regard for the balance of the phrase, confirmed by a regard for structure and cadence, impressed Goldsmith. This made the task of translating his rhetoric exactly particularly difficult: 'The Translator must not only be master of his sentiments, but also of his peculiar way of expressing them. He must have acquired a stile, correct without labour, and copious without redundancy' (Review of *The Tusculan Disputations*, in *The Monthly Review* (December 1758), *Works*, i. 132).

420 *sensible*: Goldsmith's understanding of the 'sentimental' (see below, n. to line 424) is associated with sententious gravity. Both *Davis* and *Ogden* take 'sensible' here to mean 'having sensibility; capable of delicate emotion' (*OED*, sense 9a), but Goldsmith's particular perspective incorporates an aspect, deemed 'low' by Johnson, of 'reasonable; judicious; wise'.

424 *sentiment*: speculation *L*. A significant change, suggesting that Goldsmith finally wanted to characterize Marlow as 'a man of sentiment' (i.e. strongly affected by emotional attachments), consistent with Kate's description of him at this interview as a 'mild, modest, sentimental man of gravity' (5.3.79). There are signs, though, that he may have considered Kate's part in this similarly prone to sentiment (see 2.1.469–71, 3.1.259–60).

477 *engaging*: to engage for Johnson could mean 'to induce; to win by pleasing means; to gain' (*SJ*, sense 6). This is the likely sense here, but the word also retained a trace of other shades of meaning, including one of conflict or even imprisonment.

483 S.D. *coqueting him to the back scene*: see note to Goldsmith's Epilogue, l. 16. The 'back scene' was up-stage of Drury Lane's proscenium stage and the wings. It was composed of two movable shutters on grooves that could be withdrawn to disclose a wall.

488 *Ranelagh. St James's, or Tower Wharf*: a mocking confusion of the high
and low. Ranelagh Pleasure Gardens in Chelsea (London) was an established place of entertainment (since 1742), and was much admired for its
lighting of a canal complete with gondolas. Samuel Johnson often went
there, and found it a 'place of innocent recreation' (*The Gentleman's
Magazine* (August 1765)). Moses, the vicar's son, puts an alternative
view, claiming that its fame includes its being a 'market for wives' (*The
Vicar of Wakefield*, *Works*, iv. 90).

St James's Park, just off the Mall, was much frequented by royalty, and
was definitely a place to be seen, but Goldsmith recognized its dual
nature towards dusk. The encounter with a strolling player, detailed in a
contribution to *The British Magazine* (October 1760), takes place there,
amidst those who might be 'more willing to forget that they had an
appetite than gain one' (*Works*, iii. 133). Tower Wharf summons up
commerce and industry.

493 *Pantheon, the Grotto Gardens, the Borough*: the Pantheon, on Oxford
Street, had just opened in 1772, and, according to the *Public Advertiser*
for 29 January was regarded as 'the much-talked-of receptacle of fashionable Pleasure'. The Grotto Garden, in St George's Fields, tried to provide a cut-price Ranelagh experience, and the 'Borough' of Southwark,
although once a noble district, by 1773 had attracted a mix of well-to-do
tradesmen, a range of warehouses and minor works.

495 *the Scandalous Magazine*: every month there appeared in the *Town and
Country Magazine* revelations about clandestine liaisons, where engraved
heads of the couple faced each other.

497 *the two Miss Rickets of Crooked Lane*: Crooked Lane is clearly a 'low'
address. When Lien Chi Altangi, in *The Citizen of the World*, visits Vaux-
hall Gardens, he is accompanied by a Mr Tibbs, who, on the way,
'assured us, he did not expect to see a single creature above the degree of
a cheesemonger' in the vicinity of Crooked Lane (Letter LXXI, *Works*,
ii. 294).

*head*: in this context, a striking hair-do.

502 *Ladies Memorandum Book*: Friedman locates an advertisement for
'THE LADIES Own MEMORANDUM BOOK; or Daily Pocket
Journal For the Year 1773' that was adorned with 'twelve of the
genteelest Head-dresses'.

503 *side-box*: the side-box was immediately adjacent to the thrust apron of
downstage. It was, therefore, a prime site to attract the attention of the
audience.

506 *since inoculation began*: it is unlikely that it was common practice outside
the monied classes in 1773, and, in any case, could bring on severe side-
effects that deterred others. The most prominent reason for inoculation
was to avoid the disfiguring effects of smallpox. Goldsmith gave a

graphic account of its devastation in his poem for *The Weekly Magazine* (no. 2–5 January 1760), entitled 'The Double Transformation: A Tale', detailing the 'dire disease whose ruthless power' that 'Withers the beauty's transient power':

> Lo! the small pox with horrid glare
> Levell'd its terrors at the fair;
> And rifling every youthful grace,
> Left but the remnant of a face
> (ll. 75–80; *Works*, iv. 370–1)

See also Letter XLVI (10 June 1760) of *The Citizen of the World* (*Works*, ii. 196–97).

512 *never argue . . . from his clothes*: simplify his dress so as to be more fashionable.

514 *plaster it . . . with powder*: i.e. dispense with a wig, and instead powder the hair.

518 *Gothic vivacity*: Mrs Hardcastle understands primarily the historical, rather than aesthetic, meaning: (pejoratively) disordered and medieval, rather than 'romantic' and multifarious. *OED*'s sense 4, 'Barbarous, rude, uncouth, unpolished, in bad taste', is more the standard judgement. The Gothic taste was starting, however, to gather admirers. Horace Walpole's *The Castle of Otranto. A Gothic Story* (1765) and James Beattie's poetic homage to Spenser, *The Minstrel* (1771–4) illustrate a new, contemporary interest in the non-classical past. Goldsmith regarded Gothic architecture as distracting and ultimately formless: '. . . where the eye of the spectator is presented with a number of parts, each highly finished, and separately pretty, but which, however, diminish the effect of the whole' (Review of Samuel Butler's *Genuine Remains*, for *The Critical Review* (September 1759), *Works*, i. 208). See also his translation of Voltaire's 'On Wit' for *The Bee* (20 October 1759—*Works*, i. 411).

530 *maker of samplers*: i.e. involved in a rather juvenile activity. *SJ* defines a 'sampler' as 'A pattern of work; a piece worked by young girls for improvement'.

546 *crack*: lie. An obsolete term by 1773.

548 *Blenkinsop*: presumably Mrs Hardcastle's maiden name.

560 *that waistcoat . . . genteel*: Tony Lumpkin was provided with a particularly noteworthy waistcoat in the first production of the play.

561 *prescribe . . . receipt*: an obvious sign of maternal over-protectiveness. Mrs Hardcastle not only administers the medicine ('receipt'), but orders it according to her own lay judgement ('prescribes').

564 *complete huswife*: Eliza Smith's *The Compleat Housewife* was a generally consulted authority on the management of the home. 'A Collection of Two Hundred Family Receipts of Medicines' was added for the second edition (1728). There were fourteen editions by 1769.

565 *coursing me through Quiney*: John Quincy's *Pharmacoepia officinalis et extemporanea; or, a Compleat English Dispensatory* (1718) was a standard reference work, and was on its fourteenth edition by 1769. Tony imagines that his mother had thoughts of pursuing or hunting ('coursing') him through each remedy in Quincy's manual.

574 *wild notes*: a probable allusion to Milton's praise of Shakespeare's warbling 'his native wood-notes wild' ('L'Allegro', ll. 133–4). The term was becoming characteristic of native artlessness; see James Thomson's 'Spring' (1728), where the uncertain weather at the turn of this particular season has plovers singing their 'wild notes to the listening waste' (l. 25), but not without a certain acerbic commentary: in Henry Home, Lord Kames's *Elements of Criticism* (1762), vol. ii, Section I ('Personification'), it was this very passage of Thomson's that provided an example of burlesque, i.e. an inappropriate animation of otherwise dumb nature (p. 244).

602 *as a hog in a gate*: a pig caught in a gate.

608 *Bandbox*: artificially pretty, as if she were tricked out, using ornaments from her store of hairbands or other milliner's materials from her bandbox.

614 *Anon?*: Pardon?

3.1.12 *propriety*: not directly the modern sense of decorum, but rather nearer to Samuel Johnson's senses of (1) 'Peculiarity of possession; exclusive right' and (2) 'Accuracy; justness' (*SJ*). Kate is, or seems to be, acknowledging her father's right to command.

24 *masquerade*: a masked ball or entertainment. Mr Hardcastle regards it as the epitome of London high life, and all the more suspicious for that. Goldsmith was hardly less censorious; in his essay on 'A Lady of Fashion in the Times of ANNA BULLEN compared with one of Modern Times' (*The Lady's Magazine*, October 1760), he compared a 'midnight masquerade' to a 'prolonged brag party' and found both to be 'pleasures of fashion and caprice' (*Works*, iii. 149).

32 *mauvaise honte*: acute and perhaps painful self-consciousness.

38 *Bully Dawson*: this Restoration rake had, by 1773, become known for a mixture of aggression and cowardice. Sir Richard Steele had his fictional gentleman, Sir Roger de Coverley, kick him 'in a publick Coffee-house for calling him Youngster' (*The Spectator* no. 2 (2 March 1711), in *The Spectator*, ed. Donald F. Bond, 5 vols. (Oxford, 1965), i. 8). See also the verdicts of Theophilus Lucas (in *The Memoirs of the Lives, Intrigues and Comical Adventures of the Most Famous Gamesters and Celebrated Sharpers* (1714), 40) and Tom Brown (in his 'From Bully Dawson to Bully W-' from *Letters from the Dead to the Living* (*Works* (1715), ii. 215–30)).

71 *furniture*: qualifications L. Davis traces a possible obscenity in the *1773* word, whereas *Ogden* understands simply that there is an extended housing metaphor.

87 *amused*: distracted or duped.

96 *rule of thumb*: rough and ready means; not totally calculated.

109 *bounce of a cracker*: the more direct sense is of the loud explosion of a firework (followed by *Davis*). This might be consistent with the mention of a 'Catharine wheel' at 3.1.180. Goldsmith gives Tony Lumpkin, however, several highly idiomatic phrases, and crackers are usually not negligible items. A valid sense is to follow the *OED*'s sense 4a of 'Bounce, *n.* 1' and sense 2 of 'Cracker': 'the idle boast of a braggart'.

110 *Morrice. Prance*: Move yourselves! Gee up!

119 *Lady Kill-Daylight*: an apt name for one whose habits are mainly nocturnal.

*Mrs Crump*: suggests one who's hunchbacked through constant gaming at tables.

121 *marcasites*: imitation gems. What Mrs Hardcastle fails to realize is that it is not fashion that sends the jewels to town for exchange, but rather the need for extra funds that would be raised from pawning them.

132 *parcel of old-fashioned rose and table-cut things*: motley collection of rough-cut gems.

133 *court of King Solomon at a puppet-show*: there is an obvious contrast between ancient court splendour and a modern, 'low', theatrical entertainment, yet Goldsmith was intrigued at the mock-heroic possibilities of West End puppet shows. In his essay on *The Adventures of a Strolling Player* (*The British Magazine* October 1760, *Works*, iii. 135), he recounts an early theatrical childhood spent beating a drum to punctuate puppet-show action: 'Thus the whole employment of my younger years was that of interpreter to Punch and king Solomon in all his glory'. This directly implies that a Solomon puppet appeared in such shows, and hence implies a comment on how popular entertainment vulgarizes greatness: when providing a fictional account of witnessing the coronation procession of George III and Queen Charlotte on 22 September 1761, the crush and discomfort causes his pseudonym, the 'Common Council Man', to prefer seeing 'the court of King Solomon in all his glory at my ease in Bartholomew Fair' (the site of summer theatre in Smithfield, where the booths were adjacent to trained monkeys, puppeteers, acrobats—and pickpockets) ('To The Printer', in *The Public Ledger* (24 September 1761), *Works*, iii. 178).

144 *relics*: souvenirs or mementoes.

172 S.D. Following *Ogden*, I have placed Mrs Hardcastle's exit immediately after Miss Neville's attempt to stay her: 'You shan't stir—'. *1773* has it before her speech on l. 172.

180 *Catharine wheel*: a circular firework that, when set alight, spins furiously, sending off sparks.

207 *cross-grained*: perverse, awkward.

228 *like Cherry in the Beaux Strategem*: Farquhar's *The Beaux' Strategem* (1707) is set in an inn near Lichfield. Cherry is the innkeeper's daughter, who attempts to ingratiate herself to passing nobility in order to marry well.

250 *Lion . . . Angel . . . Lamb*: names of individual rooms in an inn.

*outrageous*: disorderly, even violent; in an uproar.

267 S.D. *tablets*: notepad.

281 *disappointed in that too*: Marlow fears he may be thwarted in gaining a kiss, not that the kiss will be below expectation.

299 *mark of mouth*: the most reliable inspection to discover the true age of a horse was to look at marks on the incisor teeth.

304 *obstropalous*: a deliberately rustic colloquialism, nearest in sense to obstreperous, unruly or noisy.

316 *Ladies Club*: the most famous met in Albemarle Street during the early 1770s. Men were invited, but could never be members.

317 *Rattle*: a chatterer or amiable conversationalist. This is a suitable name for Marlow, as at 2.1.93–4 he wished to be able to 'break the ice' and 'rattle away' at will. Goldsmith's own conversation was often awkwardly maintained, and even friends depicted him as an uneasy companion, e.g. Richard Cumberland's verdict in his *Memoirs* (1806), that his 'table-talk was, as Garrick aptly compared it, like that of a parrot, whilst he wrote like Apollo; he had gleams of eloquence, and at times a majesty of thought, but in general his tongue and his pen had two very different styles of talking' (*Mikhail*, 56).

323 *Mantrap . . . Blackleg . . . Countess of Sligo . . . Langhorns . . . Biddy Buckskin*: a rather mixed company. A mantrap was a particularly vicious gin trap; a blackleg was a card sharp; the title given to Sligo was fictitious; Lang/Longhorns suggests a spiky individual, and Biddy Buckskin actually refers to Rachel Lloyd, a member of the Club.

344 *nicked seven*: a winning throw at dice.

*throw ames ace*: the lowest possible throw at dice, i.e. both aces (counting as ones).

4.1.7 *discover my name*: i.e. reveal his identity. This is a needless anxiety as Goldsmith has had both the Hardcastles call him repeatedly by name in Act 2 (he twice at 2.1.152 and 250, she six times at 483, 498, 522, 548, 549–50, and 581). It is possible, therefore, that Hastings is implying that his actual lineage might be at risk of disclosure and his acquaintance with Miss Neville, not just his surname.

20 *seat of . . . inn-door*: a post-coach carried the mail and was a most functional mode of transport. Marlow repeats the formulation at l. 61.

The likely meaning is that he regards the only safe place for concealment as a bad one: the collection point at the inn for mail.

43 *girdle*: *SJ*: sense 1—'Any thing drawn round the waist, and tied or buckled'.

70 *with a witness*: with a vengeance.

118 *liberty and Fleet Street*: Fleet Street was not yet known for its production of newspapers. It had, however, an established reputation as a location for the popular press as well as violence and vagrancy (see Pat Rogers, *Grub Street: Studies in a Subculture* (London, 1972), 153–4, and Roy Porter, *London: A Social History* (Cambridge, Mass., 1994), 204–5). More precisely, it had become notorious for factional strife. The first implementation of the Riot Act (passed in 1715) was to punish five Tory-supporting rioters who had attacked Read's 'Mug-House' (implying Whig and possibly Jacobite sympathies). Jeremy is probably aping the cant cry associating Liberty with John Wilkes, who ever since he had been prevented from taking his elected Middlesex seat in parliament by the Court (1768–9), was the subject of many a penny pamphlet, advocating an extension of the franchise and an end to the corruption of the Great.

136 *banter*: *SJ*: 'To play upon; to rally; to turn to ridicule; to ridicule'.

149 s.d. *bantering*: see note to l. 136 above.

157 *Rake's Progress*: executed 1733–5, William Hogarth's series of paintings (now in the Sir John Soane's Museum in London), depicts the ruin of Tom Rakewell, a victim of London temptations and his inability to make the best use of his inheritance. Mr Hardcastle is clearly implying the same about Marlow.

195 *caricatura in all the print-shops*: not an enviable fate; printsellers were happy to market an unflattering and exaggerated likeness to take advantage of some personal embarrassment. Henry Fielding, in his 'Preface' to *Joseph Andrews* (1742), drew a distinction between the 'exactest copying of Nature', the goal of the serious artist, and the *caricatura* that is allowed 'all Licence', where the goal is to portray 'Monsters, not Men'. It was, therefore, equivalent to 'burlesque' in writing.

196 *Dullissimo Maccaroni*: a 'Macaroni' was a fop or dandy, derived from the Italian, *macarone*, meaning one who affects a continental fashion. Marlow envisages a double problem: not only appearing in an unflattering light in the popular press but also as dull into the bargain. Friedman locates the possible source for a gallery of macaronis in Darly's Comic Prints, a series published in five volumes, 1772–3. In the anonymous letter to Goldsmith that provided notes on the first night of the play, this phrase was singled out as 'too low' (*Goldsmith Letters*, p. xli).

202 *behavour*: behaviour. Kate is lapsing into her barmaid persona with this mispronunciation.

204 *list ... subscriber*: alluding to the printed list of those who had 'subscribed' to a particular publication, i.e. those who had contributed to the printing costs by paying in advance.

239 *stooped to conquer*: conquered *L*. An alteration that reflects Goldsmith's late adoption of the play's title; see 'Introduction', pp. xxiv–xxvi.

246 *Aunt Pedigree's*: a choice of name that clearly implies a grand and rather august lineage. It may also be a common stage reference to any rich relative. William Kenrick's *The Widow'd Wife* (first staged at Drury Lane in 1767) carries a reference to a visit to an Aunt Pedigree in 2.3, where Narcissa envisages meeting eligible suitors (p. 25).

250 *fly like Whistlejacket*: a successful racehorse from the 1750s.

253 s.d. *fondle*: a (polite) caress or, as Johnson has it, 'to treat with great indulgence' (*SJ*).

268 *leave my horse in a pound*: leave a hare in her form, the dogs in full cry, or my horse in a pound *L*; a pound is an enclosure principally for animals. An anonymous letter offering advice to Goldsmith on the play derived from its first night suggests that the lines then uttered might have been nearer to *L* than the later printed versions: '(3) Tony says, I had rather leave a Hare in her form &c.&c. Would not one of the similes be quite sufficient?' (*Goldsmith Letters*, p. xl). Goldsmith evidently agreed and emended the speech for *1773*.

271 *natural humour*: though not to be understood here as direct praise of Tony, Goldsmith frequently searches for the 'natural' as a valuable touchstone, and he is an admirable corrective to undue urbanity. It should be remembered that Hastings commends Marlow for his 'natural good sense' (2.1.78), and that Goldsmith distrusted Garrick for his lack of it:

> Like an ill judging beauty, his colours he spread,
> And beplaister'd, with rouge, his own natural red.
> On the stage he was natural, simple, affecting,
> 'Twas only that, when he was off, he was acting: ...
> ('Retaliation' (1774), ll. 99–102)

The 'natural' was often set against the attitudinizing of the Sentimental, and, although the Vicar of Wakefield is an idealist in opposing swingeing capital laws and therefore an innocent, his staunch support for Natural Law is largely unchecked: 'Savages that are directed by natural law alone are very tender of the lives of each other; they seldom shed blood but to retaliate former cruelty' (*Works*, iv. 150).

275 *haspicholls*: harpsichords.

276 *parcel of bobbins*: the reference is probably to lace-making, where the spindles carrying thread (bobbins) were in constant motion.

280 *incontinently*: without delay. According to Johnson an obsolete term.

282 *Dr. Drowsy's sermons*: Tony's full education can be put off until tomorrow, much like attendance at the sermons of an inept preacher.

295 s.d. *They confer*: it is clear that they are meant to withdraw, probably upstage.

297 *print-hand*: a clear script resembling print.

298 *handles, and shanks*: Ogden interprets these as 'loops above and below the line', i.e. orthography resembling the curve of a handle and the straight line of a shank or lower leg.

318 s.d. *Twitching*: snatching from Mrs Hardcastle. One must presume that the letter was taken from Tony at some time in her last speech.

320 *feeder*: a trainer of fighting-cocks.

360 *Shake-bags and Goose-greens*: a shakebag was a large fighting-cock. Goose- green is presumably the colour of the cock, i.e. yellow-green resembling a goose turd.

369 *Bedlam*: a commonly used contraction of Bethlehem Royal Hospital, a lunatic asylum since 1676 located in Moorfields.

382 *with baskets*: basket-hilted swords were mainly used in practice. *Davis* conjectures that the dash immediately preceding indicates that 'the gentlemen half-draw their swords at this point'. It could also represent an immediate retraction of the challenge, as Tony extends it only to practice weapons.

392 *putting to*: being hitched to the coach.

395, 404, 422 s.d. [*Exit Servant*] [ . . . *Exit Servant* . . . *Exit Miss Neville [with Servant]*]: *this edn.* All authoritative printed texts and *L* omit exits for the servant or servants. If literally interpreted, this would mean three servants on the stage by 329 s.d. (where *1773* has an entrance though *L* does not). This seems excessive and also runs counter to the immediate sense of Miss Neville's implied dismissal of a servant at l. 395 and perhaps l. 404. There also seems no reason to detain the servant beyond Miss Neville's exit at 422. *Ogden* wonders whether there may be more than one, but, as this edn. indicates, a sense of rush and coercion can still be created by one servant entering three times in short order.

416 *for three years*: i.e. until she reaches her majority, at 21, and so will be able to marry without her father's consent.

429 *Your hands. Yours and yours, my poor Sulky . . . bottom of the garden*: *Davis* is correct in tracing an attempt at a quotation here, but I am not alone in being unable to locate a source. Tony presumably clasps the hands of both companions, yet the reference to being sulky is surely more addressed to Hastings than Marlow, and it is the former whom he will meet 'at the bottom of the garden'. I have therefore included in this edition firmer indication that this is the case.

5.1.3 *post coach*: see note to 4.1.20.

37 *laughing*: a significant remedy given Goldsmith's staunch advocacy for 'Laughing' as opposed to 'Sentimental' comedy (*Works*, iii. 209–13). He feared lest the sterner morality necessary to inculcate acceptable sentiments might drive laughter or humour from the stage: 'The author . . . hopes that too much refinement will not banish humour and character from our's, as it has already done from the French theatre. Indeed the French comedy is now become so very elevated and sentimental, that it has not only banished humour and *Moliere* from the stage, but it has banished all spectators too' ('Preface to *The Good-Natur'd Man*' [*Works*, v. 14]).

111 *canting*: *SJ*: *to cant*: 'To talk in the jargon of particular professions, or in any kind of formal affected language, or with a peculiar and studied tone of voice'. 'Cant', sense 1, is identified as 'A corrupt dialect used by beggars and vagabonds'.

112 *he never sat for the picture*: he does not fit the description.

5.2.9 *basket of a stage-coach*: see note to 1.1.10.

14 *varment*: dialect for 'vermin', a deliberately strong term for his mother and cousin.

24 *slough*: 'A deep, miry place; a hole full of dirt' (*SJ*).

37 *cattle*: slang for 'horses'.

54 *quickset hedge*: 'quick' because it is constructed out of already established, living plants.

66 *that kept here*: that plied their trade there, i.e. as highwaymen.

75 *Father-in-law*: i.e. stepfather.

80 *I'll cough and cry hem*: cf. l. 78, Tony occasionally echoes great literature. Here, it is probably Othello's order to Emilia that she 'cough, or cry "Hem" ' if anybody comes to disturb his conference with Desdemona (4.2.31).

81 *keep close*: stay hidden.

82 S.D. *in the back scene*: om. *L*; *Davis* helpfully notes that it would be unlikely for the set to comprise a 'tree'. It is probable that Mrs Hardcastle simply hid behind one of the wings or side-scenes on which the outline of a tree would be painted. *Ogden* suggests a mulberry, cf. l. 125 below.

*Enter Hardcastle*: the anonymous correspondent quoted by Balderston suggests that Hardcastle 'should [here] be wrapt up in a cloak with the hood up', if taking his 'night's walk', as this will better 'account for Mrs H's mistaking him for a robber' (*Goldsmith Letters*, p. xli).

103 *I'll lay down my life for the truth*: probably a version of Rousseau's motto: *vitam impendere vero*, originally in Juvenal's fourth satire (l. 91), where it was the hallmark of the noble Roman subject. Again, Tony alludes wittily and perhaps unwittingly.

5.3.25 *imputed merit*: a theological use, where a person is understood to possess (or is ascribed) merit without actual, clear, proof.

27 S.D. *from behind*: i.e. they enter from just behind the proscenium arch onto the apron stage.

35 *rustic plainness . . . refined simplicity*: a significant distinction for Goldsmith. In his depiction of the 'country inhabited by men without vice' ('The Proceedings of Providence, vindicated. An Eastern Tale', in the *Royal Magazine* (December 1759), Asem is delivered from despair by an appreciation of the inhabitants' 'antient simplicity': 'each had a house, which, though homely, was sufficient to lodge his own family . . . what they built was for convenience, and not for shew' (*Works*, iii. 63). Nature itself operated in characteristic 'simplicity' ('Preface' to Brookes's *A New and Accurate System of Natural History* (1763–4), *Works*, v. 231).

58 *catch at*: claim or snatch.

66 *uninteresting*: neither displaying interest nor engagement.

79 *gravity*: speculation L. See note to 2.1.424, where Goldsmith also removed the suggestion that Marlow might be a man of speculation, there replacing it for *1773* with 'sentiment'.

107 *Hardcastle*: L; om. *1773*, where the two lines are assigned to Mrs Hardcastle as a continuation of the preceding speech.

*when of age*: reaching your legal maturity, at 21. See 1.1.30 and note plus the denouement at ll. 94–9 below. Hardcastle keeps Tony in ignorance of his legal freedoms to aid his 'improvement' (l. 133).

109 *Mrs Hardcastle*: L; speech in *1773* assigned to Hardcastle as a continuation of preceding lines—an obvious error, as he knows all along that Tony is indeed of age.

123 *whining end of a modern novel*: 'The Novel' was a working title for the play, but Goldsmith here wished to dissociate his work from popular novels. He thought that the talent for writing novels no better than that necessary in producing a Sentimental Comedy (in 'An Essay on the Theatre' (*Westminster Magazine*, 1 January 1773), *Works*, iii. 213), and, worse, that its imaginative resources were nearing exhaustion (see 'The Life of Richard Nash' (1762), in *Works*, iii. 321).

EPILOGUE (BY DR GOLDSMITH)

This Epilogue was only finally adopted during the last few rehearsals, was used in the early performances and included in *1773*. It was a desperate expedient, however, as there had been at least five earlier versions (see note to Joseph Cradock's Epilogue reproduced on p. 225). Goldsmith, in a letter to Joseph Cradock (*c.* 16 March 1773), felt that it turned out 'a very mawkish thing' (*Goldsmith Letters*, 119).

5 *done execution*: both captivated a theatre audience and also male admirers.

7 *We have our exits and our entrances*: cf. Jaques's famous seven ages of man speech from *As You Like It* (2.7.139–41). The rest of the Epilogue is constructed on the same lines.

15 *caters*: procures food.

16 *coquets the guests*: see note to 2.1.483 S.D. To coquet is taken by Johnson to mean 'to entertain with compliments and amorous tattle; to treat with an appearance of amorous tenderness' (*SJ*).

18 *chop house toast*: possibly implying a rather cheap regard, but the status of the 'chop house' was a variable. In the 1760s, James Boswell ate regularly at Clifton's near the Temple in London and found the place cheap but also cheerful: 'You come in there to a warm, comfortable, large room, where a number of people are sitting at table. You take whatever place you find empty; call for what you like, which you get and cleverly dressed' (*London Journal*, ed. F. A. Pottle (New Haven, 1950), 112 (15 December 1762)).

19 *Cits*: mean tradesmen.

22 *Common Councilmen*: local government councillors who were stereotyped as given to lavish feasting.

25 *at Operas cries caro*: 'caro' (in Italian, dear) was a common cry of rapture at fashionable events.

26 *Nancy Dawson*: a famous and popular jig and hornpipe dancer from the late 1750s and early 1760s. The reference is probably to a jig named after her that accompanied a ballad about a runaway bride.

*Che Faro*: the aria (full title, 'che faro senza Euridice') from Act 3 of Gluck's opera, *Orfeo ed Euridice* (1762).

28 *Heinel of Cheapside*: Anna-Frederica Heinel was a noted dancer in the interludes and afterpieces of operas. Cheapside had been the most frequented market in medieval London. After the Great Fire of 1666, it was rebuilt as a more spacious area known for its goldsmiths and linen drapers—but it was still lower middle class.

35 *Female Barrister . . . Bayes*: probably contains a weak pun on the bar of law and that of the sale of drink. 'Bayes' was the character of a poet in Buckingham's *The Rehearsal* (1672) named after the laurel crown that signified pre-eminence in poetry and dramatic verse.

EPILOGUE (BY J. CRADDOCK)

Not in *L. 1773a* includes it immediately after Goldsmith's Epilogue in the front matter. Thereafter, it was moved to the end of the printed text. Craddock was a friend of Goldsmith's and had been sent the play in manuscript. Despite offering this Epilogue, Goldsmith turned it down for the actual performance, but assured him that it would be printed with the author's permission (see *Goldsmith Letters*, 118–20 (*c.* 16 March 1773)). Longer versions appear in the *Lloyd's Evening Post* for 8–10 April 1773 and then again in Craddock's *Literary Memoirs* ( (4 vols., 1826), i. 226), where there are references to several of Tony's lower-life companions: '*Pat* at the *Pigeons*' (omitted in the *Memoirs*), '*Bill Bullett*', and '*Matt Muggins*' (who becomes 'my Comrade' who had a mill in the *Memoirs*). Friedman suggests that their omission in the printed version formed an attempt 'to make the comedy more acceptable to George Colman' (*Works*, v. 87). The letter to Craddock of *c.* 16 March 1773 details the stages leading to Goldsmith's last-minute penning of the production's eventual epilogue: (*a*) Arthur Murphy sent him 'rather the outline of an Epilogue than an Epilogue' for Mrs Catley (originally asked to play Kate). An altercation ensued between her and Mrs Bulkley who, it appears, may have been the first choice for Mrs Hardcastle. (*b*) Goldsmith then composed a dialogue between the two actresses (reprinted in *Davis*, 98–100). Catley walked out. (*c*) His second attempt (in *Davis*, 101–2), just for Mrs Bulkley, was, in Colman's opinion 'too bad to be spoken', so (*d*) a fourth and, as it turned out, final epilogue was completed, in Goldsmith's own opinion, 'a very mawkish thing'—here reproduced above.

2 *nonly*: a Lumpkinism, for 'only'.

3 *blade*: *SJ*: 'A brisk man, either fierce or gay, called so in contempt.'

13 *hoikes*: more normally 'hoicks'—an incitement to hounds in hunting. Bet Bouncer probably needs no such encouragement.

15 *Sadler's-Wells*: since its reconstruction in 1765 the theatre quickly regained a certain celebrity under the ownership of Thomas Rosoman. He had retired in 1772 and was succeeded by Tom King, the ex-manager of Drury Lane. Whilst it attracted an increasingly respectable clientele, it still did not have a licence to produce plays and so was known for its musicals.

16 *roratorio*: oratorio, i.e. a semi-dramatic opera (in that it required neither scenery nor props) on a religious theme.

23 *This came . . . to be spoken*: an after-note, referring to the events noted above in the headnote.

# Wild Oats

PROLOGUE

[Introduced from *1794*]

12 *varying foil*: implying both the sense of *SJ* 2: 'Leaf; gilding' (from the French, *feuille*) and also sense 3: 'Something of another colour near

which jewels are set to raise their lustre', i.e. the elements of Shakespeare's writing are various, yet also complementary.

18 *Fancy's fairy ground*: the association of 'fairy' imagination with fancy had come to be a conventional association of Romantic excess, especially in the novels of Ann Radcliffe, who had her Hippolito feel a 'fairy dream of happiness which his fancy had formed', although he knows himself barred from a likely experience of it by losing Julia's company in *A Sicilian Romance* (1790, vol. i, ch. 3, p. 131). Similarly, St Aubert, in her *Mysteries of Udolpho* (1794), remembers his youth when 'a thousand fairy visions, and romantic images' were present to his 'fancy', giving him a sense of 'the poet's dream' (vol. i, ch. 1, pp. 40–41).

28 *generous soul*: a significant quality in Rover, recognized throughout the play; see 2.1.260 (by Lady Amaranth), 4.1.142 (by Harry) and 5.4.259. Generosity of spirit is also recognized in Harry by Lady Amaranth (3.1.53) and by Rover (5.4.284).

1.1.1 *cruizing*: to sail to and fro without any particular port to aim for. This reinforces the serendipity of the play in that the travellers obviously do not realize the true identity of their host.

4 *stoved keg*: a collapsed or breached barrel. A keg often supplied additional storage for provisions taken on board whilst on a voyage. John Dory is referring to his stomach again.

*old Dutchman*: although more often a reference to a Dutch ship, this seems to indicate a sailor of the same nationality—an old sea-salt.

13 *bluff head*: usually applied to a particularly boastful person.

20 *fallow and stubble*: arable ground set aside temporarily and not planted; as this was reaped, but not yet ploughed, it would have made for uneven and tiring progress.

21 *Gosport*: a fortified seaport, the centre of the coast's manufacture and provision of supplies, was separated from the more famous naval garrison by the mouth of Portsmouth harbour.

22 *ballast*: weight in the hold (usually of stones) to steady a ship and prevent sinking. John Dory suggests that Sir George should consider his age before chasing deserters across such unhelpful terrain.

24 *fought myself*: commanded in battle.

26 *over the King's bounty*: a bonus payment for new recruits.

27 *fingered the shot*: stolen from the ammunition store to sell ashore.

29 *piece of clinker*: the lowliest piece of material. Clinker, a mass of brick slabs fused by great heat, was often used for paving roads.

32 *in ordinary*: normally in reference to a part of the fleet under repair or decommissioned.

39  *swab*: a mild term of abuse reserved only for those fit to mop decks.

49  *dog-fish*: from the shark family, but a diminutive subspecies. John Dory is perhaps acting presumptuously.

50  *false bay*: offering security duplicitously, cf. Aphra Behn, 'The River of Pretension', from her *Poems upon Several Occasions* (1684), p. 42: 'And with a full carreer to this false Bay | I ran.'

62  *water-dog*: a hunting dog trained to retrieve shot fowl from water; in this instance, it indicates someone as happy on sea as on land.

72  *sloe juice*: drink distilled from the fruit of the blackthorn that is sharp and, notoriously, an acquired taste.

77  *bomb-boat*: also known as 'bum-boats', under the 1685 Trinity House bye-laws, a licensed scavengers' vessel, charged with cleaning the hulls of traffic on the Thames. Opportunistically, these very craft took to selling garden produce along the river, too. Such boats taking to the open seas, especially the Bay of Biscay, would, indeed, have been unwise.

88  *ballad of 'William and Margaret'*: adapted from a traditional ballad by David Mallet, first printed in 1724, it reappeared in Archbishop Thomas Percy's *Reliques of Ancient English Poetry* (1767; orig. edn., 1765). Margaret rises from her grave to remind William of his faithlessness:

> But love had, in the canker worm,
>   Consum'd her early prime:
> The rose grew pale, and left her cheek;
>   She dy'd before her time.
>
> (ll. 17–20)

He succumbs to extreme grief on her grave.

89  *dismals*: fits of melancholy.

97  *parables*: for Johnson, a parable held a neutral meaning of a 'similitude; a relation under which something else is figured' (*SJ*), yet the debate as to how best to relate holy truths had been a hot issue for seminaries in mid-century. Ephraim obviously distrusts the mediation of fiction, and the emerging orthodoxy stressed the need for simplicity. Robert Lowth, in his *Lectures on the Sacred Poetry of the Hebrews* (1773), knew that parables had the 'appellation of *enthusiasm*' (p. 79), and yet they should also 'turn upon an image well known and applicable to the subject, the meaning of which is clear and definite' (p. 225).

98  *sheer off with your sanctified poop*: go away with your sanctimonious rubbish. 'Poop' primarily indicated an animal's posterior—although it was also taken to mean what came out of it.

138  *peradventure*: perhaps.

148 *levelling*: Johnson's meaning 2 for 'leveller' noted he or she who 'destroys superiority; one who endeavours to bring all to the same state of equality' (*SJ*). Sir George remembers the efforts of the Levellers during the English Civil War's early debates on the origins of political authority. Especially due to the rhetorical pressure of pamphleteers such as John Lilburne, Richard Overton, and William Walwyn from 1647 on, the New Model Army entertained a more democratic model for self-government, intent on abolishing monarchy and the House of Lords and instituting a more popular franchise in the election of biennial parliaments.

150 *French Duke*: the revolutionary National Assembly had abolished feudalism on 4 August 1789, and all aristocratic and hereditary titles were expunged on 19 June 1790.

169 *log-book*: a formal, written, account of essential information about a voyage, including a ship's cargo, any casualties and any significant meteorological readings, handed in to the destination's Marine Office.

180 *knock 'em up*: tire immoderately.

181 *channel for the stage*: a boarding station for the stage-coach.

1.2.10 *on this scamper*: an irregular (and possibly illicit) motion, flying 'with speed and trepidation' (*SJ*).

26 *Colonel Standard . . . Tom Errand*: characters out of George Farquhar's *The Constant Couple* (1699). Standard is, according to the *Dramatis Personae*, a 'disbanded colonel, brave and generous' and Errand simply 'a porter'. Both are most certainly supporting roles at best. Errand strips Clincher Senior of his clothes in 5.2 of the play, contributing to his appearance, wrapped only in a blanket in the concluding scene (5.3), and the discomfiture of Clincher Junior.

27 *smart hat and coat-brusher*: i.e. subservient, as a servant.

33 *evil communication*: conversation or society with ill consequences.

41 *grace a prince . . . habit of quotation*] grace a prince. My poor friend has often lent me his money; though he supposed me a poor needy devil, that could never be able to pay him. He shan't know who I am till it's in my power to serve him; only the rogue always marr'd the grand design of my frolic—I had no chance among the pretty women where he was; he had the knack of winning their hearts by his gaiety. Tho' so devilish pleasant in his quotations, which on the moment he dashes in a parody whimsically opposite to every occasion as it happens (*1791–93*).

44 '*The brisk li-li-lightning I*': the opening exchanges between Harry and Rover refer to a production of George Villiers, Duke of Buckingham's *The Rehearsal* (1671), a satire on the vogue for inflated rhetoric and sentiments found most often in the Heroic Plays of John Dryden. Bayes (a thin disguise of Dryden himself) is rehearsing what seems to be a

particularly bombastic study of Heroism. In the Prologue, he has two characters called Thunder and Lightning. This line is Lightning's at 1.1; p. 10. *The Rehearsal* was a favourite afterpiece and had been played recently: at Covent Garden (from 28 September 1785), when Hull had played Johnson, and both Quick and Wilson had also been cast-members. Wilson was to take the part of Bayes and Mrs Powell the part of Chloris in the Haymarket's production of 9 August 1992.

48 *Bayes*: see note to line 44 above. Harry perhaps misrecognizes the actual speaker.

50 *'I am the bold Thunder'*: Thunder's opening line at 1.1; p. 10 of Bucking-ham's *The Rehearsal* (see note to line 44 above). Bayes requires the line to be repeated 'a little louder, and with a hoarse voice' (1.1.180–1), and Thunder obliges at line 183.

62 *'No, all in the wrong'*: indicating a comedy by Arthur Murphy, *All in the Wrong*, first produced at Drury Lane in 1761.

63 *'all round the wreken'*: George Farquhar's *The Recruiting Officer* (1706), set in Shrewsbury, is dedicated 'To All Friends Round the Wrekin'. The Wrekin is a prominent landmark, a hill in the midst of mainly flat terrain, and the phrase is a favourite Shropshire toast. The most recent Covent Garden production commenced in February 1790, when Lewis played Plume, Cubitt Kite, and Mrs Pope Sylvia.

66 *Rangers, Plumes, and Foppingtons*: very much part of the current reper-tory. Ranger appears in Dr. Benjamin Hoadly's *The Suspicious Husband* (1747); Captain Plume is a recruiting officer in Farquhar's play of the same name (1706), and Lord Foppington is a fop-role in Vanbrugh's *The Relapse* (1696). Lewis had played Ranger in the Covent Garden production of 2 January 1788, and was to repeat this from 16 September 1791.

69 *'Away! ... follows me!'*: Edgar, as Poor Tom in disguise, in Shakespeare's *The History of King Lear* (1608, 3.4.39; in *The Tragedy* (1623), 3.4.44), although the most accurate reference is probably to Nahum Tate's adaptation (1681), Act 3, p. 29. Holman was to play Edgar in the Garrick adaptation (1756) that was staged at Covent Garden on 4 November 1791 and he had already taken the part there in October 1790 and November 1789.

79 *stock purse*: a fund that supplies the common needs of a group—an idea that is very much endemic to the play.

82 *'Ay, to foreign ... bear'*: proof of two things, in that there is no equivalent to these words in Shakespeare's versions: (i) that the *King Lear* in which Rover has just appeared is probably Nahum Tate's adaptation (1681), or George Colman the elder's *The History of King Lear* (1768) that retains the lines given to Kent on his banishment by Lear in 1.1: 'Now to new

climates my old truth I bear; | Freedom lies hence, and banishment is here' (p. 6 in both versions). Garrick retains this wording at 1.2.136–7; and (ii) that his grasp of lines is approximate.

83 *car of Thespis*: Horace, in his *Ars Poetica* (275–7) claimed that Thespis took his company of actors around in a cart with their faces daubed with wine-lees. This led to his reputation as the first dramatist, although it is possible that the name was generic, referring to any dramatic poet.

91 *mystery and grand*: an ironic saying, pointing to anybody assuming an air of great secrecy. The association of grandeur and God's presence in his creation had been enshrined as a phrase as well as a cornerstone of belief in Henry More's *An Explanation of the grand Mystery of Godliness, or a true and faithfull representation of the Everlasting Gospel of . . . Jesus Christ* (1660). By 1714, though, the two words were being used in a more secular and less serious sense in John Toland's *The Grand Mystery Laid Open*, an anti-Jacobite treatise, identifying a plot to weaken the Hanoverian succession.

103 *even our acquaintance ends*: the friendship would end immediately.

2.1.29 *from the shell*: from the first days of infancy.

34 *withered hawthorn*: in the language of flowers the hawthorn was tradition-ally taken to be a symbol of hope, signifying, as it flowered, the end of winter and the onset of spring. Farmer Gammon's specimen will not flower anew.

43 *'The Economy of Human Life'*: Robert Dodsley's *The Economy of Human Life, Complete in Two Parts, translated from an Indian MS, written by an Ancient Brahmin* (1747) might prove to be a disappointment to Gammon. Far from a logical grasp on life, it celebrated the culture of the heart: 'The shadow of knowledge passeth over the mind of man as a dream; he seeth as in the dark; he reasoneth, and is deceived. But the wisdom of God is as the light of heaven; he reasoneth not; his mind is the fountain of truth' (p. xxiv).

50 *portly*: 'grand of mien' (*SJ*, meaning 1).

51 *new scratch*: a periwig, a covering for half the head.

68 *up with him*: even with him, i.e. get retribution.

69 *ringleader*: 'The head of a riotous body' (*SJ*).

98 *'Poor Tom's a-cold'*: in Shakespeare's *King Lear*, this is uttered by Edgar as Poor Tom at Scene 11, 134 (*The History*, 1608) and at 3.4.137 (*The Tragedy*, 1623). In Tate's version, it is '*Tom*'s a cold' (Act 3, p. 30) as it is in Garrick's (3.3.700).

101 *public house*: any refuge open to all, not necessarily only those licensed to sell licquor.

NOTES TO PAGES 243–246

110 *'Hear nature, ... serpent's tooth it is'*: a much adapted version of Lear's
curse on Goneril at Act 1, p. 12 in Tate's version:

> Hear Nature!
> Dear Goddess hear, and if thou dost intend
> To make that Creature fruitfull, change thy purpose;
> Pronounce upon her Womb the barren Curse,
> That from her blasted Body never spring
> A Babe to honour her—but if she bring forth,
> Defeat her Joy with some distorted Birth,
> Or monstrous Form, the Prodigy o'th'Time, ...
> How sharper than a Serpent's Tooth it is
> To have a Thankless Child! ...

Cf. Shakespeare's *The History of King Lear*, from Scene 4, 268–83; *The
Tragedy*, 1.4.254–69, and Garrick's 1.4.139–54.

126 *rumplified ... cross-grained tantarums*: rumpled (in nerves as well as
appearance) together with contrary, ill-humoured, tantrums.

143 *charity hides a deal of sins*: cf. 1 Peter 4: 8: 'For charity shall cover the
multitude of sins'. This had become proverbial and was usually entirely
laudatory, e.g. George Herbert, *Priest to Temple* (1652), xii: 'Many and
wonderfull things are spoken of thee ... To Charity is given the covering
of sins.' For Gammon, however, the primary emphasis is possibly on
charity's unrealistic and even cosmetic effects.

153 *touch him*: apprehend him.

162 *bought up ... note of hand*: accepted as payment a receipt of debt for
£30 originally incurred by Banks to another creditor.

194 *'I am the bold Thunder!'*: see note to 1.2.50.

197 *twenty pictures of his Majesty*: twenty crowns.

199 *housekeeper*: householder.

212 *Mr Shylock*: the Jewish moneylender in Shakespeare's *The Merchant of
Venice*. Rover was not alone in finding the part an amoral one. Francis
Gentleman's Shylock was 'a most disgraceful picture of human nature
... all shade, not a gleam of light' (*The Dramatic Censor, or Critical
Companion* (2 vols., 1770, i. 291]), and John Potter, in his popular *The
Theatrical Review; or, New Companion to the Playhouse* (2 vols., 1772),
found Shylock a grotesque, a 'Picture ... so disgraceful to human
Nature, that we doubt whether it ever had an Original' (i. 37).

214 *Hampshire hog*: characteristic of slovenly and thoughtless behaviour, e.g.
Thomas Flatman's 'Character of a Belly-God' from his *Poems and Songs*
(1686):

> 'For *Swines-flesh*, give me that of the *Wild Boar*,
> Pursu'd and hunted all the Forrest o're;

371

> He to the liberal *Oke* ne're quits his love,
> And when he finds no *Acorns*, grunts at *Jove*.
> The *Hampshire* Hog with *Pease & Whey* that's fed
> Sty'd up, is neither good alive nor dead.
>
> (ll. 71–6; pp. 155–6)

226 *tip*: commission to earn. Rover believes that Twitch is simply motivated by greed.

236 *stirring a fire*: being hospitable.

250 *'Madam, my master . . . his commands'*: a near accurate version of Archer's words (posing as Aimwell's servant) to Mrs Sullen in George Farquhar's *The Beaux' Stratagem* (1707): 'My master, madam, pays me; nor dare I take money from any other hand without injuring his honour, and disobeying his commands' (*The Recruiting Officer and Other Plays*, 3.3.239–41).

252 *'Run, run, . . . inexpressive she'*: the first mention of Shakespeare's *As You Like It*, the play chosen to be a charity performance by Lady Amaranth's household in Act 4. The lines are Orlando's when he turns to sonnets to hymn Rosalind's beauty (3.2.9–10).

259 *profane stage player*: the Puritan opposition to the stage had recently undergone a revival, and the word itself had stigmatized the activity. George Crabbe, in his poem *The Library* (1781), had portrayed a decay in contemporary taste, centred in the impiety of plays:

> Lo! where of late the Book of Martyrs stood,
> Old pious tracts, and Bibles bound in wood;
> There, such the taste of our degenerate age,
> Stand the profane delusions of the *Stage*.
>
> (ll. 501–4)

The association of drama with (specifically) profanity had been promoted by the Revd Jeremy Collier in a number of tracts a century before: 'But *Stage*-swearing is only to make a Profane Character more *lively* and *natural*' (*A Farther Vindication of the Short View of the Profaneness and Immorality of the English Stage* (1708), 15).

272 *bran new*: brand new.

277 *tax cart*: short for taxed cart. An open two-wheeled and springless conveyance, used for farming or trade—so small it was exempt from full taxation.

2.2.15 *'Yet my love . . . digest as much'*: a garbled memory of Orsino's distinction between men's and women's love in *Twelfth Night*:

> Alas, their love may be call'd appetite—
> No motion of the liver, but the palate—
> That suffer surfeit, cloyment, and revolt;
> But mine is all as hungry as the sea,

And can digest as much.
(2.4.96–100)

19 *eat like aldermen*: O'Keeffe noted the almost proverbial luxury of feasting found in corporation dinners in one of Nipperkin's airs, listing a catalogue of impossibilities, in his *Sprigs of Laurel* (1793):

> Show me a Right Honourable keeping to his word,
> Or a poor Poet patroniz'd by a Lord, . . .
> A Church-warden who scorns to feast upon the poor,
> Fat Aldermen, who cannot calipash [the rich, green meat to be
> found just under the turtle's shell] endure.
>
> (p. 3)

24 *'a fig for the sultan and sophy'*: Sir Wilfull Witwoud's closing line in his drunken duet with his half-brother, Witwoud, in Congreve's *The Way of the World* (1700): 'And a fig for your sultan and sophy' (*WW*, 4.1.417).

27 *'himself, in one prodigious ruin'*: an allusion to Selim's curse on Barbarossa at the close of Act 3 of John Brown's *Barbarossa: A Tragedy* (1755):

> But since Fate denies
> That Privilege, I'll sieze on what it gives:
> Like the deep-cavern'd Earthquake, burst beneath him,
> And whelm his Throne, his Empire, and himself,
> In one prodigious Ruin!
>
> (p. 52)

36 *in a white sheet*: a parish's demand for expiation when fornication was discovered involved the display of the woman in a white sheet before the congregation.

40 *'I say my . . . horrible to beedles'*: the start of a succession of allusions to Thomas Otway's *The Orphan* (1680). This is a creative misquotation, showing great swiftness of thought, of Chamont's defiance before the noble Castalio:

> I say my Sister's wrong'd;
> *Monimia* my sister born as high
> And noble as *Castalio*—Do her Justice,
> Or by the Gods I'll lay a Scene of Blood,
> Shall make this Dwelling horrible to Nature.
>
> (4.1, p. 50)

Here the rustic mock-heroism of a Blowsabella, a haymow, and Beadles (minor parish officials) cuts across Otway's heroic intensity.

41 *'Say that, Chamont'*: see above.

51 *'Then you . . . angry boy?'*: Kastril is dubbed 'the angry boy' in the *Dramatis Personae* of Ben Jonson's *The Alchemist* (1610). He has newly come to London from the country in order to learn how to quarrel, believing that there are rules to the art.

52 *So was . . . himself shaved*: a reflection upon the relative youth of William Pitt, the younger, who had taken prime ministerial office in 1784 at the tender age of 24.

59 *'I kiss'd thee ere I kill'd thee' . . . 'No way . . . upon a kiss'*: Othello's dying farewell to Desdemona at 5.2.368–9.

62 *'I've heard . . . God's creatures'*: Hamlet to Ophelia at 3.1.145–8.

66 *'Oh, that the town clerk . . . art an ass'*: the constable in charge of the watch, Dogberry, getting confused when trying to arraign Conrad and Verges in *Much Ado About Nothing* (4.2.73–4): 'O that he were here to write me down an ass!'.

69 *'Aye, to a nunnery, go'*: another phrase from Hamlet's exhortation to Ophelia (3.1.142–3).

71 *'Tis meat . . . see a clown'*: Touchstone belittling William in *As You Like It* (5.1.10).
*'Shepherd, . . . at court?'*: this time, Touchstone to Corin (*As You Like It*, 3.2.31–2).

73 *'Then thou art damn'd'*: a continuation of the above (*As You Like It*, 3.2.34).

75 *'Like an ill-roasted egg, all on one side'*: *As You Like It* (3.2.36–7). The net effect is surely not to establish a clear equivalence between Rover and the bumptious and condescending Touchstone, but rather to emphasize a distinction between a compassion for all, just demonstrated by Rover in the charity shown Banks and his family, and the pretensions to courtliness paraded by Touchstone in Shakespeare's play.

82 *'Your son? . . . him manners'*: Clifford Williams's note is broadly accurate when he identifies a reference to Justice Clodpate, that 'Country Justice, [who was also] a publick-spirited, politick, discontented Fop' from Thomas Shadwell's *Epsom-Wells* (1673). The holier-than-thou sentiments are similar, but the wording nearest Rover's is that given to Mrs Bisket when reprimanding Fribble in the play: 'Ah, thou art a good one i'faith; and thou wer't mine, I'd teach thee better manners' (2.1, p. 27).

90 *'Pillicock sat . . . loo'*: another memory of Rover's Edgar (as Poor Tom) in *King Lear*. See Tate's version, Act 3, p. 30; *The History*, scene 11.69; *The Tragedy* (3.4.72).

97 *'Thou wretch! Despite overwhelm thee!'*: Coriolanus's contemptuous dismissal of the tribune, Sicinius, in Shakespeare's play (3.1.166).

99 *'Only squint, . . . tennis ball'*: a memory of two passages from Beaumont and Fletcher's *Rule a Wife and Have a Wife* (1640), 3.1. The first is Margarita's comment to Altea that she will have freedom 'without the squint-eye of the law upon' her now she is married to Leon (p. 23). The second is Leon's defiance of the usurer, Cacafogo: 'Provoke me more, I'll beat thy blowne body | Till thou reboundst agen like a Tennis-ball' (p. 36).

103 *'Though love cool . . . son and father!'*: an approximate version of Gloucester's lament when confronted with his son, Edgar's, apparent duplicity:

> Love cools, and friendship fails.
> In Cities mutiny, in Countrys discord.
> The bond of Nature crack't 'twixt Son and Father.
> (Tate, Act 1, p. 9)

This quotation is slightly nearer a Shakespearian source: see *The History*,
scene 2.106–9 and (here below) *The Tragedy*, 1.2.104–7: 'Love cools,
friendship falls off, brothers divide; in cities mutinies; in countries, discord; in palaces, treason; and the bond cracked 'twixt son and father'.

110 *'Go, father . . . than his fellows'*: cf. Bassanio on receiving Lancelot Gobbo
into his service from Shylock's (*The Merchant of Venice*, 2.2.147, 149–
50): 'Go, father, with thy son . . . Give him a livery more guarded
[ornamented] than his fellows' '.

116 *'Thou art an honest reptile!'*: a probable allusion to Drusus's taunting of
Sejanus, not in Ben Jonson's *Sejanus*, but Francis Courtenay's adaptation
(1752), 1.1, p. 12: 'Go, thou noble reptile!'

117 *Bayes*: see note to 1.2.44.

120 *'Egad, it's . . . gone to dinner'*: a loose version of Bayes's lament that all the
players have left him to dine in 5.1 of *The Rehearsal*: 'How! are the
Players gone to Dinner? 'Tis impossible: the Players gone to dinner! I
gad, if they are, I'l make 'em know what it is to injure a person that dies
'em the honour to write for 'em, and all that' (p. 53).

126 *'Sun, moon, and stars! . . . There's the sun . . . show her tail!'*: so as to
conclude his battle between the General and Lieutenant-General, Bayes
chooses the rather abrupt expedient of a total eclipse, where a 'mid-night
darkness' invades 'the day' (5.1; p. 49). In order to demonstrate the
interposition of the moon before the sun, he has 'Earth, Sun, and Moon'
dance 'the Hey' (a kind of energetic reel) (5.1; p. 50). Rover invents, for
good measure, the participation of stars. Orbis and Luna then have a duet
that concludes with 'Orb. What means *Luna* in a veil? | *Luna Luna* means
to shew her tail' (5.1; p. 52).

129 *'I attend them . . . our mother'*: a version of Hamlet's agreement to attend
his mother at Rosencrantz's request (3.2.320): 'we shall obey, were she
ten times our mother'.

130 *stage*: stage-coach.

132 *'I am the bold Thunder'*: see note to 1.2.50.

144 *What rate is this vessel*: the rate of a ship was its official tonnage, armament, and class.

2.3.2 *hold a good thirty pounds*: accommodate an audience that would yield
thirty pounds.

7  *stand so well for pretty women*: well provided for with pretty women in the cast.

8  *Snap him at any terms*: engage him no matter what he asks for.

18  *takes the towns*: receives the attendance money.

29  *top my part*: perform the best one can.

38  *'Sir, to return to the twenty pounds'*: a reference to Sharp's request to borrow the sum off a disguised Melissa, the lover of Gayless, his master, in David Garrick's *The Lying Valet* (1741—Act 2, p. 26).

42  *step for the cast-book*: to take charge and responsibility for the prompt-book, i.e. the version recording moves and modifications of the original text during rehearsal.

56  *neater dozen*: a stronger dozen strokes of punishment.

62  *shallop*: a small boat, primarily used in shallow water to convey passengers from a seagoing ship to shore. Hence, John Dory is simply saying that he has sent a message to Lady Amaranth, announcing their arrival.

91  *'but by the care ... prevented was'*: another allusion to *The Rehearsal*: Cordelio's account of 'Peccadille's' attempts on her own life, thwarted by bystanders (3.2; p. 24).

100  *'Hear you ... absolute Shall?'*: cf. note to 2.2.86, another appropriation of Coriolanus's taunting of Sicinius: 'Hear you this Triton of the minnows? Mark you | His absolute "shall"?' (*Coriolanus*, 3.1.92–3).

104  *'More music ... than twenty hautboys'*: cf. Tom's description of Lady Godiva in O'Keeffe's own *Peeping Tom of Coventry* (1784; pub. 1787): 'I think I hear her horse's feet—the clinking of their hoofs is far sweeter than a haut-boy' (Act 2, p. 34).

106  *'Oh, such ... coronation'*: from *Peeping Tom of Coventry*, Act 2, p. 32.

108  *'I was thinking of a side-saddle'*: from *Peeping Tom of Coventry*, Act 2, p. 32. The crucial question when interpreting these quotations is one regarding recognition. How much of the source coloured the sense at this juncture—or was meant to? Whilst only mildly titillating, O'Keeffe's earlier work is still in an alternative mode to this one, bawdy rather than respectful. This third allusion, even to a spectator who had no direct knowledge of *Peeping Tom*, surely imports a more risqué shade of meaning.

120  *bigness of a Rumbo Canakin*: a small drinking vessel for a shot of rum.

121  *Ranger's dress*: a costume for the main part in Benjamin Hoadley's *The Suspicious Husband* (1747). Clifford Williams's 'Introduction' to his text of *Wild Oats* (1977) is the only serious attempt to trace the possible effects of the intertextual allusions between the play and its sources (see Introduction, p. xxxiii). On noting who Ranger was, he 'noted with some satisfaction that it was entirely apt [for Rover to dress as Ranger], for

Ranger occupied himself with amorous intrigue whilst remaining a gentleman! Not dissimilar to Rover' (p. ix).

122, 126 *'Cousin of Buckingham . . . grave man'* . . . *'Since you . . . foul-fac'd'* . . . *'Your mere . . . acquittance me'*: a near version of Richard of Gloucester's apparently reluctant (although feigned) desire to accept the crown in Shakespeare's *Richard III* (3.7.217–24).

130 *parson Palmer*: Thomas Fyshe Palmer (1747–1802), a firebrand Unitarian preacher. *1794* refers to a 'parson Sacks'. Palmer first came to national prominence after the première of *Wild Oats* with his anti-war tracts, 1793–6, for which he served at least two sentences in prison.

133 *'Aye, to the chariot! . . . for the Tigris'*: a heavily conflated version of Alexander the Great's defiance in the face of overwhelming odds in Nathaniel Lee's *The Rival Queens, or The Death of Alexander the Great* (1677–5.2., p. 62):

> Ha! who talks of Heav'n?
> I am all Hell, I burn, I burn again.
> The War grows wondrous hot, hey for the Tygris;
> Bear me, *Bucephalus*, amongst the Billows:
> O, 'tis a noble Beast! I would not change him
> For the best Horse the Sun has in his Stable . . .

3.1.4 *pound*: usually a temporary enclosure for stray or detained farm animals.

15 *beating of one brass*: probably a memory of 1 Corinthians 13: 1: 'Though I speak with the tongues of men and of angels, and have not charity, I am become as sounding brass, or a tinkling cymbal'. Ephraim's own uncharitable impulses are a telling contrast.

48 S.D. *dressed*: presumably in the garb of one who is striking. Ranger's costume (from Hoadley's *The Suspicious Husband*) should be neat and aristocratic. See note to 2.3.121.

'*'Tis I, Hamlet the Dane'*: Hamlet announces his presence at Ophelia's burial with this phrase, just prior to leaping after Laertes into the open grave (5.1.253–4).

49 *'Thus far . . . march'd on'*: Richmond, in *Richard III* (5.2.3–4).

50 *'John, . . . devouring boar'*: later in the same speech, with reference to Richard III (5.2.7).

51 *bull*: possibly a mishearing of Bucephalus in a repeat of 2.3.132–3.

58 *Spanish India-man*: a Spanish ship involved in East Indies trade, fabled to be the richest commercial opportunity.

61 *little Cupid's . . . take minutes*: i.e. they will only be accompanied by the boy-god of love and that what will there take place will be secret.

66 *younker*: a youngster, usually with a disparaging association.

78 '*A truant disposition . . . from Wirtemberg*': the 'truant disposition' is Horatio's in *Hamlet*, 1.2.168. The University is placed in Wittenberg.

83 '*Why, ma'am . . . fierce resentment*': a snatch of Henry's stirring call to arms at the gates of Harfleur: 'But when the blast of war blows in our ears, | then imitate the action of the tiger' (*Henry V*, 3.1.5–6).

87 '*I think it . . . save the mark*': Hotspur, mimicking an effete lord wary of war (*1 Henry IV*, 1.3.58–62).

91 '*Then, lady . . . beauteous flower*': Juliet to Romeo from her balcony: 'This bud of love by summer's ripening breath | May prove a beauteous flower when next we meet' (*Romeo and Juliet*, 2.1.163–4).

94 '*Excellent lady! . . . is come again*': Othello referring to Desdemona at 3.3 91–3. A rare exact quotation.

98 '*If I were . . . discord make*': from Othello's hymn of relief that Desdemona is safe after the crossing to Cyprus from Venice (2.1.190–1, 196–9)

100 '*Why, you . . . this family*': cf. Lingo's rebuke to Thomas in O'Keeffe's *The Agreeable Surprise* (1784), 2.4, p. 29: 'Why, Thomas, you fancy yourself Cardinal Wolsey in this house'. The afterpiece was a regular in the repertoire at the Haymarket, and Mrs Wells had appeared just as regularly as Cowslip. The piece had been staged over 200 times to 1800.

103, 105, 107 '*A bowl . . . Majesty*', '*You get . . . great Potentate*', '*Go, go, . . . Pomona*': a continuation of the thread of quotation from *The Agreeable Surprise*. Cowslip serves Mrs Cheshire 'some of our English cream', believing her to be deserving of the title of 'royal reverence'. Lingo confirms the mistake:

| | |
|---|---|
| LINGO | Take the glass, please, your catholic majesty. |
| MRS CHESHIRE | My catholic majesty! |
| LINGO | Cowslip, leave the presence. |
| COWSLIP | I have no more presents than the bowl of cream. |
| LINGO | Cream! you shallow Pomona! |

(2.4, p. 27)

121 '*Can'st . . . vagrant*': John to Lingo, in *The Agreeable Surprise*, 2.4, p. 27: 'Pray, bow respectfully to her'.

136 *rag and fiddlestick*: scraps and inessentials.

137 *whirlilgig*: primarily, a spinning-top, though the sense here is nearer simply to something assembled in a hurry.

144 *crow the cock . . . fowl*: to assume the role of cock of the walk (the place where barndoor fowl are fed) and lead the band of players.

150 *fiddles engaged*: the musical accompaniment contracted.

151 *overflow*: surplus, signifying a profit—if Lamp can fit them in.

163 *housewarming*: a sociable introduction of the community to a new house, usually with feasting.

175 *bully*: a term of encouragement, usually taken to indicate a brisk and enterprising individual. Given the allusion of lines 178–80 below, Rover has in mind Quince's call of 'bully Bottom' at *A Midsummer Night's Dream*, 3.1.7, and Flute's 'sweet bully Bottom' at 4.2.18.

180 *'The actors ... like to know'*: from Peter Quince's Prologue to the Mechanicals' play in *A Midsummer Night's Dream*, 5.1.116–17. The scratch nature of that performance and this is thereby highlighted—as is the need for an audience's charity.

3.2 S.D. *in a livery*: clothing that betokens being in service, e.g. '4. The cloaths given to servants' (*SJ*).

20 *shoulder my curling irons*: unpack the curling irons but not to have them ready for immediate action.

38 *runagate*: 'a fugitive; rebel; apostate' (*SJ*)

48 *All glasses reckoning ... wild with me*: one ascertained one's boat's likely speed by both timing one's progress by a half-hourglass known as a 'glass' against the pressure of a 'log' lowered at a depth of one hundred fathoms. Sir George feels he has lost his bearings.

54 *crammed*: stuffed with various seasoning.

55 *Calcavella*: a sweet white wine from Lisbon.

76 *Madeira*: a fortified wine.

81 *'A bumper ... liquor'*: a refrain from Sheridan's *The Duenna* (1775) sung by Don Jerome, Isaac, and Ferdinand (2.3.130). The full passage is

> A bumper of good liquor
> Will end a contest quicker
> Than justice, judge or vicar.
> So fill a cheerful glass,
> And let good humour pass.
> (ll. 130–4)

*The Duenna* was staged 164 times to 1800.

83 *'We'll dance ... a little'*: source untraced.

84 *rattling up*: making lively.

86 S.D. *dressed*: i.e. out of his riding garb.

97 *benefits*: a pun, associating, in Sir George's use, simple advantages, with benefit nights in the theatre, in Harry's.

99, 100 *the Fair Quaker ... The Humours of the Navy*: a reference to Charles Shadwell's *The Fair Quaker of Deal, or The Humours of the Navy* (1710), although Edward Thompson's adaptation, *The Fair Quaker* (1773) had been played more recently at Drury Lane (27 September 1783, 6 January 1785).

131 *grampus*: 'A large fish of the cetaceous kind' (*SJ*). Sir George is probably referring to John Dory's puffing and spluttering.

132 *comical roasted orange*: John's appearance would be quickly florid and mottled if he were placed in the 'fishpond' of rum and sugar that Sir George envisaged at 3.2.78–81.

146 *if you wore . . . you for this*: John would chastise Sir George even if he were a lion.

4.1.3 *they call immortal*: this view was of long standing. Ben Jonson had claimed that Shakespeare was 'not of an age but for all time!' as early as 1623 ('To the Memory of my Beloved the Author, Mr William Shakespeare', line 43). The identification of his muse as natural and fertile was at its height at this point. The *Critical Review* simply phrased what many believed: 'Every new enquiry into the dramatic works of Shakespeare renders the transcendency of his talents more conspicuous' (vol. 39 (1775), 203).

7 *origin of plays . . . delight and morality*: whilst few critics denied the claim that the plays delighted, there were several who felt that the 'morality' was rather home-spun. Samuel Johnson, in the 'Preface' to his edition (1765), felt that they were packed with 'practical axioms and domestick wisdom' from which one could construct 'a system of civil and oeconomical prudence' (*Works of Johnson*, vii: 62)—and few went further than that.

13 *tabernacle of Baal*: Baal originally signified any alternative to the God of Israel, but came to be more frequently referred to as the deity in fertility rites (see 1 Kings 14: 24; 2 Kings 1: 2–18). The Feast of Tabernacles celebrated the breaking of drought in early autumn.

25 *school for the old dragon*: for the old serpent or devil. See Revelations 12: 9: 'And the great dragon was cast out, that old serpent, called the Devil, and Satan, which deceiveth the whole world: he was cast out into the earth, and his angels were cast out with him.'

26 *primer of Belzebub*: a god of the Philistines (see 2 Kings 1: 3), who is regarded at Matthew 12: 24 as the 'prince of the Devils'.

31 *'Not the king's crown . . . man new made'*: Isabella from *Measure for Measure*, 2.1.62–5, 79–81.

40 *Miss Audrey . . . William of the Forest*: some typecasting here. Both characters are rustic inhabitants of the Forest of Arden.

44 *'The gods give us joy'*: Audrey to Touchstone in *As You Like It*, 3.3.42.

51 *Rosalind*: the main female role in the play, who teaches Orlando how to woo and eventually marries him.

53 *'Eh, what, . . . Clytus' . . . 'Why, you're like . . . laughing Gods'*: from Nathaniel Lee's *The Rival Queens* (1677), where Alexander advises Clytus:

> Let him persist, be positive and proud,
> Sullen, and dazl'd, amongst the nobler souls,
> Like an Infernal Spirit that had stole
> From Hell, and mingled with the laughing Gods.
>
> (Act 4, p. 47)

55 *'quips and ... Hebe's cheek'*: George Colman the elder's version of John Milton's *Comus* (1634; pub. 1637) was first staged at Covent Garden on 16 October 1772. It proved immensely popular, and appeared in the repertoire 215 times up to 1800. These lines are in fact incorporated from Milton's *L'Allegro*, ll. 27–9, but given to Colman's Comus in Act 2 (p. 16):

> Quips and cranks, and wanton wiles,
> Nods and becks, and wreathed smiles,
> Such as hang on Hebe's cheek.

58 *'But I'm a voice ... we must'*: an altered wording of Iago's apparent concern, on Othello's behalf, at Brabanzio's power in the Venetian state:

> Be assured of this:
> That the magnifico is much beloved,
> And hath in his effect a voice potential
> As double as the Duke's.
>
> (1.2.11–14)

60 *'By Jupiter, I swear. Aye'*: probably a conscious reversal of Lear's refusal to accept that Kent (in disguise) has been placed in the stocks by his offspring:

| | |
|---|---|
| KENT | Yes. |
| LEAR | No, I say. |
| KENT I say yea. | |
| LEAR | By Jupiter, I swear no. |
| KENT By Juno, I swear ay. | |

(*The Tragedy*, 2.2.196–7, cf. *The History*, 7.200–1 and Tate, Act 2, p. 18)

67 *'A sacrilegious thief ... in his pocket'*: some embellishment on Hamlet's diatribe against his uncle (3.4.89–91).

69, 70 *'thou owl of Crete'*: in his altercation with Nim, Pistol's actual words are 'O hound of Crete' (*Henry V*, 2.1.71). The substitution helps with the link to the 'Cuckoo's song' noted below.

*'Cuckoo's song'*: the song of spring included at the conclusion to *Love's Labour's Lost* and associated, not with the owl (the song of winter), but with 'cuckoo-buds of yellow hue' (5.2.883). Presumably, this is an addition to the performance of *As You Like It*.

77 *'Verily, I could ... of the sun'*: the nearest source located is Hannah More's *David and Goliath* (1782), that has Saul elegiac about Israel:

Where's that bold arm which quelled th'Amalekite,
And nobly spar'd fierce Agag and his flocks?
'Tis past; the light of Israel now is quench'd:
Shorn of his beams, my sun of glory sets!

(p. 83)

Its theatre history is, however, sparse, even if it enjoyed a popular literary currency.

81 *star, ribband, place or pension*: 'star' commonly referred to the decoration of the Order of the Garter, 'ribband' any state honour. Rover is likening the conspicuousness of a top part in a play to the celebrity (and security) of government honours or posts.

92 *blow me*: blow his cover, or expose him.

95 *wight*: fellow.

106 '*Nor what to say*': a reference to Shirley's bemused comment in Buckingham's *The Rehearsal* just as she witnesses the Usurpers unseat the Kings without a battle: 'I know not what to do nor what to say' (2.4, p. 18).

115 *Figuring it away*: representing, with the additional sense of showing off.

127 *high fellow*: in terms of social status. It is one of the themes of the play that such social gradation is often gratuitous.

131 *Touchstone . . . Orlando*: Rover would like to take the part of Orlando so as to play opposite Lady Amaranth as Rosalind.

153 '*If the real Simon Pure*': Simon Pure is a 'Quaking preacher' in Susanna Centlivre's *A Bold Stroke for a Wife* (1718). His 'Quaking' language is a likely model for Ephraim's phrasing. He is impersonated by Colonel Fainwell.

160 *whip her up*: bind her to some level of affection and formal assent to marriage.

188 '*Quoit him down, Bardolph*': Falstaff's instruction for Bardolph to subdue Pistol in the Eastcheap Tavern (*2 Henry IV*, 2.4.189).

192 '*My love more noble . . . of dirty lands*': part of Orsino's briefing to 'Cesario' (Viola in disguise), indicating his depth of love for Olivia (*Twelfth Night*, 2.4.80–1).

200 *competent to all my wishes*: will satisfy all his desires.

232 *standing out*: claiming.

240 *drop astern*: hold back. In nautical parlance, to do so was to fall behind, often in convoy, a lead vessel.

*buss her bob-stays*: a bob-stay was, literally, a rope used to confine the bowsprit temporarily, thus counteracting the speed from the foresails. To kiss these ropes does not make immediate sense. Sir George is just (alliteratively) encouraging Harry to pay court to Lady Amaranth.

241 *bring to, and come down straight as a mast*: to 'bring to' was to fasten down all sails when the ship was in harbour. When a ship was in the yards for repair, its mast was lowered, too.

268 *comedy squab*: a comic turn, often found in afterpieces.

272 *'Keep it up. I like fun'*: origin untraced.

277 *'Excellently well. He's a fishmonger'*: part of Hamlet's mystifying of Polonius: 'Excellent, excellent well. You're a fishmonger' (*Hamlet*, 2.2.175).

282 *'Motley's your only . . . fool in the forest'*: a rather disjointed memory of Jaques's reported encounter with Touchstone in *As You Like It*, incorporating 2.7.12–13: 'A fool, a fool, I met a fool i'th'forest, | A motley fool—a miserable world!' and 2.7.33–4: 'O noble fool, | A worthy fool—motley's the only wear'.

284 *'Salutation and greeting . . . good Audrey'*: an elision of three Touchstone phrases: 'Salutation and greeting to you all' (*As You Like It*, 5.4.39), 'Come apace, good Audrey' (3.3.1) and 'Trip, Audrey, trip, Audrey' (5.1.61).

285 *'La! Warrants. What features?'*: Audrey's comment on Touchstone: 'Your features, Lord warrant us—what features?' (*As You Like It*, 3.3.4).

287 *'A homely thing, sir, but she's my own'*: a euphemistic version of Touchstone's uncharitable verdict on Audrey: 'A poor virgin, sir, an ill-favoured thing, sir, but mine own' (*As You Like It*, 5.4.57–8).

289 *'I thank the Gods for my sluttishness'*: the reference is a little garbled:

AUDREY          I am not a slut, though I thank the gods I am foul.
TOUCHSTONE   Well praised be the gods for thy foulness. Sluttishness may come hereafter. (*As You Like It*, 3.3.33–6)

291, 292 *'My friend, Horatio' . . . 'I wear him in my . . . heart of hearts'*: part of Hamlet's appreciation of Horatio's loyalty (*Hamlet*, 3.2.69–71)

296 *'Jaffeir has discovered . . . deceive the senate'*: not a direct quotation, but certainly an allusion to Otway's *Venice Preserv'd* (1682), where Jaffeir does indeed discover a plot. The nearest equivalent is probably in 5.2, where both Jaffeir and Pierre die defiantly: '*Pierre* Now thou hast indeed been faithful. | This was done nobly—we've deceived the Senate' (p. 71). The play had just finished a short run at Covent Garden (from November 1790) in which Holman had played Jaffeir, Hull Priuli, Powel Renault, and Cubitt Spinoza.

300 *'Aye, his conscience . . . heels and run'*: a conflation of several phrases from Lancelot Gobbo's opening speech in *The Merchant of Venice*, 2.2.1–29.

312 *humming*: deceiving.

322 '*Now, by my father's son . . . crossed and crossed*' another loose rendition, this time of Petruccio's desperation at Katherine (*The Taming of the Shrew*. 4.6.6–10).

The version seen by O'Keeffe's audience would have been Garrick's *Catharine and Petruchio* (1756), and the above is found at 3.159–63.

325 '*And I say, as the saying is*': not a direct quotation, but near to the exchange between Petruccio and Katherine in the above scene:

PETRUCCIO      I say it is the moon that shines so bright
KATHERINE   I know it is the sun that shines so bright . . .
HORTENSIO (to Katherine) Say as he says or we shall never go.
(*Taming*, 4.6.4–5, 11; *Catharine
and Petruchio*, 3.157–8; 164)

327 *Charles the wrestler*: a character employed by Oliver in *As You Like It*, 1.1. to break Orlando's neck in a bout of wrestling. In 1.2, it is Orlando, however, who is the victor.

328 *trip up your heels*: throw or place an adversary off balance.

330 *undutiful chick of an old pelican*: in Christian iconography and the heraldry derived therefrom, the pelican signified piety and came to figure Christ's sacrifice, by whose blood we are saved and healed. The bird is supposed to have pecked its own breast so that it might feed its young with its own blood, but, in fact, this action is a transfer of macerated food from the sac beneath its bill.

332 *Mr Buckskin*: a pun incorporating an individual who wears the skin of a buck and also an actor, after the wearing of the high boot of that name by classical tragedians.

334 '*All the world's . . . men and women*': the opening sentiment of Jaques's famous reflection on ageing: (*As You Like It*, 2.7.139–40).

337 '*A blow, Essex, a blow*': the Earl of Essex's expostulation at having his ears boxed by Queen Elizabeth in John Banks's *The Unhappy Favourite* (1682): 'Ha! Furies, Death and Hell! a Blow! | Has *Essex* had a Blow! . . .' (3.1., p. 41). Holman played Essex and Mrs Pope the Queen in the revival from December 1790. It was repeated at Covent Garden from October 1791.

342 '*Strike me ! . . . if I don't—*': Chamont's fierce defence of Monimia in Otway's *The Orphan*:

Throw him to the earth like a dead Dog despised;
Lameness and Leprosie, Blindness and Lunacy,
Poverty, Shame, Pride, and the name of Villain
Light upon me, if, *Castalio*, I forgive thee.
(4.1, p. 48)

See note to 2.2.34–6.

**4.2.42** *establishment*: means of employment; a salary or wage.

**5.1.2** *upon our shifts*: fending for themselves.

**4** *was a hit*: was a success.

**11** *posted on the stocks*: probably the stocks here are not punitive, but rather more simply just posts.

**16** *sack*: place in a sack; appropriate.

**34** *pressed in the river*: this process of enforced, often violent, conscription targeted returning merchant seamen, who were 'pressed' still on board ship to form a crew on another. It is characteristic of O'Keeffe to spend time providing motivation for 'ruffian' behaviour.

**43** *keep out to sea*: keep out of harm's way and not be noticed. It is typical that John Dory should associate the sea with security, not with hazard.

**56** *sea-store*: provisions for survival. Again, as with John Dory, note to 5.1.43 above, Sir George transposes marine life with normal landed existence.

**5.2.34** *privateer*: 'a ship fitted out by private men to plunder enemies' (*SJ*).

**36** *Try your charge*: have your pistol primed for action.

**46** S.D. *presents the piece*: aims the pistol (rather ceremoniously).

**59** *haul up*: stand up on one's own two feet.

*crab-walk*: a bow-legged gait.

**5.3.4** *lay an execution*: impound goods by legal order.

**22** *market penny*: a perquisite earned by one who acts for another, usually in a purchase.

**47** *'tickled their catastrophes'*: origin undiscovered.

**48** *three upon one were odds, so safe's the word*: there were stiff odds as there were three ruffians opposing him, so he's fortunate to come off relatively unscathed.

**57** *hobble*: an irregular and jerky dance or walk.

**68** *'A little better, but very faint still'*: in Farquhar's *The Beaux' Stratagem* (1707), Aimwell feigns faintness in order to enter Lady Bountiful's house: 'Somewhat better—though very faint still' (*The Recruiting Officer and Other Plays*, 4.1.188).

**70** *'won't you take another?'*: probably a reference to O'Keeffe's own *The Farmer* (1788), where Jemmy Jumps tries to be clumsily hospitable with the phrase in 2.4 (p. 32). The afterpiece was very popular, being staged at Covent Garden some 130 times up to 1800. Munden had taken the part of Jemmy from December 1790.

**73** *'if you'd been fighting as I have . . . in Illyria'*: a vague allusion to *Twelfth Night*, which is set in Illyria. The calling of Sir Andrew Aguecheek's bluff in 3.4, where he is dared to a duel with the equally reluctant Viola (as Cesario), is the nearest source.

92 *Covent Garden ... beating the watch*: Covent Garden had become notorious for street fights, especially since the rapid commercial exploitation of the piazza from 1748 onwards, when the coffee houses, such as the Bedford, opened their doors. Press gangs and Mohocks (violent mobs of young tearaways) became synonymous with the area.

96 *'As you say ... it was'*: Rover is here imitating Hamlet's dismissive conversation with Polonius and Rosencrantz at 2.2.388–9: 'you say right, sir, for o'Monday morning, 'twas so indeed'.

102 *suit you with an action*: take legal action against him.

104 *'Right, suit ... not affrighted'*: part of Hamlet's advice to the Players (3.2.17–18) The timorous 'gentlewoman' is probably Ophelia: 'Alas, my lord, I have been so affrighted' (2.1.76).

105 *'Michael, I'll make thee an example'*: Othello, at the moment of Michael Cassio's dismissal: (2.3.241–4).

108 *'Thou worm and maggot of the law'*: Elder Wouldbe's attack on the legal profession—and Subtleman in particular—in Farquhar's *The Twin Rivals* (*The Recruiting Officer and other Plays*, 1703): 'Thou art the worm and maggot of the law, bred in the bruised and rotten parts, and now art nourished on the same corruption that produced thee' (4.1.117–19).

109 *'Hop me ... without my custom'*: in Shakespeare's *The Taming of the Shrew*, this is part of Petruccio's anger at his tailor: 'Go hop me over every kennel home, | For you shall hop without my custom, sir' (4.3.98–9; *Catharine and Petruchio*, 3.86–7).

118 *by the freedom*: presumably, by a distinctive lack of ceremony.

133 *footpads*: 'A highwayman that robs on foot, not on horseback' (*SJ*).

5.4.7 S.D. *Adjusts the toilet*: sets up her dressing table.

13 *They say ... black gentleman*: i.e. the Devil.

58 *Heave ahead*: Look out!

59 *like a pound of tea*: presumably, at the dockside, when unloading merchandise, the treatment would be without ceremony.

68 *Reef the foresail*: to lower by gathering or rolling up the foresail, so as to bring to a sudden halt.

69 *overset her by bringing to*: overwhelm a vessel by fastening the sail and thus bring to a standstill.

91 *impudent crimp*: an overzealous recruiting officer who seduces new conscripts on false pretences.

92 *strike my false colours*: most likely an optical expression, taken from the practice of altering inaccurate pigments in watercolours, although there

was a rarely used naval expression approximate to this usage, signifying the removal of deliberately misleading flags to reveal true colours when the time was ripe.

107 *post-captain*: holding a permanent commission as captain of a large vessel, as distinguished from temporary holders and/or officers on smaller boats.

136 *passport to Winchester bilboes*: commit him to a nearby gaol to be bound. Bilboes were long iron bars with sliding shackles fastened to a cell-floor, usually to confine the ankles of prisoners.

152 *Hold thy clapper*: as in silencing a bell, to shut up.

168 *my spear and shield*: defender.

174 *concerted*: conceived.

177 *took the bounty*: see note to 1.1.26.

*depredators*: predators.

179 *in limbo*: in temporary confinement before trial.

179, 180 *Keep them safe in limbo/ The Ruffians [are] taken off*: What, could you find no jacket to disgrace by your wearing than that of an English seaman, a character, whose bravery is even the admiration of his enemies, and genuine honesty of heart, the glory of human nature? Keep them safe. / JOHN DORY Aye, I knew the rope would be wanted, *(drives 'em off) 1791–93*.

206 *disinterested*: showing no selfish concern.

231 *Hyder Ally*: (1722–82), a Muslim ruler of Bengal, who was a powerful adversary for the British in India. See note to *She Stoops to Conquer*, 2.1.204.

*strike her toilet*: move camp.

238 *Negapatnam*: now Negapattinam in Tamil Nadu, on the south-east Indian coast. It was the site of Fort Naaden on the Coromandel, the 'Fort with the Golden Walls', owned by the Dutch, pounded by the British in 1785, and finally destroyed by them in 1805.

241 *rather act Scrub on the stage than Hotspur*: i.e. play a relatively minor role. Scrub can be found in Farquhar's *The Beaux' Stratagem* as the Sullens' servant. Hotspur is the hot-blooded (and fated) leader of insurrection in *1 Henry IV*.

243 *pair of colours*: an ensign's commission.

246 *murdered more poets than Rajahs*: mangled, by bad performances, the lines of playwrights more than any local chieftains ('Rajahs').

247 *pagodas*: likely to be gold or silver currency higher in value than rupees, although an alternative meaning could be holy images taken from a shrine.

280 *dearest Rosalind . . . our Charles*: a possible (and probably intended) confusion between the playworld and reality. Rosalind is the female lead in *As You Like It*. Charles in the play is the name of the wrestler bested by Orlando in 1.2, although here it is the suddenly discovered Christian name of Rover.

291 *candid Thespian laws*: a fair summation of O'Keeffe's play. 'Candid' here is nearest to Johnson's second sense of 'Without malice; without deceit; fair; open; ingenuous' (*SJ*). The spirit of such candour is summed up in Rover's perspective on life.

### EPILOGUE

[Introduced from *1798* on]

11 *Box-lobby Bobbies*: in order to appear to be amongst those who could afford a box at the theatre, these loungers would appear at intervals or at the end of performances without actually entering. The second edition of the popular *The Adventures of Bobby Lounge; or, The Unfortunate Levee Haunter, Related by Himself* appeared in 1791, and Richard Cumberland's *The Box-Lobby Challenge* was one of the stage hits of 1794. The invocation to Thomas Holcroft's *Innovation. A Tale of Complaint* (1806) details this type:

> Ye world of London, hear! awake!
> To you this grand appeal I make.
> Attend, each spruce box-lobby beau!
> With decent insolence appear.
> (ll. 139–42; from *Tales in Verse; Critical, Satirical,*
> *and Humorous*, 2 vols. (London, 1806), ii. 130)

12 *city frumps*: an unfashionable, probably unshapely, dame from a mercantile family.

*cork-rumps*: an old-fashioned bustle made out of cheaper materials.

13 *hops at Pewterer's Hall*: dances of a rather unmeasured nature at a City Guild gathering, with the association of rather ungenteel behaviour.

14 *Foist*: to intrude illicitly; here, without due regard to the conversation, say your piece no matter how irrelevant it might be.

36 *wring their withers*: to give grief to. Withers are a plural reference to the ridge between a horse's shoulders; to wring them would be to press the horse there with its collar when riding.

39 *for a steak of beef*: cf. in Shakespeare's play, Richard III's cry that he would swap his kingdom for the use of a horse (*Richard III*, 5.7.13).

40 *crook'd-back'd Glos'ter*: Richard III was Duke of Gloucester and, in Shakespeare's portrayal, had a twisted spine.

55 *Act Plays . . . country's good*: the running conceit here is that the jobbing

actor who performs simply to put meat on her/his table should receive
our charity. The fantasy whereby members of parliament, who are less
driven by need, would actually spend their Christmas acting (badly) to
supply another 'good' than the usual one: the public's interest, would be
instructive for them to realize how hard a life it actually was.

58 *Pierre plans treason . . . Jaffier rants*: characters from Otway's *Venice
Preserv'd* who, in this instance, might not reveal the true nature of the
actor.

61 *Jane Shore*: the unfortunate protagonist of Nicholas Rowe's *The Tragedy
of Jane Shore* (1714).

# GLOSSARY

**affirm** to tell confidently

**allay** mix a base metal with one that is superior

**ames-ace** the lowest throw in dice: two aces, counting as ones

**apostasy** a failure to live up to what one has professed

**asp** aspen tree

**asylum** refuge and shelter

**auxiliary** an accomplice or assistant

**badiner** playfully jesting

**bagatelle** a trifle; something trivial

**balloon-coach** a slow, stately, conveyance

**banter** to rally or ridicule

**basket** basket-hilted sword

**bated** held back from giving

**beaufet** an early form of sideboard on which food is displayed

**beaupot** a large decorated vase for cut flowers

**beaver** hat made out of beaver's fur

**bilboes** sliding shackles fastened to a cell-floor

**bill of lading** list or inventory of registered freight

**blade** a brisk, confident man

**blast one's fame** harm one's reputation

**blow** expose

**boatswain** officer in charge of sails and rigging on board ship

**bob** a pendant or earring

**bob-stay** rope used to confine the bowsprit temporarily to slow a vessel

**bomb-boat** scavengers' vessels, charged with cleaning the hulls of moored boats on the Thames

**bowsprit** the spar at the front of a vessel

**box-book** a record of theatre receipts

**box-lobby bobby** someone who waits just outside the box-seats either to appear amongst the best company at an interval or to steal in towards the end of the performance

**box-ticket** usually, the best seats in the house, in full view of the audience

**bread-room** (sl.) stomach

**bring to** fasten down all sails when the ship was in harbour

**buss** kiss

**bye-word** so well known as to be infamous

**cant** (v.) to talk either in an affected voice or with reference only to the jargon of a particular profession

**capstan** a wheel with long spokes comprising the winding gear for hauling sails or an anchor

**capuchin** a cloak or hood resembling the dress of a Capuchin monk

**catastrophe** a crucial change in the plot that hastens a tragic conclusion

**catch at** claim or snatch

**cause** (in a paper) case in the printed schedule

**cephalic snuff** taken to clear the head

**channel** (for the stage) a boarding station for a stagecoach

**chimerical** fantastic and illusory

**China orange** sweet-tasting orange, supposedly from China originally

**choleric** quick to anger

**chop house toast** a cheap celebrity

**circuit** a set journey for a judge who presides over the courts in a particular area

**circumbendibus** a roundabout route

**cit** low, perhaps insignificant trader

**citron-water** water with lemon peel

**civers** covers (dial.)

**clinker** lowliest piece of material

**closet** office or study

**clump** a cluster of trees or shrubs

**collector** a euphemistic word for a highwayman

**commission-day** the opening day of the assizes

**coquet** to entertain with small talk and gallantry

**cork-rump** cork padding for the seat of a dress; usually associated with unfashionable attire

**cormorant** an unthinkingly voracious individual

**counsellor** a barrister

**crack** a lie; or convivial company

**crambo** game in which each player has to provide a rhyme to the word suggested by others

**crimp** recruiting officer who deceives new recruits

**cross-grained** perverse and awkward

**crowd sail** to hoist an extraordinary number of sails so as to increase the speed of passage

**cruize** to sail or travel without a clear aim

**currente calamo** to set to and get down to work

**demur** to doubt or have scruples

**devise** (of an estate) the right to property given in a will

**discharge** acquit from debt

**dismal** fit of melancholy

**double fee** an excessive charge for services rendered by physicians or lawyers

**doux yeux** to make eyes at

**down on the nail** straightaway

**dram** an amount of spirits as is taken at one gulp

**dressing-box** a box containing cosmetics and other luxuries that might put the final touches to one's appearance

**drop astern** hold back

**drudging-box** a receptacle for any lowly household gear

**duce** devil

**eau d'arquibusade** a diluted strong liqueur

**éclat** conspicuous social brilliance

**economist** a frugal manager

**electrified** warm and ready to be attracted to other objects or bodies

**enflame a reckoning** increase a bill by having the guest cover exorbitant extra costs

**engaging** seductive

**enjouée** playful and sprightly

**esclavage** necklace composed of several rows of gold beads or precious jewels

**exciseman** an officer who inspects commodities and assesses the duty due on them

**execution** the carrying out of a legal judgment

**fallow and stubble** arable ground set aside temporarily and not planted

**false bay** offering security fallaciously

**feeder** a trainer of fighting-cocks

**ferae naturae** wild animals

**figure away** represent in an overdramatic fashion

**finger the shot** steal from ammunition store

**fleering** sneering

**flip** a warm and sweet mixture of beer and spirits

**florentine** either a savoury meat dish with spinach or a fruit cheesecake

**flout** insult

**fly-cap** an old-fashioned headdress, usually worn by the elderly, with side-flaps

**foist** cheat deftly

**gallanting** to escort and perhaps flirt with

**gauze** a fine transparent silk

**girdle** anything tied or buckled around the waist

**grampus** a large, cetaceous fish

**grand signior** the Sultan of Turkey

**grisette** innocent young woman, perhaps of a low class

**grog** a mixture of rum and water

**grumbletonian** habitual grumbler

**handle** excuse

**hogshead** a measure of sixty gallons for alcoholic drinks

**hum** deceive

**in fee** with absolute possession

**in ordinary** in dry-dock, undergoing repair or refitting

incontinently without delay

instrument a written document standing as an order or contract

japonning lacquering surfaces in a Japanese style

jaw jargon

jointure sum of money promised to the wife on her husband's death

land-carriage expensive overland haulage

lay out spend or wager

leading-string a form of reins to help babies learn how to walk

levee a formal and ritualistic rising from bed by a dignitary

liquorish lascivious

livery a uniform showing that one was in service

lodging beaten down by a great force

log-book a formal, written account of essential information about a voyage

long-robe idiomatic phrase for the legal profession

luce clarius clearly and obviously

lutestring dress of glossy silk fabric

macaroni a fop or dandy

magazine portable store

magnanimity greatness of mind or outlook; superior to trifles

marcasite imitation gem

market penny money earned by one who acts for another

masterpiece main excellence

mauvaise honte acute self-consciousness

megrim generic name for any nervous disorder

murrain disease or pestilence

muster a review of military force

nabob deputy governor in the Mogul empire; someone with great wealth

nisi prius civil suit, tried outside London

nonsuit suit likely to be withdrawn before coming to court

notable obvious and officious

omnium the whole sum of what one holds dear

overflow surplus, profit

overset overwhelm (a vessel)

own confess

pagoda gold or silver coins higher in value than rupees

pair of colours an ensign's commission

palsy-drop infusion to help alleviate a disease of the nervous system

parsonable respectable

party a game of picquet, comprising six hands

phial small bottle

pinery area for the cultivation of pineapples

pink supremely excellent

pitch upon decide to choose

pledge (v.) join in a toast

plum £100,000

poltroon coward

poop rubbish

portly grand of bearing

positive dogmatic or stubborn

post-captain a permanent commission as captain of a large vessel

post-shay a hired carriage

pound a temporary enclosure for stray farm animals

practicable realistic

prescribe a lay estimate of the correct dose of medicine

pressed conscripted

print-hand a clear written script near to the condition of print

privateer ship fitted out privately to plunder others on the high seas

propriety an exclusive right; justness

pudding-sleeve a physician

puncheon a large cask for liquids, usually a capacity of seventy-two gallons for beer

purser the paymaster of a ship

push crowd

put to hitched to a coach

qualm sudden fit of sickness or languor

quickset hedge a hedge made out of mature plants

ramble excursion with no particular goal

rappee a coarse and particularly strong variety of snuff

rate the official tonnage, armament, and class of vessel

**rattle** to speak eagerly and noisily, or (n.) one who speaks hastily

**rattle up** make lively

**reckon (a glass)** ascertain a boat's speed by checking one's progress against a half-hourglass

**reef (a foresail)** lower by gathering or rolling up the foresail, so as to bring a vessel to a sudden halt

**retainer** an authorization to represent clients of law

**ringleader** the head of an informal, and perhaps rowdy or illicit, group

**rule of thumb** rough-and-ready means

**run over** inspect minutely

**runagate** a fugitive and/or rebel

**salute-shot** the acknowledgement of another vessel by firing off single volleys and flying flags

**sampler** a piece worked upon by young girls so as to help them improve needlework

**sans-prendre-vole** a winning game of ombre where the victor succeeds without having first discarded or picked up cards

**scratch** a periwig, covering half the head

**sensibility** capacity for powerful emotion

**sergeant** a lawyer of the highest rank

*serius aut citius* sooner or later

**set down** finish an interview

**set off** present to good advantage

**shaking pudding** a jelly or blancmange

**shallop** a small boat mainly employed in transporting travellers ashore from a larger vessel

**sheer off** depart; go further off; or change direction.

**shilling ordinary** a hostelry where there was a flat rate of a shilling for a meal

**slough** a deep muddy place

**smack** a loud kiss

**smack-smooth** perfectly level

**smoked** uncovered or found out; gallop at full speed

**snap** engage on some employment

**spadille** the ace of spades in both the card games of quadrille and ombre

**statute-fair** annual fair held in a small village principally for the hiring of servants

**steerage** the cheapest rate of passage on board ship

**stingo** slang for strong liquor

**stir a fire** to be hospitable

**stock purse** a fund that supplies the common needs of a group

**stock-jobbing** buying and selling shares as one's main occupation

**stoved** collapsed or breached

**stray-vaguing** nomadic or restless

**strike a balance without errors excepted** to achieve balanced books by tacitly correcting small irregularities

**stuff** anything material

**surfeit-water** any liquid that helped digestion

**tablet** notebook

**tack an opinion** formulate an item of legal advice, usually in a written form

**take a touch** venture on something

**tax cart** shortened form of an (un)taxed cart on account of its menial use or small size

**temper** forbearance or tolerance

**termagant** overbearing and fiery

**tête** elaborate hair-piece

**tide-waiter** customs officer who collects and enforces port levies

**tight** awkward

**tintamarre** uproar or commotion

**tip** commission to earn

**toilet** dressing table

**top one's part** perform the best one can

**touch** apprehend; or steal with some deftness

**toupet coxcomb** an affected man of fashion, who wears a crest of artificial hair or topknot

**traffic** commerce

**trambooze** tramp or trudge

**tree** scaffold

**trip up one's heels** throw or place an adversary off balance

**twitch** snatch

**unbeneficed** without a living or any regular position as a clergyman

**upon one's shift** fend for oneself

**upstall** take off, flee
**valet-de-shamb** valet de chambre, i.e
    personal servant
**venal** mercenary
**venire** a summons to court
**ventre d'or** intricately woven with gold
    thread
**victual** provide food for
**voluntary cuckold** a willing cuckold,
    undergoing the disgrace for money
**votary** a devotee

**voucher** a witness
**warm** well-to-do
**whimsical** freakish and capricious
**whip (somebody) up** bind someone to
    you by affection and probably marriage
**whirligig** child's top
**wight** fellow
**wind the straight horn** blow a hunting-
    horn
**wing** graze someone by a pistol shot
**woundily** awfully

American Literature

British and Irish Literature

Children's Literature

Classics and Ancient Literature

Colonial Literature

Eastern Literature

European Literature

Gothic Literature

History

Medieval Literature

Oxford English Drama

Poetry

Philosophy

Politics

Religion

The Oxford Shakespeare

A complete list of Oxford World's Classics, including Authors in Context, Oxford English Drama, and the Oxford Shakespeare, is available in the UK from the Marketing Services Department, Oxford University Press, Great Clarendon Street, Oxford OX2 6DP, or visit the website at www.oup.com/uk/worldsclassics.

In the USA, visit www.oup.com/us/owc for a complete title list.

Oxford World's Classics are available from all good bookshops. In case of difficulty, customers in the UK should contact Oxford University Press Bookshop, 116 High Street, Oxford OX1 4BR.